MAGNOLIAS

MAGNOLIAS

NEIL G. TRESEDER

LONDON **FABER & FABER** BOSTON

PUBLISHED IN COLLABORATION WITH THE ROYAL HORTICULTURAL SOCIETY

First published in 1978
by Faber and Faber Limited
3 Queen Square London WC1
Printed in Great Britain by
Western Printing Services Ltd., Bristol

All rights reserved

BRITISH LIBRARY CATALOGUING

IN PUBLICATION DATA

Treseder, Neil
Magnolias.
1. Magnolia
I. Title
635.9′773′114   SB413.M34

ISBN 0–571–09619–0

CONTENTS

THE TEMPERATE SPECIES OF *MAGNOLIA*

SUBGENUS *MAGNOLIA*

★ These Magnolias are illustrated in the text with line drawings by Marjorie Blamey

SUBGENUS YULANIA

GENUS *MANGLIETIA*   137

GENUS *MICHELIA*   139

MAGNOLIA HYBRIDS AND CROSSES

HOW TO GROW MAGNOLIAS

MAGNOLIA CYTOLOGY

APPENDIXES

COLOUR PLATES

The colour plates appear between pages 78 and 79

PREFACE

The author gratefully acknowledges a subvention paid to the publishers by the Stanley Smith Horticultural Trust on the recommendation of its Director, Sir George Taylor. The trust was founded in 1970 and one of its first grants helped to save *Curtis's Botanical Magazine* of which it now bears half the cost. The next completed volume was dedicated to the memory of Stanley Smith 'whose love of gardens and beautiful plants prompted many munificent anonymous benefactions for the encouragement of horticulture throughout the world and whose generosity was and will continue to be especially beneficial to the Royal Botanic Gardens, Kew'.

This particular grant has greatly helped to finance the reproduction of the colour plates in this book.

The first number of *Curtis's Botanical Magazine* was published on 1 February 1787 by William Curtis (1746–99). An apothecary by profession, he was at first apprenticed to his grandfather, John Curtis, a surgeon-apothecary who had come to Alton in Hampshire in 1720. At the age of twenty William went to London where he studied at St. Thomas's Hospital and carried on an apothecary's business, which was later left to him by his employer.

In 1771 he became the first private individual to open a public botanic garden in London, on an acre of ground at the bottom of Bermondsey Street. A year later he was appointed Demonstrator of Botany to the Society of Apothecaries at the Chelsea Physic Garden, and published an English translation of the Linnaean thesis 'Fundamenta Entomologiae'. In 1774 he issued, anonymously, his first botanical publication 'Catalogue of plants growing wild in the environs of London'. The next year he published the first number of *Flora Londinensis* and his ambition was to produce a complete natural history of Great Britain, for he also became recognized as an authority on entomology and ornithology.

In 1779 Curtis opened The London Botanic Garden in Lambeth, close to the Magdalan Hospital, St. George's Fields, and in 1783 he published a catalogue of the plants growing there.

He founded *Curtis's Botanical Magazine* in 1787 and in it he published colour plates of plants then being introduced into English gardens, accompanied by a brief text which aimed at blending botanical data with historical and horticultural details.

The London Linnaean Society was founded in 1788 and Curtis became an original Fellow. In the following year he moved his garden from Lambeth to Queen's Elm, Brompton, where he kept a library for, and lectured to, subscribing members, who were also entitled to surplus plants which were grown there.

His successor, William Salisbury, removed this garden to Cadogan Place, off Sloane Street, where an arboretum was planted. Loudon recorded that in 1835 it was occupied as a subscription garden and as a nursery.

William Curtis was one of the first Fellows of the Royal Horticultural Society and took an active interest in its early years. Among the Fellows were many of his closest friends,

including Dr. John Sims, who knew him from boyhood and who edited the Botanical Magazine from 1801 to 1826. William's only child, Sarah, married his cousin, Samuel Curtis, who
was also a Fellow of the Linnaean Society and who carried on the Botanical Magazine for some
years and also published his father-in-law's lectures.

For nearly 200 years *Curtis's Botanical Magazine* has maintained, at the hands of a succession
of distinguished authors, a very high standard. Combining as it still does botanical, historical
and horticultural details, it is the recognized British authority for the majority of ornamental
plants. The many references to *Magnolia* are quoted in this book.

FOREWORD

Hitherto there have been only two monographs on Magnolias published in this country, J. G. Millais's *Magnolias* (1927) and G. H. Johnstone's *Asiatic Magnolias in Cultivation* (1955).

Millais, who included all known species, both temperate and subtropical, wrote his book at a time when many of the Asian species had not yet flowered in cultivation, so that he was unable to describe the performance of several outstanding Magnolias in this country.

Johnstone's fine monograph, now out of print, dealt only with those Asian species then in cultivation. This book is much more comprehensive in its coverage for it includes all temperate species of Magnolia introduced to cultivation from both America and Asia, with details of their performance in British gardens as well as in other parts of the world, together with the many hybrids and crosses which had flowered and been recorded up to the date of publication.

For half a century the acknowledged world authority on the *Magnoliaceae* has been veteran British botanist the late James Edgar Dandy whose authority was acknowledged by Millais way back in 1927. Dandy is perhaps best known for his masterly 'Survey of the Genus *Magnolia* together with *Manglietia* and *Michelia*' which was published in the Royal Horticultural Society's *Camellias and Magnolias Conference Report* 64–81 (1950). Before his death, he kindly consented to the publication in this book of his 'Revised Survey' which is printed on pp. 29–37.

Recent developments in Magnolia breeding have led to a growing interest in the cytology of Magnolias and a chapter on this absorbing topic has been contributed by Dr. John Wilkinson of Exeter University on pp. 209–11.

Although this book should prove useful to Magnolia enthusiasts and amateurs world-wide, the months and orientations indicated will obviously require adjustment for gardens in the southern hemisphere.

The most recent publication on *Magnoliaceae* is Dr. Stephen A. Spongberg's 'Magnoliaceae Hardy in Temperate North America' in *Journal of the Arnold Arboretum* 57, 3 : 250–312 (1976). This is a botanical treatment 'dedicated to the memory of Ernest Henry Wilson (1876–1930), indefatigable plant hunter and late Keeper of the Arnold Arboretum. It was through Wilson's efforts that many of the most ornamental taxa of *Magnolia* were introduced into cultivation in western gardens, and our knowledge of the genus and family has been greatly augmented by the specimens and information he collected on his several expeditions to eastern Asia.'

Dr. Spongberg's several changes in nomenclature have been referred to at the final up-dating of this text but not all adopted because they have not yet been generally accepted and such alterations to the text were impracticable at such a late stage. Some comments on these changes are to be found on p. 38.

Among his innovations are the adoption of (or reversion to) the original Buc'hoz names *M. heptapeta* for *M. denudata* and *M. quinquepeta* for *M. liliflora*. Such treatments add to the irritating botanical inexactitude of Linnaeus's *M. tripetala* (having three petals) which has ten or more, *M. quinquepeta* (having five petals) which normally has six, and *M. heptapeta* (having seven petals) which normally has nine; names which, to the layman's mind, make a nonsense out of botanical nomenclature.

Dr. Spongberg conforms with Blackburn's treatment of *M. stellata* as *M. kobus* var. *stellata* and upholds the status of *M. cylindrica* (provisionally) as a species. He treats *M. pyramidata* as *M. fraseri* var. *pyramidata* and *M. sinensis* as *M. sieboldii* subsp. *sinensis*, absorbing *M.* × *high-downensis* in *M. wilsonii*.

Among other hybrids he treats *M.* × *watsonii* as *M.* × *wieseneri*, *M.* × *loebneri* as *M. kobus* var. *loebneri* and absorbs both *M.* × *kewensis* and *M.* × *proctoriana* into *M. salicifolia*.

For over forty years I have been growing plants and making gardens in Cornwall and elsewhere and have had many opportunities to visit and enjoy the wonderful collections of Magnolias in such famous Cornish estate gardens as Caerhays, Trewithen, *Trengwainton, Trewidden and Lanarth. These gardens contain many of the first raisings of Magnolia species introduced by such plant hunters as George Forrest and Ernest Henry Wilson. To this list I must add Chyverton, *Lanhydrock, Werrington and *Antony House. Those marked with an asterisk have now been covenanted to the National Trust and are therefore open to the public on most spring days, as is the late George Johnstone's garden at Trewithen.

My particular interest in Magnolias dates back some twenty-five years to when the late Charles P. Raffill, then Assistant Curator at the Royal Botanic Gardens, Kew, called at our Truro nurseries shortly after visiting Caerhays and Trewithen to see them flowering. He infected me with much of his enthusiasm and we often corresponded afterwards.

I was primarily inspired to write this book when the late George Johnstone's *Asiatic Magnolias in Cultivation* became out of print. Without such an inspiration my book would not have been started, for Johnstone's magnificent monograph has proved an invaluable source of reference, containing as it does so many painstaking personal observations, diligently recorded over so many years in his famous garden at Trewithen, about six miles from Truro. Johnstone restricted his text to those Asian species then in cultivation and made but scant reference to their known hybrids. I have therefore taken up the challenge where he left off and have included in this book details of the temperate American species together with as many hybrids as I have been able to locate and check upon.

I was also inspired by Marjorie Blamey's plant paintings when she exhibited at the Cornwall Garden Society's Show at Truro in April 1966, as a result of which I commissioned her to paint a set of Magnolias for this book and I am most grateful to the owners of the many gardens who contributed flowering material for this purpose. I intended to use these as the main feature of this book but the great increase in production costs over the years has made it impossible for more than nine photographic reproductions to be included.

My third inspiration was to endeavour to propagate vegetatively the best forms of the various species and hybrids which she had painted, so that they will be available for other garden owners to enjoy in the form of grafted trees, which will not take nearly as long to begin to flower as those raised from seed.

In this country I have been able to discuss Magnolias with such experts as Mr. F. Julian Williams at Caerhays Castle, Mr. Nigel Holman of Chyverton, Mr. H. G. Hillier of Winchester, Sir Eric Savill, Mr. J. Bond and Mr. T. H. Findlay of the Crown Estates Gardens at Windsor, members of the Gardens and Herbarium staff of the Royal Botanic Gardens, Kew, and Mr. C. Brickell, Director of the Royal Horticultural Society's Garden at Wisley, who has given valuable help in checking botanical nomenclature. I am also indebted to Miss P. I. Edwards of the Botanical Library of the Natural History Department, British Museum, and members of the Herbarium staff, and to the late J. E. Dandy with whom I spent one memorable April afternoon at Kew.

Shortly after I began my task I was introduced to the American Magnolia Society which was founded in October 1963 by Dr. John M. Fogg, Jr., then Director of the Morris Arboretum of the University of Pennsylvania. The Society's Newsletters have proved an invaluable source of information as well as a means of introduction to Magnolia enthusiasts across the Atlantic.

In the course of my research I have made many friends both in this country and overseas. Some of those in the eastern states of America I was fortunate in becoming acquainted with during my visit in September 1970. Among these was that veritable mine of Magnolia information, Prof. Joseph McDaniel of the University of Illinios at Urbana, successor to Dr. John M. Fogg, Jr., as President of the American Magnolia Society. I also made the acquaintance of Dr. Fogg when I called at the Barnes Arboretum at Merion, Pennsylvania, after visiting the National Arboretum at Washington, D.C., and being shown round the Magnolia collection by six-foot-six Bill Kosar who has bred some interesting hybrids. My thanks are due also to the Magnolia Society's Secretary/Treasurer Philip J. Savage, Jr., with whom I spent a most interesting day inspecting some of the finer Magnolias in the Detroit (Michigan) area before seeing his own very comprehensive collection at Bloomfield Hills, Michigan. They have allowed me to quote freely from their contributions to Magnolia literature.

Later I visited the Brooklyn Botanic Garden on Long Island, New York, home of some interesting new Magnolia hybrids between the American *M. acuminata* and the Chinese *M. quinquepeta*. I also met Dr. Benjamin Blackburn who showed me around the Willowwood Arboretum of Rutgers, the State University, at Gladstone, New Jersey, where I was able to discuss with him his theory that *M. stellata* is a diminutive and multitepalled form of *M. kobus*. At the Arnold Arboretum of Harvard University, Boston, I saw the grafted perpetuation of Sargent's original introduction of *M. kobus* var. *borealis* and was given permission to collect seeds from the many Magnolias which were fruiting freely there.

In other overseas countries I acknowledge the assistance of Dr. Carlo Stucchi of Cuggiono, Milan, for his endeavour to trace the origin of *M.* 'Lennei' in Italian archives, also for his translations of Italian documents; and in France to the librarians of the Muséum National d'Histoire Naturelle, Paris, for contributing to my research into early introductions of *M. grandiflora* into France, together with the history of the Soulangiana hybrids and *M.* × *wieseneri*.

Many of my enquiries in Japan have been answered by Mr. K. Wada of the Hakoneya Nurseries, Yokohama, with whom I spent two memorable days visiting Cornish gardens in March 1967; others by Prof. Haruo Ohyama of the Botanical Gardens of the University of Tokyo and latterly Professor of Meiji University, and by Dr. Tsuneshige Rokujo of the same city. While in South Korea I visited Cheju Do (formerly known as Quelpart Island) an outpost of the Japanese *M. kobus*.

In Australia my main contact has been Mr. Cyril H. Isaac, nurseryman of Noble Park, Victoria, who, until his retirement, propagated and distributed Magnolias on a wholesale scale to other Australian nurseries and garden centres. I am also indebted to Miss E. Pickard and her colleagues of the Truro Secondary Modern School for assisting me in translating correspondence and photocopies of Magnolia documents from France and Germany. The final copy editing of the manuscript, and the proof reading, have been the responsibility of Mrs. Barbara Ellis, for whose help I am very grateful. To the many others, too numerous to mention, who have assisted me with my enquiries, I extend my grateful thanks.

NEIL G. TRESEDER

Falmouth
Cornwall

THE ORIGIN OF THE NAME *MAGNOLIA**

Pierre Magnol (1638–1715) was an eminent French botanist who suffered for many years under the persecution of Protestants by the Catholic regime of that period. Eventually he became Professor of Medicine and Prefect of the Botanical Gardens at Montpellier. His *Botanicum Monspeliense* (1676, 1686, 1688) listed in alphabetical order under his system of polynomials, plants of the Montpellier region, Hérault, Southern France.

Magnol became highly esteemed among contemporary botanists so that Charles Plumier (1646–1704) in *Plantarum Americanarum Genera* 38, t. 7 (1703) coined the name *Magnolia* to commemorate him and applied it to a West Indian species now known as *Talauma dodocapetala* (Lam.) Urban. Although this belongs to the family *Magnoliaceae* it is generically distinct on account of differences in the fruit.

The celebrated Swedish botanist Carolus Linnaeus (1707–88), introducer of the binomial system on which modern nomenclature is based, reviewed the genus *Magnolia*. Linnaeus possessed the 1688 edition of Magnol's work which he considered one of the best Floras then published and, in his *Genera Plantarum* 62 : 456 (1737) and subsequent works, he took up Plumier's generic name *Magnolia*. However, as he had only scanty information about Plumier's Martinique plant, he based his own generic description on the North American species *M. glauca* L., later known as *M. virginiana* L., which was already established in many English gardens. By so doing he unintentionally transferred the name *Magnolia* from a tropical genus to one which includes temperate species and is popular in cultivation. But for this error Magnol's name, together with that of Magnolia, would be unknown today to all but a few professional botanists.

Subsequently Linnaeus made use of Magnol's *Botanicum Monspeliense* in his *Species Plantarum* (1753) and later published his dissertation *Flora Monspeliensis* (1756–9) using the binomial nomenclature and Linnaean sexual system of classification so that Magnol's work became of lasting nomenclatural importance.

---

* Reproduced here from *Festschrift fur Claus Nissen* 612–50 (1974) by kind permission of Prof. W. T. Stearn of the British Museum of Natural History. Prof. Stearn's contribution to this Festschrift, honouring Dr. Claus Nissen as a bibliographer and historian of biological iconography, links the two publications of Magnol and Linnaeus. He draws attention to the large number of beautiful illustrations of *Magnolia* in Nissen's monumental work *Die Botanische Buchillustration* (1951).

Magnolias are known to be among the most ancient of flowering plants. Their fossil remains have been found in rock formations of the Tertiary Period dating back more than one hundred million years. Throughout the intervening ages, during which most other races of plant have evolved, Magnolias have remained relatively unchanged.

Magnolia flowers are of simple structure, with free carpels and numerous stamens, attached in spiral formation to a convex receptacle. Because there is usually no distinction between sepals and petals these floral leaves are termed 'tepals' and are arranged in whorls of three.

The open, saucer-like blooms, this lack of differentiation between sepals and petals, and the spiral arrangement of their stamens, represents the most primitive form of flower structure. Apart from the tropical *M. coco* there are no nectar glands, though the flowers of most Magnolias are more or less fragrant.

When the flowers open, the reproductive organs become fully exposed and the stamens split open to shed their pollen, but by this time the stigmas have withered and become dry for they are usually only receptive while the flowers are closed. How then are Magnolia blooms fertilized so that they set seed? It has been found that they are largely pollinated by flower beetles (*Nitidulidae* species) which crawl between the overlapping tepals into the warm, sheltered environment of the flower chamber, and it is probable that other insects likewise seek food and shelter there. It seems likely, however, that they can only assist in pollination when they have previously visited older flowers and become smeared with pollen. They would then be attracted by the fleshy sugary tissues of the sticky, beak-like stigmas, which curve outwards from each free carpel within the unopened blossoms, and pollination would take place. Pollen is rich in protein and may also form part of the diet of these insects.

Beetles are known to have been plentiful in the Tertiary Period, millions of years before bees, wasps, moths and butterflies evolved, though they were preceded by dragonflies, mayflies, silver-fish and springtails. It is fascinating to contemplate that Magnolias and their contemporary beetle pollinators still survive, relatively unchanged by the passing of such an incomprehensible period of time in our planet's history.

Dr. E. E. Leppik of the Plant Genetics and Germplasm Institute, United States Department of Agriculture, attributes the relatively slow evolutionary rate of Magnolia flowers to the equally slow sensory development of their beetle pollinators. Under 'Morphogenic Stagnation in the Evolution of *Magnolia* Flowers', in *Phytomorphology* 25, 4 : 451–64 (1975), he points out that the damaging effect caused by beetles feeding on the flower tissues is minimized by the continuous development of protective devices on ovaries, fruits and leaves. They feed on pollen, food hairs and soft tepals. He observes that a nectar-like sugary fluid is excreted between the stigmas on *M. grandiflora* while the leaves have a hard epidermis which protects them from beetle damage.

Dr. Leppik explains that, in the first stage of opening, the beetles walk on to the pistils without damaging them while the ovaries are protected with a thick layer of unripe stamens which are not yet edible. The sticky stigmas can become readily inoculated by pollen grains adhering to the beetles' bodies from mature flowers visited earlier, then fertilization takes place and the inner tepals close to protect the young reproductive organs. At this stage beetles may start to chew these guard tepals but by the following day they reopen, the anthers dehisce, and the stamens fall apart on to the expanded outer tepals where they may be readily eaten by beetles and gathered by honey bees. Beetles may also devour the tepals which are no longer necessary to the fertilized flower. Meanwhile the rapidly developing carpels become protected by woody tissue and stiff hairs which make them immune to beetle damage.

Dr. Leppik recorded that the second most frequent visitor on the flowers of *M. grandiflora* were the pollen-collecting honey bees and he considers some species of Magnolia, including *M. heptapeta* (*denudata*), to have adapted their flowers to hymenopterous visitors, thereafter having changed much in floral form and size. Although Magnolia flowers have no visible nectar guides they emit distinctive odours which attract pollinators to certain points. In 1960 Dr. A. von Aufsess showed that on *M. kobus* the basal part of the flower emits a stronger odour than the peripheral part. This odour may guide pollinators to the stamens and pistils, thus favouring the process of fertilization.

Veteran Kew botanist, Dr. J. Hutchinson, classified the plant kingdom into two great divisions or *Phyla*, one comprising herbaceous and the other woody plants. He considered the order *Magnoliales* to be the most primitive of the woody *Phylum* from which all other dicotyledons have evolved. The simple structure of Magnolia flowers certainly indicates an affinity to the monocotyledons and they may well represent the demarcation between dicots and monocots.

Add to this romantic background the fact that Magnolias bear the largest individual flowers of any tree or shrub capable of outdoor cultivation in temperate regions, that they are often borne precociously on bare stems well in advance of leaf growth, that they will flourish in a wider range of soils than rhododendrons and camellias, varying in stature from large shrubs to vast trees usually with fragrant flowers, and then their importance in our gardens becomes manifest.

The bark of most of the Magnolia species and hybrids emits a pleasant resinous aroma when cut, bruised or crushed while that of several species has medicinal properties.

In temperate climates it should be possible to grow at least some species or hybrid Magnolia in all but the coldest and most exposed environments. Although they generally prefer a neutral-to-acid soil, most of them will tolerate alkaline conditions, some being perfectly at home on chalk. While some can withstand hot, dry summers with prolonged periods of drought, others seem to prefer cooler and moister conditions in woodland shade. The large-leaved species demand maximum wind shelter, while those with small leaves will tolerate considerable exposure, especially if they are naturally bushy and low growing like *M. stellata*.

Their flowering season varies from early spring to late autumn, some continuing in prolonged succession throughout this period. Though not among the easiest of trees and shrubs to establish, they normally live to a greater age than many other ornamentals, and, although some species, such as *M. campbellii*, may take from twenty to thirty years to flower from seed, most of them begin to bloom before they are ten years old, while some produce their first flowers when only two or three years old and may be available as young plants with flower buds. Some Magnolias make excellent second-storey plants to form a foil for rhododendrons and camellias.

I hope that this book will encourage many more gardeners to plant Magnolias, and that they will be planted more extensively by the responsible authorities in our public parks as well as in the grounds of churches, county halls, factories, hospitals, institutions, sanatoria and schools where there is usually ample space and an incentive to grow trees likely to live to a great age. I have noticed in America that one of the best places to see veteran Magnolias is in cemeteries for these are one of the few places immune to the destructive powers of property developers. Indeed, why not plant a Magnolia tree in *your* local cemetery Garden of Remembrance?

Climatic considerations

City dwellers tend to look upon the climate of the south-west of England as warmer and milder than elsewhere in the British Isles but this is not always so. London is blessed with the highest mean average temperature in the British Isles, in spite of the fact that, in still, winter weather, a smoky pall shuts out the warming rays of the sun, so that the day temperature is often lower than that of the surrounding countryside. By the end of March the south-west of England tends to lose the climatic advantage bestowed upon it by the adjacent seas, and the advent of spring is often delayed by cooling winds, sometimes of gale-force velocity. Consequently Magnolia time at Kew is often a week or more earlier than their peak period in Cornwall.

Deciduous Magnolias are remarkably tolerant of the polluted atmosphere associated with industrial areas and city environments, though there is no doubt that conditions in our cities have greatly improved in recent years, for there is no longer a sooty deposit on the leaves of trees and shrubs at Kew Gardens and in the London parks.

The higher temperatures recorded in towns and cities result largely from sun heat, absorbed by most forms of mechanical transport. Also there is a very rapid run-off of rainfall into drains an off-peak, night-storage heater. To this latent heat must be added the effect of power stations, gas works, factories, central-heating installations and the constant stream of hot gases emitted by most forms of mechanical transport. Also there is a very rapid run-off of rainfall into drains and sewers so that cooling due to evaporation is mainly of short duration and the atmosphere is therefore less humid than in adjacent rural areas.

Microclimate is a term used to indicate a restricted area which normally maintains a higher mean average temperature than that of adjacent sites. These favoured environments may be as restricted as the south or west face of a wall or as extensive as a city or industrial area which becomes virtually frost-proofed through its polluted atmosphere acting as a baffle to the rapid heat loss by radiation on clear winter evenings. On frosty mornings this climatic advantage of our big cities must be clearly demonstrated to those who commute regularly from outlying residential areas.

Katabatics is the science of atmosphere drainage. Cold air is denser and therefore heavier than warmer air. It therefore pours slowly down to the lowest level available, spreading out in a shallow layer over a wide valley or estuary or becoming trapped in the form of an invisible lake of considerable depth in a narrow valley which forms a frost pocket. Miniature frost pockets are often formed where ground slopes down to garden walls or hedges, also by screens of trees or by buildings or by embankments constructed to carry roads or railways.

It is wise to anticipate this invisible trapping of cold air and to try to avoid planting the earlier Magnolias in such environments.

The shade tolerance of Magnolias mentioned in the text may seem confusing to the less experienced planter. By *partial shade* one implies a situation where much of the overhead exposure to direct sunlight is at least partly filtered by the branches and foliage of taller trees. Alternatively *part-time shade* exists where the site is screened from direct sunlight for part of the day by adjacent trees, buildings or by rising ground.

Because Magnolias are so tolerant of polluted atmospheres the precocious Asian species and their hybrids should be planted far more extensively in our public parks. To ensure that they attain their full stature they should be provided with adequate summer irrigations, especially where the soils are sandy and the rainfall below 30 in. (76 cm).

Have you ever pondered on the lines of that old song hit of the 1920s? 'Is it true what they say about Dixie? Do the flowers really bloom all the time? Do the "Sweet Magnolias" blossom round everybody's door?' . . . Well, I'm told on good authority that they do not! However some few native plants of *M. virginiana* still survive at Magnolia, Massachusetts (now part of the Greater Boston Metropolitan Complex), where the Revd. Cotton Mather is reputed to have discovered that outpost stand of this species soon after it was named as the type plant of the genus *Magnolia* by Linnaeus.

According to Prof. J. C. McDaniel, President of the American Magnolia Society, writing in the Society's *Newsletter* 7, 1 : 7 (1970), no less than seventeen places in the United States are named 'Magnolia'. 'American Magnolias are native near most but not all the numerous towns having the name "Magnolia" or some combination of it. Alabama, with at least six of the eight U.S. species growing wild within its borders, is perhaps the state where more different ones can be seen. Appropriately, it has post offices named Magnolia (36754), Magnolia Springs (36555), and Magnolia Terminal (36755).

'Texas duplicates Alabama's first two, Magnolia (77355) and Magnolia Springs (75957). Other "Magnolia" post offices are listed by the American Zip Code Company for the states of Arkansas (71753), Delaware (19962), Illinois (61336), Iowa (51550), Kentucky (42757), Maryland

(21101), Minnesota (56158), Mississippi (39652), New Jersey (08049), North Carolina (28453), and Ohio (44643). The Magnolia in Massachusetts (with the northernmost wild *M. virginiana*) is a substation of the Gloucester post office (01930).

'A few *M. × soulangiana* trees grow in Magnolia, Illinois, and that may be true of Magnolia, Iowa. The Minnesota town could probably cultivate *M. kobus* and *M. acuminata*, while the ones in Ohio and Kentucky would have a wider range of species.

'It would be interesting to trace the origin of these place names more fully. The Illinois, Iowa and Minnesota towns probably adopted the name for its pleasant sound. Those in Massachusetts, New Jersey, Delaware and Maryland, are, or were, associated with stands of *M. virginiana*. The Arkansas town is considered not to be in native *M. grandiflora* territory, like those in Texas, Mississippi and Alabama, but there are big trees in it dating from about the time of settlement.'

Some readers may have heard of the Magnolia Warbler and wonder what affinity it has with American Magnolias. Apparently very little for, according to Oliver L. Austin's *Birds of the World*, 'The Magnolia Warbler is an inhabitant of northern Spruce, Hemlock and Balsam forests at nesting time. Its discoverer, the pioneering Alexander Wilson, collected the type specimen in a Magnolia tree at Mississippi, and gave it its inappropriate name.'

This book on Magnolias is intended for the owners of modest gardens as well as grand ones. There is virtually no garden too small to accommodate a Magnolia of some kind, even if it has to be restricted occasionally, an operation which can well be performed at flowering time by bringing the beauty of the unfolding flower buds into the house, where their amazingly rapid development can be watched at close quarters.

Any garden with space for an apple, pear or plum tree can grow one of the larger tree Magnolias, most of which demand less space at ground level than that eventually required by some of the popular Soulangiana hybrids which often grow into vast bushy trees with a spread of twice their height.

One rarely sees deciduous Magnolias trained against walls yet many of them readily adapt themselves to this treatment. *M. stellata* in its various forms is one of the best since it responds to spur pruning immediately after flowering. Both *M. × wieseneri* (*watsonii*) and *M. × soulangiana* 'Lennei' tend to produce long gangling branches which lend themselves to horizontal training, espalier fashion, along the face of a wall or fence. A post and wire fence is often better than a wall because the plant is more likely to be able to spread its roots on both sides and be less likely to suffer from lack of moisture during the summer. In either position avoid growing bedding plants within their root range, since Magnolias are surface rooting and therefore resentful of soil disturbance once they become established.

Why not plant an orchard of Magnolias? You can always buy fruit, but the fantastic floral display from a collection of Magnolia trees is something which money cannot buy; but careful planning and patience are necessary. A spacing of twenty-five feet is sufficient if those of erect and spreading habit are alternated.

The natural distribution of Magnolias is confined to the northern hemisphere, apart from a few of the tropical species, whose range is marginally transequatorial at high altitudes. The family is divided geographically into two groups, one American and the other Asian, both of which include tropical species which are not within the scope of this book.

Many of the finest Magnolias are found in China, a country endowed with the richest and most widely diversified flora of all temperate regions of the world. When the last great ice age wiped out all vegetation in most of Europe and the northern part of North America, eastern Asia escaped completely this devastation and, as a result, there are more kinds of trees, shrubs and non-woody plants in China than in all other countries of the northern hemisphere combined.

With the rise of the Himalayan Mountains in the comparatively recent geological past, there developed a large area of abundant moisture, borne by winds from the southern seas. Consequently an exceedingly rich flora developed in the provinces of Yunnan, Szechwan and Kansu (the former province of Sikang) in western China where many of the most beautiful species of Magnolia originated.

The American species are to be found in an area extending down the eastern side of North America, southwards from the Canadian border. They have flowers which are white, cream or yellow and, as these appear with the leaves, they are not generally as conspicuous as those of their Asian cousins, many of which flaunt their fragrant flowers on branches still in their winter nakedness. Some of these are very large and richly coloured, in shades of pink or purple, so that it is not surprising that, with one exception, the popularity of the earlier American introductions waned rapidly when the first Asian Magnolias flowered in our gardens.

That single exception was *M. grandiflora*, one of the most noble of large-leaved evergreen trees, which also boasts the largest individual blossoms borne by any evergreen tree or shrub from temperate zones. It has achieved world-wide popularity and has become one of the most widely planted of evergreen ornamentals, being very tolerant of hot, dry summers. In leaf size it is eclipsed by the Asian *M. delavayi* but that species is less hardy and bears somewhat disappointing flowers.

The author is indebted to the late J. E. Dandy, long acknowledged as the world botanical authority on the genus, for the publication in this book of his 'Key to the Subgenera and Sections of *Magnolia*' on p. 27 which is followed by a revised edition of his 'Survey of the Genus *Magnolia* together with *Manglietia* and *Michelia*' on pp. 29–37. Alas, Dandy died without completing his monograph on the Magnoliaceae upon which he had continued to work almost up to the time of his death in November 1976. He was looked upon by his colleagues as a perfectionist who was not readily satisfied, even with his own efforts. Generally he was in favour of preserving a moratorium on plant nomenclature and sought to avoid the changing of botanical names merely to conform with the rule of priority of publication.

More enlightened readers will also find much to interest them in Dr. Wilkinson's 'Cytological Considerations' on pp. 209–11. The author has added details of the chromosome counts for each species at the ends of the chapters, also for most of the hybrids.

Throughout the preparation of this manuscript Marjorie Blamey's paintings have proved a most useful source of comparison and reference to floral detail, especially at times when Magnolias were out of bloom. Unfortunately the cost of high class colour reproduction of these paintings prevented us from including all of them in this book, but it has been possible to use colour photographs of nine of them and some fifty of her line drawings. However, the author will continue to try to find ways and means of publishing the paintings, either as single colour plates or in the form of a supplementary volume.

Bud orientation in Magnolias

In the spring of 1971, Dr. P. Allison, Pathologist of the Morris Arboretum, Merion, Pennsylvania, noticed that all the flower buds on a Magnolia tree were pointing in the same direction. David P. Earnshaw investigated this phenomenon on numerous Magnolia trees over the two following years. His conclusions, published in the *Newsletter of the American Magnolia Society*, 12, 1 : 13 (1976), were that certain members of genus *Magnolia* do act in this manner: they point approximately N. 15 °E.

He found that the bud bending is not due to an adjustment of the bud on the pedicel but to a distortion of the bud axis. In the northern hemisphere the south side receives more solar radiation than the north side. This produces a temperature difference between the two sides and the tepal tissues grow faster on the warmer side.

This bending of the bud axis occurs in Magnolias which have convolute tepals. Because of the tight overlapping of tepals, which are rolled tightly together, the force of the stronger tissue growth on the south side causes the axis of the flower buds to bend towards the north. The phenomenon can be observed only just before the buds open. Measurements indicate that they treble in length during the fourteen days before the flowers develop.

Earnshaw's conclusions were verified by negative results to tests for the effect of photoperiodism and magnetropism. In tests using artificial illumination and complete shielding of southern light, the tepal tissues swelled on the side closest to the energy source. It was shown that tepal colour had no effect on the cause of the bending.

Small thermistor beads implanted on the bud tissues on the north and south sides of flower buds showed a temperature variation of 15 °F. (8·3 °C.) during daylight hours. Bud bending was recorded on all of the precocious-flowering Magnolias with large flowers (i.e. *M. heptapeta (denudata)*, *M. quinquepeta (liliflora)* and their hybrids *M.* × *soulangiana* cultivars). No bending was recorded on the smaller-flowered *M. kobus* and *M. salicifolia* among early flowering kinds, nor on the later flowering *M. acuminata* var. *subcordata*, *M. fraseri*, *M. grandiflora* and *M. tripetala*.

An apparently quite independent observation of this phenomenon in the southern hemisphere was reported by Arthur W. Headlam in notes on 'Magnolias in Melbourne' in the Royal Horticultural Society's *Rhododendrons 1974 with Magnolias and Camellias* p. 87. While photographing a plant of *M. quinquepeta (liliflora)* he noticed that the points of the sickle-shaped flowers invariably leaned to the south (away from the sun) and he confirmed this happening on a number of plants of this species in other gardens.

As might be expected, the earliest references to Magnolias concerned their medicinal qualities and examples in oriental literature preceded the first Western recording by several centuries. Not only were the Chinese more advanced in their civilization than any Western country but they had Magnolias growing literally at their doorsteps, whereas it was not until after the Spanish conquest of Mexico that the first Magnolia was described by a Western observer.

Dr. Joseph Needham, F.R.S., foremost British authority on oriental history, tells me that Chinese drawings and botanical descriptions of mediaeval type still extant go back at least to the eleventh century. The *Cheng Lei Pen Tshao* (Reclassified Pharmaceutical Natural History), originally the work of Thang Shen-Wei, was published in 1083, to be followed by progressively larger versions in 1108 and 1249. These natural histories contain primitive drawings of three species of Magnolia. The mediaeval text still awaits the difficult task of translation.

Hou-phu (*M. officinalis*) is said to have been extensively cultivated for centuries, especially in Szechwan, not only for the flowers but for the thick bark, which is used as a tonic drug commanding a high price. Dr. H. L. Li in *The Garden Flowers of China* appears to confuse this Chinese species with the Japanese *M. hypoleuca* so that his reference to a red form may apply to that species and not to *M. officinalis*. No red form of either species is known in cultivation but a pink form of *M. hypoleuca* is growing at the Royal Horticultural Society's Garden at Wisley, also in the gardens in Windsor Great Park.

Mu-lan (Woody Orchid) is *M. quinquepeta* (*liliflora*). Apart from its use as a drug-plant, it is said to have been much used as a grafting stock. The practice whereby the emperor's gardeners maintained a prolonged supply of container-grown flowering plants of *M. heptapeta* (*denudata*) for the royal palaces is mentioned elsewhere in this book. There seems little doubt that these would have been grafted plants of selected forms of the species and *M. quinquepeta* (*liliflora*) would be an obvious choice of understock to achieve a dwarfing influence.

Hsin I, also called *Yu-lan* (Jade Orchid) is *M. heptapeta* (*denudata*). Dr. Li describes this as 'the most showy species of Magnolia, native to China, where it has been cultivated at least since the T'ang dynasty (A.D. 618–906) and is now widely found and planted in Chinese gardens. In temple grounds huge specimens of great age are frequently seen and these gnarled old Magnolia trees are greatly cherished. The petals are used for food, and medicinal preparations are also obtained from other parts of the plant.'

Now let us return to the Western world. Following the Spanish conquest of Mexico a vast array of fact and fiction filtered into the mother country from the lips and pens of soldiers, sailors and settlers. In order to procure an accurate account of his new possessions, Philip II of Spain commissioned, in 1570, his court physician Francisco Hernandez to undertake the first scientific expedition to Mexico to study the natural, ancient and political history of New

Spain. Elsewhere Hernandez had been preceded by Gonzalo Fernandez de Oviedo, who became known as 'First Naturalist of the New World' for the descriptions and drawings which he made, as early as 1535, of native plants growing mostly in Hispaniola and Tierra Firme.

Hernandez was given the title of Protomedico of the Indies, and he was assisted by his son. No doubt their task was simplified by the influence of the Aztec culture. By 1575 his five-year term was up and he had completed for publication six folio volumes of text and ten of drawings but, realizing that his task was still incomplete, he stayed on for a further two years, assisted by a resident Spanish physician named Lopez.

Late in 1577 (the year in which Drake sailed from Plymouth in the *Pelican* which he later renamed the *Golden Hinde*) Hernandez set out on his return voyage, leaving copies of his manuscript in Mexico. By this time he was exhausted by his arduous labours and in failing health. He died soon after reaching Spain.

For reasons which can be only surmised, his voluminous work was not published but was bound elaborately and deposited in the Escorial, in the library of the Royal Monastery.

For a time it seemed that his records and very name would pass into oblivion for they seemed ill fated. First of all the editing and publication of the records was delayed for several years until Philip II ordered his Neapolitan physician, Dr. Nardo Antonio Reccho, to prepare an extract from Hernandez's notes of whatever related to the science of medicine; but this was not published either, for shortly after he returned to Naples to begin the task, Reccho died. Then a friar, Francisco Ximenez, discovered the second copy of Hernandez's manuscript in the Convent of Huaxtepec, from which he extracted and translated from Latin to Spanish those parts which he considered most useful and interesting, and had it printed in Mexico City in 1615, to provide a much needed medical guide for the haciendas and towns of Mexico which had no means of medical aid.

Following the death of Reccho his extracts from Hernandez's manuscript and drawings were purchased by Prince Frederico Cesi, founder of the Academi di Lincei.

Then, between 1629 and 1651, members of the Academy of Lincei re-edited the material which Reccho had extracted, and published it in three editions containing annotated descriptions of 412 plants, with drawings of some 650, under the title *Nova Plantarum Historia Mexicana* (1651). Under the Mexican (Nahuatl) vernacular name *Eloxochitl* was printed a crude drawing of a branch of a Magnolia without a flower. The bark is deeply ringed with prominent petiolar (leaf) scars which indicate that it is *M. dealbata*, a species akin to *M. macrophylla* and the only deciduous species to be found in the tropics.

The Aztec name *Eloxochitl* is derived from *elotl* (green ear of corn with husk) and *xochitl* (flower) referring presumably to the young flower surrounded by its spathaceous bract. The corn referred to would be, of course, Indian corn or maize (*Zea mays*) which originated in that part of the world.

It is not known whether the latinized text was that of Hernandez, or added some seventy years later by Johannis Terrentius of the Academy of Lincei, whose name is printed beneath the plate on p. 376 in capitals as large as those of the page heading. The description lacks any reference to a medicinal usage and may well have been concocted to replace the original Hernandez text which Reccho must have extracted, and which Ximenez presumably published, in Mexico, in 1615. Freely translated it reads: 'Here we see the branch of a tree with leaves of the Banana, which are a deep colour on one side and very pale on the other, as with the Olive. The branch bears nodes where the leaves have fallen just as with the trunk of the Palm. There are many veins on the underside of the leaves which are clustered together at the tip of the branch.'

The earliest Western record of the bringing into cultivation of a member of the Magnolia family is to be found in Aztec history. The Mexican *Talauma mexicana* was known to the Aztecs as *Yolloxochitl*, meaning heart-flower, referring to the shape of the flower buds. According to Emily W. Emmart's annotations to her translation of the *Badianus Manuscript*, an Aztec Herbal of 1552, this was among the plants sent by Pinotl from Cuetlaxtlan to be planted in the famous garden of Huaxtepec at the time that it was enlarged by Tlacaelol, brother of Montezuma (1466–1520). Hernandez illustrated the tree and described its medicinal properties under *De Yoloxochitl Aristochyea*.

It was unfortunate that the learned members of the Academy of Lincei did not attempt to edit and publish the whole of the original Hernandez records for, in 1671, fire destroyed the library of the Escorial palace in which they were stored. It seems likely that they had merely made use of the large collection of woodcuts which may well have been the residue of Reccho's arbortive efforts. It is difficult to explain their actions otherwise.

Here one would expect this story to end, but lo and behold a hitherto unknown copy of Hernandez's original manuscript, but without the drawings, was unearthed more than 200 years after their author's death, by no less an authority than the official Spanish historian, Juan Bautista Muñoz, from among the archives at the Jesuit Colegio Maximo in Madrid.

From this fresh source an edition of his complete works was begun by the leading Spanish botanist of that day, Don Casimiro Ortega, director of the Botanical Gardens in Madrid. But of this only three volumes appeared and these omitted the notes on animals and minerals. Perhaps it was intended that these should be tackled later by experts in those respective fields. Ortega's three volumes were published under the title *Francisci Hernandi medici atque historici Philippi II Hisp. et Indiar. regis et totius novi orbis, archiatri opera, cum edita, tum inedita.* Matriti (1790). (The works, not only those published but also those unpublished, of Francisco Hernandez, doctor and historian of Philip II, King of Spain and the Indies, and of the whole new world. Matriti 1790.)

No further attempt appears to have been made to compile a fully comprehensive edition of Hernandez's monumental undertaking until 1959 and 1960 when the Universidad Nacional de Mexico published the first three volumes of an edition which promises to include all of his surviving works. These volumes should bring to light for the first time many of the observations so painstakingly recorded four centuries earlier.

The Hernandez natural history expedition was the first ever sent out by a government and this account of the attempted publications of his records reflects the many personal, physical and financial difficulties which confronted the Spanish authorities at a time when the art of printing was still in its infancy.

In this decade an expedition to collect seed of *M. dealbata* was undertaken in October 1975 by veteran timber-grower Mr. George A. Pfaffman of Citronella, Alabama. Mr. Pfaffman had made numerous trips previously into Mexico, primarily for the purpose of collecting forest tree seeds in the higher altitudes of that country. He drove to the Mexican state of Hidalgo via Tamazunchale to Chapulchuacan, a small town about twenty miles farther south and a somewhat lesser distance from the San Luis Potosi border. There he hired a guide and drove on for several miles before setting off on foot up the steep mountain slopes until they came across a fair number of trees of the Magnolia which they were seeking, apparently close to where Mexican botanist Dr. J. Rzedowski collected herbarium material twenty years earlier. The climb was quite an achievement for a man of his eighty-five years to accomplish at such an altitude.

Mr. Pfaffman reported that the trees, which did not exceed 30 ft (9 m), were all basal growths from larger specimens which had been felled several years earlier. There was no sign of either fruit cones or seedling plants. He learned from his guide that they were felled not for timber but to facilitate the harvesting of the flower buds. He understood that the flowers were sold in the towns for home decoration. One cannot help wondering whether this demand is stimulated by either an obscure religious significance or a herbal remedy possibly dating back to the early Aztec civilization.

One can appreciate that, because the flowers arise from the tips of the shoots along slender and very brittle branches, the only practical way to harvest them on a commercial scale would be after felling the tree.

It is indeed fortunate that *M. dealbata* shares with other Magnolias a pronounced power of regeneration from the base of the trunk. No doubt the time of felling, just when the sap begins to rise, is opportune for speedy recovery growth, but it is not surprising that this Magnolia is listed as one of the Mexican cloud forest plants threatened with extinction.

Mr. Pfaffman reported that the area was subject to winter freezes but he also came across quite tall plants of a tree tomato with edible spindle-shaped fruits (probably *Cyphomandra betacea*) which is an indication that these frosts were not severe. He also learned that the flowers opened in May, which corresponds with the flowering of the closely related *M. macrophylla* in the greater part of its natural range. In the absence of seed he had to be content with a handful of young shoots which were wisely passed on to more experienced hands for attempts at propagation.

The author is indebted to Mr. Harold Hopkins of Bethesda, Maryland, for an early report on Mr. Pfaffman's remarkable expedition, recorded during a long telephone conversation with him on his return to Citronella. Mr. Hopkins raises the query as to whether the flowers of *M. dealbata* invariably have purple spots similar to most races of *M. macrophylla*. The only flowering specimen in the U.S. National Herbarium at the Smithsonian Institute has spots. It was collected in 1906 by Conzatti from a more southerly area on the Sierra de Ixtlan, Oaxaca.

Since these notes were written Mr. Pfaffman has contributed his own account of his expedition in *Newsletter of the American Magnolia Society* 11, 2 : 8–15 (1975). This includes a progress report on attempts at propagation by Prof. J. C. McDaniel at the University of Illinois, Urbana.

Like so many of our trees and shrubs, the finest Magnolias come from Asia, found within a great triangle formed by Japan to the east, the Indian Himalayas to the west and Indonesia to the south. The first Magnolia to be introduced into Europe was *M. virginiana* from the New World, now the United States, in 1688 and it is the American continent which is their other home. Here they are found in an area stretching from northern South America, up through Central America and the eastern seaboard of the United States to the Canadian border. Within these two vast areas of the world botanists recognize about eighty species of Magnolia, twenty-six of them in America and the remainder in Asia.

The first Magnolias from America

Henry Compton (1632–1713), Bishop of London and of the North American Colonies, was one of the great gardeners of his day. According to Stephen Switzer in *Ichnographia Rustica* (1718) 'This reverend Father was one of the first that encouraged the importation, raising, and increase of exotics, in which he was the most curious man in that time.' In his garden at Fulham Palace, Compton built up an unrivalled collection of foreign plants, many of which originated in the outermost reaches of his enormous diocese—the American Colonies.

He sent John Bannister (1654–93) to Virginia to preach the gospel and Bannister became one of his most successful plant collectors. In 1688 he sent back the Sweet Bay Magnolia which was originally named by botanists *Laurus tulipifera* – the Laurel-leaved Tulip Tree. This name was retained until 1731 when the English botanist Mark Catesby referred it to the genus *Magnolia*.

Mark Catesby (1679–1749), naturalist and artist, sailed to America in 1710 and stayed there for nine years, during which he built up a collection of botanical specimens and paintings said to have been the most perfect ever brought to this country. Upon his death his collections passed on to Sir Hans Sloane, founder of the British Museum. Catesby's *Flora Caroliniana* was published in 1741 while a selection of his paintings appeared in *Natural History of Carolina, Florida and the Bahama Islands* which was published posthumously in 1771.

The first Magnolias from Asia

Thirteen hundred years ago the Buddhist monks of central China collected specimens of the native *M. heptapeta* (*denudata*) from the wild and planted them in their temple gardens, calling them 'Yulan' meaning Lily Tree. It is probable that a religious significance sprang up around the simple beauty of the large white flowers which appeared before the leaves in spring and it is reasonable to assume that this was one of the first flowering trees to be used as a garden feature.

The flowers of *M. heptapeta* (*denudata*) were often pictured on early Chinese porcelain, paintings and tapestries as a symbol of candour and purity. It is probable that this Magnolia was introduced from China into Japan by the monks during the T'ang Dynasty (A.D. 618–907) during which there was a cultural exchange between the two countries.

It is natural that a considerable amount of improvement took place over the centuries by the selection of improved forms of this plant. According to J. C. Loudon in *Arboretum et Fruticetum Britannicum* I : 279 (1838) 'This tree is said to be a native of the southern provinces of China; and to be extensively cultivated there in the gardens of the emperor, and in those of all eminent persons who can afford to procure it. It began to be cultivated in China in the year 627; and from that time it has always held the very first rank, as an ornamental tree, in their gardens. It is not only planted in the open ground, and allowed to attain its full size, but dwarfs are kept in pots and boxes and forced throughout the winter, so as to keep up a perpetual supply of bloom in the apartments of the imperial palace. So highly is this tree valued, that a plant in flower presented to the emperor, is thought a handsome present, even from the governor of a province.'

There appears to be conflicting evidence as to which Asian Magnolia was the first to be grown in this country. In his 'Revised Survey' (p. 29) J. E. Dandy awards this distinction to the tropical *M. coco* which is too tender for inclusion in the main text of this book. It is unique in being the only Magnolia with nectar glands. It is said to have been introduced in 1786 by Lady Hume of Bury, Hertfordshire, and is much valued in the tropics as a pot plant on account of its fragrance. The nodding white flowers are ephemeral, lasting like mayflies for only one day. They open at dusk and a solitary flower is said to perfume a whole apartment. At one time it was thought that it might prove hardy enough for outdoor cultivation (*Curtis's Botanical Magazine*: 977 (1807) as *M. pumila*).

According to *Curtis's Botanical Magazine* the date of introduction of *M. heptapeta* (*denudata*) (the Chinese Yulan or Lily Tree) by Sir Joseph Banks was 1780 (1789 according to Loudon). If so this Magnolia preceded *M. coco* by several years and, after centuries of cultivation in China and Japan, it became available for distribution in the Western world. Sir Joseph Banks (1746–1820) had been botanist with Captain Cook on his first round-the-world voyage from 1768 to 1771.

M. heptapeta (*denudata*) was long known as *M. conspicua*, the name bestowed on it by the British botanist R. A. Salisbury in 1806. The name *denudata* was later restored by reason of priority since it had been cited by the French botanist Desrousseaux in 1791. However, in 1976 leading American botanists decided to interpret the rule of priority in nomenclature to the extreme and reverted to the even earlier name, *M. heptapeta* (Buc'hoz 1779), which had been disregarded by several generations of botanists because it originated from a false description.

For the same reason they reverted to the faulty Buc'hoz name *quinquepeta* for the dark-purple *M. liliflora* which was introduced in 1790 from China or Japan. It was these two species that Soulange-Bodin, a retired French cavalry officer, mated about 1820 to produce the race of hardy hybrids, known botanically as *M.* × *soulangiana*, which have done more to popularize

Magnolias than any of the original species. It is fortunate that they were eagerly sought after and propagated by wholesale nurserymen, not only in England and France but also in Holland and Belgium, so that they soon became widely distributed throughout Europe and ultimately overseas.

In the latter half of the nineteenth century five species were introduced from Japan, notably *M. stellata* to the United States in 1862, and thence to Britain, and one species from the Indian Himalayas, *M. campbellii*, in 1868.

It was not until the turn of the present century that great plant collectors such as Ernest Henry Wilson and George Forrest penetrated into western China, and introduced into our gardens such Magnolias as *M. campbellii* subsp. *mollicomata*, *M. sargentiana* var. *robusta*, *M. sprengeri* and *M. dawsoniana*, all with very large flowers, opening on naked branches, sometimes long before the leaves appear. Some have immense upward-poised blossoms, their huge outer tepals opening almost horizontally to form large saucer-shaped bases surmounted by the inner ones, which at first remain furled vertically around the sexual organs, either in the form of a cone (as in *M. campbellii*) or like a dome (as in its subspecies *mollicomata*).

The early introduction of *M. virginiana* from America in 1688 was to be shortly followed by the sensational *M. grandiflora* with its larger glossy leaves and immense fragrant white flowers, which open here usually in late summer and autumn, somewhat later than in its native habitat. This Magnolia became much sought after by owners of the great eighteenth-century gardens, not only in England but also in France and Italy. It so eclipsed the somewhat diminutive but hardier and equally fragrant *M. virginiana* that the popularity of this species waned into oblivion and it became virtually lost to cultivation, at any rate as far as British gardens were concerned.

Further introductions, together with importations of seeds and plants, were interrupted from 1771 to 1780 by the American War of Independence but were revived with increasing demands between 1780 and 1800. Because all other American Magnolias open their white, cream or yellow flowers after they come into full leaf, it is not surprising that they likewise became eclipsed following the introduction, in 1790, of the precocious-flowered *M. heptapeta* (*denudata*) and *M. quinquepeta* (*liliflora*), which gave rise, some thirty years later, to the first generation of the Soulangiana hybrids.

There are still several known Asian temperate species to be introduced into cultivation including *M. amoena*, *M. biondii* and *M. zenii*. As these come from western China it may well be many years hence before they are growing in our gardens, a sad case of plants becoming involved in international politics. However *M. cylindrica*, a Chinese species listed in the *Camellias and Magnolias Conference Report* (1950) as not in cultivation, is now flourishing in our gardens, though certain aspects of this new introduction do not correspond with herbarium material which the author has examined, nor with Wilson's field notes.

Several of the Asian species of Magnolia share a Sino-Himalayan distribution, extending along the Himalayas from Nepal or Sikkim in the west to north-west Yunnan in the east, while in North America we find a considerable north-to-south range for *M. virginiana*. It is not surprising therefore that representatives, from close to the extremes of the natural ranges of some of these species, show considerable differences from a horticultural point of view though botanists insist that these are not of specific importance.

At this stage the horticulturist begins to feel frustrated at the lack of valid botanical names whereby he may distinguish, on his labels and in his catalogues, the different forms of a species. These may vary from the type in such important matters as the approximate age at which they are likely to flower, the relative date of their flowers' opening and of their growth initiation, as well as such other distinguishing features as the presence or absence of pubescence on their leaves and young shoots and the colour of their flowers.

Botanical classification is decided by botanists on criteria mostly very different from those used by gardeners, and botanical nomenclature is governed by the International Code★. Where supplementary nomenclature is required by horticulturists the Horticultural Code★ provides recommendations, which are virtually rules, so it is up to the plantsman to try to abide by them in his endeavours to find practical solutions to his problems.

★*Regnum Vegetabile*, a series of publications for the use of plant taxonomists published by the International Bureau for Plant Taxonomy and Nomenclature, of the International Association for Plant Taxonomy, Utrecht, Netherlands. The two referred to in the book are the *International Code of Botanical Nomenclature* (1972) and the *International Code of Nomenclature of Cultivated Plants* (1969).

Drawings A, B, C and D show the various stages of development of a flower of *M. campbellii* subsp. *mollicomata*: A shows the unfolding of the hairy *perules* (1) to reveal the *spathaceous bract* (2). B shows the shedding of the perules and the splitting of the spathaceous bract to reveal one of the *tepals* (3). C shows a flower dissected to reveal the various organs. D shows the *gynandrophore* and *peduncle* after the floral parts have fallen away. E shows the *adnate stipules* (*M. sinensis*) and F *free stipules* (*M. nitida*). G shows growth buds of *M. campbellii* and its subspecies *mollicomata*. H shows a fertile fruit cone and method of seed dissemination.

The flowers of Magnolias are always stalked. The *peduncle* (4), or flower stalk proper, comprises the *internodes* (5) or spaces between the *nodes* (6) which separate the uppermost foliage leaf from the perianth or tepals of the flower. There are always at least two such internodes.

At each node of the peduncle there is initially a spathaceous bract which falls off before the flower opens, leaving an *annular scar*. Thus the number of spathaceous bracts is one fewer than the number of internodes and, when the peduncle comprises only two internodes, there is only one spathaceous bract. These bracts consist of a petiole plus a pair of adnate (attached) stipules.

The perianth often shows no differentiation between petals and sepals, hence the term tepal, which was coined by Johnstone and which has since become the recognized term for these floral organs. The tepals are arranged in two or more whorls each of which may have from three to six tepals. Sometimes the outer whorl is reduced in size and/or texture in the form of a false calyx. The tepals leave prominent *tepal scars* (7) when they fall away.

The position in Sections *Yulania* and *Buergeria* is complicated by the fact that the flowers are precocious (i.e. appear before the leaves). The over-wintering bud is protected by perules which enclose not only the flower with its peduncle and spathaceous bract, but also the internodes below the peduncle which will bear new foliage leaves and young axillary shoots.

The uppermost internode, between the perianth and the bract (or uppermost bract), varies in length. When Johnstone was writing his book he wanted to call this internode the pedicel, but J. E. Dandy pointed out to him that this would be incorrect, as this term is generally applied to the ultimate stalk of a single flower within an inflorescence, a collective arrangement which does not occur in *Magnoliaceae*. Consequently Johnstone compromised by adopting the term 'pedicle' (8) and the author has continued its usage in the text of this book.

Drawings E and F show the young growths which are, at first, protected by stipules which are deciduous, falling away to leave *annular scars* (9) around the nodes. The stipules are either free from the *petioles* (10) or more or less *adnate* (attached) to them (11). These fall away to leave *stipulary scars* (12).

The *androecium* (13) or male part of the flower is composed of numerous free stamens. These are spirally arranged in the form of a boss around the base of the *gynoecium* (14) or female organ, which protrudes in the form of a column or cone composed of numerous carpels which are also spirally arranged. The stamens usually split open (dehisce) *laterally* (15) to shed their pollen. In some Magnolias they dehisce *introrsely* (16) or inwards as in *M. delavayi*. The term *gynandrophore* (17) denotes the column bearing the stamens (androecium) and pistils (gynoecium). The tepals, at least as regards the outer whorls, are strictly cyclic, but the leaves, bracts, stamens and carpels are always spirally arranged.

The *growth buds* (18) are at first protected by *bracts* (19) which fall away to leave further annular scars. The spathaceous bract usually protects both a growth bud and a *leaf bud* (20) each with its own furry bract.

The *petiole* (21) or leaf stalk supports the *leaf blade* (22). The shoots of most Magnolias are dotted with conspicuous *lenticels* (23) or breathing pores which become covered with corky shields.

The fertile fruit cone (Drawing H) usually turns red or pink upon ripening and may vary in length on different species from 1 in. (2·5 cm) or so to 8 or 9 in. (20·5 or 23 cm).* They are often considerably distorted owing to irregular fertilization of the ovules within the *carpels* (24). When the fruit cones are ripe the fertile carpels dehisce along the *dorsal suture* (25) so that the ripe *seeds* (26) become partially exposed. They vary in colour from pink to scarlet or crimson according to species. There are usually not more than two seeds per fertilized carpel, and, when the carpels split open, they become suspended temporarily by short silken threads which are extensions of the *raphe* (27). This suspension of the seeds probably provides a greater opportunity for wind to play a part in their dissemination than if they fell freely to the ground upon ripening.

* The metric equivalents of measurements have been generally shown to the nearest half centimetre thus: 6 in. (15·5 cm). Altitude conversions and tree dimensions from feet to metres have been similarly approximated in most instances.

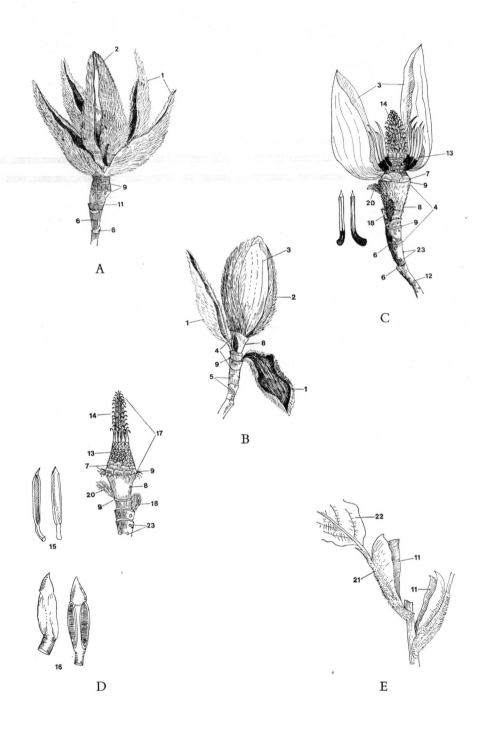

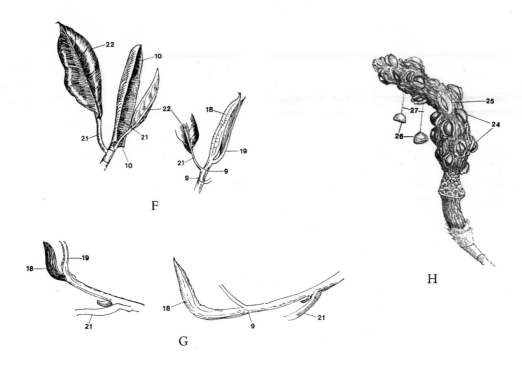

F

G

H

Key to Drawings A *to* H (half natural size)

1 Perule
2 Spathaceous bract
3 Tepal
4 Peduncle
5 Internode
6 Node
7 Tepal scars
8 Pedicle
9 Annular scar
10 Free stipules on leaf
  petioles of *M. nitida*

11 Adnate stipules on leaf
  petioles of *M. sinensis*
12 Stipulary scar
13 Androecium
14 Gynoecium
*15 Stamens of *M. campbellii*
  showing lateral dehiscence
*16 Stamens of *M. delavayi*
  showing introrse
  dehiscence
17 Gynandrophore

18 Growth bud
19 Bract
20 Leaf bud
21 Petiole
22 Leaf blade
23 Lenticels
24 Carpels
25 Dorsal suture
26 Seed
27 Raphe

★ Natural size.

GLOSSARY OF BOTANICAL TERMS

giving the sense in which they are used in this book

Acuminate With the apex suddenly narrowed and tapering to a point.

Adnate Attached close to base.

Adpressed (*appressed*) Lying flat.

Androecium The male part of the flower – the stamens.

Annular Ring-shaped.

Anther That part of the stamen containing the pollen.

Anthesis Pollen-shedding.

Apex, Apices Tip, tips.

Apiculate With the apex ending in a short, sharp, but not a stiff, point.

Auriculate Having ear-like lobes.

Axil Angle between leaf and stem.

Axillary Growing in the axil, the normal position of lateral branches.

Caducous Deciduous (perules).

Calcifuge Avoiding calcareous (chalky or limy) soils.

Callus Thickened skin forming at base of cuttings and at other cut or damaged portions of the stem, branch or trunk.

Calyx Outer members of perianth of flower when differentiated into sepals and petals.

Cambium Growth tissue between wood and bark.

Campanulate Bell-shaped.

Carpel A single pistil which develops into the seed-container (follicle in Magnolias).

Chartaceous Of the texture of writing paper.

Chlorosis, Chlorotic A yellowing of the leaves due to chlorophyll deficiency.

Chromosome Fibrillar bodies of definite number formed during nuclear division, dividing by fission into new groups and contributing to form the daughter nuclei.

Ciliate Fringed with hairs.

Clone All plants propagated vegetatively from one select individual or from its vegetatively propagated progeny.

Cordate Heart-shaped.

Coriaceous Leathery.

Cross A plant bred from different forms or races of the same species.

Cultivar Garden variety, or form found in the wild and propagated as a clone.

Cuneate Wedge-shaped.

Cytology Study of the protoplasmic nucleus of a cell.

Deciduous Not persistent.

Decurrent Running downwards.

Dehisce Open, as the carpels and stamens when ripe.

Diurnal Lasting for twenty-four hours.

Dorsal On the back.

Elliptic Oval, widest in middle, narrowing equally to both ends.

Emarginate Notched at the apex.

Ephemeral Lasting for only a day.

Evanescent Quickly fading.

Fastigiate With branches closely parallel and erect.

Filament The stalk of a stamen (bearing the anther).

Florescence Flowering state.

Foliar Of the leaves.

Follicle A ripe carpel opening along one suture only.

Genus Group of plants usually containing several species having common structural characteristics distinct from those of all other groups.

Glabrescent Becoming glabrous or nearly so.

Glabrous Without hairs.

Glaucous Covered with a bluish-white or bluish-grey bloom.

Gynandrophore Column bearing the stamens (androecium) and the pistils (gynoecium). The torus.

Gynoecium   The female part of the flower – the pistils.

Hybrid   A plant resulting from a cross between two different species.

Indigenous   Native to.

Indumentum   Hairy covering – e.g. pubescence.

Internode   The space on a stem between two nodes or joints.

Introrsely   Towards the centre of the flower – used to describe the dehiscence of anthers.

Lanceolate   Lance shaped.

Lenticel   Breathing pore, later becoming a corky scab.

Lenticellate   Having lenticels.

Marcescent   Withering but not falling.

Meiosis   Phase of nuclear change in germ cells.

Mucro   Short abrupt extension beyond apex of leaf, drip-tip.

Nematodes   Eelworms. Microscopic soil organisms.

Nodding   Bending over from perpendicular but not fully pendent.

Node   Joint. Part of stem from which a leaf arises.

Oblanceolate   Inversely lanceolate.

Obovate   With the outline of an egg, broader end at *apex*.

Obtuse   Blunt (angle of over 90°).

Ovate   With the outline of an egg, broader end at *base*.

Ovule   Female cell which, after fertilization, becomes a seed.

Pedicle   Small stalk-like structure – used here for the internodes at the apex of the peduncle immediately below the flower.

Peduncle   Stalk of a single flower or of an inflorescence. In *Magnolia* the internodes, usually two in number, between the uppermost foliage leaf and the perianth of the flower, with the node which carries the spathaceous bract, or the annular scar where it grew.

Pendent   Hanging from its support so as to be fully inverted.

Perianth   The outer or non-essential organs of the flower, including the sepals and petals – referred to in this book as the tepals, since there is no distinction between petals and sepals in *Magnolia*.

Perule   Structure (formed of modified stipules) enclosing and protecting the flower bud.

Petaloid   Like a petal.

Petiolar Scars   Annular scars at nodes of branchlets, where the petiole and stipules were attached.

Petiole   Leaf stalk.

Pistil   A single female organ of the flower comprising ovary, style and stigma.

Precocious   Flowering before the leaves develop.

Pruinose   With waxy bloom.

Pubescent   Clothed with short hairs or down.

Raphe   Cord of tissue by which one seed is attached to the inside of the follicle.

Reticulate   With veins patterned like network.

Retuse   Applied to a leaf having a shallow notch at its rounded tip.

Rugose   Puckered or wrinkled.

Rugulose   Somewhat wrinkled.

Sepal   A segment of the calyx.

Septate   Having partitions.

Somatic Cells   Normal vegetative cells which are not specially modified for the purpose of sexual reproduction.

Spathaceous Bract   Resembling a spathe – here applied to a bract enclosing one flower. Protective spathe-like sheaths enclosing flowers and falling away to leave an annular scar or scars. When the peduncle comprises only two internodes there is only one spathaceous bract.

Spathulate   Spoon shaped.

Spatulate   Rounded at top and long-attenuated to base.

Species   Group subordinate in rank to Genus.

Stamen   Single male organ of the flower.

Stigma   That part of the pistil that receives the pollen.

Stipitate   Stalked.

Stipules   Two appendages to the petiole, one each side.

Stomatic   Referring to the stomatic pores in the undersurfaces of leaves and young stems.

Style   The middle portion of the pistil between ovary and stigma.

Subcordate   Somewhat heart-shaped.

Suture   Inner or outer edge of a carpel.

Temperate   Other than tropical or arctic.

Tepal   A segment of a perianth which is not clearly differentiated into sepals and petals.

Tepaloid   Like a tepal.

Tomentose   Thickly hairy or with matted hair.

Tomentum   A covering of dense, matted hairs.

Trihybrid   A seedling bred from a species and a hybrid of two other species.

Verticillate   Arranged in a whorl, forming a ring around a common axis.

Villous   Having long soft hairs, usually curved.

Whorl   A ring of organs all on one plane.

The late J. E. Dandy, recognized as the leading world authority on Magnolias since J. G. Millais's *Magnolias* was published in 1927, had, before his death, kindly allowed the author to publish in this book a revision of his masterly 'Survey of the Genus *Magnolia* together with *Manglietia* and *Michelia*', which was first published by the Royal Horticultural Society in *Camellias and Magnolias Conference Report* (1950).

During the twenty-seven years which have elapsed since the original publication, quite a number of discoveries have been made among tropical Magnolias, though none of these affects the cultivated temperate species within the scope of this volume.

Some minor changes have been made in plant nomenclature. As from the publication of the 1952 edition of the *International Code of Nomenclature of Cultivated Plants*, all specific epithets should begin with small letters (e.g. *Magnolia kobus* not *Magnolia Kobus*). Where specific epithets commemorating persons are in the genitive singular they should end in -*ii* (men) or -*iae* (women) (e.g. *M. wilsonii* not *M. wilsoni*) unless the personal name ends in a vowel (including y and j in certain Slav languages) or -*er*, in which case they should end in -*i* or -*ae* (e.g. *M. ashei*, *M. fraseri*).

Another change involves the specific epithet for *M. obovata* which now reverts to *M. hypoleuca* while *M. cordata* is now accepted as a form of *M. acuminata*. Several more recently proposed changes involve the changing of *M. denudata* to *M. heptapeta* and *M. liliflora* to *M. quinquepeta*.

In his 'Revised Survey' Dandy found it necessary to change the names of one of his sections, also one of his subgenera. In so doing he explained that, whereas the name *Magnoliastrum* which he used in his 1950 'Survey' was correct at that time, the International Botanical Congress, in 1954, decided the type-section must bear an epithet repeating the generic name, as had been the practice with subgenera. Hence Section *Magnoliastrum* now becomes Section *Magnolia* and since Dandy considered that Reichenbach's groups, published in 1841, are subgenera, not sections, the epithet of the second subgenus in his Key must be changed from *Pleurochasma* Dandy to *Yulania* (Spach) Reichb. However, the sectional epithet *Yulania* still stands as it designates the typical section of the Subgenus *Yulania*.

Dandy therefore divided the genus into two subgenera, *Magnolia* and *Yulania* (Pleurochasma). These were subdivided into eleven sections, with their general distribution in eastern Asia and the Americas north of the equator. In each of the subgenera Dandy has a section with species from the temperate parts of both North America and eastern Asia.

The Subgenus *Magnolia* includes some Asian evergreen species but these are not in the same botanical section as the American ones and none of them is likely to be quite as hardy as the American *M. grandiflora*.

Of the twenty-six recognized American species, eighteen belong to the Section *Theorhodon*, including *M. grandiflora*. The remaining seventeen species in this section are divided between the continental uplands and the high islands, southward to the slopes of Cerro Roraima in the Guiana highlands of Venezuela. The author has included notes on the Mexican *M. schiediana* (p. 78), hitherto spelt *schiedeana* which was the spelling used by Schlechtendahl in 1864. But R.H.S. botanist, Mr. C. D. Brickell, Director of Wisley, considers this to be an orthographical error which should be corrected under Article 73 of the Botanical Code because it involved the use of a wrong connecting vowel. The correct connecting vowel for epithets taken from a man's name is 'i' (e.g. *soulangiana* derived from Soulange-Bodin).

Dandy limited the small Section *Magnolia* (*Magnoliastrum*) to *M. virginiana* (*M. glauca*) the American Sweet Bay.

The third section is the deciduous *Rytidospermum* which includes five species from the eastern United States and one from the mountains of southern Mexico allied to *M. macrophylla*, while the Asian members are *M. hypoleuca* (*M. obovata*), *M. officinalis* and *M. rostrata*.

In the second subgenus, *Yulania*, there are the two wholly Asian sections, *Yulania* and *Buergeria*, together with *Tulipastrum* which contains one Chinese species, *M. quinquepeta* (*liliflora*), and one American species, *M. acuminata* (including *M. cordata*).

In the *Newsletter of the American Magnolia Society* 8, 1 : 3–6 (1971) Dandy contributed a re-edited version of his *Classification of Magnoliaceae*, the original having been published in Dr. John Hutchinson's *The Genera of Flowering Plants* 1 : 50–7 (1964). In this he wrote: 'A constant feature of the family is the deciduous stipules which leave annular scars at the nodes; they are either free from the petiole or more or less adnate to it. Another constant feature is the presence on the peduncle of one or more deciduous spathaceous bracts which leave similar scars. There is no doubt that these bracts consist of a petiole plus a pair of adnate stipules, and that the adnate condition is primitive. In no case is there any transition between bracts and tepals. The stamens and carpels, like the bracts and foliage leaves, are always spirally arranged; but the tepals, at least as regards the outer whorls, are always strictly cyclic.

'*Geographical Distribution.* The *Magnoliaceae* have a markedly discontinuous distribution and they once occupied a much larger area of the earth's surface, fossil remains being well marked and widely distributed. These are found in Tertiary deposits in the Arctic Circle, Greenland, Europe and the central plains of North America. The advent of the ice ages probably destroyed the greater part of the family, those now remaining occurring in S.E. North America, the West Indies, Central America to E. Brazil, and in S.E. Asia. The family contains no austral elements, though in South America and the Malay Archipelago it extends via mountain-ranges and plateaux into the southern hemisphere. Its greatest concentration of species is in S.E. Asia, in the region extending from the E. Himalaya eastwards to China and southwards to Java.'

KEY TO SUBGENERA AND SECTIONS OF *MAGNOLIA*

by J. E. Dandy

A. Anthers dehiscing introrsely; flowers neither precocious nor with a much reduced (calyx-like) outer whorl of tepals; leaves evergreen or deciduous: fruit various –

Subgen. *MAGNOLIA*; type *M. virginiana* L.

  B. Stipules adnate to the petiole, leaving a scar on its upper surface:

    C. Leaves evergreen; flower-buds at first enclosed in one or more spathaceous bracts which leave as many annular scars on the peduncle; Asian species:

      D. Fruiting-carpels short-beaked, the beak not dorsally flattened –

Sect. *Gwillimia* DC; type *M. pumila* Andr. = *Gwillimia indica* Rottl. ex DC. = *M. coco* (Lour.) DC.

      DD. Fruiting-carpels long-beaked, the beak forming a dorsally flattened lanceolate coriaceous appendage and finally becoming more or less recurved –

Sect. *Lirianthe* (Spach) Dandy; type *Lirianthe grandiflora* (Roxb.) Spach = *M. pterocarpa* Roxb.

    CC. Leaves deciduous (sometimes persistent in the American section *Magnolia*); flower-buds at first enclosed in a single spathaceous bract which leaves a single annular scar on the peduncle:

      E. Leaves crowded into false whorls at the ends of the branchlets, usually large or very large; Asian and American species –

Sect. *Rytidospermum* Spach; type *M. umbrella* Desr. = *M. tripetala* (L.) L.

      EE. Leaves not crowded into false whorls at the ends of the branchlets:

        F. Anthers with the connective produced into a short acute appendage; leave sdeciduous or sometimes persistent, glaucous on the undersurface; American species –

Sect. *Magnolia*; type *M. virginiana* L.

        FF. Anthers with the connective blunt or retuse and not normally produced into an appendage; leaves deciduous, the under-surface pale-green or somewhat glaucescent; Asian species –

Sect. *Oyama* Nakai; type *M. parviflora* Sieb. & Zucc. = *M. sieboldii* C. Koch.

  BB. Stipules free from the petiole, the latter unscarred; leaves evergreen:

    G. Tepals subsimilar in texture; fruit ellipsoid to oblong, sometimes distorted; leaves with a more or less elongated petiole:

      H. Gynoecium sessile; American species –

Sect. *Theorhodon* Spach; type *M. grandiflora* L.

      HH. Gynoecium usually shortly stipitate; plants entirely glabrous; Asian species –

Sect. *Gynopodium* Dandy; type *M. nitida* W. W. Sm.

    GG. Tepals of the outer whorl much thinner in texture than those of the inner whorls; fruit more or less cylindric, usually distorted; leaves with a comparatively short petiole; Asian species –

Sect. *Maingola* Dandy; type *M. maingayi* King.

AA. Anthers dehiscing laterally or sublaterally; flowers precocious and/or with a much-reduced (calyx-like) outer whorl of tepals; leaves deciduous; fruit cylindric or oblong, usually more or less distorted –

Subgen. *YULANIA* (Spach) Reichb.; type *Yulania conspicua* (Salisb.) Spach = *M. denudata* Desr. [= *M. heptapeta* Buc'hoz]

I. Tepals subequal; flowers appearing before the leaves, white to rose or rose-purple; Asian species –

Sect. *Yulania*

II. Tepals very unequal, those of the outer whorl much shorter and simulating a calyx:

  J. Flowers appearing before the leaves; inner (large) tepals white, sometimes tinged with rose or purple; Asian species –

Sect. *Buergeria* (Sieb. & Zucc.) Dandy; type *Buergeria stellata* Sieb. & Zucc. = *M. stellata* (Sieb. & Zucc.) Maxim. [= *M. kobus* var. *stellata* Blackburn]

  JJ. Flowers appearing with or after the leaves; inner (large) tepals purple or green to yellow; Asian and American species –

Sect. *Tulipastrum* (Spach) Dandy; type *Tulipastrum americanum* Spach = *M. acuminata* (L.) L.

A REVISED SURVEY OF THE GENUS *MAGNOLIA* TOGETHER WITH *MANGLIETIA* AND *MICHELIA*

by J. E. Dandy

[*In order to make the text more readily understandable to the layman, the abbreviated botanical references found in the original text have been transcribed in full.*]

Subgenus *MAGNOLIA*

Magnolia subgenus *Magnolia*; based on *Magnolia* Linnaeus, *Species Plantarum* 1 : 535 (1753) and *Genera Plantarum* Edition 5 : 240 (1754)

Section *Gwillimia* de Candolle

Magnolia sect. *Gwillimia* de Candolle, *Regni Vegetabilis Systema Naturale* 1 : 455, 548 (1817)

This is a large section of the genus, with about sixteen species in south-east Asia, ranging from southern China through Indo-China to the Philippines. The species are very similar in appearance to species of the tropical genus *Talauma*, which differs chiefly in having a different type of fruit. Indeed so close is the resemblance that in the absence of fruiting material the generic position of some of the species remains uncertain. The only temperate species in the section is *M. delavayi*, of Yunnan, and this is the only one of real interest to gardeners, by whom it is especially valued on account of its handsome evergreen foliage. It has been in cultivation for about seventy years. Another species, *M. coco* (formerly called *M. pumila*), has the distinction of being the first Asian Magnolia to be grown in this country (1786), but it is not hardy and in any event has no great horticultural merit. The other species of the section include *M. henryi* (the largest-leaved evergreen Magnolia), *M. fistulosa*, *M. paenetalauma*, *M. championii*, *M. nana*, *M. pachyphylla* and *M. albosericea*.

Section *Lirianthe* (Spach) Dandy

Magnolia sect. *Lirianthe* (Spach) Dandy in *Camellias and Magnolias Conference Report*: 68 (1950); based on *Lirianthe* Spach, *Histoire Naturelle des Végétaux, Phanérogames* 7 : 485 (1839)

There is only one species in this section: *M. pterocarpa*, a tree of India and Burma, remarkable for the long flattened beaks which terminate the fruiting-carpels. The species is tropical and not suitable for cultivation in our climate.

Section *Rytidospermum* Spach

Magnolia sect. *Rytidospermum* Spach, *Histoire Naturelle des Végétaux, Phanérogames* 7 : 474 (1839)

This section contains nine species of deciduous trees and is one of the two sections which occur both in Asia and America. Its most striking character is the whorl-like arrangement of the leaves, because of which the American species have long been known as Umbrella Trees. Except for the tropical *M. dealbata* all the species are in cultivation. Three series can be recognized, one Asian and the other two American, and each contains three species.

The Asian series comprises *M. hypoleuca, M. officinalis* and *M. rostrata. M. hypoleuca* (often known as *M. obovata*) is a well known species in cultivation; it is native of Japan and is the easternmost of the Asian species. Closely allied to it, but differing in the colour of the branchlets and the size of the fruit, is *M. officinalis*, a Chinese species which was at first identified as *M. hypoleuca* and may be found in gardens under that name. This tree appears to occur wild in east China, but further west it is found only in cultivation; it is remarkable for the fact that its leaves are often bilobed at the apex. *M. rostrata*, distinguished by its longer-beaked fruiting-carpels and rufous indumentum, grows in north-western Yunnan and adjacent parts of south-eastern Tibet and north-eastern Upper Burma. When first introduced into cultivation it was believed to have precocious flowers, but this was due to a misapprehension: the flowers, as always in this section, appear after the leaves.

The first of the two American series of this section comprises *M. tripetala, M. fraseri* and *M. pyramidata* the two latter being characterized by their auriculate-cordate leaves and complete lack of hairs. *M. tripetala*, the original Umbrella Tree, is one of the oldest-established Magnolias in cultivation, but like most of the other American species it has gone out of favour; it is indigenous to the Appalachian and Ozark mountain systems of the eastern United States. *M. fraseri* has a more restricted distribution in the southern Appalachian Mountains. Very closely allied to *M. fraseri* is *M. pyramidata*, a plant of the coastal plain of the south-eastern United States. This species was introduced into Britain as long ago as 1806, but it is doubtful whether any trees survive.

The other American series includes three closely allied species remarkable for the enormous dimensions attained by the leaves, which are the largest in the genus. Best known is *M. macrophylla*, which is native of the south-eastern United States in the region of the southern Appalachian and Ozark Mountains. Its leaves may attain over a yard (1 m) in length, and the flowers also are very large. *M. ashei*, described in 1926 from the coastal plain of north-west Florida, is very closely related to *M. macrophylla*. It was introduced into cultivation at the New York Botanical Garden by J. K. Small, and in an article entitled 'A Magnolia as a New Border Plant' he has described how plants in cultivation flowered when only about one foot (30·5 cm) tall! The species also behaves like this in the wild state, but normally it is a shrub or small tree up to a height of about twenty-five feet (7·5 m). Another close ally of *M. macrophylla* is *M. dealbata*, from the mountains of southern Mexico, which is notable as the only deciduous

Magnolia found in the tropics; it is not known in cultivation. Very surprisingly this Mexican species is the earliest recorded Magnolia, having been described and figured by Hernandez as long ago as 1651.

Section *Magnolia* (formerly *Magnoliastrum*)

Magnolia sect. *Magnoliastrum* de Candolle, *Prodromus* 1 : 80 (1824) emend.

This section, originally founded by De Candolle to include all the American Magnolias, is now restricted to a single species, *M. virginiana*, the type of the genus. *M. virginiana* is a very distinct and easily recognized species, differing widely from *M. grandiflora* in its glaucous leaves and adnate stipules. Its home is in the region of the Atlantic coastal plain in the eastern United States, and two geographical varieties are sometimes recognized. The northern (typical) variety, which is the one usually found in cultivation, extends from Massachusetts to eastern Florida; it is a shrub or small tree, the leaves deciduous or sometimes persisting. The southern variety, *M. virginiana* var. *australis*, ranges from North Carolina to Texas. It grows to a larger size than the typical variety and its leaves are more persistent, while the young branchlets and flower stalks are densely hairy. *M. virginiana* has the distinction of being the first Magnolia to be brought into cultivation (1688).

Section *Oyama* Nakai

Magnolia sect. *Oyama* Nakai, *Flora Sylvatica Koreana* 20 : 117 (1933)

This is a group of deciduous shrubs or small trees confined to temperate east Asia. There are four species, all in cultivation and deservedly popular on account of the beauty of the flowers, in which the usually white tepals contrast pleasingly with the purple-red stamens and green carpels. The easternmost species, and the oldest one in cultivation, is *M. sieboldii* (well known under the name *M. parviflora*) which is found in Japan, Korea, Manchuria and the eastern Chinese province of Anhwei. There is a striking gap between the distribution of *M. sieboldii* and that of the allied species in western China. Two of these, *M. sinensis* and *M. wilsonii*, occur in western Szechwan, but whereas the former is known only from a single locality, *M. wilsonii* is wider spread and extends into northern Yunnan. *M. sinensis*, like *M. sieboldii*, has leaves which are mostly of an obovate type. In *M. wilsonii*, however, the leaves are chiefly of an ovate or elliptic type, as they are also in *M. globosa*, the most western species of the section, which extends from eastern Nepal along the eastern Himalayas to extreme north-western Yunnan.

Section *Theorhodon* Spach

Magnolia sect. *Theorhodon* Spach, *Histoire Naturelle des Végétaux, Phanérogames* 7 : 470 (1839)

This is the largest of the American sections, having about eighteen species. These are all ever-green trees, often growing to large dimensions, and it is unfortunate that with one exception they are all tropical and not suitable for cultivation in our climate. The exception is *M. grandi-flora*, a native of the south-eastern United States in the region of the coastal plain. *M. grandiflora* was one of the first Magnolias to be brought into gardens (by 1732), and until the coming of *M. delavayi* was the only hardy evergreen species. It has retained popularity as an evergreen, and numerous garden forms have been developed especially in the south of Europe where the species is more at home. The allies of *M. grandiflora* form two series of tropical species, one of which is confined to the Greater Antilles in the islands of Cuba, Hispaniola and Puerto Rico, while the other extends on the mainland from Mexico through Central America to northern South America.

The tropical series on the mainland begins in the north with the Mexican *M. schiediana*. Then, in geographical order, come *M. sharpii* (from eastern Mexico), *M. guatemalensis* (from Guatemala), *M. yoroconte* (from Honduras), *M. poasana* (from Costa Rica), *M. sororum* (from Panama) and *M. ptaritepuiana* (from the mountains of south-eastern Venezuela). All these appear to be closely related to *M. schiediana*.

The West Indian series contains about eight species, including the following: *M. cubensis*, from eastern Cuba; *M. domingensis*, *M. emarginata* and *M. ekmanii*, all from Haiti; *M. pallescens* and *M. hamorii*, from the Dominican Republic; *M. portoricensis*, from western Puerto Rico; and *M. splendens*, from eastern Puerto Rico. *M. splendens* is notable for its beautiful indumentum of shining appressed hairs, contrasting remarkably with the entirely glabrous *M. portoricensis* which inhabits the western end of the same island.

Section *Gynopodium* Dandy

Magnolia sect. *Gynopodium* Dandy in *Curtis's Botanical Magazine* 165 : sub t. 16 (1948)

The species of this small Asian section are characterized by a usually shortly-stalked gynoecium, a complete lack of hairs, and comparatively small glossy evergreen leaves with free stipules. Geographically they range from south-eastern Tibet to south-eastern China and the island of Taiwan (Formosa). The only one in cultivation is *M. nitida*; its home is in north-western Yunnan and adjacent parts of south-eastern Tibet and north-eastern Upper Burma – a dis-tribution very similar to that of *M. rostrata*. *M. kachirachirai*, an allied species from Taiwan, is tropical and not a likely proposition for gardeners. It has smaller leaves and flowers than *M. nitida*. The other species of the section are not yet fully understood; they are distributed in south-eastern China and include *M. lotungensis*.

Section *Maingola* Dandy

Magnolia sect. *Maingola* Dandy in *Curtis's Botanical Magazine* 165 : sub t. 16 (1948)

This is a tropical Asian section, of great interest botanically but containing no species suitable for cultivation in our climate. The species are evergreens, with short-petiolate leaves and free stipules. In some species the gynoecium is shortly stalked as in Section *Gynopodium*, but the fruit resembles that of the next subgenus. The geographical range of Section *Maingola* extends from Assam to Indo-China and the Malay Archipelago, farther south, in fact, than any other section of *Magnolia*. There are about fourteen species, including the following: *M. griffithii*, from Assam and Upper Burma; *M. pealiana* and *M. gustavii*, both from Assam; *M. annamensis*, from Annam; *M. maingayi*, from the Malay Peninsula and Sarawak; *M. aequinoctialis*, from Sumatra and *M. macklottii*, from Sumatra and Java. The last named is the southernmost of all Magnolias, either in Asia or America.

Subgenus YULANIA (Spach) Reichenbach (formerly PLEUROCHASMA)

Magnolia subgenus *Yulania* (Spach) Reichenbach in *Der Deutsche Botaniker* 1 : 192 (1841); based on *Yulania* Spach, *Histoire Naturelle des Végétaux, Phanérogames* 7 : 462 (1839)
Magnolia subgenus *Pleurochasma* Dandy in *Journal of the Royal Horticultural Society* 75 : 161 (1950)

Section *Yulania*

Magnolia sect. *Yulania* (Spach) Dandy in *Camellias and Magnolias Conference Report*: 72 (1950)

This is without doubt the finest section of *Magnolia* from a garden point of view. The flowers are precocious with nine or more large tepals which vary in colour from white to rose or rose purple; and the trees when in full flower are objects of surpassing beauty. There are five or more species, distributed in temperate east Asia from the eastern Himalayas to eastern China, but not extending to Japan. The oldest species in cultivation is the white-flowered Yulan, native of east China but long cultivated in many parts of that country as well as in Japan; it is now called *M. denudata*,★ but it has also been known by a variety of other names such as *M. heptapeta, M. precia, M. conspicua* and *M. yulan*. In central China, in the region of western Hupeh, western Honan and eastern Szechwan, the place of the Yulan is taken by *M. sprengeri*, of which two or three forms are in cultivation. Some plants of *M. sprengeri* are white flowered, while in others the flowers are rose or rose purple – a variation which occurs also in *M. campbellii* and the other western species of the section. Two of these western species are found in

---

★ In 1976 this name gave way to *heptapeta*.

western Szechwan. One of them, *M. dawsoniana*, is apparently a very rare species for it has been collected in only one locality. The very closely allied *M. sargentiana*, however, has a wider range, occurring also in northern Yunnan. This is a magnificent species, rivalling *M. campbellii* in size and beauty of flower; it was introduced into cultivation by Wilson in 1908 along with *M. dawsoniana*. *M. campbellii*, another striking species, is the westernmost representative of the section, its geographical range extending from Nepal along the eastern Himalayas to western Yunnan. The type of *M. campbellii* came from the Sikkim Himalayas, and it was from here that the species was originally brought into cultivation in 1868. Specimens from the eastern end of the range (western Yunnan and extreme south-eastern Tibet) have been named *M. mollicomata*, and plants from Forrest's seed collected in this area are in cultivation. As often happens in species with this distribution (Himalayas to west China) the plants from the two extremes of the range show differences, the significance of which is open to different interpretations. It must be borne in mind, however, in this case as in others, that the individuals in cultivation, numerous though they may be, are the progeny of but a few wild plants from the two extremes of the range and do not represent a fair sample of the wild population *in toto*. To my mind the differences which exist between the *mollicomata* forms and typical *M. campbellii* are not of specific value.

In addition to the species mentioned above, two others have been described which are apparently closely allied to the Yulan and therefore belong to this section. *M. zenii*, from the neighbourhood of Nanking in southern Kiangsu, has white tepals with a purple base. *M. amoena*, from north-western Chekiang, is described as having pink flowers. I have not seen specimens and am unable to make any further botanical comment on these plants; but whatever their taxonomic status they appear desirable subjects for cultivation.

Section *Buergeria* (Siebold & Zuccarini) Dandy

Magnolia sect. *Buergeria* (Siebold & Zuccarini) Dandy in *Camellias and Magnolias Conference Report*: 73 (1950); based on *Buergeria* Siebold & Zuccarini in *Abhandlungen der Mathematisch-physikalischen Classe der Königlich Bayerischen Akademie der Wissenschaften* 4, 2 : 186 (1846)

This is another temperate Asian section and, like the last, is precocious flowered and very popular in cultivation. It differs technically from Section *Yulania* in the form of the perianth, the tepals of the outer whorl being much reduced in size and forming a small 'calyx'. The prevailing flower colour is white though there is sometimes a tinge of rose or rose purple. There are five species: three in Japan, one in eastern China and one in north-central China. The three Japanese species are *M. kobus*, *M. salicifolia* and *M. stellata*, all well known in cultivation. *M. kobus*, the most widely distributed of the three, falls into two geographical varieties which are both in cultivation. Typical *M. kobus* inhabits southern Japan and is found also in Cheju Do (Quelpart Island) off the coast of Southern Korea. The more northern variety *borealis* occurs in northern Japan (Hokkaido and northern Honshu); it is a bigger tree with larger leaves and flowers and is said to be the hardiest of the Asian Magnolias in cultivation. *M. salicifolia*, which as its name implies has willow-like leaves, has a more restricted distribution than *M. kobus* and does not reach the northern island of Hokkaido; two forms of it are in cultivation, one of which has a fastigiate habit. *M. stellata*, which is said to be spontaneous in the islands of Honshu and Kyushu, is a very distinct species on account of its flowers, which have numerous tepals giving the characteristic starry effect; these are typically white, but forms are grown in which the tepals are more or less deeply suffused with pink. The two Chinese species of the section are not familiar to gardeners, though both have been brought into cultivation. *M. biondii* (*M. aulacosperma*), which was one of the species brought to the Arnold Arboretum from China by Wilson in 1908, is the northernmost of Chinese Magnolias, with a range extending from Shensi to western Honan, western Hupeh and eastern Szechwan, and it should certainly be hardy; like *M. salicifolia* it is a 'willow-leaved' species with white flowers. The other Chinese species is *M. cylindrica*; its home is in eastern China, from southern Anhwei to northern Fukien, and it appears to be most closely allied to *M. kobus*.

Section *Tulipastrum* (Spach) Dandy

Magnolia sect. *Tulipastrum* (Spach) Dandy in *Camellias and Magnolias Conference Report:* 74 (1950); based on *Tulipastrum* Spach, *Histoire Naturelle des Végétaux, Phanérogames* 7 : 481 (1839)

This is one of the two sections of *Magnolia* which are common to Asia and America. It resembles Section *Buergeria* in the reduction of the outer whorl of tepals to a small 'calyx', but differs in the form and colour of the inner tepals which are purple, green or yellow. The leaves are deciduous, appearing either before or along with the flowers, so that the latter are never truly precocious as in Sections *Yulania* and *Buergeria*. There are two species, one Asian and one American, and both have long been in cultivation. The American species, which has green or yellow flowers, is *M. acuminata* (including *M. cordata*). *M. acuminata*, known as the Cucumber Tree on account of the form of the unripe fruit, is the most widely distributed of American Magnolias and the only one which reaches Canada where it occurs in extreme south-eastern Ontario. Its range extends through the Appalachian and Ozark mountain-systems of the eastern United States from New York southwards.

The Asian species of this section is *M. liliflora*,* which has also been known as *M. quinquepeta*, *M. purpurea*, *M. discolor* and *M. gracilis*, and was at one time wrongly named *M. obovata*. It is a very distinct species with purple flowers and has long been cultivated in China and Japan along with the Yulan, with which it has had a close and tangled association in botanical literature. Unlike the Yulan, however, *M. liliflora* is unknown in the truly wild state, though it is believed to have originated in eastern China and probably in the temperate region south of the Yangtze River. Again unlike the Yulan, *M. liliflora* has no close allies in Asia, and it is my opinion that,

---

* In 1976 this name gave way to the earlier name *quinquepeta*.

despite the contrast in flower colour, the affinities of this species are with the American *M. acuminata* with which it agrees closely in both vegetative and floral structure.

Manglietia

Manglietia is an Asian genus of about twenty-five species, very closely allied to *Magnolia* from which it differs technically in the greater number of ovules in the carpels. The range of the genus extends from the eastern Himalayas across southern China, and southwards through Thailand and Indo-China to Malaysia where the southern limit is in Java. It is not known to reach Japan or Taiwan. Most of the species are tropical or of tropical type and the geographical distribution suggests that only five species are of interest to gardeners. Three of these, *M. insignis*, *M. hookeri* and *M. forrestii*, have been introduced into cultivation by Forrest, but the only one which can be regarded as at all hardy is *M. insignis*. This is a widely distributed species extending from the central Himalayas into south-central China and north-western Tongking. Wallich, who originally described the species from Nepal, remarked that 'It is scarcely possible to contemplate a more magnificent object than this noble tree exhibits, both when it is covered with flowers and in fruit . . . the accumulated fragrance of the innumerable blossoms, with which this tree is covered at one and same time, extends to a great distance'. This is no mean eulogy from a man who saw very many fine plants in his time, and it is to be hoped that the species will live up to it in cultivation; it has flowered in a Cornish garden in recent years. The other two species of *Manglietia* which have been introduced into cultivation are *M. hookeri* (from Upper Burma and western Yunnan) and *M. forrestii* (from western and southern Yunnan). There are two species of the genus, not yet introduced, which may have possibilities as garden plants, namely *M. szechuanica* (from western Szechwan) and *M. duclouxii* (from north-eastern Yunnan). All these species of *Manglietia* are evergreen trees, showing great uniformity in both vegetative and floral structure.

Michelia

Michelia differs from *Magnolia* and *Manglietia* primarily in having axillary flowers, and another important character lies in the gynoecium which is always stalked. This is a large genus of about forty-five species, confined to Asia and predominantly tropical. Its geographical range extends from India and Ceylon eastwards through southern China to Japan, and southwards through Thailand and Indo-China to Malaysia with the southern limit in Java. The leaves are evergreen, and as the flowers are borne in the leaf axils instead of only at the ends of the branchlets as in *Magnolia* they are produced more profusely than in that genus, though on the average their size is much smaller.

Michelia champaca, the type of the genus, is a well known cultivated tree in the tropics and has highly scented yellow flowers. It was introduced into Britain as long ago as 1779 but is not hardy; its distribution as a wild plant extends from India to Indo-China. Another non-hardy species, *M. figo* (formerly known as *Magnolia fuscata*) was introduced into Britain in 1796. This species is native of south-eastern China and is widely cultivated in warm countries.

Of the species which may be considered hardy in cultivation the finest is *Michelia doltsopa*, in which the white or yellowish flowers are of fair size and are at first enclosed in beautifully rufous-tomentose spathaceous bracts. Its geographical range extends from Nepal to western Yunnan. An allied species of similar distribution is *M. velutina* (*M. lanuginosa*), in which the leaves are densely hairy beneath. This species was introduced to Kew from Sikkim about 1855 and flowered in the Temperate House in 1875; I have no record of its being grown out of doors. *M. compressa*, a native of Japan and Taiwan, is the hardiest species of *Michelia* in cultivation, but its flowers are disappointingly small. It was introduced into Britain in 1894.

The remaining species of *Michelia* are, as already indicated, chiefly tropical; but there are a few which, judged from their temperate distribution, might prove hardy if introduced. In Yunnan, for example, there are *M. microtricha*, an ally of *M. doltsopa*, and *M. yunnanensis*, which is allied to *M. figo*; while in Szechwan are *M. wilsonii* and *M. szechuanica*, both of which belong to the same group as *M. doltsopa*. At present the horticultural merit of these plants is a matter only for speculation★.

★ James Edgar Dandy (1903–76) joined the Herbarium staff at Kew in 1925 where he worked for two years as assistant to the late Dr. John Hutchinson, who was then elaborating a new system of classification for flowering plants. He gave Dandy the opportunity to revise three genera, one of which was *Magnoliaceae*. Magnolias became his main future interest and he was the acknowledged world authority.

In 1927 he moved from Kew to the British Museum (Natural History) in Cromwell Road, London, where he was Keeper of Botany from 1956 to 1966. Long after his official retirement he continued his botanical work at the Zoological Museum at Tring, Herts, maintaining regular weekly visits to the Herbarium and Library in which he had worked for almost 40 years.

He constantly maintained the high standard of scholarship associated with the British Museum (Natural History) and became almost morbidly reluctant to publish his continually revised works which were never, for him, quite perfect enough. Consequently the monograph on the *Magnoliaceae*, upon which he had worked for nearly half a century, remains unpublished.

After a short illness, he died on 10 November 1976. It is sad he did not survive to proof-read his contribution as he had insisted that he should when he revised it for publication in this book.

Both amateur and professional growers of Magnolias will be wondering who has rocked the boat of Magnolia nomenclature and for what reasons. Some of the proposed changes adopted recently in America by Dr. Stephen Spongberg, and also by *Hortus III*, are taxonomical and therefore the concern of the professional botanist. These include the recognition of Dr. Benjamin Blackburn's treatment (1955) whereby *M. stellata* becomes *M. kobus* var. *stellata* which leads to *M.* × *loebneri* being relegated from hybrid status to M. *kobus* var. *loebneri*. Then a veritable cascade of demotions in rank has been recommended by Dr. Spongberg's treatment of *M. salicifolia*, whereby he has scuttled *M.* × *kewensis*, together with *M.* × *proctoriana* and *M.* × *slavinii*, to sink them among the variants of that species.

In all of these cases we should accept without criticism the conclusions of those who have made far more profound studies of Magnolia taxonomy than any layman, but some other proposed changes in nomenclature are open to criticism.

For many years we have come to know *M. denudata* and *M. liliflora* by these self-descriptive specific epithets which, in spite of their latinized form, readily conjure up mental images of these two quite different species. The same can never be said of the names likely to replace them, when *M. heptapeta* (seven petalled) replaces the name *denudata* which has nine tepals and when *M. quinquepeta* (five petalled) replaces the name *M. liliflora* which never has fewer than six petaloid tepals and sometimes as many as nine, in addition to the usually three sepaloid tepals of the false calyx.

When these names become universally accepted future listings will express the parentage of the *M.* × *soulangiana* grex as *M. heptapeta* × *M. quinquepeta* which would satisfy the accepted priority either of alphabetical sequence or that of the female parent first since, until recently, there were no known hybrids of this parentage where *M. quinquepeta* (as *M. liliflora* or under one of its other earlier names) was the female or seed parent. (Prof. J. C. McDaniel has recently raised seedlings from a reverse cross.)

It can, of course, be argued that the first of such botanical inexactitudes was published even earlier (in 1759) when that venerable creator of modern botanical nomenclature, the Swedish botanist Carolus Linnaeus, gave the name *tripetala* to a Magnolia known to him only in the form of a very accurate painting which had been made in America by the English botanist Mark Catesby and which had been published in *Flora Caroliniana* 2 : 80 (1741). Catesby's plate clearly depicts a flower with nine tepals, the six innermost ones poised more or less vertically around the stigmatic column while the outermost three are reflexed sub-horizontally, in a manner which Catesby described as *petalis exterioribus dependentibus*, adding 'flowers white, ten to eleven petals, the three outermost pale green, later hanging downwards'. Had Linnaeus named it *M. trisepala* he would have satisfied both botanists and horticulturists but, strange to relate, nobody appears to have criticized the selection of such a misleading specific epithet for a Magnolia which later became the type species of Section *Rytidospermum*.

Quite a different story can be told concerning the *heptapeta* and *quinquepeta* which were coined by the French botanist P. J. Buch'hoz just two centuries ago. In 1779 he published in *Plantes Nouvellement Découvertes* 21 : t. 19, fig. 2, under his newly invented name *Lassonia quinquepeta*, a flower which had been obviously copied from a Chinese impressionist representation of the plant known long since as *M. liliflora*; but the stigmatic column, so characteristic of Magnolia flowers, had been replaced by a flattened boss of stamens. The same type of configuration appears at fig. 1 for a plant (intended to represent *M. denudata* but with only seven tepals) which he christened *Lassonia heptapeta* and, to make matters worse, the outer whorl of tepals is shown in the form of a fringed calyx. *Lassonia* was later merged with *Magnolia*. The Buc'hoz practice, of publishing inaccurate drawings and paintings taken from artistic representations of Chinese flowers of which he had no other knowledge and of applying to them botanical names of his own creation, caused him to fall into ill repute, not only among other botanists of his own generation, but also among those who succeeded him. Thus it came about that a fellow botanist, with an obvious sense of humour, decided to commemorate his name in a new genus with an evil odour: *Bucozia foetida*★ (subsequently renamed *Serissa foetida*).

Consequently, succeeding generations of botanists, when reviewing the family Magnoliaceae, have chosen to ignore the early Buc'hoz nomenclature. Thus it was that, in 1913, American botanist Dr. Rehder dismissed the Buc'hoz name and description as being 'manca falsaque', inadequate and false, when he adopted the name *denudata* which has since become established in botanical literature as the accepted specific epithet for this Magnolia.

In 1934 the late J. E. Dandy contributed notes on 'The Identity of *Lassonia* Buc'hoz' in *Journal of Botany* 72 : 101–3, that genus which had been founded by the French botanist Buc'hoz in *Plantes Nouvellement Découvertes*: 21 (1779) and named in honour of M. de Lassone who was physician to the French royal household.

For more than a century *Lassonia* had been completely ignored by other botanists until it appeared in the *Appendix to the Index Kewensis* 2, 1289 (1895) where it was designated 'Genus spurium Magnoliacearum'.

Dandy discussed the misleading Buc'hoz epithets *heptapeta* and *quinquepeta* and argued that they are not more so than Linnaeus's epithet *tripetala* for a Magnolia with nine to twelve or sometimes fifteen tepals. He considered that they were legitimately published and, being the oldest for these two species, 'they necessitate name changes that are particularly undesirable because the nomenclatural history of the plants concerned is already very complicated'.

_____

★ *Curtis's Botanical Magazine* describes this plant under *Lycium japonicum* thus: 'The flowers are somewhat like jasmine but without scent, as is the whole plant if not bruised, but if you strongly squeeze a flower bud or tip of a young shoot betwixt your thumb and finger you will perceive a smell highly disgusting which Kaempfer likens to human ordure.'

He considered that the Buc'hoz discrepancies in the published descriptions are fully accounted for by defects in the drawings. From the drawings Buc'hoz counted seven tepals ('pétales') in the white-flowered species which he then named *L. heptapeta* (it normally has nine, or occasionally ten to twelve, subequal tepals); and five in the purple-flowered species which he named *L. quinquepeta* (it normally has six to twelve plus three small outer ones which represent the false calyx). Dandy then proceeded to list 'the necessary new combinations for the two species . . . along with their most important synonyms' under *Magnolia heptapeta* (Buc'hoz) Dandy and *M. quinquepeta* (Buc'hoz) Dandy.

All of this was published over forty years ago, and, although these names have been used on a few rare occasions (the 'Purple Eye' clone of *M. denudata* received an R.H.S. Award of Merit as *M. heptapeta* in 1926 probably from Dandy's naming), they were completely ignored by Millais (1927) and disregarded by Johnstone (1955). Even Dandy avoided their use in his 'Survey of the Genus *Magnolia*' (1950) referring to them only as early synonyms for *M. denudata* and *M. liliflora* respectively.

But it was only a matter of time before one of a younger generation of botanists would decide to apply rigidly the rule of priority of publication which has led to so many changes in plant nomenclature in the past.★ Originating as they do from the Arnold Arboretum of Harvard University, an establishment recognized from the time of Sargent, Rehder and Wilson, as one of the leading world authorities on *Magnoliaceae*, it seems certain that these changes in nomenclature will be eventually adopted, no matter how unpalatable they may seem. Another change involves *M.* × *watsonii* which now becomes *M.* × *wieseneri*.

★ The Eleventh International Botanical Congress was convened at Seattle in August 1969 and resulted in the publication of the *International Code of Botanical Nomenclature* (1972). The preamble states 'The only proper reasons for changing a name are either a more profound knowledge of the facts resulting from adequate taxonomic study or the necessity of giving up a nomenclature that is contrary to the rules.'

Section 3 deals with the Rule of Priority under which Article 11 governs the treatment for the names of species which reads 'For any taxon below the rank of genus, the correct name is the combination of the earliest available legitimate epithet in the same rank with the correct name of the genus or species to which it is assigned.'

Article 62 reads 'A legitimate name or epithet must not be rejected merely because it is inappropriate or disagreeable, or because another is preferable or better known, or because it has lost its original meaning'. Article 14 contains an escape clause applicable to the names of ranks superior to that of species and reads 'In order to avoid disadvantageous changes in the nomenclature of genera, families, and intermediate taxa entailed by the strict application of the rules, and especially of the principle of priority in starting from the dates given in Art. 13, [May 1753 in respect of most groups of plants] this Code provides lists of names that are conserved (*nomina conservanda*) and must be retained as useful exceptions. Conservation aims at retention of those generic names which best serve stability of nomenclature.'

THE TEMPERATE SPECIES OF *MAGNOLIA*

SECTION *MAGNOLIA*

(formerly *Magnoliastrum*)
A. P. de Candolle in *Prodromus* 1 : 80 (1824)
type species *M. virginiana*

This section was founded by French botanist A. P. de Candolle in 1824 to embrace all of the American species, but it is now restricted to *Magnolia virginiana*, which is also the type species of genus *Magnolia*. This was the first Magnolia to be introduced into cultivation in England, some 300 years ago.

Dandy explains that the name *Magnoliastrum* which he used for this section in his 1950 'Survey' was correct at that time. However, in 1954 the International Botanical Congress decided that type-sections must bear an epithet repeating the generic name, as had been the practice with subgenera. Hence Section *Magnoliastrum* has to become Section *Magnolia*.

North American Sweet Bay or Swamp Bay

MAGNOLIA VIRGINIANA Linnaeus

C. Linnaeus in *Species Plantarum* 1 : 535 (1753)
M. Catesby in *Flora Caroliniana* 1 :39 (1741)
SYN. *M. glauca* Linnaeus in *Systema Naturae* 10, 2 : 1082 (1759)
J. E. Dandy in *Curtis's Botanical Magazine* 173 : t. 457 (1964–5)
Plates 1 and 2

Today the popular American name is Sweet Bay but in the past other common names included Swamp Bay, Swamp Laurel, Swamp Magnolia, Swamp Sassafras and Beaver Tree. The name Beaverwood (Bieberbaum) was applied generically to the Magnolia family by the German botanist Hartweg in *Hortus Carlsruhanus* (1825), but in America this term was specifically applied to *M. virginiana* because beavers are very fond of eating the stems and roots. According to Loudon, the early inhabitants of the marshy country in which this Magnolia occurs made a tincture from the bark for use in chronic rheumatism and as a medicine for treating coughs, colds and fevers.

As it is primarily a plant of low, wet woodlands it is not surprising that several of the common names cited refer to its supposed swamp-loving nature. However it requires aeration and seems to prefer other than waterlogged ground. In cultivation it seems to grow best in soils which are moist without being perpetually soggy; in fact it flourishes in a wide variety of soils and situations. A rich, sandy loam, liberally laced with sphagnum peat, seems to suit it well. Like many other trees and shrubs it would, no doubt, tolerate waterlogged soil conditions during its period of winter dormancy.

The Sweet Bay Magnolia occurs along the east coast of America from Florida and Texas northward to Pennsylvania, New Jersey and locally in eastern Massachusetts. It therefore has a wide natural distribution, and is consequently somewhat variable both in stature and in the persistence of its leaves. It also varies considerably in its ultimate height and is best described as a partially evergreen shrub or small tree with smooth slender shoots and hairy buds. In typical shrubs the leaves are from 3 to 5 in. (7·5 to 12·5 cm) long, more or less glossy above and glaucous white beneath, finally almost glabrous. When young the undersurfaces may be silky pubescent and this condition persists on the foliage of many trees in the southern variety. Catesby in *Flora Caroliniana* 1 : 39 (1741) described the leaves as 'pale green, having their backsides white' and here lies the reason for the synonym *glauca*.

The more northerly forms at maturity are often deciduous, shrubby and slower growing than the more fully evergreen southerly form var. *australis*, which attains the stature of a tall tree.

The fragrant creamy-white flowers are globular, 2 to 2½ in. (5 to 6 cm) in diameter, usually but not invariably with eight tepals, plus three or four greenish sepaloid ones of papery texture. The tepals are obovate, 1½ to 2 in. (4 to 5 cm) long, and turn deeper cream with age. They begin to open in June and are usually at their peak in late July with some plants continuing to bloom into September. The gynoecium or stigmatic column is ovoid and the hooked stigmas are usually of a reddish colour while the androecium is composed of orange-brown stamens. The flowers are diurnal, opening for the first time in the mid to late afternoon, closing at night, and opening finally on the second day, when the stamens shed their pollen. The earlier flowers develop from quite fat, furry terminal buds, which begin to open as the leaves appear almost in the manner of some fully deciduous kinds. The secondary flowers develop from relatively small non-furry buds which enlarge to produce flowers of normal size some weeks later. The fruit cones (Plate 1) of some trees turn bright red in late summer and open to reveal scarlet seeds in brilliant contrast to the lustrous foliage. Vigorous plants often begin to flower when only three or four years old from seed.

There are some multitepalled forms and it would appear that the description in L. H. Bailey's *Cyclopedia of Horticulture* (1919) of *M. virginiana* as having 'nine to twelve petals' may have referred to one of these, or perhaps the 'sepals' were included in this count. Some plants have produced flowers with as many as twenty tepals, together with some petaloid stamens, and such a form would be well worth propagating vegetatively such as the 'Havener' clone described later.

Some flowers have a greenish glow at the base of their tepals while others are cream and a few have a perceptible pink flush. Philip Savage, Jr., writing in *Newsletter of the American Magnolia Society* 4, 2 : 3 (1967), recorded that he had observed that the pinkish variant referred to usually had an above average number of tepals. At the Barnes Arboretum, at Merion, Pennsylvania, there is a tree of *M. virginiana* with unusually rough, fissured bark.

M. virginiana grows to timber dimensions from Florida to Texas where it forms a considerable proportion of the Magnolia lumber produced by the smaller sawmills.

It is known to have been grown in 1688 in the gardens at Fulham Palace by Dr. Compton while Bishop of London (1675–1713) and may well have been sent or brought to him by the Revd. John Bannister whom he had sent out to America as a missionary. According to early reports it seldom set fertile seed in this climate.

Miller's Gardener's Dictionary Edition 1 (1731), published prior to the Linnaean Nomenclature of 1753, gives the name *Tulipifera arbor Virginiana* and records a tree fifty years old and fifty feet tall in the Wilderness in the gardens of the Right Honourable the Earl of Peterborough at Parsons Green near Fulham, where it had been drawn upwards by proximity to other trees. This was probably one of Bishop Compton's raising for they must have been neighbours. Miller reported that this Magnolia 'was formerly kept in pots and tubs and housed in winter with great care, in which arrangement the plants made but poor progress'.

At Kew, on the lawn opposite the Wild Garden, there are two shrubby specimens of *M. virginiana* which produce a long succession of fragrant creamy-white flowers from July to late October.

This species is now but rarely met in English gardens though there seems to be a revival of interest in its cultivation. It is certainly one of the best Magnolias for smaller gardens, combining as it does distinctive leaves with their blue-white undersides and a long succession of very pleasantly-scented flowers at a time when they are unlikely to be damaged by bad weather. Their fragrance has been described by American authoress Louise Wilder in *The Fragrant Path* (1932) as 'one of the best outdoor scents – cool and fruity and sweet'. American Magnolia enthusiast Philip J. Savage, Jr., of Bloomfield Hills, Michigan, wrote on this topic: 'There is Attar of Roses in it. There is certainly lemon and perhaps orange, and more than a hint of iced tea' – surely enough to whet any gardener's thirst for a plant of the Sweet Bay Magnolia!

The southern form was first published as *M. virginiana* var. *australis* by Sargent in 1919 and was raised by Ashe to specific rank in 1931, but the leading world authority on the genus Magnolia, British botanist J. E. Dandy, did not concur with Ashe when he drew up his 'Survey of the Genus *Magnolia*' which was published with the Royal Horticultural Society's *Camellias & Magnolias Conference Report* in 1950. (Dandy's 'Revised Survey' is published on pp. 29–37 of this volume.) Sargent described *M. virginiana* var. *australis* as being distinguished by its larger tree size, more persistent leaves and densely hairy branchlets and flower stalks. He recorded its distribution as ranging from North Carolina to Florida and Texas. It has more slender petioles which are subject to winter breakage especially when the leaves are ice coated.

The leading American authority on *M. virginiana* is undoubtedly Prof. J. C. McDaniel of the Department of Horticulture of the University of Illinois. The author is indebted to him for permission to quote quite freely from his correspondence and published notes. He records that, from his own personal observations, *M. virginiana* var. *australis* is not always tree-like, nor always fully evergreen, and that its leaves vary in shape and size, but he finds that it always has a different, more intense, more lemon-like fragrance than var. *virginiana*, opens its flower buds later in the day, and has paler almost white pollen. He also finds that it differs by being usually self-sterile to a high degree, though it can be fertilized by another clone of its variety, or by var. *virginiana*.

In an article entitled 'Variations in the Sweet Bay Magnolia' which was published in the *Morris Arboretum Bulletin* 17 : 7–12 (1966) Prof. McDaniel reported on his findings, not only in tracking down the more remote outposts of this widely scattered species, but also on some of the different forms which he had come across in cultivation.

In a letter to the author he wrote: 'I have been restudying the *M. virginiana* complex as it grows from Massachusetts to southern Florida, west to eastern Texas and inland to Tennessee. I am now in agreement with Mr. Dandy that its variations together comprise only one species, but I believe that there is at least a major variety difference. The southern variety (distributed from Georgia, westward and southward) agrees only roughly with Sargent's var. *australis* description and I think he (and Fernald later) erred in giving it a distribution around Wilmington, North Carolina, or even into south-eastern Virginia. The Carolina-Virginia trees may be pubescent, but otherwise are like typical var. *virginiana*.'

He reported that 'this typical glabrous and deciduous form does not occur naturally in the states west of Georgia, and it seems rare even there. Its total native population (in Massachusetts and New York to Georgia) is probably much less than that of var. *australis* in the southern U.S., though var. *virginiana* seems the more common variety in cultivation.'

Until 1966 no natural occurrence of forms intermediate between var. *virginiana* and var. *australis* had been reported in areas where their natural ranges coincided, but Prof. McDaniel had recorded the existence of many plants of an ambiguous form in cultivation, which he considered distinct and uniform enough to be worthy of a separate forma status under *M. virginiana* var. *virginiana*. Then in 1966 he found this intermediate wild form native around Wilmington, North Carolina where it is predominant.

In the article mentioned he listed their key points of separation thus:

1. Var. *australis* has much paler pollen than var. *virginiana*, while 'intermediates' have pollen like var. *virginiana*.

2. Flower odour consistently differs, being more lemon-like in var. *australis*.

3. Flowering, and apparently vegetative growth, starts three or more weeks later in the spring with var. *australis*.

4. Var. *australis* flower buds in June open around 7.30 p.m., about two hours later than buds on var. *virginiana*, and close the same evening an hour or two later than those of var. *virginiana*. (Some, at least, of the 'intermediate' plants also have bud-opening near sunset.) All day-old flowers reopen and shed pollen the following afternoon, but with a similar time difference between the taxa. In var. *australis* at least, flowers can reclose again, before reopening permanently on the third afternoon.

5. Fruits of var. *australis* are slower to mature than those of var. *virginiana* and the 'intermediates', taking about ninety days from flowering time, compared to seventy days for the others, while those from Texas sources are less slow. At an inland outpost around Bethel Springs, Tennessee, he later found an early maturing population of var. *australis*.

6. Var. *australis* usually has one or a few trunks dominant and rather erect, with a crown spread, even when open-grown, usually less than half the tree height. Var. *virginiana* and the 'intermediates' have more tendency towards a multi-stemmed condition, with diverging trunks and a total crown spread often greater than half their height.

Prof. McDaniel decided that the fresh flowers provide a much more certain means of identification than winter leaf retention. He considers that if a plant of flowering age retains many green leaves on its upper branches in March, and shows dense pubescence on last year's shoots, it is probably var. *australis*. If it is a tree over 50 ft (15 m) tall then it is almost certainly of this southern form of the species.

Prof. McDaniel has been instrumental in collecting and distributing seed from selected mother plants of *M. virginiana* to which he has given clonal names, thereby to identify them. Some are being introduced as vegetatively-propagated cultivars.

McDaniel's 'Havener' clone of var. *virginiana* (Plate 2) has large multitepalled cream flowers, tinged pinkish inside, and comes from a cultivated specimen at Mount Pulaski, Illinois, which has proved to breed remarkably true from seed. His 'Mayer' clone is a shrubby form from Champaign, Illinois, with comparatively small fruit cones and narrow leaves, the seedlings of which have reproduced its dwarf habit. Several have begun to flower when just over two years old. His 'Hensel' clone, a tree planted on a farm near Princeton, Illinois, in 1912, has relatively large flowers and the most fertile fruit recorded for the whole genus. Not only are the fruit cones relatively large but they frequently have three and sometimes as many as five seeds per carpel whereas the norm is two. He showed me a fruiting branch from this tree on which the leaves were remarkably broad with recurved margins like an inverted spoon.

Another interesting form of *M. virginiana* is among those grown and propagated by the Tennessee Valley Nursery at Winchester, Tennessee, where several similar plants appeared among seedlings from New Jersey. This is a compact-growing clone with white-backed leaves which are broadly heart shaped or retuse (having emarginate tips) which will make a most interesting foliage plant when it comes into circulation among nurserymen.

Prof. McDaniel also has some compact Texas seedlings of var. *australis* with twisted, emarginate leaves.

One form of *M. virginiana* var. *australis*, his 'Crofts' clone, is an evergreen from Polk County, Tennessee, at 1,600 ft (487 m) which, he says, may be the highest altitude at which var. *australis* or any other native Sweet Bay Magnolia occurs. Its progeny may therefore prove very useful. 'Crofts' and many seedlings with this as a parent have highly lustrous upper leaf surfaces.

The 'Henry Hicks' clone of var. *australis* is a tree which was presented by the late Long Island nurseryman Henry Hicks to the Arthur H. Scott Horticultural Foundation at Swarthmore College. It has been well tested for hardiness and leaf persistence, remaining evergreen in winters with −17 °F. (−27 °C.) temperatures, with David G. Leach at Brookville, Pennsylvania. It has required grafting for its propagation, but some 'Henry Hicks' seedlings (crosses with other var. *australis* clones or with the 'Mayer' clone) are proving easily rooted as cuttings.

Prof. McDaniel concludes that some clones of *M. virginiana* var. *australis* are hardier than Sargent and later Rehder suggested, since they succeed in central Illinois to the northern border of United States Department of Agriculture Zone 6a – average winter minimum temperature −10 °F. to 0 °F. (−23 °C. to −17 °C.). Some clones are likely to prove hardier than most forms of *M. grandiflora*.

In the East Texas to Arkansas region grows a larger-leaved but less frequently evergreen race of var. *australis*, often with larger flowers than the *M. virginiana* var. *australis* from east of the Mississippi River. Breeding is being continued at the University of Illinois with inter- and intravarietal crosses between some of the more extreme *M. virginiana* forms.

Pollination of *Magnolia virginiana* by honey bees and other *Hymenoptera* was reported by Prof. McDaniel in the *Newsletter of the American Magnolia Society* 4, 1 : 8 (1967). He observed insects visiting newly opened and older flowers, the latter having free pollen which was being transferred on to the receptive stigmas of the former.

Somewhat surprisingly *M. virginiana* was omitted from *Curtis's Botanical Magazine* until as recently as 1965, although it was known in cultivation in England as long ago as 1688. Dandy explained this oversight through what he termed 'an accident of mis-identification'. In 1820 John Sims had figured, at Tab. 2164, a plant which he thought to be a large-flowered variety of this species and which he named *M. glauca* var. *major*. However this plant was identified in 1876 by C. de Vos as a hybrid *M. tripetala* × *M. virginiana* under *M.* × *thompsoniana*, and such identification has been in general use since that date.★

Although *M. virginiana* is found in acid soil areas it will tolerate considerable alkalinity when grown in cultivation.

Probably the finest specimen in England is that in the Cambridge University Botanic Gardens which is about 30 ft (9 m) tall and 20 ft (6 m) across.

Cytologically, *M. virginiana* is a diploid with 2n = 38 chromosomes.

★ Dr. S. A. Spongberg's treatment for *M. virginiana* in *Journal of the Arnold Arboretum* 57, 3 : 265–6 (1976) dismisses any recognition of var. *australis* 'inasmuch as most of the characters are ill defined morphologically and are clinal over the range, a utilitarian taxonomy does not appear to result from the recognition of a southern variety'. Prof. McDaniel counters this by pointing out, in *Newsletter of the American Magnolia Society* 13, 1 : 25 (1977), 'the one difference that persists in herbarium specimens is the longer pedicel (internode between peduncle and flower) noted by Dr. F. S. Santamour, Jr., and characteristic of the *virginiana* populations indigenous west or south from Savannah, Georgia'. [In this book the term 'pedicle' has been used in preference to 'pedicel' for the reason given on p. 18.]

SECTION *GWILLIMIA* de Candolle

A. P. de Candolle in *Regni Vegetabilis Systema Naturale* 1 : 455, 548 (1817)

type species *M. coco (pumila)*

This, the largest section of the genus, comprises some sixteen species but only one of these, *M. delavayi*, is temperate. The remainder have a wide distribution in south-east Asia but, being tropical, are therefore outside the scope of this book.

M. coco is tropical and is unique in being the only Magnolia with nectar glands.

The species in this section are all evergreen and have stipules adnate to the petioles and distinguished from Section *Lirianthe* by the short-beaked fruiting carpels with beaks not dorsally flattened.

Delavay's Magnolia

MAGNOLIA DELAVAYI Franchet

A. R. Franchet in *Plantae Delavayanae* 33 : 9,10 (1889)

J. G. Millais in *Magnolias*: 104–6 (1926)

T. A. Sprague in *Curtis's Botanical Magazine* 135 : t. 8282 (1909)

G. H. Johnstone in *Asiatic Magnolias in Cultivation*: 145–7 (1955)

W. J. Bean in *Trees & Shrubs Hardy in the British Isles* Ed. 8, 2 : 649 (1973)

Plate 3

This Magnolia was discovered by the great French plant collector Père Jean Delavay near Langkong in 1886. It was introduced by Wilson from southern Yunnan in 1899, just ten years after Franchet's publication, and first flowered under glass at Kew in 1908, so that, when grown in such an advantageous environment, it may commence to flower at a relatively early age.

Wilson recorded it growing in open situations or in scrub on both sandstone and limestone formations. In view of the near-tropical latitude and relatively low elevation 4,000 to 8,000 ft (1,200 to 2,400 m) according to Bean, and 5,000 to 11,000 ft (1,500 to 3,300 m) according to Johnstone, it seems remarkable that such a large-leaved evergreen should have proved sufficiently hardy for outdoor cultivation in the milder parts of the British Isles. Evergreen woody plants from the Sino-Himalayan region have rarely proved hardy from altitudes much below 10,000 ft (3,000 m).

M. delavayi has the largest leaves of any evergreen temperate species or hybrid, up to 12 in. (30 cm) long by 6½ in. (16·5 cm) wide. They are coriaceous, being of a very stiff, parchment-like texture, in fact almost resembling thin plastic.

The mature leaves are of a deep sea-green colour, ovate to oblong in shape and somewhat rounded at the base. The upper surfaces are glabrous or smooth while the undersides are pubescent. The young shoots carry the same colouring as the leaves and are dotted with large white lenticels.

For a plant with such spectacular foliage the flowers of *M. delavayi* are somewhat disappointing. The great dome-shaped buds look full of promise but, alas, they open only briefly and at night and last for but twelve hours before they begin to fade. The nine fleshy tepals are creamy white, the larger exterior three are shaded lime green on their outer surfaces and completely enclose the erect flower bud up to the time of opening. They turn buff and become leathery in texture, reflexing to a sub-horizontal position in the form of a false calyx. When the flower is fully expanded it measures about 7 in. (18 cm) across. The tepals are concave and incurved along their margins especially towards their tips. When the flower opens the broad conical gynoecium is of a pale creamy-buff colour while the stamens are a rich creamy yellow. They become shed into the goblet-shaped flower cup and are partly retained by the concave form of the tepals. The flowers are sparsely produced at the tips of the shoots and open spasmodically from mid July to September.

Johnstone recorded the fruit-cones of *M. delavayi* as being 4 to 8 in. (10 to 20·5 cm) long and ovoid oblong in shape but this description seems inaccurate. The sterile cones are nearly heart shaped and as broad in their widest part as they are long, averaging 1½ in. (4 cm) each way. They are dark brown when dry with buff-yellow indumentum between the sharply-beaked carpels. The seeds are relatively small and difficult to find without pulverizing the cones when they closely resemble the woody portions of the crushed carpels. It seems reasonable to suppose that fully fertilized cones would be broader than their length and that freshly ripened seeds would be just as conspicuous as in other species of Magnolia. This species seems to set seed very sparingly in cultivation and it is usually difficult to propagate by other means apart from layering. Consequently, like *M. nitida* it seems likely to remain a scarce item unless a more ample source of seed can be found.

Johnstone observed and recorded the manner in which the stamens shed their pollen within the flower chamber before the outer tepals unfold, while the stigmas do not appear to become receptive until after the tepals have fallen. In this respect *M. delavayi* differs from most if not all other temperate species.

In the great Cornish woodland garden at Caerhays *M. delavayi* grows into a vast tree-like bush over 40 ft (12 m) tall by as much across and does not suffer from branch brittleness which is the curse of so many Magnolias. It is remarkably wind-tolerant for such a large-leaved evergreen and there are several specimens flourishing along the south wall of the Castle facing Veryan Bay, alongside *M. grandiflora* 'Goliath'. How unfortunate that neither of these normally bear fertile seed in this climate, for the possibility of raising a hybrid between them, however remote, is not impossible.

Where space and climate permit, it looks better when grown away from and not crucified against a wall. It is hardy at Kew where there is a good bushy specimen against the wall of the Herbaceous Garden between the Reference Museum and the Rock Garden. The plant in Windsor Great Park was cut to ground level by the arctic winter of 1962-3 but has since recovered.

The species will flourish in a wide range of soils and situations. In a lecture to the Royal Horticultural Society in 1967 on 'Trees at Highdown' (situated on the chalk soil of the Sussex Downs), Sir Frederick Stern said: 'Another plant bought at Sir James Veitch's sale at Coombe Wood in 1912 was *Magnolia delavayi*, introduced by E. H. Wilson on his first journey in China in 1900; it was planted against the south wall of a house. . . . The large evergreen leaves looked most attractive and there were hopes that the white flowers would be so too, but alas the flowers are poor and fleeting. It has grown into a large spreading tree now 36 ft (11 m) high and 2 ft (61 cm) in girth on the main stem.'

An even more remarkable example of the lime tolerance of *M. delavayi* was noticed by the author during an advisory visit which took him to a garden the leeward side of some extensive sand-dunes on the north shore of the mouth of the Cornish River Camel opposite Padstow. On an adjacent plot a property developer had bulldozed away the perimeter screen of natural blackthorn and wild privet to construct an approach road to a new building site in a large established garden. There, in a clearing now fully exposed to the north and east, was a fine bushy specimen of *M. delavayi* which had suffered severe wind damage on its exposed face through this sudden loss of natural shelter. As far as could be seen it was growing in a soil composed largely of wind-blown dune sand which has a very high calcium content derived from tiny particles of pulverized sea shells. (Dune sand is the main source of agricultural lime in most parts of Cornwall and its importance to farmers gave rise to the construction of canals and later to railways as a means of transporting this material to inland depots mainly for agricultural use.)

This plant was examined more closely several years later, by which time it had adapted itself considerably to the more exposed conditions by a marked reduction in the size of its leaves and more bushy nature of its recent growth. Indeed it contains more promising material for cuttings than has been noticed in any other plant of this species and has also proved much easier to root.

From the recorded date of its introduction in 1899 to its first flowering in 1908 we can deduce that it attains florescence from seed in nine to ten years, which is about half the time normally taken by its American cousin *M. grandiflora*.

M. delavayi has shown a remarkable power of recovery from severe winter damage and mature plants seldom lose more than the unripened tips of their shoots even when defoliated by a severe winter.

The bark on the trunk and main branches is greenish grey in colour but, being rough and fissured, it may appear much darker in bad light. The prominent lenticels expand and spread until the branches become completely pockmarked with them so that the green shoots become overlaid with brown. The young shoots are densely covered with light chestnut hairs, as are those of *M. grandiflora*.

Cytologically *M. delavayi* is a diploid with 2n=38 chromosomes whereas *M. grandiflora* is a hexaploid with 2n = 114 chromosomes.

SECTION *RYTIDOSPERMUM* Spach

Magnolia sect. *Rytidospermum* Spach, *Histoire Naturelle des Végétaux, Phanérogames* 7 : 474 (1839)
type species *M. tripetala*

This section shares with *Tulipastrum* the peculiarity of having representative species occurring in both Asia and America. Its most distinguishing feature is the whorl-like arrangement of the leaves at the tips of the shoots, which has given rise to the name Umbrella Tree commonly used in America. The flower buds are at first enclosed in a single spathaceous bract which leaves a single annular scar on the peduncle.

The tight apical leaf whorls appear to be devoid of axillary buds and, when lateral shoots do develop, they appear to arise from dormant buds on the older shoots. Because of these characteristics the Magnolias in this section are not as easy to graft or bud as are those of other sections dealt with in this book.

The manner in which the leaves are clustered towards the ends of the shoots is termed 'apical dominance'. It is thought to be due to a large amount of complex growth-regulating substances, known as auxins, moving down from the apices of the shoots and inhibiting the growth of lateral buds.

All species in this section are in cultivation with the exception of the tropical *M. dealbata* from the mountains of southern Mexico. This, the only deciduous tropical species, holds the honour of having been the first Magnolia to be recorded in a Western language for it was described and figured by the Spanish botanist Francisco Hernandez about 1575 during the first government-sponsored scientific expedition ever undertaken. For reasons related in the Introduction his drawings and notes were not published until 1651.

In his 'Revised Survey' Dandy recognizes three series within this section, one Asian and two American:

ASIAN SERIES
M. hypoleuca (obovata)
M. officinalis
M. rostrata

AMERICAN SERIES 1
M. tripetala
M. fraseri
M. pyramidata

AMERICAN SERIES 2
M. macrophylla with subsp. *ashei*
M. dealbata

ASIAN SERIES OF SECTION *Rytidospermum*

The three species in this series are so remarkably similar as to be readily confused. All grow to sizeable trees with large leaves and have heavily-scented creamy-white flowers, which usually fade to buff and tend to be hidden by the terminal leaf whorls when viewed from below.

Their confusion has been added to by the fact that, apparently, both the Japanese *M. hypoleuca* and the Chinese *M. officinalis* have been grown together for timber and medicinal purposes in China and so there is every likelihood that natural hybrids have arisen to add further complications to the identification of the true species.

Japanese White Bark Magnolia
Ho-no-ki in Japan

MAGNOLIA HYPOLEUCA Siebold & Zuccarini

(Referring to the greenish-white undersurfaces of the leaves)

P. F. von Siebold & J. G. Zuccarini in *Abhandlungen der Mathematisch-physikalischen Classe der Königlich Bayerischen Akademie der Wissenschaften* 4, 2 : 187 (1846)

S. A. Skan in *Curtis's Botanical Magazine* 132 : t. 8077 (1906)

J. E. Dandy in *Baileya* 19, 1 : 44 (1973) explained his reason for this change of name thus:

'SYN. *Magnolia obovata* Thunberg in *Transactions of the Linnaean Society of London* 2 : 336 (1794) *nomen illegitimum*, pro parte (as to the description but excluding the Kaempfer synonyms); et sensu Rehder & Wilson in Sargent, *Plantae Wilsonianae* 1 : 406 (1913)'

Plate 4

Dandy continued: 'Until 1913 *Magnolia hypoleuca* Siebold & Zuccarini (1846) was the accepted name for this Japanese species well known in cultivation. In that year, however, the earlier name *M. obovata* Thunberg (1794) was adopted for it by Rehder and Wilson on the ground that Thunberg's own specimen, on which his short description was based, is identical with *M. hypoleuca*. Their identification is correct; the specimen, consisting of a sterile branchlet with four leaves, is preserved in Thunberg's herbarium. But this specimen is not the only element involved in *M. obovata*. The species, as delimited by Thunberg, also included the plants figured by Kaempfer in his plates 43 and 44 (published in 1791 by Banks), and these, as pointed out by Rehder and Wilson themselves elsewhere in their account of Wilson's Magnoliaceae, were already the types respectively of the names *M. denudata* Desrousseaux and *M. liliflora* Desrousseaux, both published in 1792. Thus Thunberg proposed a new name, *M. obovata*, for a species which according to his own citations, already had two available names, one of which, according to the International Code of Botanical Nomenclature, he should have adopted. Article 63 of the code states that "A name is illegitimate and must be rejected if it was nomenclaturally superfluous when published, i.e. if the taxon to which it was applied, as circumscribed by its author, included the type of a name or epithet which ought to have been adopted under the rules." The name *M. obovata* is, in fact, doubly illegitimate, because the species as delimited by Thunberg included the types of both *M. denudata* [*M. heptapeta*] and *M. liliflora* [*M. quinquepeta*]. *Magnolia obovata* must therefore be rejected, and the name *M. hypoleuca* stands as correct.

'This may not be to the liking of growers brought up on the name *M. obovata*; but it is amusing to reflect that when I first began to study *Magnolia* gardeners were still fulminating about having (as they then believed) to drop the name *M. hypoleuca* in favour of *M. obovata*!'

The above extract was contributed by the late J. E. Dandy to *Baileya* 19, 1 : 44 (1973) and was reproduced in *Newsletter of the American Magnolia Society* 9, 4 : 4–5 (1973). It explains the reasons for this example of a typical botanical seesaw in plant nomenclature.

This large-leaved Japanese tree species is distinguishable from its Chinese counterpart *M. officinalis* by having leaves which are predominantly obovate (hence its synonym), their undersides being coated with a silvery-grey pubescence and with pronounced purple shadings along the usually glabrous petioles and young shoots. This colouring is absent on *M. officinalis*, the petioles and young shoots being greenish yellow. *M. hypoleuca* differs from *M.*

rostrata in the absence of the reddish-fawn indumentum which clothes the buds and young leaves of that species.

In *Plantae Wilsonianae* 1 : 392, Rehder and Wilson drew attention to the longer gynandrophore of *M. hypoleuca*, while the bright-red fruit cones are not only larger than those of *M. officinalis*, being 5 to 8 in. (12·5 to 20 cm) long compared with 4 to 4½ in. (10 to 11·5 cm) but they are also differently shaped and the ripe carpels have shorter beaks than *M. rostrata*, these being usually less than ¼ in. (5 mm) in length.

In 1913 Rehder and Wilson, under *Magnoliaceae* in Sargent's *Plantae Wilsonianae* 1 : 403, wrote under *M. liliflora*: 'The name *M. obovata* used by almost all authors for *M. liliflora* must now replace *M. hypoleuca* Siebold & Zuccarini, for Thunberg's description of *M. obovata* and part of its synonyms refer to *M. hypoleuca* and his type specimen represents this species.' The remainder of their text seems to add further confusion to an already confused situation. Little wonder that, in 1968, J. E. Dandy decided that the species under consideration should revert once more to *M. hypoleuca* after a lapse of over half a century.

The heavily-scented white waterlily-like flowers, opening in June after the leaves have developed, are up to 8 in. (20·5 cm) across with six to nine obovate tepals of a leathery texture. Those in the outer whorl are similar but shorter and are sometimes tinted pink outside. The inner tepals fade to creamy yellow. The stamen filaments are bright crimson, and form, with the yellow anthers, a circular boss 3 in. (7·5 cm) across, which characteristic is likewise displayed in *M. × wieseneri*, the putative hybrid of *M. hypoleuca* and *M. sieboldii*, long known as *M. × watsonii*.

Introduced in 1878 (other authorities give 1884 and 1893), it was recorded by Millais in *Magnolias* as having first flowered about 1905 in the garden of a Mr. Chambers at Haslemere, Surrey, and that shortly afterwards this tree was struck by lightning and killed.

There is a fine specimen at Trewidden near Penzance about 50 ft (15 m) high which was planted about 1893 and was recorded to have been flowering freely by 1906.

This Magnolia is reported to grow to its largest size in the forests of Hokkaido (Yezo) where it attains heights up to 100 ft (30·5 m) and is highly valued for its light, soft, easily worked timber. It is one of the hardiest of the great tree Magnolias and, although somewhat gaunt in appearance as a young plant, it makes a fine specimen tree if planted in good deep soil in a sheltered and sunny situation.

The tree has an almost antediluvian appearance, with its prominently annular-scarred and lenticelled stems and the remarkably primitive appearance of its flowers with their thick spoon-shaped tepals. Philip Savage aptly describes their exotic fragrance as 'the odor of all tropical fruits and perfumes combined in one, Tutti-frutti'.

The earliest mention in *Curtis's Botanical Magazine* was when J. D. Hooker first described *M. × watsonii* in February 1891. He referred to *M. hypoleuca* as having 'robust branches, large oblong leaves, densely pruinose and thinly hairy beneath, and more or less biennial in duration'. It is apparent that he was referring to a specimen growing in the Temperate House at Kew since the leaves are deciduous and not biennial when plants of this species are grown in the open.

The foliage of this Magnolia is remarkably durable when cut sprays are placed in water either for indoor decoration or for the show bench. The author recalls a large flowering branch of *M. hypoleuca*, which was exhibited under canvas at the Royal Cornwall Show at Wadebridge in June 1970 by Mr. Nigel Holman of Chyverton near Truro. The leaves remained unblemished after more than two days of gruelling heat, in spite of the fact that they were, as yet, in an immature condition. Branches adorned with fruit cones (Plate 4) can form quite sensational cut material when displayed in a suitable setting where bold material is required for indoor decoration.

In the garden at Antony House, Torpoint, Cornwall, Sir John Carew Pole has planted trees of *M. hypoleuca* and *M. officinalis* within easy distance for comparison.

M. hypoleuca has a distribution from the Kuril Islands and Hokkaido southward to Kyushu and the Ryukyu Islands up to 5,600 ft (1,700 m).

There is a specimen of this Magnolia growing in the local park in the Czechoslovakian town of Pruhonice near Prague. According to Eng. Vladimir Vasak of the Botanical Institute of the Czechoslovak Academy of Science at Pruhonice, the tree is one of Japanese origin (Shirasawa, Tokyo) which was raised and cultivated in the nurseries of the Czech Dendrological Society between 1910 and 1916 and is now about 55 ft (16 m) tall with a trunk girth of 3 ft (90 cm) at a height of 3¼ ft (1 m). Vasak gave these details in '*Magnolia hypoleuca* in Nature and in Cultivation' in *Newsletter of the American Magnolia Society* 9, 1 : 3–6 (1973).

His article includes an account of a botanical expedition which he joined in 1968 which visited the island of Kunashir in the southern Kurils. A substantial part of the island remains covered with primeval forests in which grow many stately specimens of *M. hypoleuca*. The expedition was organized by the Botanical Department of the Sakhalin-Complex Institute of the Academy of Sciences of the USSR. The article lists the plants which grow on Kunashir in association with *M. hypoleuca* at the northern limits of its natural distribution. Kunashir lies very close to the eastern shore of the northern Japanese island of Hokkaido.

Cytologically *M. hypoleuca* is a diploid with 2n = 38 chromosomes.

Medicinal Magnolia
Ancient Chinese name *Hou-phu*

MAGNOLIA OFFICINALIS Rehder & Wilson

A. Rehder & E. H. Wilson in Sargent, *Plantae Wilsonianae* I : 392 (1913)

SYN. *M. hypoleuca* L. Diels in Engler, *Botanische Jahrbücher* 29 : 321–2 (1900) not of Siebold & Zuccarini

Plate 5

This Magnolia differs from *M. hypoleuca* in having smaller flowers of somewhat irregular shape, with narrower and less substantial tepals of varying width, from nine to fifteen in number, shaped rather like those of the American *M. tripetala*, with incurved margins and wrinkled surfaces. The green gynoecium has hooked, creamy-yellow styles while the stamens and filaments of the androecium are not only far fewer but much less colourful than those of the Magnolia described previously. The deeply ribbed 'sepals', which constitute the false calyx, have the colour and appearance of light brown paper. The flowers open about midsummer, after the leaves have fully developed, and emit an almost overpowering scent.

The stout, swollen shoots are pockmarked with large, rounded or shield-shaped leaf scars reminiscent of the horse chestnut (*Aesculus* species) and these provide an interesting stem pattern which is noticeable to a lesser degree on *M. tripetala*.

The very large, deciduous leaves are elliptic obovate, 12 to 15 in. (30·5 to 38 cm) long by 7 in. (18 cm) wide with rippled margins, rounded apices and long petioles and are of a paler green than those of *M. hypoleuca*. They are greenish grey below, the undersurfaces losing much of their original pubescence, excepting on the midrib and veins. They are arranged in terminal whorls as are those of other members of this section.

The growth buds are green with purplish pubescence, while the flower buds are a warm greenish brown. The leaf stalks and young shoots are yellowish green.

Discovered by Dr. A. Henry in eastern Szechwan, in 1885, *M. officinalis* was first found by E. H. Wilson in western Hupeh when on a Veitch expedition in 1900. He also collected seed for the Arnold Arboretum from the north and south of Ichang (in Kiangsi province) in 1907. One of his photographs shows this species as a small deciduous tree with very erect branches and fastigiate sucker growths arising from the base of the trunk.

Pink forms assumed to be of this Magnolia have flowered in several English gardens. On 8 June 1971 the Royal Horticultural Society gave an Award of Merit to one exhibited by the Crown Estate Commissioners from the Gardens in Windsor Great Park. Material from this tree was examined by the author in August 1972 and when considered with the Table of Comparisons at the end of this chapter it was identified as a form of *M. hypoleuca*. Mr. C. Brickell, botanist and Director of the R.H.S. Garden, says that the specimen at Wisley has never been examined botanically but he suspects that it is referable to *M. hypoleuca*.

M. officinalis var. *biloba* differs only in the shape of its leaves which are deeply emarginate or notched at their apices. The winter buds are golden. Wilson reported this form from Kiukiang in the province of Kiangsi at the foot of the ascent to Kuling, and at Ningpo, while A. Henry recorded it in eastern Szechwan.

It was apparently first introduced from China in 1936 following its listing by the Lu Shan Arboretum and Botanical Garden at Kuling, in Kiukiang (Chiu-chiang) close to where Wilson recorded it. In the Arboretum's *Descriptive Catalogue of Chinese Tree Seeds* (1936–7) it was described as 'Deciduous tree introduced for the first time, leaves obovate, 1 to 1·5

ft [30·5 to 46 cm] long, whitish beneath, with a deep notch at tips, flowers pale yellow or greyish yellow, fragrant, 5 to 7 in. [12·5 to 18 cm] across, cup-shaped, *appearing before leaves* in April to May. Very handsome tree of pyramidal shape with showy flowers.'

This Magnolia flowers with and *not* before the leaves (as stated in the Chinese description) as do all other members of Section *Rytidospermum*, and no climatical difference could conceivably alter this process.

Mr. H. G. Hillier tells me that his nursery imported seed of *M. officinalis biloba* from Lu Shan in 1936 from which five seedlings were raised. He retained three and sent one to Bodnant and one to Wisley. These trees have since flowered and fruited so that a limited supply of young plants has become available.

M. officinalis is commonly cultivated on the mountain slopes of Hupeh and Szechwan for the medicinal qualities of its bark and flower buds and is known as the Hou-po or Hou-phu tree. Its cultivation for medicinal purposes dates back well over 1,000 years. In the *Cheng Lei Pen Tshao* (1083), probably the earliest Chinese Pharmaceutical Natural History and originally the work of Thang Shen-wei, there is a primitive drawing of this Magnolia.

The removal of the bark causes the death of the trees but it is probable that use is also made of the timber, which is soft yet durable. An infusion of the bark yields a cure for coughs and colds and is used as a tonic during convalescence. A similar extract is made from the flower buds and used as a medicine for feminine ailments.

Owing to this demand for its bark, most of the natural trees have been destroyed, so that it has become extremely rare except in cultivation in western China, though it is said to be found in the forests to the east. Because of its large and rather papery leaves, *M. officinalis* requires maximum wind shelter if it is to attain its finest proportions. In more exposed situations it will, in most seasons, present an unhappy wind-riven appearance. In a suitable environment it may attain a height of 70 ft (21 m) or more with grey, ash-like bark.

According to S. S. Chien and W. C. Cheng in *Contributions from the Biological Laboratory of the Scientific Society of China* 9 : 282 (1934) 'this variety differs from the type not only in the bi-lobed leaves but also in the appressed pubescence on the undersurface of leaves. The tepals are smaller than those of the type species.'

M. officinalis was first named *M. hypoleuca* in 1900 by L. Diels under *Magnolia* in Engler, *Botanische Jahrbücher* 29 : 321, whereby these two species became confused horticulturally if not botanically.

This might have been the source of Dr. Li's name (in *The Garden Flowers of China*) for the Magnolia under consideration here. *M. officinalis* has not figured to date in *Curtis's Botanical Magazine*.

Cytologically *M. officinalis* is a diploid with 2n = 38 chromosomes.

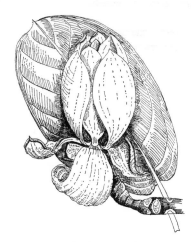

Beaked Magnolia
(referring to the carpels of the fruit cones)

MAGNOLIA ROSTRATA W. W. Smith

W. W. Smith in *Notes from the Royal Botanic Garden, Edinburgh* 12 : 213 (1920) excluding description of the flowers.

G. H. Johnstone in *Asiatic Magnolias in Cultivation*: 137–40 (1955)

It is distinguishable from *M. hypoleuca* and *M. officinalis* by the buds and young leaves being thickly clothed in a rufous indumentum or pubescence, also by the ripe carpels of the fruit cones having stiff beaks up to ¼ in. (8 mm) in length and by the very small pink seeds.

M. rostrata attains a height of about 80 ft (24·5 m) in its native habitat, with a smooth ash-grey bark. In cultivation it may seldom attain such dimensions. The abnormally stout shoots present a somewhat gaunt and grotesque appearance after leaf fall and this is partly due to the prominent petiolar scars which encircle them and which remain visible on the stouter branches and even on the main trunks of mature trees.

In 1926 Capt. F. Kingdon-Ward collected herbarium material from a tree on the Burmese-Tibetan border (K. W. No: 6783) which he recorded as having such prominent transverse grooves or fissures in the bark as to give it a remarkable palm-like appearance.

M. rostrata appears to have a somewhat limited natural range which roughly coincides with that of *M. nitida*. It has the most westerly distribution of the three species in this series of Section *Rytidospermum*, ranging from the Tsangpo Gorge at the eastern extremity of the Himalayas, into north-west Yunnan and adjacent parts of south-eastern Tibet and north-eastern Upper Burma. It was first discovered in Yunnan by George Forrest in 1917.

The foliage of *M. rostrata* is coppery green until fully expanded and is the finest of all Asian species, measuring up to 20 in. (51 cm) in length by 8½ in. (21·5 cm) in width. The leaf shape is obovate oblong, broadly rounded at the tip and, because of their chartaceous or parchment-like texture, they rival in effect the somewhat larger but papery-textured leaves of the American *M. macrophylla*. The undersides are glaucous, the midrib and veins being coated with erect chestnut brown hairs which are bent over at the tips. The flowers are somewhat disappointing, being disproportionate to the size of the leaves, which effectively screen them from view below.

The flower buds are enclosed in a purple-green spathaceous bract which hardens before falling. The flowers usually have eleven tepals, the three outermost ones reflexing and assuming a pinkish tinge on their upper surfaces with green shadings beneath. There are normally eight inner tepals and these are creamy white and of a fleshy texture, remaining for a while in the form of an upright cone over the gynoecium, while the reddish-purple stamens and filaments of the androecium are visible through the gaps between their narrowing bases. In poise and shape they more closely resemble the flowers of the *M. campbellii* series than any other Magnolia in this section, but they are not conspicuous because they open after the leaves have developed. Apparently it was at first much confused with *M. mollicomata*. Sir William Wright Smith published the original description in *Notes from the Royal Botanic Garden, Edinburgh* 12 : 213 (1920) but he was in fact referring to the flowers of *M. mollicomata*, the herbarium material having been confused. Reginald Farrer likewise confused these two Magnolias when he found *M. rostrata* in Upper Burma in 1919. They assumed that the flowers were larger, precocious and consequently more sensational than they are, and they did not visualize that they would be borne above the umbrella-like whorls of enormous leaves and virtually invisible from below. The melon-scented flowers are fugitive and extremely frost tender so that the production of fertile fruit cones is an irregular occurrence even in the more favoured Cornish gardens.

The coloured styles are arranged in spirals up the

conical column of the gynoecium producing an attractive pattern against the pale green carpels. The filaments and stamens are incurved towards its base. The peduncles are green and dotted with elongated creamy lenticels.

The fruit cones are quite spectacular, being slender and erect, about 5 in. (12·5 cm) long and 2in. (5 cm) in diameter, the beaks of the carpels becoming curved and claw-like. Each fertile carpel contains one or two small flesh-coloured seeds. After maturity the cones turn from red to brown and later bend over till they eventually hang upside down like fir-cones if they are not blown off the branches by winter gales. The seeds are the smallest of the genus and often number several hundred per cone. Seedlings take about fifteen years to attain florescence.

Johnstone in *Asiatic Magnolias in Cultivation*: 138–9 drew attention to the very numerous bud scales protecting the terminal growth buds in winter. As with the spathaceous bracts which protect the flower buds, these are modified stipules arising from the leaf petioles. Johnstone observed that whereas one might expect a leaf to develop at the base of each bud scale, the majority are suppressed while still undeveloped, becoming detached from the petioles immediately above the attachment of the stipules while still inside the bud. Further dissection of the growth bud revealed that all but the last few leaf blades were similarly shrivelled and fell off at the slightest touch leaving stipulary scars. This phenomenon is doubtless due to *apical dominance* referred to in the introductory notes to Section *Rytidospermum* on p. 49.

Unfortunately *M. rostrata* is very vulnerable to wind damage, for not only are the branches brittle, but the huge leaves are readily torn before they have matured to a parchment-like texture. It is therefore a tree for the milder and most sheltered gardens where its huge, stiff leaves will provide a sub-tropical effect unrivalled by any other Magnolia from temperate regions. There is a fine specimen in Sir Charles Cave's garden at Sidbury Manor near Sidmouth, Devon, which is believed to have been planted about 1935.

Forms of *M. rostrata* with pink flowers have been reported. One example, which flowered at Exbury in 1935, no longer survives. *M. rostrata* has not figured to date in *Curtis's Botanical Magazine*.

Cytologically *M. rostrata* is a diploid with 2n = 38 chromosomes.

TABLE OF COMPARISONS

	M. hypoleuca (M. obovata)	M. officinalis	M. rostrata
SHOOTS	Shaded purple with elongated lenticels and conspicuous annular scars. Growth buds glabrous.	Stout and swollen, greenish yellow becoming light yellowish grey with prominent shield-shaped leaf scars. Growth buds green with purplish pubescence.	Abnormally stout and lenticellate. Growth buds glabrous.
BARK	Smooth purplish grey.	Light ash grey.	Smooth ash grey. Often showing petiolar scars.
LEAVES	Predominantly ovate, apiculate or roundly pointed at apex; base obtuse, averaging 8 to 18 in. (20·5 to 46 cm) long by 4 to 8 in. (10 to 20·5 cm) wide. Pruinose becoming glabrous.	Very large elliptic obovate, averaging 12 to 15 in. (30 to 38 cm) long by 6 to 7 in. (15 to 18 cm) wide. Papery texture, apple green sometimes bi-lobed at apex.	Reddish-fawn indumentum on young leaves. At first coppery green, developing a parchment-like texture when mature, averaging 20 in. (51 cm) long, by 8½ in. (21·5 cm) wide.
LEAF UNDERSURFACES	Silvery grey or glaucous blue green. Densely pruinose and thinly hairy.	Greenish grey with grey hairs along midrib and veins.	Glaucous. Midrib and veins coated with chestnut hairs.

	M. hypoleuca (M. obovata)	M. officinalis	M. rostrata
PETIOLES	Shaded purple, rounded, up to 2 in. (5 cm) long, usually glabrous.	Greenish yellow 1 in. (2·5 cm) long, usually pubescent.	2¾ in. (7 cm) long, light green, stained bronze. Stout, glabrous.
FLOWERS	Very long gynandrophore, gynoecium light green. Filaments and pistils bright crimson forming boss 3 in. (7·5 cm) across. Pedicle glabrous. Thick spoon-shaped creamy-white tepals. Heavy exotic fragrance, June and July.	Smaller and irregular in shape resembling *M. tripetala* but whiter. Tepals nine to fifteen; margins in-incurved and wrinkled. Gynoecium green with hooked creamy-yellow stigmas. Deeply ribbed sepaloid tepals resemble light-brown paper. Flowers cup shaped; scent almost overpowering. June. Pedicle pubescent.	Stamen filaments reddish purple. Tepals usually eleven, outer three reflexing, tinted pink on upper surface, greenish beneath. The eight inner tepals form a dome over the gynandrophore as in *M. campbellii*. Melon scented, fugitive. June to July.
FRUIT CONES	5 to 8 in. (12·5 to 20·5 cm) long with short-beaked carpels. Perpendicular, red until mature. Carpels heavily spotted fawn, the basal ones are concave and decurrent along the floral axis to form an attenuated base. Seeds bright red.	4 to 5 in. (10 to 12·5 cm) oblong, rounded at base, due to basal follicles being convex and not decurrent along the axis. Seeds bright red.	Slender and erect 5 in. (12·5 cm) long. Long-beaked carpels with very small pink seeds. Cones bend over to inverted position when mature.

AMERICAN SERIES I OF SECTION *Rytidospermum*

As with the Asian species in this section, the leaves of these Magnolias are borne in terminal whorls at the ends of the shoots. *M. fraseri* and *M. pyramidata* are very closely allied, both have auriculate-cordate leaves and complete absence of hairs. The type species of this series is *M. tripetala* which is also the type species of Section *Rytidospermum*.

Umbrella Tree

MAGNOLIA TRIPETALA Linnaeus

M. Catesby in *Flora Caroliniana* 2 : 80 (1741)
C. Linnaeus in *Systema Naturae* 10, 2 : 1082 (1759)
   Species Plantarum 2, 1 : 756 (1763)
F. Pursh in *Flora Boreali-Americana* 2 : 381 (1814)
A. F. Michaux in *North American Sylva* 3 : 90 (1819)
SYN. *M. umbrella* Desrousseaux, L. A. J., in *Encyclopédie Méthodique, Botanique* 3 : 671 (1791)

Plate 6

This misnomer originated in 1759 when Linnaeus referred to Mark Catesby's *Magnolia amplissimo flore albo, fructo coccinea* in *Flora Caroliniana* which had been published in 1741. The coloured plate 80* clearly shows a flower with six inner tepals standing more or less vertically around the stigmatic column, also three outermost ones in a fully reflexed poise in the form of a false calyx and which Catesby described as *petalis exterioribus dependentibus* 'Flowers white, ten

---

* In some copies plate 80 has been transposed with plate 61 (*M. grandiflora*) but this was not so in that which was scrutinized by the author when preparing these notes.

to eleven petals, the three outermost pale green, later hanging downwards'. The author finds it difficult to appreciate why Linnaeus should have decided upon a name which implied that this Magnolia had only three 'petals'. Had he named it "*M. trisepala*" he would have satisfied both botanists and horticulturists.

This Magnolia is remarkable for its somewhat evil-smelling flowers, the odour being almost unbearably goat-like if cut blooms are kept in a closed room overnight. It is a small deciduous tree, up to 30 or 40 ft (9 or 12 m) in its native haunts, but usually somewhat smaller in British gardens. It has a pronounced tendency to replace its main branches periodically by sending up vigorous shoots from the base. In this manner it seldom forms a sizeable main trunk excepting close to ground-level. It produces a spreading open-branch system with stout young shoots of gaunt winter appearance to which the Virginian-American name Elkwood referred.

The wood is soft, spongy and brittle, with a disagreeable aroma when cut in a sappy condition. The bark is grey, smooth and polished. The shoots are swollen and pocked with leaf scars at intervals where successive generations of leaf whorls have developed in previous seasons. The leaves are very large, up to 20 in. (51 cm) long by 10 in. (25·5 cm) wide, broadly oblanceolate and tapering acutely at both ends. They have 1- to 2-inch (2·5 to 5 cm) petioles and are strongly ribbed, with pale pubescent undersurfaces when young. They form a parasol or umbrella-like shape when they curve downwards at the ends of the long, straight shoots. The tapering bases of the leaves distinguish this from other large-leaved American Magnolias.

The flowers open after the leaves have developed in May and June and have from nine to sixteen narrow creamy-buff tepals which are paler on their upper surfaces. The larger exterior ones become pendent in the form of a false calyx. The short column of the gynoecium is green with brown styles which match the incurved stamens. The flowers lack the elegance and poise associated with those of the Asian species and usually present a somewhat ragged, asymmetrical appearance. The large rosy-red fruit cones often provide an attractive display in early autumn.

A particularly good sixteen-tepalled form with larger than usual leaves was described and pictured by Philip J. Savage, Jr., in the *Newsletter of the American Magnolia Society* 4, 2 : 3 (1967). He reported that the flowers were of dinner-plate size when they were opened out flat. This cultivar was named and registered as 'Bloomfield' in 1974. It was raised from a Pennsylvania seed source. *M. tripetala* 'Bloomfield' is unusual in having white to pale-pink fruit cones. This appears to have been the first cultivar name to be applied to a seedling of *M. tripetala*. In the same year Prof. J. C. McDaniel registered the name 'Woodlawn' for a large-fruited tree in Woodlawn Cemetery, Urbana, Illinois, notable for its exceptionally large fruit cones which measure up to 5 in. (12·5 cm) by 2 in. (5 cm). These colour in August and were photographed by the author when he visited the site with Prof. McDaniel in September 1970. The photograph (Plate 6) was published in the *Journal of the Royal Horticultural Society* 97, 8 : 342, Fig. 162 (1972) in notes on a lecture on 'Magnolias and their Cultivation' given by the author in March of that year. The colour plate quoted gave rise to a comment in a letter from J. E. Dandy: 'They don't look like *M. tripetala* to me – more like *M. hypoleuca*; but perhaps the photograph is deceiving.' It was in fact printed sideways and the likeness is quite remarkable, though on closer scrutiny they are seen to be smoother and lighter in colour than cones from that Japanese species.

The fruit cones are normally about 4 in. (10 cm) long, conical and of a bright rosy-red colour when mature, the carpels opening to reveal the scarlet seeds which hang briefly at the ends of slender white threads before falling. The seeds germinate readily if cleaned and sown while fresh, or given moist storage in the bottom of a domestic refrigerator with or without the removal of their fleshy outer coating. The young trees usually begin to flower in about seven or eight years.

Magnolia tripetala occurs in eastern North America in the Allegheny region, from Pennsylvania southward on the wooded slopes of the Appalachian and Ozark mountain ranges.

It was introduced into British gardens in 1752 and it is believed to have first flowered in the garden of Peter Collinson at Mill Hill, London, on 24 May 1760. It has not figured in *Curtis's Botanical Magazine*.

It has proved to be one of the hardiest of the American Magnolias, presenting quite a tropical appearance with its whorls of huge leaves and polished brown shoots. It is extremely cold tolerant, flourishing in the Detroit area without winter damage and fruiting regularly.

Cytologically *M. tripetala* is a diploid with 2n = 38 chromosomes.

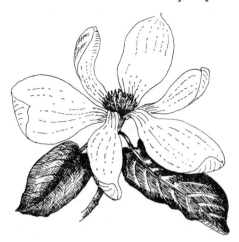

Fraser's Magnolia
Ear-leaved Umbrella Tree

MAGNOLIA FRASERI Walter

T. Walter in *Flora Caroliniana*: 159 (1788)
John Sims in *Curtis's Botanical Magazine* 30 : t. 1206
  (1809)
SYNS. *M. auriculata* Bartram
  M. auricularis Salisbury

The specific name commemorates John Fraser, who sent many North American plants to England between 1780 and 1810, including this Magnolia.

The second common name cited is also indicated by the synonym provided by Bartram's name *M. auriculata*, the distinctive feature of this Magnolia being the deep auricles or lobes at the bases of the leaves at the points of insertion of the petioles. They are pale green, obovate, spatulate, being widest near the apex, then gradually pointed. Their deeply auriculated bases are formed by long, narrow lobes which overlap the petioles. The leaves are 8 to 10 in. (20·5 to 25·5 cm) long and 4 to 6 in. (10 to 15 cm) wide, but often much larger on young vigorous trees. They are clustered so closely at the tips of the shoots that they appear whorled or verticillate. Their upper surfaces have an almost iridescent sea-green sheen while the undersides are pale green and glabrous. The young shoots are purplish red with white lenticels.

The growth habit is influenced by the same apical dominance referred to in the introduction to this section, but this species produces a greater mass of slender wiry branches than any other member species. In some parts of America this Magnolia attains a height of 40 to 50 ft (12 to 15 m) with a straight trunk 12 to 15 in. (30·5 to 38 cm) in diameter. Michaux described how the trees which he en-countered usually had straight sheer trunks for half their height, after which the branches radiated widely, with relatively few side shoots, thus giving the trees a peculiar and distinctive appearance whereby they were readily identifiable from a distance, even in winter. The type normally met with has fragrant creamy-white flowers 6 to 8 in. (15 to 20 cm) across although much larger sizes have been recorded. They open several weeks before those of *M. tripetala* and *M. macrophylla* with much yellower colouring in cold seasons.

This Magnolia was described by Dr. John Sims in *Curtis's Botanical Magazine* 30 : t. 1206 (1809). The colour plate shows quite a large pale yellow flower of ten broad tepals, the outer ones being shaded lime green. The gynandrophore is green and the petioles have dark-purple stipulary bracts. It seems probable that this was a selected form which had been propagated by grafting or layering and distributed on this side of the Atlantic in the same manner as the elusive *M. cordata*, though the richer colouring might be due to lower temperature and light and intensity at flowering time.

M. fraseri was discovered by William Bartram, the son of John Bartram who, in 1731, had established a nursery on his farm on the bank of the then beautiful and unpolluted Schuylkill River in eastern Pennsylvania, and who, in 1736, set out on his first long plant-collecting trip through the wilderness as far as Lake Erie in the north-west corner of the state. Such expeditions were repeated over a period of many years and were later continued by his son. There is some disparity about the date of the first introduction. Loudon gives 1786 but other authors as early as 1762. Loudon recorded that Mme Lemonnier, the widow of Michaux's patron and friend, had, in 1800, described a tree growing in her garden which was then 9 (2·5 m) tall and had already flowered. It usually attains florescence at from five to six years, so this specimen might well have been raised from seed sent from America in 1786.

There are also varied reports of its natural habitat. J. E. Dandy gives it a restricted distribution in the southern Appalachian Mountains and Dr. John Fogg, Jr., in his paper 'The Temperate American Magnolias' in *Morris Arboretum Bulletin* 12, 4 : 51–8 (1961) stated that *M. fraseri* 'grows in swamps and bottomlands from Georgia and Alabama north to West Virginia and Virginia'. He reported that it flourishes in cultivation in the Philadelphia region and is hardy as far north as Massachusetts. His notes on the species are illustrated by two photographs taken at the Barnes Arboretum in Merion, Pennsylvania.

J. C. Loudon, in his *Arboretum et Fruticetum Britannicum* 1 : 277 (1838) recorded its sparse distribution as being 'confined to a particular part of the Alleghenies, nearly 300 miles [480 km] from the sea', growing 'on the steep banks of rivers which rise in these lofty mountains', and that some natural stands of this Magnolia were 150 miles (240 km) apart.

Michaux wrote: 'I have nowhere found it so abundant as on the steepest part of the lofty mountains of North Carolina, particularly those which were called by the inhabitants Great Father Mountains and Black and Iron Mountains.' He reported that 'the soil was brown, deep, and of an excellent quality', and that this Magnolia was found to 'multiply so fast from seed that a thousand plants might be collected in a single day. . . . The atmosphere in these regions is continually charged with moisture from the number of torrents which rush down from the summits.'

M. fraseri was sent to Loddige's nurseries at Hackney, London in 1786. In his *Travels through South and North Carolina*: 338 (1791) William Bartram wrote: 'This exalted peak I named Mount Magnolia, from a new and beautiful species of that celebrated family of flowering trees, which here, at the cascades of Falling Creek, grows in a high degree of perfection.

'This tree (or perhaps rather shrub) rises eighteen to thirty feet [5·5 to 9 m] in height. There are usually many stems from a root, or source, which lean a little, or slightly diverge from each other, in this respect imitating *M. tripetala*; the crooked wreathing branches arising and subdividing from the main stem without order or uniformity; their extremities turn upwards, producing a very large rosaceous, perfectly white, double or polypetalous, flower, which is of most fragrant scent. This fine flower sits in the centre of a radius of very large leaves, which are of a singular figure, somewhat lanceolate, but broad towards their extremities, terminating with an acuminate point, and backwards they attenuate, and become very narrow towards their bases, terminating that way with two long narrow ears, or lapels, one on each side of the insertion of the petiole. The leaves have only short footstalks, sitting very near each other at the extremities of the floriferous branches, from which they spread themselves after a regular order, like the spokes of a wheel; their margins touching or lightly overlapping upon each other, form an expansive umbrella, superbly crowned or crested with the fragrant flower, representing a white plume. The blossom is succeeded by a very large crimson cone, or strobile, containing a great number of scarlet berries, which, when ripe, spring from

their cells and are, for a time, suspended by a white silky web or thread. The leaves of these trees which grow in a rich humid soil when fully expanded and at maturity, are frequently about 2 ft [61 cm] in length and 6 to 8 in. [15 to 20·5 cm] where broadest.'

From this quotation of Bartram's field notes it would appear that *M. fraseri* makes a smaller, but larger-leaved tree in the very humid conditions which he described, whereas Michaux recorded much larger specimens with proportionately smaller leaves and flowers. Rehder in *Manual of Cultivated Trees and Shrubs* 2 : 246 (1940) described the leaves as obtusely pointed and the mature fruit cones as having the tips of the carpels incurved.

There is a good specimen at Kew in the Azalea Garden and there is a specimen almost 70 ft (21·5 m) tall at Leonardslee in Sussex.

Cut material of this species was exhibited by Lord Aberconway and the National Trust Gardens, Bodnant, at Chelsea Flower Show on 25 May 1971. It had mahogany-brown stems and the flowers had incurved strap-shaped tepals, those of the outer whorl turning creamy buff. The styles were green and the stamens were buff.

Philip J. Savage, Jr., writing in the *Newsletter of the American Magnolia Society* 6, 1 : 6 (1969) referred to the way in which the surfaces of the young leaves on the new growth of *M. fraseri* 'refract light in an unusual way, something like gasoline looks floating on water. It isn't a gloss, it's a slight iridescence, and gives the harpoon-shaped young leaves a look of real distinction. . . . Its branches are wiry and slender, and the leaves, which mature in a great range of sizes, sway and dance on their long, red, petioles throughout a well filled and shapely crown.' He found that with good culture and in full sunlight it will often begin to flower in five or six years from seed. The earlier flowers open when the leaves are only a few inches long and are therefore quite spectacular. Their scent is like mild Sweet Bay (*M. virginiana*).

At Caerhays there is an unusual form of *M. fraseri*, which has the opening flowers coloured lime green. This was exhibited by Mr. F. Julian Williams at the Cornwall Garden Society's Show at Truro on 26 April 1972. It is of course possible that this richer colouring (which was also evidenced by the *Curtis's Botanical Magazine* Plate 1206 referred to earlier), might be due to our climate being cooler and often cloudier at flowering time, compared with conditions normally prevailing at that season in its native environment.

Cytologically *M. fraseri* is diploid with 2n = 38 chromosomes.

Pyramidal Magnolia

MAGNOLIA PYRAMIDATA Bartram

W. Bartram in *Travels through South and North Carolina*: 338 (1791)

John Sims in *Curtis's Botanical Magazine*: t. 1208 (1809)

F. Pursh in *Flora Americae Septentrionalis* 2 : 382 (1814)

SYN. *M. fraseri* var. *pyramidata* (Bartram) Pampanini in *Bulletino della R. Societa Toscana di Orticultura* 40 : 230 (1915)

A North American deciduous species allied to *M. fraseri* but of smaller stature, making a slender, pyramidal tree from 30 to 35 ft (9 to 10·5 m) high, flowering a few days earlier than *M. fraseri*, also smaller in its flowers and fruits. The leaves are described as being smooth, rhombic obovate and abruptly acute, rather gradually pointed at the apex, glaucescent beneath, of thinner texture and with petioles shorter than those of *M. fraseri*. They are about 8 in. (20·5 cm) long by 4 in. (10 cm) wide. The fragrant flowers are creamy white and 3 to 4 in. (7·5 to 10 cm) across, of loose formation with narrow, reflexing, strap-like tepals. This species ripens its fruit cones earlier than any other Magnolia. It is said to flower at quite an early age from seed.

They are distinguished from *M. fraseri* by their shorter stamens, shorter gynoecia and hence shorter fruit aggregates. R. E. Miller in 'The deciduous Magnolias of West Florida' in *Rhodora* 77 : 64–75 (1975) states that 'there is a gradual transition between *pyramidata* of Florida and *fraseri* of the mountains since the Alabama and Georgia plants form a continuous sequence from north to south in these states'.

It was first described by William Bartram but, owing to lack of clarity in his description, the author citation is often given to Frederick Pursh, who described it again some twenty-three years later.

William Bartram wrote: 'I discovered, in the maritime parts of Georgia, particularly on the banks of the Alatamaha, another new species of Magnolia, whose leaves were nearly of the figure of those of this tree' (referring to his description of *M. fraseri*) 'but they were much less in size, not more than 6 or 7 in. [15 or 18 cm] in length and the strobile [cone] very small, oblong, sharp-pointed, and of a fine deep crimson colour; but I never saw the flower. These trees grow straight and erect, 30 ft [9 m] or more in height, and of a sharp conical form, much resembling the Cucumber Tree (*M. acuminata*) in figure.'

M. pyramidata is found in south-west Georgia, the panhandle of Florida, southern Alabama and south-eastern Mississippi. It has also been reported in Louisiana and south-eastern Texas. It was introduced into England in 1806 by William Bartram.

In Don's *Miller's Dictionary* 1 : 83 (1811) the white flowers of *M. pyramidata* are described as having 'nine lanceolate, pointed petals and three spreading sepals, opening in May and June'.

J. C. Loudon, in his *Arboretum et Fruticetum Britannicum* 1 : 278 (1838), wrote: 'It is extremely difficult to propagate [which is done by inarching on *M. auriculata* (*M. fraseri*)] and it is, in consequence, very sparingly distributed over the country.'

Apparently *M. pyramidata* replaces the closely related *M. fraseri* in the forests of the coastal plain. It has never been common in cultivation and Dandy has expressed doubt as to whether it still survives in any British or European garden. Next to *M. macrophylla* subsp. *ashei* it is probably the second rarest of the United States species or subspecies. It shares with the closely related *M. fraseri* a pronounced sensitivity to poorly drained soils.

George Nicholson recorded having seen a tree of this Magnolia growing in the gardens of the Trianon in France in 1887. It is probably less hardy than *M. fraseri* with which it has been confused.

Dr. Robert L. Egolf of the University of South Florida, at Tampa, described an interesting hunt for this species in the *Newsletter of the American Magnolia Society* 4, 1 : 6 (1967) in notes entitled 'Two Rare American Magnolias'. He gave a detailed account of his searches for *M. pyramidata* and *M. ashei*. His quest eventually led him, in 1963, to Torreya State Park in Liberty County, on the banks of the Apalachicola River. This is situated about sixty miles west of Tallahassee, in the north-west panhandle of Florida and is relatively isolated and unspoilt. The park was established to protect one of the rare stands of *Torreya taxifolia*, the stinking cedar, a conifer with stiff, sharply pointed leaves. *Taxus floridana*, the rare Florida yew is also found there.

After an hour's search, Dr. Egolf came across a specimen of *M. pyramidata* and several small saplings, but no seed. In the following year he revisited the site at the end of July and found both species of Magnolia in fruit. The cones of *M. ashei* were mature but not yet open, while those of *M. pyramidata* were less mature, being rose pink and not yet ripe. He collected cones of each species and subsequently germinated their seeds.

Dr. Stephen Spongberg treats *M. pyramidata* as *M. fraseri* var. *pyramidata*. His main distinctions are: the shorter stamens of *pyramidata* $\frac{1}{8}$ to $\frac{1}{4}$ in. (4 to 6 mm) long, the smaller gynoecia $\pm\frac{1}{2}$ in. ($\pm$1·5 cm) long at anthesis and their correspondingly shorter fruit cones $1\frac{1}{4}$ to $2\frac{1}{4}$ in. (3·5 to 5·5 cm).

Cytologically *M. pyramidata* is a diploid with $2n = 38$ chromosomes.

AMERICAN SERIES 2 OF
SECTION *Rytidospermum*

This series includes two closely allied species, remarkable for the enormous size of their leaves, which are the largest in the genus. Only one of these, *M. macrophylla* and its subspecies *M. ashei*, are under consideration here, since the second species in the series, *M. dealbata*, is tropical. A recent expedition to collect and introduce *M. dealbata* is described in the introductory chapters of this book.

Big Leaf Magnolia

MAGNOLIA MACROPHYLLA Michaux

A. Michaux in *Flora Boreali-Americana* 1 : 327 (1803)
John Sims in *Curtis's Botanical Magazine* 48 : t. 2189 (1820)
Plate 7

This king of the American Umbrella Trees has the largest leaves of any Magnolia, resembling those of a banana and measuring up to 3 ft (91 cm) in length, by almost 1 ft (30·5 cm) wide, arranged in the form of enormous umbrellas which are a ghostly white on the undersurfaces.

M. macrophylla grows into a round-headed tree up to 60 ft (18 m) tall, with stout, spreading branches which are downy when young. The trunks of mature trees are often free of branches for 40 ft (12 m) above ground. Primarily a native of the deep South of the North American continent, it is reported to be in danger of extinction through intensive forestry management. It is usually found growing in the deep alluvial soils of creek bottoms, in sheltered valleys and on the lower hill slopes. In its ideal environment the trunks are tall and straight, the leaders pushing their way into the upper canopy until able to swamp competing branches of adjacent trees by the sheer size of their mature foliage.

These huge leaves are light green above, silvery grey and downy beneath and of thin, papery texture. They are oblong obovate, obtuse and somewhat auriculate at the base. The young shoots are pubescent and of a pale-silvery shade of lime green. The flowers are proportionately large, larger indeed than those of any other tree in North America, larger even than those of *M. grandiflora*. They open after the leaves have developed and are at first cup shaped, 10 to 12 in. (25·5 to 30·5 cm) across, fragrant, with six thick, creamy-white tepals, on most forms the inner three are tinted purple towards the base. The giant flowers are said to shine out through the forest, in spite of the huge leafy parasols on which they nestle. They fade to a parchment colour. The rose-coloured fruit cones are globose ovoid and pubescent, $2\frac{1}{2}$ to $3\frac{1}{2}$ in. (6 to 9 cm) long. The white (unspotted) form is found in Cullman and Winston counties, Alabama; in the Homochito Hills of southern Mississippi and a stretch of country between there and Woodville.

M. macrophylla is of very limited distribution from Tennessee west of the Cumberland River and in a small district of North Carolina about 12 miles (19 km) south-east of Lincolnton, 250 miles (400 km) from Charleston. The most northerly native trees are in Jackson County, Ohio.

A tree with leaves of such dimensions obviously requires maximum wind shelter, such as the environment of sheltered woodland, with a rich, moist, neutral-to-acid soil.

It attains florescence in about fourteen years from seed. Etienne Soulange-Bodin, breeder of the famous Soulangiana Magnolia hybrids from 1820 onward, published a paper in the *Annales de L'Institut Royal Horticole de Fromont* 3 : 150–1 (1831) entitled 'Beau Phénomène de Fructification, *Magnolia macrophylla – Magnolia yulan*'. He reported that his tree of *M. macrophylla* had begun to flower at fourteen years from seed and had fruited freely at sixteen years. He also reported on his abortive attempts to hybridize it with pollen from *M. discolor* (a form of *M. quinquepeta* (*liliflora*).

According to André, the elder Michaux, who first discovered it in 1759, *M. macrophylla* was often found in company with *M. tripetala* from which it is readily distinguished by its larger size and smooth white bark.

J. C. Loudon drew attention to 'the stipules in this species, and the manner in which they envelope the unexpanded leaves . . . The stipules are large, and placed mainly upon the petioles of the leaves; yet the office of the stipules borne by the petiole of any leaf is not to envelope and protect that leaf, but the leaf next inward to it. The outermost wrappers of the leaf buds are stipules upon the rudiments of petioles.' (*Arboretum et Fruticetum Britannicum* 1 : 271 (1838).)

In America several superior forms have been selected and registered as named cultivars but, because all species in section *Rytidospermum* are difficult to propagate vegetatively, it is unlikely that any of them will become widely distributed. They include 'Holy Grail' by D. Todd Gresham (1963) and 'Whopper' by J. C. McDaniel (1974) both with purple spots, the latter with up to nine tepals and up to 18 in. (46 cm) across when opened flat. He has also selected an all-white form growing in the Arboretum of the J. J. Audubon Foundation currently in the care of Sara and Frank Gladney, at Gloster, Mississippi, where the native woods have several impressive seedling trees, and registered it as 'Sara Gladney'.

Prof. J. C. McDaniel, a proven expert with the grafting knife, reports in *Newsletter of the American Magnolia Society* 11, 2 : 4 (1975) 'Usual tree grafting methods are not as feasible . . . on account of their thick pith and rather thin wood. I prefer a thin chip-bud on stocks of half inch or larger diameter and buds taken from last year's well-developed stems, if budding is to be done in spring. For August-early-September work buds may be taken from current year's stems. In either case, overwrap the inserted bud with polyethylene plastic film for about three weeks. After that, the spring set buds may be forced into growth the same season.' With *M. macrophylla* cultivars he reported his best results on established seedlings of the same species.

M. macrophylla was introduced into English gardens in 1800. It received the coveted First Class Certificate of the Royal Horticultural Society a century later. It is believed to have first flowered in the garden of James Vere in July 1819.

For creating a bold subtropical effect in a sheltered situation *M. macrophylla* has no rival among deciduous woody plants hardy in the temperate zone. The young foliage, like that of other Magnolias, is somewhat frost tender, as are the unripened shoots of young trees.

In England there is a fine specimen of *M. macrophylla* in the garden at Embley Park near Romsey, another at Exbury, both in Hampshire.

As with all other members of Section *Rytidospermum*, *M. macrophylla* is a diploid with 2n = 38 chromosomes.

Ashe's Magnolia
MAGNOLIA MACROPHYLLA subsp. *ASHEI* (Weatherby) Spongberg

A. C. Weatherby in *Rhodora* 28 : 35 (1926)
S. J. Spongberg in *Journal of the Arnold Arboretum* 57, 3 : 268–9 (1976)

This Magnolia was not distinguished from *M. macrophylla* until 1926. It is perhaps best described as a diminutive form of that species, attaining less than half the ultimate height, 26 ft (8 m) compared with 60 ft (18 m), with what is termed 'subappressed pubescence' on the undersides of the midribs of the leaves. The flowers are smaller with tepals 4 to 6 in. (10 to 15 cm) long, compared with 5 to 8 in. (12·5 to 20·5 cm), the tepal shape usually acute or acutish. It is generally agreed that, whereas the fruit cones of *M. macrophylla* are globose, those of subspecies *ashei* are cylindrical or sub-cylindric to ovoid, and the stamens are shorter ⅜ to ½ in. (11 to 13 mm).

The elevation of this Magnolia to specific rank in 1926 created considerable confusion as to the natural ranges of the two 'species', both of which had hitherto been considered as *M. macrophylla*. Later it became generally recognized as a variety of that species and the name was altered to *M. macrophylla* var. *ashei*. It has been recently given official recognition as a subspecies.

The existence of *M. ashei* suddenly came to the fore when J. K. Small introduced it to the New York Botanical Garden and wrote about it in an article entitled 'A Magnolia as a New Border Plant' in the *Journal of the New York Botanical Garden* 34 : 151–2 (1933). He described how this Magnolia began to flower at only 1 ft or so (30·5 cm) tall when raised from seed. Apparently it also behaves in this manner in the wild, though it ultimately grows into a large tree-like shrub over 20 ft (6 m) tall.

M. macrophylla subsp. *ashei* is endemic to the panhandle of north-western Florida where it is most frequently encountered in the Knox Hill region of Walton County. According to H. Oscar Harrison of De Funiak Springs, Florida, the local name for this Magnolia in the Euchee Valley area of Walton County is Cow Cucumber.

Dr. Robert L. Egolf, of the University of South Florida, in the *Newsletter of the American Magnolia Society* 4, 1 : 6 (1967) described how, in 1963, he located *M. ashei* in relative abundance in the Torreya State National Park in Florida, together with a sparse stand of the equally rare *M. pyramidata*. He recorded that *M. ashei* was 'scattered irregularly along the slopes of ravines, but nowhere where the ground had a tendency to be wet or swampy. The trees grow as part of the underwood in company with *Ostrya virginiana*, *Halesia tetraptera*, *Aesculus pavia*, *Taxus floridana* and *Torreya taxifolia*. None of the specimens seen exceeded 20 ft (6 m) in height and usually had crooked, leaning trunks, 2 to 5 in. (5 to 12·5 cm) in diameter, occasionally divided near the base, and very sparingly branched. None of these trees was bearing fruit at the time.'

He returned to the site in late July 1964 and was able to collect seed of both species of Magnolia. He reported that 'the cones of *M. ashei* collected were not of the very narrow cylindrical form usually described, but were long-ovoid and considerably smaller than the cones of *M. macrophylla*, with fewer carpels. . . . It is noteworthy that no seedlings of *M. ashei* could be found, although a search was made.'

It appears that *M. ashei* was not introduced into English gardens until 1948/9. George Johnstone described its first flowering in the *Journal of the Royal Horticultural Society* 78 : 288–9, Fig. 90 (1953). Plants were raised from seed in his garden at Trewithen, near Truro, Cornwall, in 1949 and planted out in February 1950. A seedling given to Treve Holman at Chyverton, Zelah, near Truro, was transferred to the sheltered angle of a wall in March 1951. In May 1952 the first flower bud was apparently pushed off by an adjacent growth bud which it closely resembled.

The plant was only 19 in. (48 cm) high when it flowered on 8 June 1953. The flower bud was remarkably pointed and opened to a cup-shaped flower 8 to 10 in. (20·5 to 25·5 cm) in diameter, the two pale-green sepaloid tepals quickly withering. The six white tepals were in two whorls of three. The androecium was green with white stamens and the gynoecium cream with pale-brown stigmas. The scent was described as resembling that of *M. wilsonii*. A double form is reported to be growing in the botanical garden of the Henry Foundation at Gladwyne, Pennsylvania.

M. macrophylla subsp. *ashei* has not taken kindly to cultivation in the sheltered woodland gardens in Cornwall where Asian species grow to such perfection. Here the best specimen is probably that at Trewithen which, by 1977, had grown into a small bushy tree some 12 ft (3·7 m) in height and spread. It apparently prefers an open situation and hotter and drier summers than are usually experienced in Cornwall.

Cytologically *M. ashei* is the same as *M. macrophylla* being a diploid with 2n = 38 chromosomes.

SECTION *OYAMA* Nakai

T. Nakai in *Flora Sylvatica Koreana* 20 : 117 (1933)
SYN. *Cophanthera* J. E. Dandy in *Curtis's Botanical Magazine* 159 : sub. t. 9467 (1936)
type species *M. sieboldii* (*parviflora*)

This section was named Oyama in 1933 by the Japanese botanist Professor T. Nakai, who selected *M. sieboldii* (as *M. parviflora*) for the type species. In 1936 Dandy, unaware of Nakai's citation, proposed the epithet *Cophanthera*, alluding to the characteristic blunt or rounded anthers which distinguish its member species. They are also distinguishable by their pendent fruit cones.

The Oyama Magnolias are deciduous shrubs or small trees, their nodding or pendent white flowers being either cup shaped or saucer shaped, opening when the leaves are mature to display their crimson

or purple stamens.

Their combined natural distribution covers a wide area, extending from the eastern Himalayas to eastern China, south-west Manchuria, Korea and southern Japan.

This section comprises four species: *M. sieboldii* (*parviflora*), native of Japan, Korea, Manchuria and the eastern Chinese province of Anhwei; *M. sinensis* which has only been recorded in a confined area in Szechwan; *M. wilsonii* likewise found in Szechwan but with a natural distribution extending into eastern Sikang (Kansu) and northern Yunnan and *M. globosa* which is to be found from Sikkim along the eastern Himalayas as far as the north-western corner of Yunnan.

M. × wieseneri (*M. × watsonii*), an assumed hybrid between *M. sieboldii* and *M. hypoleuca* (*obovata*), is known in Japan as *Ukesaki Oyamarenge* which means 'upward-facing Oyama Magnolia'.

All four species fruit freely in cultivation and, since they normally begin to flower at five to seven years of age, seed seems to be the best method of propagation. If, however, one wishes to perpetuate a particularly fine form, then vegetative propagation by layering, cuttings or grafting must be used.

M. × *highdownensis*, an assumed hybrid between *M. sinensis* and *M. wilsonii*, is described on p. 181. Seedlings have somewhat variable bark colour and leaves more or less intermediate between those described for these species. The extent to which they hybridize where their natural range coincides in Szechwan is open to speculation. There appear to be a lot of these intermediate forms in English gardens.

Cytologically all Oyama Magnolias are diploids with 2n=38 chromosomes.

Siebold's Magnolia
Oyamarenge in Japan
Tennyoka in China

MAGNOLIA SIEBOLDII

M. sieboldii C. Koch in *Hortus Dendrologicus*. Magnoliaceae 4 (1853)

SYNS. *M. parviflora* P. F. von Siebold & J. G. Zuccarini in *Abhandlungen der Mathematisch-physikalischen Classe der Königlich Bayerischen Akademie der Wissenschaften* 4, 2 : 187 (1846)

J. D. Hooker in *Curtis's Botanical Magazine* 121 : t. 7411 (1895)

M. oyama A. Kort in *Revue de l'Horticulture Belge* 31 : 258–9 (1905)

M. verecunda G. Koidzumi in *The Botanical Magazine of the Tokyo Botanical Society* 40 : 339 (1926)

Plate 8

A large deciduous shrub or small tree bearing nodding or horizontal, cup-shaped flowers, white and fragrant, later opening flat to reveal their crimson stamens. The shortness of the internodes below the perianth distinguishes *M. sieboldii* from other species in Section *Oyama*.

Originally named *M. parviflora* in 1846 by Siebold and Zuccarini, this name was discarded in favour of *M. sieboldii*, which had been given to it by C. Koch in 1853, because the name *parviflora* had been used by Blume in 1825 for *Michelia figo* (*Magnolia fuscata*). Under the homonym rule of the International Code of Botanical Nomenclature, which was agreed in 1930, *M. parviflora* had to be discarded. Priority was therefore given to Koch's epithet *sieboldii*.

Not only does this Magnolia flower in May and June when the last of the spring ones are finishing, but it continues intermittently until August; thereby its flowers are most likely to escape frost damage even if the earliest ones are caught. It is also more wind tolerant than most Magnolias, largely due no doubt to its later growth commencement and flower initiation. It is considerably lime tolerant but is not suitable for thin chalky soils.

The flowers are $3\frac{1}{2}$ to 4 in. (9 to 10 cm) across when fully expanded, with nine tepals, some of the outer ones reflexing. The numerous stamens form a magenta-purple collar around the green gynoecium. It is a somewhat variable species and several multi-tepalled forms have been recorded. The flowers have an almost horizontal poise so that they 'look you in the face' as Millais so aptly worded it.

It fruits freely even as a young plant, the small semi-pendent crimson fruit cones later displaying their scarlet seeds.

Wilson's photograph No. 137, taken on one of his plant-hunting expeditions in China, shows a bush 8 by 12 ft (2·5 by 3·5 m) growing near Taiyudo province, north Heiam (Anhwei), at an altitude of 3,000 ft (915 m).

Although the flowers of *M. sieboldii* are somewhat smaller and less fragrant than those of *M. sinensis*, it is probably the most popular member of Section *Oyama* on account of its remarkably long flowering season. It layers more readily than most Magnolias.

Perhaps the most distinctive feature of the flowers is their comparatively long stalks or peduncles which tend to arch upwards as the flower buds develop, owing to their tips being trapped by the leaf stipules which form the perules. When the buds are ultimately released, and their tepals are able to unfurl, one or more of the outer ones gradually reflexes outwards so that the form of the mature flowers is asymmetrical.

Although *M. sieboldii* does not normally exceed

10 ft (3 m) in height in cultivation it was reported up to 20 ft (6 m) by Wilson in north-east Korea. Under ideal conditions it tends to spread itself into a vast thicket by layering its lower branches. Millais in *Magnolias* recorded a specimen at Caerhays 24 ft (7·5 m) across which was believed to have been planted there in 1912. Johnstone in *Asiatic Magnolias in Cultivation* recorded a far larger specimen at Duffryn, Glamorgan, which measured 78 ft (23·5 m) across. Both examples are doubtless attributable to the sheltered and humid microclimates of these vast woodland gardens.

In *Curtis's Botanical Magazine* 121 : t. 7411 (1895) Hooker described the manner whereby *M. parviflora* (now *M. sieboldii*) differs from *M. × watsonii* (now *M. × wieseneri*) 'by being smaller in all its parts with fewer nerves on the leaves and longer peduncles (stalks) to its flowers; to which may be added the absence of the yellow margin of the leaves and the fewer carpels'. He recorded it as 'a native of the alpine region of the Japanese island of Nippon, recorded from Mounts Hakone and Hego-san and from the foot of the volcano of Wunyen'. He gave the origin of the plant from which the drawing was made as having been purchased in 1893 from the Yokohama Gardener's Association. It flowered in June 1894 in the Temperate House of the Royal Botanic Gardens, Kew. The flower shown on Plate 7411 is *upward facing* so the artist must have assumed that its nodding poise was due to wilting and decided to correct it!

The flower of the Magnolia depicted as *M. parviflora* by Keisuke Ito on Fig. 11 in his *Figures and Descriptions of Plants in the Koishikawa Botanical Garden* (1884) is in its correct nodding position but it is a multitepalled form with twenty-two tepals compared with the norm of nine, so it requires the Japanese cultivar name 'Kwanso'.

The Japanese text to Keisuke Ito's Fig. 13 translates: 'Distributed deep in the mountains in different parts of Japan. Found on Mount Miura in Nagano Prefecture, in the Nagawa area and in the mountains area of Hagiso in Nagano Prefecture, on Mount Yufu in Ooita Prefecture, on Ohmine (Big Peak) of Mount Yoshino in Nara Prefecture, etc. Ohmine is also known as Oyama and hence this Magnolia is referred to as the Oyama Magnolia.

'It is also said to have come from China in 1673. . . . There are two different kinds in the colour of the anthers, red coloured and purple coloured. Red coloured ones are said to be the Chinese species which came from China in 1673. . . . The Chinese name for this Magnolia is *Tennyoka*.'

Johnstone referred to a form of *M. sieboldii* with scarlet rather than crimson stamens which he recalled having seen exhibited from a Scottish garden several years previous to 1955 at one of the Royal Horticultural Shows in London. This could well have been of the Chinese form referred to by Keisuke Ito.

M. sieboldii 'Variegata', with leaves variegated white, originated on Mount Chiisan, Korea, and was recorded by the Japanese botanist T. Nakai in *Flora Sylvatica Koreana* 20 : 120 (1933).

Philip J. Savage, Jr., has drawn my attention to Sowerby's collection of this Magnolia (as *M. parviflora*) on the northern bank of the Yalu River in southern Kirin, Manchuria, in 1915. In *Notes de Botanique Chinoise* (1950), which was published by the Musée Heude, Shanghai, I. V. Kosloff contributed 'Notes on Plants Collected by Mr. Arthur de Carle Sowerby in Eastern China'. Sowerby's specimens are in the Heude Herbarium.

Kosloff stated that this Magnolia 'Grows in Japan, Southern Manchuria in its northern part under Mukden, and in northern Korea'. In a letter to Philip Savage dated 15 June 1953, Sowerby wrote: '*Magnolia parviflora* grows in huge shrubs in stream valleys throughout the hills from the neighbourhood of Mukden south-east to the right bank of the Yalu'. Mukden is now Shenyang so this would be about latitude 42 °N and make this distribution of *M. sieboldii* the most northerly location recorded for a Magnolia on the Asian continent.

In correspondence with the author in January 1971 Mr. K. Wada of Hakoneya Nurseries, Yokohama, Japan, reported having come across supposed hybrids between *M. sieboldii* and *M. grandiflora*.

There are conflicting opinions concerning the lime tolerance of this species. Since the related *MMs. sinensis*, *wilsonii* and *× highdownensis* are reported to tolerate chalky soils, it seems reasonable to suppose that *M. sieboldii* would share this lime tolerance. This supposition is strengthened by Dr. Stephen Spongberg's treatment (1976) of *M. sinensis* as *M. sieboldii* subsp. *sinensis*. On the contrary, Karl Flinck, who grows Magnolias in Sweden, suggests treating *M. sieboldii* like a rhododendron, in well-drained acid porous soil with a mulch and some shade. Chlorosis – that sickly pallor of the foliage – can be caused not only by excesses of lime, or of potash, but also from a potash deficiency, and this may have misled some growers of this species.

Cytologically *M. sieboldii* is a diploid with 2n = 38 chromosomes.

Globe-flowered Magnolia

MAGNOLIA GLOBOSA Hooker & Thomson

J. D. Hooker & T. Thomson in *Flora Indica* 1 : 77–8 (1855)

SYNS. *Yulania japonica* var. *globosa* (Hooker & Thomson) P. Parmentier in *Bulletin Scientifique de la France et de la Belgique* 27 : 258, 336 (1896)

M. tsarongensis W. W. Smith & G. Forrest in *Notes from the Royal Botanic Garden, Edinburgh* 12 : 215 (1920)

J. E. Dandy in *Curtis's Botanical Magazine* 159 : t. 9467 (1936)

Plate 9

A wide-ranging species occurring along the Himalayas from Sikkim eastward to north-west Yunnan at altitudes between 8,000 and 11,000 ft (2,400 to 3350 m). This Magnolia differs from other members of Section *Oyama* in having spectacular leaves, their large size and elegant shape being accentuated on the Chinese form by the chestnut-coloured felting which clothes the bud stipules, young shoots and petioles.

The flowers are pleasantly scented and somewhat smaller than those of other members of Section *Oyama*. They do not develop into the pendent white saucers characteristic of *M. sinensis* and *M. wilsonii*. Instead they usually form white egg-shaped cups, fleetingly tinted at the edges with pale pink. The nine to ten tepals are in three whorls and the flowers open in a nodding or sub-horizontal poise. The stamens are crimson to reddish purple and the gynoecium is green.

In Cornwall they are often disappointing because they tend to brown off if dampened by dew or rain, which seems to affect both buds and flowers. The

short, pendent fruit cones at first green, turn pink and later brown with scarlet seeds. These are freely produced even from flowers which have become 'browned off'. Seedlings usually begin to flower at from seven to ten years of age.

M. globosa grows into a vast spreading bush. Johnstone cited a plant in his garden at Trewithen in Cornwall which was 24 ft (7·5 m) across and 14 ft (4·5 m) tall when about thirty years old. Although relatively few would-be planters are likely to have such an ideal soil and environment in which to plant and grow Magnolias, it would probably require judicious pruning to restrict its spread in most gardens.

The two more-or-less distinct forms of this Magnolia, which represent the species in cultivation at the present time, have been raised from seed collections made at the approximate extremes of its extensive natural range. Although the species was originally discovered by J. D. Hooker, along with the sensational *M. campbellii*, during his botanical exploration of the Sikkim Himalayas about 1854, *M. globosa* was not introduced into cultivation until 1919, when George Forrest collected herbarium specimens and later seed in the Tsarong region of south-eastern Tibet. So in 1920 it was described as a new species *M. tsarongensis* and plants of this form now growing in our gardens originated from his seed collection number F. 21722, whereby the less hardy Chinese form of *M. globosa* became the first to be grown in cultivation.

It is distinguished by its early leafing and pronounced covering of reddish-brown hairs on the younger branches, petioles and midribs of the undersides of the leaves. This early growth initiation makes it susceptible to frost damage so that it is only suitable for planting in the milder gardens in this country.

The hardier Indian form does not appear to have been introduced until about 1930. Johnstone recorded that the Trewithen specimen was raised by the late Dr. J. Cromar Watt from seed collected in the Lachung Valley in Sikkim. He grew it under glass in his garden at Aberdeen where it began to flower in June 1937. A photograph of this plant, taken at its first flowering, is shown in Fig. 17 facing p. 116 in *Asiatic Magnolias in Cultivation*. This plant was later sent to Trewithen and planted in the garden in 1939. According to Hooker and Thomson in *Flora Indica* 1 : 78 (1855), *M. globosa* attains the greatest elevation, and penetrates farther into the interior of the Himalayas, than any other Magnolia.

Distinguishing features of the western and eastern forms of *M. globosa*:

	Indian (Western) Form	Chinese (Eastern) Form (*M. tsarongensis* Smith & Forrest)
GROWTH INITIATION	Comes into growth late.	Comes into growth early.
BUD STIPULES	Glabrous.	Very noticeably rufous pubescent.
YOUNG SHOOTS	Green, glabrous.	Densely felted with rufous pubescence.
PETIOLES	Glabrous.	Felted.
LEAF UNDER-SIDES	Reddish golden between veins.	Silvery grey between veins.
WOOD	Ash brown.	Reddish fawn.

It should be borne in mind that these details are from but few individuals and come from the two extremes of the vast natural range of this species. Intermediate forms are certain to exist and may one day be introduced into cultivation. The quite pronounced differences in indumentum and, what is of vital importance, in relative hardiness, make it advisable to distinguish these two geographical forms horticulturally even if such distinction is considered unnecessary botanically. In most seasons the Chinese form is in full leaf by the time its western counterpart shows signs of growth.

Cytologically *M. globosa* is a diploid with 2n = 38 chromosomes.

Chinese Oyama Magnolia

MAGNOLIA SINENSIS (Rehder & Wilson) Stapf

Otto Stapf in *Curtis's Botanical Magazine* 149 : sub. t. 9004 (1923)

SYNS. *M. globosa* var. *sinensis* A. Rehder & E. H. Wilson in Sargent, *Plantae Wilsonianae* 1 : 393 (1913)

M. sieboldii subsp. *sinensis* (Rehder & Wilson) Spongberg in *Journal of the Arnold Arboretum* 57, 3 : 279 (1976)

A large shrub or spreading, bushy tree up to 20 ft (6 m) high, originally collected by Dr. E. H. Wilson under his number W.1422 in 1908. It was found in moist woodland thickets on Wa Shan near Wen-chuan-hsien in western Szechwan. Wilson was on a plant-hunting expedition sponsored by the Arnold Arboretum of Harvard University, Boston, Massachusetts, so this must have been one of the collection of Magnolias sent by the Arboretum's director, Prof. Charles S. Sargent, to the French nurseryman Léon Chenault at Orléans in 1913 for propagation and distribution. According to Hillier's *Manual of Trees & Shrubs*, before 1930 this plant was distributed by Chenault as *M. nicholsoniana*.

M. sinensis has fawn bark and oval to orbicular leaves which are usually rounded at their apices, 3 to 7 in. (7·5 to 18 cm) long by 2 to 5½ in. (5 to 14 cm) wide: deeply veined and bright green above, their undersides are clad with a velvety-grey felting and conspicuous silky hairs, especially along the midribs. They are usually larger and paler than those of the *M. sieboldii* and develop a leathery texture as they mature.

The very fragrant white flowers appear after the leaves in May and June. They have from nine to twelve tepals and are pendent and saucer shaped, from 3 to 5½ in. (7·5 to 14 cm) across when fully expanded. The stout peduncles are downy and have bract scars situated about their middle. The contrasting bosses of rosy-crimson stamens around the bases of the bright-green gynoecia are most attractive.

Although naturally of spreading habit, *M. sinensis* can be encouraged to form a small shapely tree by judicious pruning, as has been demonstrated with a plant on our nurseries which was given to the author by the late P. D. Williams of Lanarth in the early 1930s.

In the cloudy wet summer of 1972 a solitary hot cloudless day in mid July caused severe burning of the most recently developed leaf on each shoot without damaging the growing points. The leaves had developed to almost double their normal dimensions because of the prevailing weather conditions.

Although botanists consider *M. sinensis* to be more nearly related to *M. globosa*, the observant plantsman sees a closer resemblance to *M. sieboldii* and to *Magnolia* × *highdownensis*, which is assumed to be a hybrid between *M. sinensis* and *M. wilsonii* and is described in detail in the chapter on Magnolia Crosses and Hybrids. In order to assist in the identification of these very similar Magnolias the author has drawn up a Table of Comparisons overleaf.

The fruit cones of *M. sinensis* are generally larger than those of *M. wilsonii* being pale pink, pendulous and later marcescent, about 3 in. (7·5 cm) long, with scarlet seeds usually in pairs. It has the largest flowers of any Magnolia in Section Oyama and, in spite of the location in which it was found, it is not only tolerant of hot dry conditions, but it will grow on chalky soils.

Plants raised from seed normally commence to flower in from five to seven years so that unless one comes across a particularly good form there appears to be no advantage in resorting to the costly process of grafting, or layering.

Dr. Stephen A. Spongberg in *Journal of the Arnold Arboretum* 57, 3 : 279 (1976) treats *M. sinensis* as *M. sieboldii* subsp. *sinensis*. He explains that 'The fact that subsp. *sieboldii* is wide-ranging in nature while subsp. *sinensis* is widely disjunct and apparently restricted to a small area of northwestern Szechwan Province suggests that the species once was more widely distributed and the Szechwan population(s) has become morphologically differentiated as a result of geographic isolation'.

Cytologically a diploid with 2n = 38 chromosomes.

Wilson's Magnolia

MAGNOLIA WILSONII (Finet & Gagnepain) Rehder

A. Rehder in Sargent, *Plantae Wilsonianae* 1 : 395 (1913)

Otto Stapf in *Curtis's Botanical Magazine* 149 : t. 9004 (1923)

SYNS. *M. parviflora* var. *wilsonii* A. Finet & F. Gagnepain in *Mémoires publiés par la Société Botanique de France* 1, 4 : 39 (1906)

M. nicholsoniana A. Rehder & E. H. Wilson in Sargent, *Plantae Wilsonianae* 1 : 394 (1913)

M. taliensis W. W. Smith in *Notes from the Royal Botanic Garden, Edinburgh* 8 : 341 (1915)

M. liliifera var. *taliensis* (W. W. Smith) R. Pampanini in *Bulletino della R. Societa Toscana di Orticultura* 41 : 137 (1916)

M. wilsonii f. *nicholsoniana* (Rehder & Wilson) A. Rehder in *Journal of the Arnold Arboretum* 20 : 91 (1939)

M. wilsonii f. *taliensis* (W. W. Smith) A. Rehder in *Manual of Cultivated Trees and Shrubs* 2 : 249 (1940)

This is perhaps the most distinctive species in Section *Oyama*, being of more erect growth, with slender young shoots at first coated with pale brown felt, the bark becoming smooth and usually of a dark purple-brown colour in the second year. The longer, narrower, pointed leaves are well spaced, of a distinctive deep sea-green colour, usually with pronounced ripples along the margins and sometimes velvety-brown beneath. In suitable conditions it will form a small tree of up to 25 ft (7·5 m) in height and has been found to be comparatively lime tolerant.

The main flower flush is in May and June when this Magnolia becomes draped overall with large pendent white flower cups about 4 in (10 cm) across, the edges of the nine tepals becoming recurved along their margins. Very often in August a second crop of fragrant flowers appears which apparently open from retarded buds, the development of which was arrested at the time of the main display. Even when the earliest flower buds are damaged by a late frost, some seem to escape to produce flowers at the normal time.

At first the flower buds are erect and they do not begin to bend over from the base of the peduncle until they are released from the last protecting perule. Still enclosed in their spathaceous bracts, they gradually attain the more-or-less pendent position in which they continue to develop. The peduncles have prominent scars left by the spathaceous bracts. The stamen colouring is somewhat variable, from rich red to rosy purple, while the gynoecium is light green. Both the leaf stalks (petioles) and the flower stalks (peduncles) are coated with tan-coloured hairs.

M. wilsonii was discovered by Dr. E. H. Wilson growing at an altitude of 7,000 to 9,000 ft (2,100 to 2,700 m) in woods and thickets south-east of Tachienlu in western Szechwan in 1904, but he did not collect seed until four years later when he also sent home *M. sinensis*. Its natural distribution also extends into eastern Sikang (now Kansu) and northern

Species	Habit and Stature	Shoots	Leaves
M. sieboldii (syn. M. parviflora)	Up to 10 ft (3 m)	Slender, downy, later glabrous and light brown.	Broad elliptic, 4 to 6 in. (10 to 15 cm), large, *base roundish, apex abruptly pointed.* Veins seven to nine pairs. Dark green above, glaucous downy beneath (usually with a rust-coloured pigmentation). Stalks downy $\frac{1}{2}$ to $\frac{3}{4}$ in. (11 to 19 mm).
M. globosa Indian Form from Sikkim	10 to 20 ft (3 to 6 m)	Brownish velvety when young. Branchlets yellow brown weathering to chocolate brown.	Large, oval, shortly pointed. 4 to 10 in. (10 to 25·5 cm) long. Dark glossy green, reddish downy midrib, downy beneath, generally with rufous pubescence. Late leafing.
var. *tsarongensis* = M. globosa Chinese Form from north-western Yunnan		Densely clothed with tawny pubescence.	Paler green, turning yellow in autumn. Early leafing, therefore frost tender.
M. sinensis (syn. M. globosa sinensis) (syn. M. nicholsoniana of gardens). Western Szechwan in one location.	Up to 20 ft (6 m). Very spreading habit. Tolerates full sun and chalky soils.	Covered with silky hairs when young. Light-fawn bark.	Obovate, *oval to roundish*, 3 to 7 in. (7·5 to 18 cm) long, 2 to $5\frac{1}{2}$ in. (5 to 14 cm) wide. Bright green above, velvety glaucous beneath. *Larger than M. sieboldii* and tomentose with silky hairs beneath especially along midrib. Tough and somewhat leathery. No rust-coloured pigmentation.
M. wilsonii (syn. M. nicholsoniana of Rehder & Wilson) Szechwan, into Kansu and northern Yunnan	Up to 25 ft (7·5 m). Prefers shade or semi-shade.	Slender, brown felted. Bark dark purple brown.	Elliptic. Ovate lanceolate to narrowly oval, pointed 3 to 6 in (7·5 to 15 cm) long, *narrower than in M. sieboldii.* Dull green above *velvety brown beneath* when young, later with yellowish or silvery pubescence.
M. × highdownensis (M. sinensis × M. wilsonii)	Up to 20 ft (6 m). Very spreading habit. Most vigorous of this group		Somewhat variable, often more pointed than either putative parent, more or less pubescent beneath.

Flowers white, fragrant, opening with the leaves. Anthers blunt or rounded	Months	Fruits pendent
Nodding, cup shaped, 3 to 4 in. (7·5 to 10 cm) across. Tepals usually six, obovate, concave 2 in. (5 cm) long. Stamens rosy purple or crimson, *spreading*, pedicles downy 1 to 2½ in. (2·5 to 6 cm) long. Very short internode below the perianth.	May to August	1½ to 3 in. (4 to 7·5 cm) long. Pink, horizontal, later pendulous.
Cup shaped or egg shaped, globose, creamy white 2½ to 3 in. (6 to 7·5 cm) across, nodding on long peduncles. Anthers deep pink to crimson ½ to ¾ in. (12 to 17 mm) long.	June Flowers tend to brown badly even when still in bud, especially in damp weather.	2 to 2½ in. (5 to 6·5 cm) long, crimson, drooping.
	May to June	
Pendent, saucer-shaped, 3 to 5 in. (7·5 to 12·5 cm) across. Tepals nine (sometimes twelve). Oblong ovate 1 to 2 in. (2·5 to 5 cm) wide. Stamens rosy crimson. Larger and more fragrant than *M. sieboldii*.	May to June	3 in. (7·5 cm) pendulous, pale pink.
Cup shaped, more pendent than *M. sieboldii*. 3 to 4 in. (7·5 to 10 cm) across, nodding, fragrant. Tepals usually nine, obovate, incurved, up to 2½ in. (6 cm) long, 1¾ in. (4·5 cm) wide. Stamens rich red to rosy purple, ¼ to ½ in. (9 to 12 mm) long.	May to June, sometimes with secondary flowering in August from retarded buds. Best in shade.	*Purplish pink* 2 to 4 in. (5 to 10 cm) long. Carpels beaked.
Nodding horizontally, smaller than *M. sinensis*, globular.	May to June	

Yunnan. The 1904 collection was under the Veitch Expedition No. 3137 while a second collection was made when he returned to the same locality four years later sponsored by the Arnold Arboretum (Wilson No. 1374).

M. wilsonii differs from the Section *Oyama*'s type species *M. sieboldii* by its more slender growth, darker-coloured shoots, narrower leaves and larger, more pendent flowers.

It prefers moist, shaded or semi-shaded situations and its tall, graceful, open-branched habit enables it to display to full advantage its large pendent white flower cups, so that one can gaze upwards into the blossoms and admire their contrasting crimson stamens. It can be gradually pruned and trained to form a single-stemmed standard tree with a cascading head.

In California the leaves of *M. wilsonii*, when grown under the high shade of oak trees, are reported to produce autumn colouring rivalling that of *Cornus florida*. The author can find no similar record from English gardens.

As with other members of Section *Oyama*, *M. wilsonii* is readily raised from seed, the plants flowering in five to seven years. The pendent cones are 2 to 4 in. (5 to 10 cm) long and purplish pink in colour, later turning brown, with beaked carpels. The scarlet seeds are usually in pairs and, as with other Magnolias, they become temporarily suspended by fine threads which are the unrolled spirals of the raphe.

At Maidwell Hall, between Northampton and Market Harborough, there is a screen of *M. wilsonii* which was mentioned by Johnstone (1955). In 1971 it was described as being some 15 or more ft (4·5 m) tall, the plants being in echelon, about 6 ft (2 m) apart and somewhat overgrown by near-by trees. Maidwell Hall has been, for the past thirty-five to forty years, a preparatory school for boys. These Magnolias, along with several other species, were planted by that eminent gardener, Oliver Wyatt, while he was headmaster.

Several double-flowered forms have been recorded. These include a plant grown at Wakehurst Place, Sussex, and another at Westcroft Gardens in Michigan. The latter appeared indifferent to below zero temperatures in midwinter but was killed by a freak October frost of 17 °F (−8·3 °C).

Referring to the name *M. nicholsoniana* bestowed upon this species by Rehder & Wilson in Sargent, *Plantae Wilsonianae* 1 : 394 (1913), the author clearly recalls a Magnolia bearing this name in the late P. D. Williams's garden at Lanarth, Cornwall, in the 1930s. It differed from *M. wilsonii* in having shoots which remained bright green and glabrous during their first winter. Apparently this plant succumbed to wartime neglect for no trace of it has since been found. W. J. Bean in *Trees and Shrubs Hardy in the British Isles* Ed. 1, 3 : 225 (1933) says that Chenault first distributed *M. sinensis* under the name *M. nicholsoniana* in 1920 but that this name was later regarded as a synonym for *M. wilsonii*.

Johnstone in *Asiatic Magnolias in Cultivation*: 120 mentioned such a Magnolia and wrote: 'the name *M. nicholsoniana* had been given to a form of *M. wilsonii* which it was subsequently determined could not be separated specifically, thus it comes about that *M. nicholsoniana* appears as a synonym of both *M. sinensis* and *M. wilsonii*.'

In the eighth edition of W. J. Bean's *Trees & Shrubs Hardy in the British Isles* Ed. 8, 2 : 674–5 (1973) Desmond Clarke has added some interesting references to particularly good forms of this somewhat variable species. He cites the best example as growing above The Slips at Wakehurst Place, Sussex, which originated as a seedling from Caerhays, and was awarded the R. H. S. First Class Certificate in 1932. He mentions also a plant at Quarry Wood, near Newbury in Berkshire, raised from seed received from Rowallane, Co. Down, Northern Ireland. Mr. Clarke tells us that the form which received an Award of Merit in 1925 as 'Borde Hill form' was raised from seed collected in China and still survives, but is now considered inferior to many raised since from seeds off plants grown in cultivation.

In the types of *M. taliensis* and *M. nicholsoniana* now merged in *M. wilsonii* the leaves are glabrous except on the midrib and main veins, also on *M. nicholsoniana* the leaves are oblong obovate, cuneate at the base, the young wood is yellowish grey and the flowers have twelve tepals while those of the type usually have nine.

The same author drew attention to the variations in growth habit and leaf pubescence which he had observed within this species. In some examples the leaves are heavily felted on the undersurface as with *M. sinensis* while in others the leaves are smaller with very little pubescence (f. *taliensis* W. W. Smith).

This was another of the Wilson collection of Magnolias, the entire stocks of which were sent by Sargent from the Arnold Arboretum to French nurseryman Léon Chenault in 1912 with instructions to propagate by grafting and to distribute as widely as possible.

Cytologically *M. wilsonii* is a diploid with 2n = 38 chromosomes.

SECTION *THEORHODON*

E. Spach in *Histoire Naturelle des Végétaux, Phanéro-games*, Les Magnoliacées 7 : 470 (1839)
type species *M. grandiflora*

Comprising some eighteen species, all of which are evergreen, this is the largest of the American sections. All but *M. grandiflora* are tropical and therefore outside the scope of this book, though the most northerly form, the Mexican *M. schiediana* may prove worthy of trial in our more favoured gardens.

M. grandiflora was among the first species to be introduced to British and European gardens. It has retained its popularity for over 250 years and many selected seedlings have been named as cultivars, especially in France and Italy where the climate more closely approximates that of its native habitat. According to Dandy, the Mexican *M. schiediana* resembles *M. grandiflora* more closely than any other member of Section *Theorhodon* and is the only other species in the section with 114 chromosomes. Plants believed to be of this species, raised from seed collected in northern Tamoulipas, are being tested in several parts of the United States and one of these has proved hardy enough to survive in the open at Seattle. The author has therefore seen fit to include some brief notes on *M. schiediana* at the end of this chapter.

The distribution of the seventeen or so tropical species in this section is given in Dandy's 'Revised Survey' on p. 32.

Large-flowered Magnolia
Southern Magnolia
American Bull Bay

MAGNOLIA GRANDIFLORA Linnaeus

C. Linnaeus in *Systema Naturae* 10, 2 : 1082 (1759)
M. Catesby in *Flora Caroliniana* 2 : t. 61 (1741) as
M. altissimo, flore ingenti candido

John Sims in *Curtis's Botanical Magazine* 45 : t. 1952 (1818)

Plates 10 and 11

The natural range of *M. grandiflora* is restricted to the southern part of the United States and extends from central Florida along the Gulf of Mexico to eastern Texas and Arkansas thence northward to eastern North Carolina. Nowhere does it grow far inland from the Atlantic Ocean or the Gulf of Mexico. It attains a height of 60 to 90 ft (18 to 27 m) and a trunk diameter of 2 to 3 ft (61 to 91 cm) in this region of considerable summer rainfall, heat and humidity. It is usually found growing on well-drained hummocks or bottom land in rich, moist soil. In the past *M. grandiflora* was valued for its timber so that it is doubtful whether any virgin stands still exist though there are large second-growth specimens to be found.

The large fragrant creamy-white flowers last for two days. They are cup shaped on the first day of opening, then on the second day the anthers are shed and are held by the saucer-like form of the tepals. The flowers are proportionate to the bold glossy leaves and the ultimate tree-like stature is of great longevity. It is remarkably wind, heat and drought tolerant for such a large-leaved evergreen. Its ability to withstand such extremes is doubtless due to a great extent to the rusty indumentum which protects the stomatic or transpiratory pores on the undersurfaces of the leaves. These are usually shed in spring when two years old.

It has been planted extensively in gardens as far north as Philadelphia and New York but north of Washington it requires a protected environment.

Probably cultivated more widely than any other evergreen ornamental tree, it is the only broad-leaved evergreen with conspicuous flowers which can be grown in such a wide range of climatic conditions. It has been extensively planted in India and Japan. It is also found in China where it is grafted on to *M. heptapeta*.

The date of introduction of this Magnolia into the British Isles and Europe was some time before 1732, which was the date published by J. C. Loudon in his *Arboretum et Fruticetum Britannicum* (1838) and widely accepted since by other authors.

The generic name *Magnolia* was not adopted by the famous Swedish botanist Carolus Linnaeus until 1753 when he cited *M. virginiana* as *M. glauca* for the type species, which had been introduced into Europe from America as early as 1688.

He did not name *M. grandiflora* until 1759. How then did contemporary botanists refer to this evergreen ornamental at the time of its introduction? In 1731 the first edition of *The Gardener's Dictionary* by Philip Miller was published in London. On page 82 he described under *Tulipifera virginiana* the plant we now know as *M. virginiana* and added: 'There is also another *species* of this tree which has been lately brought into England. This is esteemed one of the most beautiful trees in America where they usually grow in moist swampy woods and do often rise to the height of sixty feet [18 m] or more. The leaves are much larger than those of our Common Laurel, and are of a light green colour; the flowers, I am told, are very large of a whitish colour and very fragrant. . . . It is in beauty from May to November and the leaves, always remaining green, do afford an elegant prospect in winter. They are of quick growth and generally rise with straight stems, which is a great addition to their beauty and, since they are hardy enough to endure the cold of our climate in the open ground, I doubt not but in a few years we shall have the pleasure of seeing its beautiful flowers, there being several trees planted in the gardens of some curious persons near London where they have borne the cold *of the three last winters*★ without shelter and do make considerable progress every year. . . . This tree must also be obtained in plants from abroad and increased by layers. . . . for *seeds have not succeeded in any part of Europe where they have yet been sown.*★ . . . In the woods of America, where they naturally grow, it is very difficult to find young plants, the cattle being so fond of 'em that they generally eat off their tops soon after they appear above ground. But in little islands which are furrowed by rivulets so that cattle can't easily get in there are great numbers of these plants. Therefore whoever would procure a quantity of them must always have recourse to such places as are infrequented by cattle.'

Miller's reference to plants of *M. grandiflora* in gardens near London having '*borne the cold of the last three winters without shelter*' indicates that the date of introduction was not later than 1728. He also recorded, using its common name, the 'Laurel-leav'd Tulip-tree', that it 'is at present very rare in England, though formerly, there were several of these trees in the gardens of the Bishop of London at Fulham, and those of the Duchess of Beaufort at Chelsea; but these have been since lost so that there are very few of them to be seen in the English gardens. The largest tree of this kind which I know at present, is in the gardens of Mr. Peter Collinson at Peckham, which has produced a great number of

flowers the three years past. This sort is propagated by layers for the seeds do never come up if sown in England; the layers should remain undisturbed two years, by which time they will take root, and may be taken off in the spring.' It appears to have been introduced as saplings and not as seed.

In *The Gardener's Dictionary* Edition VII (1759) Miller recorded a further description of this Magnolia prior to Linnaeus naming it *M. grandiflora* thus: '*Magnolia foliis lanceolatis persistentibus caule erecto arboreo* Fig Plant Tab 172. *Magnolia* with evergreen spear-shaped leaves and an erect tree-like stalk. This is the *Magnolia altissima flore ingenti candido* of Catesby. Tallest *Magnolia* with very large white flower, commonly called Greater *Magnolia* or Tulip Tree with a Laurel Leaf. . . . Grows in Florida and South Carolina . . .

'There were a great number of young plants in England before the year 1739 but a great part of them were destroyed by that severe winter and since then there have been few good seeds sent to England, so that there are very few left to be purchased at present. . . .

'Our seasons are not warm enough to bring the fruit to maturity so that we can never hope to see the trees adorned with them which is a great beauty to them in their native soil.'

In Philip Miller's *Figures of Plants* 2 : 115 (1760), Plate CLXXII (172) drawn by I. Miller, shows a branch with an open flower while below it are two of the buds, a fruit cone showing the seeds suspended from the carpels on their thread-like appendages, and drawings of the floral parts.

Miller wrote: 'The largest tree of this kind which I have met with in England is in the garden of Sir John Colliton of Exmouth in Devonshire, which has produced flowers for several years.' (Plate 10.)

In J. C. Loudon's *Gardener's Magazine* 11, 6 : 70 (1835) an interesting history of this Magnolia was published. 'The information was communicated to the author by Mr. R. Glendinning, head gardener to Lord and Lady Rolle of Bicton and was dated 28 December 1834. This tree was mentioned by Miller in 1759 as the oldest tree of its kind in England. Glendinning reported through the kindness of Lady Rolle thus: "The Information of Thomas Tupman respecting the original Plant of the Exmouth Magnolia: He says that his father was gardener to Sir Francis Drake;★ that soon after the death of Sir J. Colliton, who lived at Exmouth he, (Tupman's father) left his place and rented the garden in which the Magnolia tree grew, off a Mr. Zorn (the then

---

★ The italics are mine.

★ Obviously a descendant of the original.

proprietor) with an agreement that he was to make layers of the tree at half a guinea a plant. Zorn made five guineas.

' "The garden afterwards came into the hands of a Mr. Davis, a mercer of Exeter. This was about forty years ago [1794]. Mr. Davis sent a labouring man named Skinner to cut down an old apple tree and, through the man's ignorance, the beautiful Magnolia was, by mistake, levelled to the ground. The trunk of the tree was about five feet [1·5 m] in height and it was one foot, six inches [46 cm] in diameter. Tupman remembers a scaffolding erected about it in his father's time on which tubs were placed to propagate it by layers."

'A small part of Exmouth lies in the parish of Withycombe Rawley (Raleigh) in which parish the garden and premises of the said Sir J. Colliton were situated.'

Sir John Colliton's property where this Magnolia grew was Rill Manor which stood at the rear of North Street, Exmouth, close to the main Exeter road. The Exmouth coat of arms, granted under Letters Patent dated 12 February 1947 is superimposed by a fortified tower flanked by flowers and leaves of the Exmouth Magnolia. The scroll beneath the coat of arms bears the Latin motto 'Mare ditat flores decorant'. ('The sea enriches the flowers adorn.')

In *Curtis's Botanical Magazine* the Exmouth Magnolia was described thus in 1817 by Dr. John Sims under *M. grandiflora* var. *lanceolata* alongside Plate 1952: 'Long laurel-leaved Magnolia of South Carolina and Florida. Must be esteemed to be one of the finest trees in the world; growing with a straight trunk two feet [61 cm] in diameter to upwards of seventy feet [21·5 m] high, and forming a regular head; it bears a profusion of flowers, which perfume the air far around with a most agreeable scent; and in the autumn, the fruit, a kind of cone containing scarlet seeds which drop from their cells and remain suspended by a thread, is scarcely less attractive.

'This variety, the *lanceolata* of *Hortus Kewensis*, is generally known among the Nurserymen by the name of the Exmouth Magnolia.'

Although the description gives nine tepals as a norm for this cultivar, Plate 1952 of a flower from a tree in the garden of John Walker, Esq., at Arnos Grove, Southgate, shows three plus three large outer ones with nine smaller petalodes.

At Antony House near Torpoint, Cornwall, there is a considerable planting of *M. grandiflora* as free-standing specimens. Two, which are trained on the wall flanking the forecourt, are obviously very old and may well date back to the mid 1700s. The house

was completed in 1731 and is the residence of Sir John and Lady Carew Pole.

In 1838 Loudon recorded a similar history for another specimen of this Magnolia: 'The first tree of *Magnolia grandiflora* to be brought to England is said to have been planted in Gray's nursery at Fulham which was founded early in the 18th century, and all old trees of the kind in the country are said to have been propagated from it. The tree died about 1810; but its trunk, which measured four feet ten inches [1·5 m] in circumference, was till very lately, preserved. The branches extended over a surface twenty feet [6 m] in diameter, it was as many feet high and in the blossoming season, which lasted generally two or three months, it perfumed the whole neighbourhood. It was surrounded by stages from the ground to its summit, on which were placed pots containing layers for propagation. It was the number of these, and the exhaustion they caused, which killed the tree.'

M. grandiflora first flowered in Sir Charles Wager's garden in 1737. If this plant had been raised from seed and it took the normal twenty years or more to flower the date of its introduction into England could well have been before 1717.

Peter Collinson (1693–1768), Quaker, botanist and linen draper, who lived at Ridgeway House, Mill Hill, near Hendon in Middlesex, recorded: 'In 1759 there were, in the American Grove at Goodwood [near Chichester, Sussex] two fine great Magnolias [*M. grandiflora*] about 20 feet [6 m] high, that flowered annually' adding that his own tree of that species was raised from seed and first flowered in 1760 when twenty years old. Apparently the Goodwood Magnolias were destroyed on the Duke of Richmond's death, for Collinson wrote in 1768 that they no longer existed and that all movable articles had been sold. One wonders if the Magnolias could have been among them! The soil at Goodwood is thin and overlying chalk. Collinson also recorded that a tulip tree (*Liriodendron tulipifera*) which he gave Sir Charles Wager flowered for the first time when it was thirty years old in 1756.

The earliest introduction of *M. grandiflora* into Europe was almost certainly the once-famous Maillardière Magnolia of Nantes. The romantic history of this tree was described in *Société Nantaise d'Horticulture et Recherche*: 131–46 (1849). In this we read 'The Maillardière Magnolia, the first of its kind in France, was brought over from North America in 1731, and given to M. René Darquistade, Lord of La Maillardière, who was mayor of Nantes, first in 1735, then for a second time in 1740. This tree, then quite small, was placed in the Orangery.'

(Apparently it was thought to be a form of the common laurel, *Prunus laurocerasus*.)

'This date of the introduction of the Magnolia to Nantes, determined in a note by M. le Sant as the year 1731, does not conform with the reference which we have been given by M. de la Bretesche, the actual owner of La Maillardière, who according to a family tradition, can trace back this original Magnolia to about the year 1711. According to this tradition, this plant when quite small, was placed in the Orangery, where it remained for about twenty years, becoming progressively larger, but without any flowers. Then in 1731, the tree having attained a size too large for the greenhouse, the gardener decided to destroy it, and this course would have been carried out in his master's absence but for the remarkable circumstances which saved it. Fortunately his wife intervened and persuaded him to let her replant it near the mansion beside the dovecot, where it would be sheltered from the north winds. Although the gardener was convinced, as most people were at the time, that plants from the New World could not succeed in the open in that climate, he reluctantly gave in to his wife's pleadings and let her replant it in the place which she had suggested. A few years later it began to flower and details of the beauty of its great blossoms and their delightful perfume spread far and wide so that it was visited each season by botanists and horticulturists from all over Europe. For a long time it was known as the Laurel Tulip Tree until the genus was given the name *Magnolia* by Linnaeus.

'In 1793 the fatal civil warfare of La Vendée spread fire and devastation among the chateaux on the left bank of the Loire including La Maillardière, but the tree survived in spite of being badly burned, scarred with bullets and partly covered with rubble from a collapsed wall.

'After such a narrow escape from destruction the local botanists and horticulturists decided on a plan to try to propagate it by layering. So, in 1795, scaffolding was placed around the top of the Magnolia to support three boxes of soil, into each of which four or five shoots were layered. The trunk circumference at 1 metre [3¼ ft] above ground level was then 1 metre [3¼ ft]. The successful rooting of these layers ensured the continued existence and future distribution of *Magnolia grandiflora* 'La Maillardière' throughout France. By 1848 the tree had attained a height of 11 metres [36 ft] and had a trunk circumference of 1 metre, 55 cm [5 ft] above ground but was dying back through a bark infection at ground level.'

One would expect the nurserymen of Nantes still to grow this plant but it appears to have been superseded by the slightly later introduction of *M. grandiflora* 'Gallissonnière' which dates back to about 1745. It was named after the estate of Roland-Michel, Baron de la Gallissonnière, a lieutenant-general of marines, who travelled extensively in parts of America then possessed by France and who became Governor of Canada in 1749. One cannot help wondering if it was he who brought the original introduction to La Maillardière, for in the course of his travels, he brought home and established in his garden near Nantes many new species of trees and shrubs from abroad.

Probably the oldest surviving specimen of *M. grandiflora* in Europe today is in the garden of the Orto Botanico of the University of Padua in Italy. Brief details of this veteran tree have been supplied to the author by Professor C. Cappelletti, Director of the gardens. Its earliest recorded dimensions were measured in 1887 when its height was 56 ft (17 m) and its trunk circumference at 3¼ ft (1 m) above ground was 5½ ft (1·5 m). Eighty years later, and after having been pruned several times, it had a height of 59 ft (18 m) and a trunk circumference of 7 ft 10 in. (2·75 m) at 3¼ ft (1 m) above ground.

In America the native *M. grandiflora* was popularly planted in front of early homesteads in the lower South but whereas other types of tree were invariably grown with bare trunks to provide maximum shade for man and beast, it was common practice to peg down the lower branches of this magnolia so that they rooted as layers. Apart from providing replacement plants if and when required, such treatment would make the tree virtually indestructible by abnormal winds. It was found that layers transplanted best not in autumn or spring, but in July and August after the removal of half the leaves to reduce transpiration.

Carl R. Amason writing from Calion, Arkansas, described this old southern manner of growing *M. grandiflora* in *Newsletter of the American Magnolia Society* 11, 2 : 22 (1975). The fallen leaves were brush-broomed underneath the interior of the tree at least once a week. The brush-brooms which he describes were similar to the English besom or birch-broom. He refers to the fine old trees in front of homesteads in South Arkansas and North Louisiana and recalls that one of the luckiest things that can happen to a child down South is to have access to one of these noble old magnolia trees in which to climb and play.

M. grandiflora has proved to be one of the most heat tolerant of the temperate broad-leaved evergreen trees and has been more widely planted throughout the world than any other Magnolia. In colder climates it should have good drainage to ensure adequate ripening and hardening of the season's growth before winter. Even in climates as cold as that of Michigan, *M. grandiflora* is reported to survive with wall or tree protection, but in the open the tree dies of dehydration caused by winter wind and sun when the roots are frozen and incapable of absorbing soil moisture. If protected from cold drying winds and bright winter sun, and mulched to prevent deep freezing of the soil around its roots, it will survive and flourish. It is best espaliered against a sheltered wall. It has the disadvantage of being prone to snow damage since the clustered formation of the large evergreen leaves tends to trap large masses of snow so that the branches are liable to become badly smashed especially if it freezes upon them.

There is a fine collection of trees of *M. grandiflora* in Spring Grove Cemetery, Cincinnati, Ohio where the minimum winter temperature often falls below 0 °F. (−17·8 °C.).

M. grandiflora displays a tremendous capacity for variation, not only in growth habit but also in the shape, size, colour, gloss and pubescence of the leaves as well as in the shape and number of the tepals, also the size, shape and length of season of the flowers.

While it is not surprising that the older named cultivars are of English and French origin there have been many clones selected and named in the United States of which a few are listed here.

American Cultivars of *M. grandiflora*

'Alabama Everblooming' Leaves lanceolate. A long-flowering clone from Cullman, Alabama.

'Baby Doll' A diminutive clone from Tampa, Florida.

'Cairo' (pronounced Karo) (Plate 11) Named after the most southerly city in the state of Illinois at the confluence of the Ohio and Mississippi rivers. Believed to have been brought up the rivers as a seedling from Louisiana or Mississippi nearly a century ago, the original tree stands at 2808 Washington Street, Cairo, Illinois, in front of the next house north of 'Magnolia Manor'. Its distinguishing characteristics are its very highly polished leaves with hyaline margins and midribs, reminiscent of the Asian *M. nitida* but much larger. Flowers bowl shaped with nine white acutely-tipped tepals. Fruit cones colour red where exposed to the sun. The tree stands winter temperatures below 0 ° F.(−17·8 °C.) with little foliage discoloration. Selected for registration and propagation by Prof. J. C. McDaniel and described in the *Morris Arboretum Bulletin* 17 : 61–2 (1966)

Charles Dickens' (Plate 11) Named after the present owner of the site of Britton's old nursery at Esthill Springs between Winchester and Tullahoma in Franklin County, Tennessee; the original tree was calculated to be 103 years old in 1967. Differs from the typical *M. grandiflora* in its broad, glossy and flexible leaves and its magnificent display of bright-red fruit cones which are larger than usual and more ovoid with oblong seeds. A curious tetraploid with 76 chromosomes whereas *M. grandiflora* is hexaploid with 114 chromosomes. Prof. J. C. McDaniel suggests that it may have *M. macrophylla* in its ancestry. It is difficult to root from cuttings.

'Edith Bogue' This cultivar seems to have a reputation for easy propagation and hardiness in the States. It originated as a tree sent from Florida in 1920 to Miss E. A. Bogue at Montclair, New Jersey.

'Little Gem' A seedling raised from local seed at Candor, North Carolina, by Warren Steed of Steed's Nursery, Candor, and named in 1966. A strikingly compact evergreen tree of distinctive narrow and columnar habit recorded as being only 4 ft (1 m) wide when 14 ft (4·5 m) tall at sixteen years. Leaves elliptic to oval 5½ by 2 in. (14 by 5 cm) lustrous dark green with heavy rust-coloured indumentum beneath. Flowers smaller than average, cup shaped, opening over a long period. Roots readily from hardwood cuttings in intermittent mist. Flowers as a young plant.

'Madison' A selection from Madison, Alabama, with lanceolate leaves and a long-flowering season. I saw a young tree which had survived three winters against a wall at Urbana, Illinois, in September 1970.

'Russet' (U.S. Plant Patent No. 2617) A clone raised by the Saratoga Horticultural Foundation in California and selected for vegetative propagation in 1952. The undersurfaces of the leaves and petioles, together with the young shoots and buds of the current season, are densely coated with velvety, orange-brown, suede-like tomentum which is said to be particularly attractive in artificial light. The twelve-tepalled flowers are 6 to 8 in. (15 to 20·5 cm) in diameter.

'Saint George' Has well-russeted leaves and creamy-white flowers with twenty-two to twenty-five tepals.

'Saint Mary' Originated as a seedling purchased from Joseph Vestal & Son, Little Rock, Arkansas, by the Glen Saint Mary Nursery, Florida, about 1905. It was first named and catalogued by W. B. Clarke & Company of San José, California, in 1940–1. Has lustrous wavy-margined leaves. Has flowered at Detroit, Michigan.

'Samuel Sommer' (U.S. Plant Patent No. 2015) Another cultivar raised and patented by the Saratoga Horticultural Foundation and named after the President of the Board of Trustees. It was selected for propagation in 1952 on account of its unusual leaves which are large and leathery with golden-green midribs, primary veins and margins, which contrast with the glossy dark-green surfaces. The twelve-tepalled flowers are exceptionally large being 10 to 14 in. (25·5 to 35·5 cm) in diameter, when fully open. Has survived temperatures down to −12 °F. (−24·4 °C.) and tornado winds at Reinhardt College, Waleska, Georgia.

'Santa Cruz' A clone selected in California by the late D. Todd Gresham who described it as having ivory-white flowers averaging twenty-two tepals and 9 in. (23 cm) in diameter with a strongly pervasive lemon fragrance.

'Variegata' A fine variegated-leaved form from Alabama.

Some English and European Cultivars of *M. grandiflora*

'Exmouth' (var. *lanceolata* Aiton, var. *exoniensis* Loddiges) This is a cultivar that has held its popularity in English gardens and nurseries for over two centuries and, as one might expect, some of the finest surviving specimens are to be found in Devonshire where it first became known. It is characterized by its vigorous erect growth, with long narrow leaves which tend to recurve along their edges and lose much of the rusty indumentum from their undersurfaces as they mature. It flowers freely over a long period from July to late autumn if planted in a hot, sunny situation. The flowers, which have upwards of eighteen tepals, some of which are petaloid stamens in the form of additional narrow tepals.

'Ferruginea' This has shorter and stiffer leaves than 'Exmouth', their undersides being densely coated with rust-coloured indumentum. It has a bushier habit with a tendency to produce most of its flowers high up and out of reach.

'Gallissonnière' A cultivar much propagated by French nurserymen on account of its hardiness. It produces large cup-shaped flowers.

'Gloriosa' A compact-growing cultivar with broad leathery leaves. It bears flowers of great size and substance, up to 14 in. (35·5 cm) in diameter.

'Goliath' Distinguishable by its shorter and broader leaves which are blunt ended with a tendency to twist and undulate, later becoming bullate with glabrous undersurfaces. Some garden owners consider this form superior to 'Exmouth' and it has a bushier habit, the large flowers being globular with very broad incurved tepals. There is a photograph of a flower in Millais's *Magnolias*: 136. Selected and named by the Caledonia Nursery, Guernsey.

'Nanetensis Flore Pleno' The Nantes Double Grandiflora bears immense flowers, some of the outer stamens being modified to petalodes in the form of additional tepals of varying lengths and widths.

'Tréyvei' A very hardy floriferous clone of French origin with slightly curled glossy leaves. Originated at the nursery of M. Tréyve at Trévoux near Lyon.

'Undulata' A French cultivar with a pronounced tendency to produce wavy-margined leaves.

A freak form of *M. grandiflora* named 'Biflora' which produced two flowers on most of its peduncles was listed by M. Tréyve in 1860 and described by R. Pampanini in *Bulletino della R. Societa di Orticultura* 41 : 77 (1916).

M. grandiflora may be grafted successfully on to deciduous understocks; the Japanese do so on to *M. kobus*, the Americans on to *M. acuminata* and the Chinese on to *M. heptapeta*. Most of the cultivars listed may be rooted as half-ripe cuttings in intermittent mist with bottom heat. It is on record that leaf cuttings can be rooted in water in a narrow-necked glass on a semi-dark shelf in a warm room. Such cuttings must have a 'heel' of the wood attached with the axillary bud. It is reasonable to suppose that leaves off the previous year's shoots would respond better than less mature ones.

Dr. Stephen A. Spongberg in 'Magnoliaceae Hardy in Temperate North America' *Journal of the Arnold Arboretum* 57, 3 : 264 (1976) draws attention to the septate pith of branchlets of *M. grandiflora* whereas *M. delavayi* has continuous pith.

McDaniel draws attention to the short stipular scars readily seen on the bases of newly abscissed petioles or leaf stalks on many cultivars of *M. grandiflora* including 'Exmouth'. He points out that by Dandy's definition, the *absence of* stipular attachment to the petioles is diagnostic of Section *Theorhodon*.

That *M. grandiflora* pollen will sometimes fertilize flowers of *M. virginiana* was demonstrated in 1930 by Oliver M. Freeman while he was attached to the U.S. National Arboretum at Washington, D.C., as Associate Botanist. Hybrids between these two species are discussed and described elsewhere in this book (pp. 153–5) under the Freeman Hybrids. The same cross has since been repeated by Prof. J. C. McDaniel and others using both *M. virginiana* var. *virginiana* and *M. virginiana* var. *australis* as seed parents. McDaniel points out that emasculation is unnecessary because the stigmas probably only remain receptive for about twelve hours and the stamens do not shed any pollen until the stigmas have become incapable of supporting pollen germination. Any resulting seedlings which are hybrids can be readily identified because of their larger evergreen leaves which usually lack the glaucous undersurface colouring typical of *M. virginiana*.

M. grandiflora has 114 chromosomes in its somatic cells which is more than any other native North American species. Among temperate species this hexaploid or six-fold number is matched only by Magnolias of the Asian Section *Yulania*. Prof. McDaniel points out that *M. grandiflora* has co-existed with *M. virginiana* var. *australis* for thousands if not millions of years and that they also overlap in flowering season. He reasons that, while *M. grandiflora* is normally self-fertile, *M. virginiana* var. *australis* appears to be highly incompatible to its own pollen. It will, in the wild, as well as in cultivation, sometimes be cross-fertilized with *grandiflora* pollen. Some such hybrids would eventually survive to reach sexual maturity and produce viable seeds and from such beginnings would exist the possibility of introgression into the adjacent race of *M. grandiflora*.

Professor McDaniel in *Newsletter of the American Magnolia Society* 7, 2 : 4–7 (1970) contributed a fascinating detective story entitled 'Did *Magnolia grandiflora* borrow some genes?' He points out that this species has more chromosomes (114 in somatic cells) than any other U.S. native species in subgenus *Magnolia* and that this hexaploid or six-fold number is matched in the other subgenus, *Yulania*, only by members of Section *Yulania*, all of which are of Asian origin. These include *M. campbellii*, *M. dawsoniana*, *M. heptapeta* (*denudata*), *M. sargentiana* (and var. *robusta*) together with *M. sprengeri*.

So far this high level of ploidy has been found to be exceeded only by some of the later generations of *M. × soulangiana* which have been rated up to octoploid (eight-fold) level and even higher. McDaniel argues that such a high number of chromosomes can accommodate a continuing high degree of genetic diversity. He points out that other species of Subgenus *Magnolia*, occurring within the same natural range as *M. grandiflora*, include *M. virginiana* (most consistently) with *M. macrophylla* and *M. tripetala* less frequently. He draws attention to the relative ease whereby Oliver M. Freeman hybridized

M. virginiana and *M. grandiflora* at the U.S. National Arboretum at Washington D.C. in 1930 (as detailed under the Freeman Hybrids in the third section of this book). This breeding has been repeated since by McDaniel as well as by other Magnolia breeders. These hybrids are tetraploid with a four-fold chromosome number of 2n = 76 in their somatic cells.

Such a plant would be less fertile than a Magnolia which is naturally tetraploid but it could possibly back-cross with an adjacent *M. grandiflora* or *M. virginiana* and, if the progeny exhibited even a small degree of fertility, this could open the way toward later generation recombinations with either species whereby a relatively small number of genes are contributed by the second parent in the primary cross. This process is termed introgressive hybridization. However with this particular *M. virginiana* × *M. grandiflora* combination there may be a barrier to continued recombinations of the hybrids with *M. virginiana*. These backcross hybrids have been found to be triploids (2n = 57 chromosomes) and they share the sterility commonly found in triploid plants. Similar sterility is reported by Kosar and Santamour for the group of triploid hybrids of *M. quinquepeta* × *M. stellata* bred at the U.S. National Arboretum by De Vos & Kosar. (See under the De Vos & Kosar Hybrids.)

However *M. grandiflora* × Freeman Hybrids should be approximately pentaploids with 2n = 95 chromosomes in their somatic cells, as were the original *M. × soulangiana* hybrids which gave rise to F2 generation seedlings (e.g. 'Lennei' and 'Rustica Rubra'), which can sometimes function at hexaploid level. Such hexaploids of *M. grandiflora* × Freeman Hybrids should be able to back-cross readily with *M. grandiflora* with the possibility of giving rise to extensive seedling populations of introgressed *M. grandiflora* possessing partially *M. virginiana* chromosomes and genes and some phenotypic characters attributable to *M. virginiana* ancestry.

McDaniel considers that the normally hexaploid plants of *M. grandiflora* may sometimes constitute what is called a 'compilospecies', having compiled an assortment of genes (and variability) derived from other species belonging to the same subgenus *Magnolia*. He reasons that most of its outcrossing was with *M. virginiana* var. *australis* but suggests that the fertile tetraploid 'Charles Dickens' (2n = 76), with its broad leaves and large broad fruits, indicates the likelihood of some *M. macrophylla* ancestry in its genetic make-up. He cites the presence of short stipular scars (to be seen upon close examination of the leaf petioles which have just abscissed) and points out that the *absence* of such stipular attachment to the petioles is diagnostic of Section *Theorhodon* to which *M. grandiflora* is assigned.

The majority of Magnolia species endemic to the United States belong to Section *Rytidospermum*. They have clearly adnate stipules which means that these detach to leave a distinct scar part way up the petiole in addition to that which encircles the stem at each node.

The fourteen or so tropical members of Section *Theorhodon* occur south of the border. They are mainly quite local in their distribution, each in its own little niche at high altitudes in the mountains of tropical America, extending from Mexico to Venezuela, with an island series from Cuba to Puerto Rico. The exception is *M. schiediana* which is widely scattered among the mountains in several Mexican states in both Gulf and Pacific drainage areas. Besides approaching the extreme Texas range of *M. grandiflora* it is the only other American hexaploid species (2n = 114 chromosomes).

McDaniel reasons that though native Magnolias do not now occur in the intervening hot droughty country which flanks the Rio Grande, both *M. schiediana* and *M. grandiflora* (or their common ancestor) could have grown there in the distant past, when central Texas had a climate moist and cool enough to support fir and spruce forests.

Cytologically *M. grandiflora* is a hexaploid with 2n = 114 chromosomes.

Schiede's Magnolia

MAGNOLIA SCHIEDIANA Schlechtendahl

D. F. L. Schlectendahl in *Botanische Zeitung* 22 : 144 (1864)

P. C. Standley in *Contributions from the National Herbarium* 5 : 275 (1926)

This Magnolia is reported to be widely scattered among the mountains in several Mexican states in both Gulf and Pacific drainage areas. It is the most northerly of Mexican Magnolias, extending into Tamoulipas to north of the Tropic of Cancer in the Sierra Madre Oriental, near Gómez Farias, and still farther north where Dr. F. G. Meyer collected it.

M. schiediana is considered to be more closely related to *M. grandiflora* than any other tropical species. It was discovered by Schiede between San Salvado and Jalapa in 1829 and named after him by Schlechtendahl in 1864. It has the widest distribution and is the most variable of the Mexican Magnolias.

M. schiediana attains the stature of a large evergreen tree, the shoots and branches ringed with the scars of the fallen stipules. The creamy-white flowers have nine tepals and are 5 to 6 in. (12·5 to 15 cm) across.

M. schiediana and *M. grandiflora* are the only two American Magnolias with 114 chromosomes. Though less pubescent and smaller flowered than *M. grandiflora* the resemblance is said to be close enough to cause confusion.

Because of its affinity to *M. grandiflora* and the possibility that a high altitude and northerly form may prove to be on the borderline of hardiness in the more favoured temperate environments, the author feels optimistically justified in including these brief notes.

A seedling raised from seeds collected by Dr. F. G. Meyer in the Sierra Madre Oriental of northern Tamoulipas, and thought to be of this species, has proved hardy enough to survive in the open at the University of Washington Arboretum at Seattle. Dandy has since expressed the opinion that this is probably a *species nova* as yet undescribed.

The leaves of a cutting-raised plant which was received from the Arboretum in 1969 are narrower than those of most forms of *M. grandiflora* and taper evenly at both ends. The upper surfaces are matt, not glossy and the undersides are glabrous, not felted. The growth buds are covered with silvery adpressed hairs and the stipulary scars which encircle the stems are more conspicuous than is usual on *M. grandiflora*.

According to J. N. Rose, the Tepic vernacular name for this Magnolia is *Corpus* and a concoction of the flowers is used there as a remedy for scorpion stings.

Cytologically *M. schiediana* is a hexaploid with 2n = 114 chromosomes.

1. *Magnolia virginiana*

2. *Magnolia virginiana* 'Havener'

3. *Magnolia delavayi*

4. *Magnolia hypoleuca*

5. *Magnolia officinalis*

6. *Magnolia tripetala* 'Woodlawn'

7. *Magnolia macrophylla*

8. *Magnolia sieboldii*

9. *Magnolia globosa*

10. *Magnolia grandiflora* 'Exmouth'

11. *Magnolia grandiflora* 'Charles Dickens' (above)
'Cairo' (below)

12. *Magnolia nitida*

13. *Magnolia heptapeta (denudata)*

14. *Magnolia campbellii*

15. *Magnolia campbellii*

16. *Magnolia campbellii* 'Landicla'

17. *Magnolia campbellii alba*

18. *Magnolia campbellii alba*

19. *Magnolia campbellii* subsp. *mollicomata*

20. *Magnolia campbellii* subsp. *mollicomata* 'Lanarth'

22. *Magnolia campbellii* subsp. *mollicomata* 'Borde Hill'

21. *Magnolia campbellii* subsp. *mollicomata* 'Lanarth'

23. *Magnolia campbellii* subsp. *mollicomata* 'Lanarth'

24. *Magnolia dawsoniana* 'Chyverton'

25. *Magnolia sargentiana* var. *robusta*

26. *Magnolia sargentiana* var. *robusta*

27. *Magnolia sargentiana* var. *robusta alba*

28. *Magnolia sprengeri* 'Diva'

29. *Magnolia sprengeri* var. *diva* 'Copeland Court'

30. *Magnolia stellata*

31. *Magnolia stellata* 'Rubra'

32. *Magnolia stellata* 'Waterlily' with *Magnolia* × *loebneri* 'Ballerina'

33. *Magnolia salicifolia*

34. *Magnolia kobus*

35. *Magnolia acuminata*

36. *Magnolia acuminata*

37. *Magnolia acuminata* 'Klassen'

38. *Magnolia acuminata* var. *subcordata*

39. *Magnolia quinquepeta (liliflora)* 'O'Neill'

40. *Magnolia* 'Caerhays Surprise'

41. *Magnolia × loebneri* 'Spring Snow'

42. *Magnolia* 'Moresk'

43. *Magnolia* 'Caerhays Belle'

44. *Magnolia* × *soulangiana* 'Lennei'

45. *Magnolia* × *thompsoniana*

46. *Magnolia* × *thompsoniana* 'Urbana'

47. *Magnolia* × *veitchii* 'Peter Veitch'

48. *Magnolia* × *wieseneri (watsonii)*

SECTION *GYNOPODIUM* Dandy

J. E. Dandy in *Curtis's Botanical Magazine* 165 : sub t. 16 (1948)
type species *M. nitida*

This small section comprises as yet only two species, *M. nitida* with a distribution very similar to that of *M. rostrata*, from north-western Yunnan and adjacent parts of south-eastern Tibet and north-eastern Upper Burma, at altitudes between 7,500 and 12,000 ft (2,300 to 3,500 m) and *M. kachirachirai*, an allied tropical species from Taiwan, which does not concern us here. Other Magnolias from south-east China may be added to this section when plant exploration can be resumed in that country.

Members of Section *Gynopodium* are characterized by their stalked gynoecia, complete absence of hairs and comparatively small, glossy, evergreen leaves with free stipules.

Glossy Magnolia

MAGNOLIA NITIDA W. W. Smith

W. W. Smith in *Notes from the Royal Botanic Garden, Edinburgh* 12 : 212 (1920)
J. E. Dandy in *Curtis's Botanical Magazine* 165 : t. 16 (1948)

Plate 12

In appearance and botanical detail *M. nitida* differs considerably from any other temperate Magnolia in cultivation. The small dark-green leaves have remarkably highly polished upper surfaces, as though lacquered, and, when held up to strong light, they display what is termed *hyaline* margins – fine hair-lines as of glass or silver – to use an unintentional play upon words. The young leaves are even more spectacular with their shining bronze-red colouring. How rightly named is *M. nitida* – the glossy Magnolia.

In many ways this species resembles the closely related genus *Michelia*, from which it differs in bearing its flowers exclusively at the tips of the shoots, whereas those of *Michelia* are both terminal and axillary (from the axils of the leaves). It shares with members of that genus a characteristic which distinguishes it from all other temperate Magnolias as yet in cultivation: the stalk which separates the androecium from the gynoecium. It differs from other Asian Magnolias in cultivation in having free stipules which, instead of being attached to the petioles, are attached to the nodes of the shoots on which they leave prominent scars.

The fragrant primrose-yellow flowers fade somewhat as they mature and usually have a carmine-purple streaking on the backs of the outer tepals. The flowers normally open in March and April. The mature flowers are about 3 in. (7.5 cm) across and have nine to twelve tepals which are obovate spatulate with pointed apices. The stamens are creamy yellow and incurved towards the base of the stalked (stipitate) gynoecium. The flower buds are glabrous green, shading to reddish brown, and later turning rich plum purple (Plate 12).

The fruit cones are remarkable in remaining a vivid shade of lime green when ripe, the carpels splitting longitudinally to display brilliant orange seeds, not scarlet as in most Magnolias. They emit a resinous aroma. The cones average 3 in. (7.5 cm) in length. They are supported by the stalk of the gynoecium, a characteristic which is much more apparent than at flowering, when it is often not readily discernible without dissecting a flower.

M. nitida usually forms a tall erect shrub or small tree with rough grey-brown bark. It seems to prefer a mild moist climate, resenting cold winds more than frost. In Cornwall severe winters may defoliate and even kill the tips of the shoots and the flower buds, but the plants recover if left unpruned until after growth begins. At Caerhays the older specimens of this Magnolia were 25 ft (7.5 m) tall by 18 ft (5.5 m) wide at the end of 1970. A more columnar form at Lanarth has flowers which lack the purple shading on their outer tepals.

M. nitida is very difficult to strike from cuttings and it does not graft readily although it is certainly not incompatible with deciduous understocks. Consequently the majority of the few plants which become available originate from seed. The time taken for a seedling to reach florescence is about fifteen years.

M. nitida was first discovered by George Forrest on the Salween-Mekong divide in north-west

Yunnan in 1917, at 10,000 to 11,000 ft (3,050 to 3,350 m).

It is of interest that the prominent petiolar rings which scar the shoots of *M. nitida* are likewise a prominent feature in *M. rostrata,* which shares the same distribution.

Cytologically *M. nitida* is a diploid with 2n = 38 chromosomes.

Subgenus *Yulania* (Spach) Reichenbach (formerly *Pleurochasma*)
M. Subgen. *Yulania* (Spach)
H. G. L. Reichenbach in *Der Deutsche Botaniker* 1: 192 (1841); based on
Yulania E. Spach in *Histoire Naturelle des Végétaux, Phanérogames* 7 : 462 (1839)

SECTION *YULANIA* (Spach) Dandy

J. E. Dandy in *Camellias and Magnolias Conference Report*: 72 (1950)
type species *M. heptapeta (denudata)*

This section includes all the deciduous temperate species with large precocious flowers and therefore contains the most spectacular of Magnolias, flowering as they do in their winter nakedness, often several weeks before the leaves appear.

The flowers show no distinction between sepals and petals, hence the adoption of the term *tepal*. These are nine or more in number and range in colour from white to crimson or purple on different trees. The anthers dehisce laterally or sublaterally to shed their pollen. The species in this section are distributed in temperate east Asia from the eastern Himalayas to eastern China. Many have immense upward-poised blossoms, their large outer tepals opening almost horizontally to form huge saucer-shaped bases surmounted by the inner ones, which at first remain furled vertically around their sexual organs, usually in the form of a cone.

The section was named after the oriental *Yulan*, meaning Lily, applied by the Chinese to the type species *M. heptapeta*, latterly known as *M. denudata*. The name *Yulania conspicua*, was proposed for this Magnolia by the British botanist R. A. Salisbury in 1806 and adopted by the French botanist E. Spach in *Histoire Naturelle des Végétaux, Phanérogames*, Les Magnoliacées 7 : 462 (1839). Later German botanist H. G. L. Reichenbach adopted the name *Yulania* for one of the two subgenera of the species *Magnolia* in *Der Deutsche Botaniker, Magnolia* 1 : 192 (1841).

When J. E. Dandy compiled his authoritative 'Survey of the Genus *Magnolia*' in 1950 it was thought that Reichenbach's groups were sections, so he proposed the name *Pleurochasma* for this second subgenus in *Journal of the Royal Horticultural Society* 75 : 161 (1950). The name *Yulania* now replaces *Pleurochasma* and therefore applies both to the second subgenus and to the first section therein.

In addition to the type species *M. heptapeta (denudata)*, other species included in Section *Yulania* are the upward-facing flowered *M. campbellii* together with its subspecies *M. mollicomata* also *M. sprengeri*,

and three with informal, nodding flowers, *M. dawsoniana*, *M. sargentiana* and *M. sargentiana* var. *robusta*. It is possible that additional species may be added later since both *M. amoena* and *M. zenii*, whose introduction is still awaited from eastern China, are thought to be closely allied to *M. heptapeta (denudata)*. Brief descriptions of these two species have been added to the end of this section.

Naked Magnolia or Lily Tree
Yulan in China

MAGNOLIA HEPTAPETA (Buc'hoz) Dandy
Adopted from *Lassonia heptapeta* P. J. Buc'hoz in *Plantes Nouvellement Découvertes* 21 : t. 19 (1779)
J. E. Dandy in *Journal of Botany* 72 : 103 (1934)
S. A. Spongberg in *Journal of the Arnold Arboretum* 57, 3 : 285–6 (1976)
SYNS. *M. denudata* L. A. J. Desrousseaux in Lamarck, *Encyclopédie Méthodique, Botanique* 3 : 675 (1791)
M. conspicua R. A. Salisbury in *Paradisus Londinensis* 1 : t. 38 (1806). John Sims in *Curtis's Botanical Magazine* 39 : t. 1621 (1814)
M. yulan R. L. Desfontaines in *Histoire des Arbres et des Arbrisseaux* 2 : 6 (1809)

Plate 13

This, the first Magnolia to be brought into cultivation, is native of eastern China, though long cultivated throughout both China and Japan.

In *Mémoires concernant l'Histoire, les Sciences. . . . des Chinois, par les Missionaires de Pé-Kin* (1778), P. M. Cibot published the earliest known and most apt Western description of this Magnolia under *Le*

Yulan. 'It is said to resemble a naked Walnut Tree with a Lily at the end of every branch.' This description was quoted by R. A. Salisbury in *Paradisus Londinensis* 1 : t. 38 (1806).

Thirteen hundred years ago the Buddhist monks of central China collected plants of their native Yulan or Lily Tree from the wild and planted them in their temple gardens. It seems likely that a religious significance sprang up around the simple beauty of the large white flowers which appeared before the leaves in spring, so that this was probably the first flowering tree to be used as a garden feature.

The Chinese, who had developed a love of culture and refinement at a very early date, were among the first to plant ornamental trees and shrubs in their gardens. It seems that this Magnolia was introduced from China into Japan by the monks during the T'ang Dynasty (A.D. 618–906) along with their native fruits the orange, peach, plum, quince and loquat, when there was a prolonged period of cultural exchange between the two countries.

Even as early as the fourteenth and fifteenth centuries Chinese artists liked to figure the Yulan on many of their paintings, porcelains, carvings and embroideries. Dr. H. L. Li in *Garden Flowers of China* wrote of *M. heptapeta* (*denudata*): 'The Yulan (Jade Orchid) is the most showy species of all. It has been cultivated in China at least since the T'ang Dynasty (618–906) and is now widely planted in gardens all over the country. . . . The Yulan Magnolia is native to central China and wild plants are still being found in the forests.' The tepals were used as food and medicinal preparations were obtained from other parts of the plant.

Plant hunter E. H. Wilson reported this species in Kiangsi province in thickets at an altitude of 4,000 ft (1,200 m). He said that it was common around Kuling, but only in the form of bushy sucker growths springing from the stumps of felled trees. It is also said to be indigenous from south-east Kiangsu to south-west Hunan.

It is likely that a considerable amount of improvement took place over the centuries through the selection of the best forms of this Magnolia. It was first introduced into English gardens by Sir Joseph Banks in 1780, whereupon, after centuries of cultivation in China and Japan, it became available for distribution throughout the Western world.

In *Plantes Nouvellement Découvertes*: 21 (1779) the French botanist Buc'hoz published as *Lassonia heptapeta* on t. 19 Plate 1 a flower bearing little resemblance to the Magnolia with which it was later identified (when *Lassonia* became merged with *Magnolia*) for, not only does it have only seven tepals instead of nine, but the protruding gynoecium is replaced by an irregular mass of stamens and, to make matters worse, the outer whorl of tepals is shown as a fringed calyx! Clearly the plate is from a Chinese impressionist painting which bears but little botanical likeness. Three years earlier he published a coloured reproduction without a botanical name in *Collection Précieuse* 1 : t. 4 (1776) which represents the same Magnolia, to be followed some ten years later by a further coloured plate as *Lassonia heptapeta* (*heptapetala*) in *Le Grand Jardin de L'Univers* t. 131 (1785) referring to the plant as 'l'Iulan blanc'.

For more than a century *Lassonia* was completely ignored by other botanists until it appeared in the *Appendix to the Index Kewensis* 2, 1289 (1895) where it was designated 'Genus spurium Magnoliacearum'.

Successive generations of botanists ignored and despised Buc'hoz and thus it was that, in 1913, American botanist Dr. Rehder dismissed the Buc'hoz name and description as being 'manca falsaque', inadequate and false, when he adopted Desrousseaux's name *denudata* which has since become established in botanical literature as the accepted specific epithet for this Magnolia.

Then in 1934 J. E. Dandy contributed notes on 'The Identity of *Lassonia* Buc'hoz' in *Journal of Botany* 72 : 101–3, that genus founded by Buc'hoz in *Plantes Nouvellement Découvertes*: 21 (1779) and based on the two now well-known species of Magnolia which he had named *L. heptapeta* Buc'hoz and *L. quinquepeta* Buc'hoz and which were known to him only from Chinese drawings. (He named the genus in honour of M. de Lassone who was physician to the French royal household.)

Dandy discussed the misleading Buc'hoz epithets *heptapeta* and *quinquepeta* and argued that they are not more so than Linnaeus's epithet *tripetala* for a Magnolia with nine to twelve or sometimes fifteen tepals. He considered that they were legitimately published and, being the oldest for these two species, 'they necessitate name changes that are particularly undesirable because the nomenclatural history of the plants concerned is already very complicated'.

He considered that the Buc'hoz discrepancies in the published descriptions are fully accounted for by defects in the drawings. From the drawings Buc'hoz counted seven tepals ('petales') in the white-flowered species which he then named *L. heptapeta* (it normally has nine, or occasionally ten to twelve subequal tepals), and five in the purple-flowered species which he named *L. quinquepeta* (it normally has six to twelve plus three small outer ones which represent the false calyx). Dandy then proceeded to list 'the necessary new combinations for the two species . . .

along with their most important synonyms' under *Magnolia heptapeta* (Buc'hoz) Dandy and *M. quinquepeta* (Buc'hoz) Dandy.

All of this was published over forty years ago, and although these names have been used on a few rare occasions (the 'Purple Eye' clone of *M. denudata* received an R.H.S. Award of Merit as *M. heptapeta* in 1926 most likely from Dandy's naming), they were completely ignored by Millais (1927) and disregarded by Johnstone (1955). Even Dandy avoided their use in his 'Survey of the Genus *Magnolia*' (1950) also in his 'Revised Survey' (1970) on pp. 29–37 in this volume, referring to them only as early synonyms for *M. denudata* and *M. liliflora* respectively.

The reasons for the adoption of the Buc'hoz nomenclature of 1779, almost two centuries after the original publication, are contained in the footnote to p. 40. The author makes no apology for having repeated in this chapter (and in that on *M. quinquepeta* on pp. 130–5) part of the account given under 'Some comments on recent changes in Magnolia nomenclature' on pp. 38–40, which may be missed by the more cursory reader.

Over the intervening years, British botanists had managed to preserve a moratorium or *status quo* for plant nomenclature but, with so many equally misleading specific epithets in established use, they were eventually outvoted by their American associates at the Eleventh International Botanical Congress at Seattle in 1969 which led to the publication of the 1972 *International Code of Botanical Nomenclature*. As a result two of the most important and popular species of Magnolia have become saddled with ridiculous epithets which, with that of Linnaeus's *M. tripetala*, will constitute a trio of botanical inexactitudes which must be perpetuated for ever.

M. heptapeta rarely sets seed but has been found to do so readily when fertilized by other Magnolia pollen. It was the female or seed-bearing parent from which Chevalier Soulange-Bodin bred successive generations of his *M. × soulangiana* race of Magnolia hybrids between 1820 and 1840, the pollen parent being a form of *M. quinquepeta* then known as *M. purpurea*. The breeding of these hybrids is discussed under 'Magnolia Hybrids and Crosses'.

In some seasons *M. heptapeta* tends to produce secondary flowers in July and August as do many cultivars of *M. × soulangiana*. It is remarkable that these are often suffused with rose or purple whereas the main flowers are almost pure white. It is difficult to layer and is usually grafted or budded on to seedlings of *M. kobus* by Japanese nurserymen and on to young *M. × soulangiana* by the Dutch.

A good hardy clone of *M. heptapeta* has been distributed by Mr. K. Wada of the Hakoneya Nurseries, Yokohama, Japan. Philip Savage grows Wada's form of *M. heptapeta* in his Magnolia collection at Bloomfield Hills, Michigan, and finds it slower and later to open its flowers than other forms which he has tried. They are therefore more likely to escape frost damage.

At Caerhays there is a pink form of *M. heptapeta* which was planted in 1925 and might well have originated from one of Forrest's seed collections. It is more arborescent than is usual with the white form, though this might well be due to its seedling origin. In 1970 it had a clear 10 ft (3 m) trunk with a girth of 3 ft 10 in. (1·15 m) at 3 ft (91 cm) above ground-level. The flowers have nine to eleven tepals which are flushed rose at the base and up the midrib, giving an overall pink effect when viewed from below. The stamens are tinted pink with purple filaments. The styles are long, curled, creamy white, and the carpels bright green. It is said to produce very long fruit cones.

Wilson contributed notes on 'The Chinese Magnolias' in the *Gardeners Chronicle* 3, 39 : 234 (1906) in which he reported having seen 'one or two giants 80 ft [24·5 m] or more [of this Magnolia], with enormous trunks and widely spreading branches. One such tree I saw in full flower early in May, and if it bore one flower it bore ten thousand!' He said that the fruit cones were spindle shaped and often 8 in. (20·5 cm) long. The bark is known as Wu P'i and constitutes an important drug, considered by the Chinese to be a tonic and stimulant.

This Magnolia was long known in our gardens as *M. conspicua*, a name published by R. A. Salisbury in *Paradisus Londinensis* 1 : t. 38 (1806). But French botanist L. A. J. Desrousseaux had described it earlier as *M. denudata* under *Magnolier* in Lamarck, *Encyclopédie Méthodique, Botanique* 3 : 675 (1791) and, as this represented the original publication of a latinized binomial under *Magnolia* which conformed with the Linnaean Nomenclature of 1753, it had priority, although his description was faulty as to colour. This species has, in fact, masqueraded botanically under no less than ten different names since Engelbert Kaempfer first described it under the oriental name *Mokkwuren* in his *Amoenitatum Exoticarum*: 845 (1712), adding the latinized *flore albo* to indicate that it had white flowers. However some eighty years later considerable confusion was caused by Joseph Banks, who accidentally interchanged Kaempfer's plates of *M. heptapeta* (*denudata*) and *M. quinquepeta* (*liliflora*) in his *Icones Selectae Plantarum, quas in Japonia Collegit Engelbertus Kaempfer*: tt. 12–14 (1791). This unfortunate error also confused Desrousseaux who, in the same year, described the flowers of *M. heptapeta* as red and those of *M. quinquepeta* as white.

Described by Dr. John Sims as *M. conspicua* in *Curtis's Botanical Magazine* 39 : t. 1621 (1814), *M. heptapeta* is recorded as having been introduced to the Western world by Sir Joseph Banks in 1780. However J. C. Loudon in his *Arboretum et Fruticetum Britannicum* gives 1789, as does *Hortus Kewensis* and this has been copied apparently by other authors including W. J. Bean in *Trees and Shrubs Hardy in the British Isles* Ed. 4, 2 : 68 (1925) and J. G. Millais in *Magnolias*. If *Curtis's Botanical Magazine* is incorrect then the first Magnolia introduction would have been of the tropical *M. coco (pumila)* in 1786.

Plant collector George Forrest, who was responsible for the discovery and introduction of many species of Magnolia, contributed the third chapter 'Magnolias of Yunnan' in John G. Millais's book *Magnolias*. He recorded that in Yunnan Magnolias were most often planted in the grounds surrounding many of the larger temples and guild-houses and that *M. heptapeta* (then known as *M. conspicua*) flowered in late January and February before the winter frosts were gone. He described the flowers as appearing 'much before the foliage, are 6 to 7 inches [15 to 18 cm] in diameter, fragrant, and of a clear ivory white, in fine contrast to the drab grey of the bark'. He added that there was no evidence of it being indigenous to that area.

M. heptapeta differs from other introduced species of Section *Yulania* in having fewer tepals (nine as compared with usually twelve or more), and somewhat smaller flowers, which are at first erect and campanulate, but later the tepals open sometimes to a horizontal position. They measure from 3 to 4 in. (7·5 to 10 cm) in length and are usually obovate and concave, being rounded at the apex and narrowed to a spatulate base which is sometimes faintly flushed pink. In some forms the tepals are narrower and more pointed.

M. heptapeta grows into a large arborescent shrub over 30 ft (9 m) in height, sometimes taking over a century to do so. It is a long-lived species and specimens of 150 years or more are on record in English gardens. In China there are reported to be ancient specimens as much as 50 ft (15 m) high.

One of the largest specimens in England is that in the Rectory garden as Little Saxham near Bury St. Edmunds. Believed to have been planted about 1850, this Magnolia was measured in 1948 as approximately 36 ft (11 m) high, with a maximum spread of 34 ft (10·5 m) and a trunk girth of 4 ft (1 m) at 3 ft (91 cm) above ground-level.

A very good form, referred to earlier and distributed by Robert Veitch & Sons of Exeter, is said to have originated as a seedling given by J. C. Williams of Caerhays Castle, Cornwall, to Peter Veitch. It has been given the clone name 'Purple Eye' because of the pronounced basal flush and rosy-purple stamens. It has nine broad tepals of a particularly fleshy and weather-proof texture which splay out horizontally with recurved margins, the inner three flushed purple towards the base along their outer surface. There is also a faint trace of the same shading on the six outer ones. The stamens are buff with purple filaments, while the gynoecium is green with very long, pale-green, incurved styles. The peduncle is covered with long silky hairs. The leaves of this form are very broad and rounded, being up to 9½ in. (24 cm) long by 6½ in. (16·5 cm) across. This form usually flowers seven to ten days later than the type normally met with in English gardens and is thought by some authorities to be of hybrid origin, possibly of the Soulangiana grex.

M. heptapeta is hardier than most Magnolias though the open flowers are prone to frost damage. It blossoms freely as a young plant and is not fussy about soil conditions provided it is supplied with ample humus in the form of peat, leaf-mould or composted vegetation where the terrain is sandy or alkaline.

Millais in *Magnolias* reported that it was hardy as a free-standing tree as far north as Derbyshire but that farther north it should be given the protection of a wall. When planted in the open *M. heptapeta* looks best against a dark background of sombre conifers, as a contrast to the creamy-white flowers gleaming in the spring sunshine. There is a subtle mandarin quality about them.

The flower buds are conspicuous throughout the winter with their grey, shaggy-haired perules. They respond quickly to a spell of mild weather in late February or early March and are then liable to be frost damaged should the weather change. Consequently a cold February and March tends to suit them best so that their opening is delayed until a prolonged spell of milder weather prevails.

The veteran tree of *M. heptapeta* at the Goldsworth Nursery of Walter C. Slocock Ltd., at Woking in Surrey, which Johnstone recorded as having been planted in 1815 and which in 1948 measured 35 ft (10·5 m) high by as much across, has since died. When it began to show signs of decline one of its outer branches was layered to provide a replacement. According to information supplied to the author by Mr. J. A. Slocock in September 1972, this replacement specimen had then attained an estimated height of 24 ft (7·5 m) with a spread of 30 ft (9 m) and the six main branches had circumferences of 18 to 24 in. (46 to 61 cm) at 3 ft (91 cm) above ground-level.

At Antony House, Torpoint, on the Cornish side of the River Tamar opposite Devonport Dockyard, there is an extensive planting of *M. heptapeta* along one of the lawns. The flowers show purple shadings towards the base of the tepals, but these are not as broad as in Veitch's 'Purple Eye' cultivar.

Cytologically *M. heptapeta* is a hexaploid with 2n = 114 chromosomes.

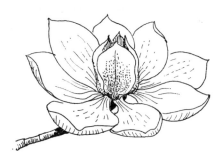

Campbell's Magnolia

MAGNOLIA CAMPBELLII Hooker & Thomson

J. D. Hooker and T. Thomson in *Flora Indica* 1 : 77 (1855)

J. D. Hooker in *Curtis's Botanical Magazine* 111 : t. 6793 (1885)

G. H. Johnstone in *Asiatic Magnolias in Cultivation*: 48–52 (1955)

SYN. *M. campbellii* subsp. *campbellii* Johnstone

Plates 14, 15 and 16

This species was named by J. D. Hooker in 1855 after Dr. Archibald Campbell, who was Political Resident at Darjeeling, close to where Hooker had seen extensive mountain flanks covered with this tree during his Himalayan travels.

M. campbellii ranges along the Sikkim Himalayas from eastern Nepal to northern Assam at altitudes between 7,000 and 11,000 ft (2,100 to 3,350 m). It is not surprising therefore that considerable differences should exist between representatives from opposite ends of this elongated distribution. While botanists do not consider these differences to be of specific importance, they are of very great importance to members of the gardening fraternity who grow or propose to grow them in their gardens.

The eastern race of *M. campbellii* was named *M. mollicomata* in 1920 by Sir William Wright Smith at the Edinburgh Botanical Garden, when he was classifying herbarium specimens brought back from western Yunnan by plant collector George Forrest.

Consequently it has become generally known under this name wherever it has been grown, but unfortunately this quite innocent acceptance of a distinct name, for what is to plantsmen a distinctive race of Magnolia, has proved a source of considerable embarrassment to some botanists. Apart from the important fact that it normally flowers about a fortnight later than most trees of the western form, and is consequently less susceptible to frost damage, it also has a reputation for attaining florescence in as little as half the time. This difference, which could be anything from ten to thirty years, is of vital importance to garden owners, especially those who may not begin to take a serious interest in gardening until they reach the age of retirement.

So here we have two races of Magnolia which, though classified botanically as one species, are sufficiently distinct horticulturally to make it desirable to separate them. It is important that the Magnolia enthusiast and would-be planter should know whether the tree, which he or she proposes to purchase, is likely to flower within ten years or twenty years and also whether it will come into flower very early in the year or a few weeks later when the weather is likely to be more favourable.

In 1947 the late C. P. Raffill, while Assistant Curator at the Royal Botanic Gardens, Kew, bred about a hundred crosses between these two races of Magnolia. They are discussed in detail under the Sidbury-Raffill Group of Crosses (p. 167). (Apparently a similar race of crosses was raised some twenty years earlier at Sidbury Manor in Devonshire.)

Words cannot adequately describe the elegant beauty of this Queen of Magnolias. The fat, ovoid flower buds are borne erectly at the tips of the shoots. They develop slowly during the winter and are protected by several layers of furry perules which are densely pubescent, with short hairs standing out from the surface while longer ones lie flat beneath them. As milder weather approaches, these perules are gradually shed until only the innermost spathaceous bracts remain to enclose the flowers. In subdued light these bracts seem black instead of dark grey, with a satiny sheen beneath their covering of lighter-coloured hairs, and they split down both sides to reveal the vivid pink colour of the tepals. The opening buds are almost egg shaped and their discarded furry spathaceous bracts often hang in two halves beneath the opening tepals, until the flowers are almost spent. Their great beauty lies in their elegant poise, the eight outer tepals opening to form bowls before reflexing horizontally like huge saucers, while the four inner ones remain closed like enormous rosebuds. These four inner tepals then bulge outwards at the base, thus permitting pollen-bearing insects to enter the flower chamber and reach the now receptive stigmas, which they still shield. Pollen may also be transferred by a combination of gravitation and wind from the stamens of fully opened flowers higher up the tree, for no pollen is shed until the stigmas in a particular flower have begun to wither, so that direct pollination and fertilization cannot occur.

Johnstone referred to a peculiarity in the pollen-shedding stage of *M. campbellii*, which the author has been unable to verify. He recorded that the stamens of *M. campbellii* shed pollen *before* the four inner tepals unfurl, but the author has failed to observe free pollen on the anthers of any flowers from numerous trees of this species until they have become virtually spent, and sometimes not before they have shed their tepals, leaving only the gynandrophores at the ends of the peduncles.

The same applies to all other precocious Magnolias which have been examined. One cannot help wondering if this phenomenon was observed on a flower which had been removed from a tree several hours previously and which had reacted in this manner. Col. Johnstone was probably the most painstaking observer of Magnolias of all time, his powers of observation being concentrated, no doubt, through his many years of enforced inactivity after he was crippled in a hunting accident when only thirty-one.

The outer tepals of the earliest flowers of *M. campbellii* are often arrested in their opening by adverse weather conditions so that they do not reflex to a horizontal plane. Even when considerably damaged by slight frost and gales, this is often not apparent from a distance, and the general effect is still quite startling. The added beauty of the gyn-androphores does not become apparent until the flowers begin to fade. The stout filaments which carry the stamens are rosy magenta while the slender stigmatic column or gynoecium is green with small crimson styles.

In cultivation it is one of the earliest Magnolias to flower, a doubtful privilege which it shares with the even more sensational magenta-purple Magnolia, hitherto known to gardeners as *M. mollicomata* con-variety *williamsiana*, which the author has renamed *M. campbellii* Lanarth Group to conform with current botanical opinion.

Dr. W. Griffith first described and pictured *M. campbellii* in 1838. His drawing was published posthumously sixteen years later in *Icones Plantarum Asiaticarum* 4 : t. 656 (1854). It was the white form of the species, which he had discovered in the Bhutan Himalayas near Tongsa at an elevation of 8,000 ft (2,440 m), flowering during the third week in March. His latinized description was published in his *Itinerary Notes* (published under *Posthumous Papers*) 2, 153 : 755 (1847–8). A translation of this appears on p. 91.

The first coloured plates of the pink *M. campbellii* were published by J. D. Hooker and T. Thomson in *Illustrations of Himalayan Plants*: tt. 4, 5 (1855). Thirty years later Hooker (then Sir Joseph Hooker) recorded in *Curtis's Botanical Magazine* 111 : t. 6793 (1885) that Griffith's *Posthumous Papers* did not reach England until after the publication of his *Illustrations of Himalayan Plants*.

Surely Griffith's *Posthumous Papers*, printed in Calcutta by order of the Government of Bengal in 1847–8, would have reached England long before 1855, though it is possible that the plate published in 1854 arrived too late to affect Hooker's citation. Hooker had spent a considerable time in the Sikkim Himalayas and reported having seen flanks of mountain-sides turn pink with massed displays of *M. campbellii*. He had probably already committed himself to naming the species which might otherwise have commemorated Griffith.

Hooker's plate of *M. campbellii* in *Curtis's Botanical Magazine* shows a very light pink flower with sixteen rather narrow tepals and a boss of erect yellow stamens, shaded orange at the base, which almost eclipse the gynoecium. He recorded that the flower was 'sent from Mr. Crawford's well-known garden at Lakeville near Cork in 1878'. This in-dicates that the species must have been introduced about 1855.

Johnstone, in *Asiatic Magnolias in Cultivation*: 51, referred to the faulty impression presented by Hooker's plate, which suggests that all of the tepals open together in the manner of a waterlily. He sug-gested that this might be explained by the flower's opening while in transit to the artist so that, when it was unpacked and placed in water, all sixteen tepals opened together. This does in fact happen to *M. campbellii* flowers when they are cut and left out of water or left in a warm room.

In the description which accompanies the plate Sir Joseph Hooker wrote: 'This, the noblest species of the genus, was, before the destruction of the grand forest that clothed the higher elevation of the outer ranges of the Sikkim Himalayas, by far the most notable tree of the district, and I have seen the flanks of a mountain rose-coloured in spring from its abundance and habit of flowering before the de-velopment of the leaves. . . . It is now growing scarce in Sikkim, whereas when I was in that country upwards of thirty years ago, it was one of the commonest trees at about 8,000 to 9,000 feet [2,400 to 2,700 m] in the hills near Darjeeling.'

Writing on 'Flowers of the Valley of Nepal' in the *Journal of the Royal Horticultural Society* 89 : 294–300 (1964), G. A. C. Herklots reported that *M. campbellii* was then very rare in that area because it was much sought after for firewood, so that an untouched tree probably did not exist.

Kingdon-Ward, writing also in the *Journal of the Royal Horticultural Society* 52 : 16 (1927), reported: 'Though we saw scores of trees [of *M. campbellii*] in the forests above Gangtok [near Darjeeling], they were all white flowered.' He said that the pink form was 'rare and local'.

Unfortunately this Magnolia usually takes twenty-five years or more to attain florescence, by which time it will probably have reached a height of over 30 ft (9 m), the first flowers being invariably on the topmost shoots. One has to wait even longer before any are borne on the lower branches closer to eye level. The moral therefore is to plant it if possible at the foot of a bank or terrace where the first flowers may be admired to greater advantage.

Surely it is this very long period of adolescence which adds to its risk of ultimate extinction, since it attains considerable dimensions before it reaches sexual maturity, by which time it may well have succumbed to the woodsman's axe.

The author reasons that by grafting *M. campbellii* on to understocks of *M. mollicomata*, which often attains florescence at ten years, or on to *M. sargentiana* var. *robusta*, which often does so at twelve to thirteen years, this long and frustrating waiting period will at least be halved and the ultimate stature of the plant to some extent restricted.

In the Strybing Arboretum at San Francisco grafted Magnolias such as *M. campbellii* have been flowered when ten years old and only 5 ft (1·5 m) tall, by being severely root-bound in containers. It is also probable that the flowering of Magnolias can be hurried by a temporary strangulation of the main trunk, by ringing with wire for a period of eight to ten weeks in July. The Hon. Lewis Palmer reporting on 'A Cold Chalk Garden Throughout the Year' in the *Journal of the Royal Horticultural Society* 92, 1 : 12, 13 (1967), wrote that once a Magnolia, so treated, begins flower production, it will continue to flower each year thereafter.

One would imagine that plants raised by layering the shoots of a mature tree would begin to flower as soon as they were re-established, yet in practice they take about twenty years. One such specimen, in Mr. Nigel Holman's garden at Chyverton near Truro, produced four blooms at its first flowering and twenty-six in the following season. It was planted as a large layer about five years old in 1953 and did not flower until 1967.

In cultivation at least, *M. campbellii* appears to be highly sterile to its own pollen. The rarity with which mature trees produce fertile fruit cones cannot be explained entirely by unfavourable weather conditions at the time of flowering, nor by lack of suitable insects so early in the year, since both gravitation and wind must also act as agents capable of transferring pollen from the stamens of fully matured primary flowers on to the now receptive stigmas of those which have just reflexed their outer tepals.

Similar self-unfruitfulness has been reported from America by Prof. J. C. McDaniel of the University of Illinois in connection with most trees of *M. acuminata* but this has been attributed latterly to a lack of pollinating beetles, since fertile fruit cones were produced after unopened flowers had been hand-pollinated with pollen from those which had already opened and commenced to shed pollen.

The production of fertile fruit cones on *M. campbellii* is not unusual where two or more trees, unrelated by grafting or layering, have been planted reasonably close. This is demonstrated by three trees in the National Trust Garden at Lanhydrock near Bodmin, Cornwall, which are growing in an open situation on the lawn. These are also unusual in having pubescent flower stalks or peduncles.

J. G. Millais in *Magnolias* said that the best specimen of *M. campbellii* which he had seen in Cornwall was at Bosahan, 'where in March 1921 it had five hundred blooms. It is a fine tree of forty feet [12 m] and was planted in 1888.' The Bosahan tree still survives, in spite of the fact that the old mansion, against which it grew, has been demolished. However it is still largely protected by the new house and the tree has had expert surgery so that it should survive for a very long time to come.

In the famous Cornish Magnolia garden of Lanarth, on the Lizard Peninsula, there is a tree growing against the west gable end of the rear wing of the house with the back driveway running over the tree's roots. In spite of this seemingly unsuitable situation, its flowering branches now overtop the chimney pots and overhang the driveway, dappling it with fallen pink and white tepals in March (Plate 15).

Millais also mentioned the two large specimens of *M. campbellii* in the gardens of Leonardslee and South Lodge, Horsham, each of which was said to be 40 ft (12 m) high in 1926. I saw the Leonardslee tree in flower in 1967 and thought it must be one of the largest specimens in cultivation.

When Veitch's old nursery at Exeter was transferred to Alphington on the outskirts of the city in 1930, the tree which first flowered in 1905, was sold to the owner of an Irish garden.

In the garden of the late the Hon. Mrs. Bell, Fota Island, near Cork, there is a fine specimen of *M. campbellii* which was planted in 1870 and was over 70 ft (21·5 m) high in 1967.

At Caerhays Castle in Cornwall a tree of this Magnolia had reached the age of forty years in 1968 without having attained florescence. There, *M. campbellii* is considered to be one of the most brittle members of the Magnolia family but this may be due to their being drawn upwards by proximity to adjacent beech trees.

There are two specimen trees of *M. campbellii* at Kew. The finer of the two, with the deeper pink flowers, originated from the Calcutta Botanic Garden in March 1904 and was planted near the Victoria Gate. The present authorities do not consider that it flowers regularly as late as reported by W. M. Campbell, the then Curator, and recorded by Johnstone in *Asiatic Magnolias in Cultivation*: 49. The second specimen is in the centre of a collection of different Magnolias near the Azalea Garden. This tree is more spreading in habit, the flowers being a little larger and paler than those of the former and the tepals are somewhat larger and narrower than on other forms examined. According to the *Royal Botanic Gardens Newsletter* 60 : 5 (1973) two specimens which were raised as grafts from the deep pink *M. campbellii* subsp. *campbellii* by the Temple of Bellona (No. 170–04, Calcutta) flowered for the first time in 1973, sixteen years from grafting. One was planted by No. 1 House and the other near the Victoria Gate. The understocks were seedlings of the same subspecies.

M. campbellii in Windsor Great Park first flowered in 1962, producing nine blooms in that year and more than five times as many the following season.

In 1968 Lord Strathcona told the author that a plant of *M. campbellii* planted in his garden on the Isle of Colonsay in 1932 produced its first flowers in 1959.

There is a very dark-flowered tree of *M. campbellii* growing in the Botanical Garden at Darjeeling, India. Messrs. Hillier & Sons of Winchester have a tree propagated vegetatively from it to which they have given the clonal name 'Darjeeling'.

A seedling from the same Indian tree in Sir George Jessel's garden at Goudhurst in Kent has been recently accorded the cultivar name 'Betty Jessel'. It received a First Class Certificate at an R.H.S. show in April 1975. This tree first flowered when twenty-three years of age. It is perhaps the latest-flowered form the author has yet come across and may, on this account, be more suitable for colder localities. The author examined a flower which the owner kindly sent to him on 6 May 1969. It was the nearest approach to crimson that he had seen in a Magnolia and remarkable too because the deeper colouring *appeared* to be on the *upper* surface of the tepals, whereas other forms examined have much paler upper surfaces often fading to white, the richer colouring being on the exterior (undersides) when they have reflexed to form the saucer which gives the flowers such an elegant poise.

Sir George Jessel reports that his *M. campbellii* 'Betty Jessel' had attained a height of about 30 ft (9 m) in thirty-one years and that it bore nine flowers in its twenty-third year. The flowers on his tree begin to open about the middle of April and the tree has never shown any sign of coming into leaf until some time after flowering.

The author recorded a good late-flowering form of *M. campbellii* flowering at Trewithen on 28 April 1969. Mrs. Johnstone said that it was given to her husband (the late George J. Johnstone, author of *Asiatic Magnolias in Cultivation*) by the late E. K. Elmhirst of Dartington Hall, Totnes, Devon. It did not begin to flower until after Col. Johnstone's death. In correspondence with the author, Mr. Elmhirst recalled that, towards the end of the Second World War, he was staying at the United Services Club in Calcutta. The seed from which the Trewithen tree was raised was given to him by a Professor of Botany, who was then Head of the Botanic Garden in Calcutta and who had recently returned from a botanical expedition in the foothills of the Himalayas, either in Nepal or possibly Bhutan. At this time E. K. Elmhirst made the acquaintance of professional plant hunter F. Kingdon-Ward who was then staying close by. Kingdon-Ward told him that he had spotted, on one of his trips, a form of *M. campbellii* with almost scarlet flowers. He had marked it for subsequent seed collection but, when he returned to the area at the appropriate time, he could not locate the tree.

So far we have not discussed either the relative hardiness of *M. campbellii* or its growth characteristics. With most forms of this Magnolia, flowering begins at that very uncertain weather period when winter is giving way to spring, which may vary from mid February onward, according to locality and season. The flowers are therefore very prone to frost damage, as indeed are those of most other Magnolias. Consequently trees are often found growing against walls, but they seem to shun such cosseting by growing vigorously away from the shelter intended for them, and at the same time reaching constantly upward, until their topmost branches are well clear of all protection, to display their huge, deep pink, cup-shaped blooms against the perfect foil of a clear blue sky.

In American gardens the flowers of *M. campbellii* are reported to be often frost damaged in western Oregon and Washington, but even if this happens in two years out of three the rewarding sight of a tree in full flower in a good season is quite beyond adequate description.

Johnstone referred to its remarkable power of recovery from complete frosting of its young foliage in May, but the same can be said of other deciduous Magnolias.

The young leaves, which usually appear some time after the last tepals have fallen, are bronze tinted, while mature ones vary considerably in size, shape and indumentum on different trees. Sir Joseph Hooker, in his notes on *M. campbellii* in Sikkim, wrote: 'Young plants have the leaves perfectly glabrous; those of the older trees are more or less silky on the undersurfaces'; but this course of events has not always held good in our gardens. They average 8 to 12 in. (20·5 to 30·5 cm) long by 3 to 5 in. (7·5 to 12·5 cm) wide. Their shape is elliptic or narrowly ovate, the apex terminating in a short point and the base usually rounded. The undersurfaces are usually, though not always, pubescent, especially when young.

Hooker described the bark of trees of *M. campbellii* which he saw as being almost black, but trees in cultivation in this country have bark of quite a light silvery grey. This dark colouring may have been caused by a covering of algae.

When trees attain florescence their hitherto sparse and open-branched appearance begins to change with the production of more side shoots. Continued apical shoot development is arrested by the formation of flower buds so that the growth impulse becomes diverted laterally to induce branch initiation from hitherto dormant growth buds.

The most prevalent form of *M. campbellii* in English gardens today is probably that which was propagated by grafting in the early 1900s, when Peter Veitch had a nursery in New North Road between the two railway stations at Exeter, Devon. This tree attained florescence in 1898 and its propagation and subsequent history is described elsewhere in the appropriate chapter (p. 204). Until recently, the only form grown in Britain has been the pink one which, because of its almost sterile nature, has had to be propagated by grafting or layering. It is therefore

likely that many plants, especially those of lower, bushy habit, are grafted trees which became distributed by the one of the few nurseries which persevered in raising stocks of such a difficult subject, for even in the hands of the most skilled propagators the results were uncertain and failures on an average must have outnumbered successes.

Millais mentioned that 'Mr. R. Gill of Penryn, Cornwall, who has a son in the Himalayas, has imported some seed and managed to raise a few plants, so he may be encouraged to get some more and distribute a fair stock of the species.' Richard Gill's nephew, Mr. Bernard Gill, who now runs this old family nursery business, told the author that his uncle, Norman Gill, was trained at Kew and took a post as curator in one of the Indian botanic gardens. From time to time he went on plant hunting expeditions in the Himalayas and sent home seed of rhododendrons, and occasionally of Magnolias, the seed travelling in charcoal in sealed tins.

He recalls that, on one occasion, a considerable quantity of seed of *M. campbellii* which had failed to germinate, was dumped on the nursery rubbish heap. A year or two later a mass of seedlings appeared and these were carefully retrieved and grown on. He also recalls importing two-year seedlings of this and other Magnolias from India, and managing to potestablish about 50 per cent of them.

One of the finest forms of *M. campbellii* (Plate 16), which the author has examined and photographed, is in the garden of the old Vicarage at Gulval, near Penzance, where it has relatively little protection from Mounts Bay. It was planted about 1937 by the late Vicar's wife, Mrs. Buckley, who recalls that it first flowered fifteen years later, so it must be a grafted tree. The flowers, which open to a formal cup-and-saucer shape, are particularly large and have very broad, spoon-shaped, heavy textured tepals of a rich pink, fading to pale pink and white on the upper or inner surfaces. This Magnolia bore its first two flowers in its fifteenth year, followed by twelve in the following season. It has since flowered profusely each March. It is a large bushy tree with horizontal branches flowering to ground-level.

A deeper coloured *M. campbellii* grows at the front of the terrace wall at Rosillian, Flushing, across the mouth of the Penryn River from Falmouth in Cornwall. It has very large cup-and-saucer flowers, which usually begin to open a week or two later than a second and slightly paler form near the opposite corner of the house. This garden also boasts several mimosas (*Acacia dealbata*) which flower at about the same time as the Magnolias.

The late G. H. Johnstone, in a chapter on 'Magnolias' which he contributed to W. Arnold-Forster's *Trees and Shrubs for the Milder Counties*: 231 (1948), wrote of *M. campbellii*: 'The *cup-shaped* flowers are upright on the trees.' This tends to confirm the author's contention that most forms have cup-shaped flowers, while others produce wide cup-and-saucer blossoms, though climatic conditions at the time of flowering may have some effect on the extent to which the eight outer tepals reflex.

The author knows of several fine specimens of *M. campbellii* which have either outgrown or survived longer than the protecting walls against which they were originally planted. They still flower as prolifically as ever except after the more exposed branches have become stripped of foliage by an unusually late gale before the leaves have matured in late May or early June. Such a specimen can be seen in the National Trust's Garden, Overbecks, which overlooks the mouth of the Kingsbridge Estuary at Salcombe, on the South Devon coast.

More than one tree of *M. campbellii* has been successfully re-erected after being blown over by an abnormal wind during winter, though such an occurrence would almost certainly prove fatal had they been in leaf. The large tree at Killiow House, near Truro, suffered in this manner many years ago and was supported by wire hawsers attached to a steel collar around the uppermost section of the trunk.* The specimen in David Trehane's garden at Trehane near Tresillian, Truro, has a large swelling at the base of the trunk where it was grafted and has partly rotted away to leave a considerable cavity. It is amazing that such a large tree could have survived with such a mechanical weakness since the branch canopy must transfer very considerable wind stresses right down to its roots.

In Australia a tree in Mr. W. J. Simpson's garden at 'Wayside', Frankston, near Melbourne, was reported by Arthur W. Headlam in 'Magnolias in Melbourne' *Rhododendrons 1974 with Magnolias and Camellias*: 86, to have commenced to flower only eight years after planting. Mr. Simpson tells me that it originated as a layer which he imported from Duncan & Davies of New Plymouth, New Zealand, in 1962 when it was quite a young plant with a single stem and small root system. He reports that the several older trees of *M. campbellii* from various other sources had shown no sign of flowering by early 1977. The soil at 'Wayside' is deep and sandy

---

* Since these notes were compiled this tree has been blown down again and had to be destroyed.

and the garden slopes steeply down to the cliff-top. The tree in question is sited in a very open situation.

Cytologically *M. campbellii* is a hexaploid with $2n = 114$ chromosomes.

White Campbell Magnolia

MAGNOLIA CAMPBELLII ALBA

W. Griffith in *Posthumous Papers* 2, 153 : 755 (1848) and in *Icones Plantarum Asiaticarum* 4 : t. 656 (1854)
SYN. *M. campbellii* White Form
Charles Williams in *Journal of the Royal Horticultural Society* 76 : 218 (1951)
Plates 17 and 18

'Gaze down in wonder on the dark forest, lit by thousands of milk white glowing cups, hung like beacons in the bare trees, and be silent.' So wrote that famous plant hunter F. Kingdon-Ward in *Pilgrimage for Plants* (1960) when he first saw the white form of *M. campbellii* flowering in its native Sikkim.

Only those of us who have been fortunate enough to see a specimen tree of this wonderful Magnolia, bearing its large precocious ivory-white blossoms, can begin to imagine the impact of the spectacle of a whole forest of them flowering in the fading light.

The white form of *M. campbellii* was discovered in 1838 by Dr. William Griffith (1810–45), assistant surgeon on the Madras establishment of the East India Company. In the course of his assignments he travelled extensively in Assam, Burma, Bhutan, Afghanistan and the neighbouring countries, embracing nearly the whole extent of the East India Company's extra-peninsula possessions and adding large collections in every branch of natural history, especially in botany.

In 1837 he was appointed surgeon to the Embassy to Bhutan then about to depart on an expedition to

Khasyah and the Bhutan mountains under the charge of Major Pemberton. With him Griffith traversed 400 miles (644 km) of Bhutan country, returning to Calcutta about the end of June 1838, Dr. Griffith recorded that they stayed at Tongsa, in the Bhutan Himalayas, at an altitude of 8,000 ft (2,440 m) from 13 to 22 March 1838 and mentioned in his notes 'a Magnoliaceous tree with exquisitely fragrant blossom'.

Griffith eventually exhausted himself with his long and arduous journeys throughout India, during which he suffered several bouts of fever. Upon his death, at the early age of thirty-five, his specimens and *Itinerary Notes* were bequeathed to the East India Company, and remained in the vaults of India House until they were published, by order of the Government of Bengal at Calcutta in 1847 and 1848, under the title *Posthumous Papers*.

The Magnolia which Griffith discovered, described and depicted in 1838 was the white form of the species named *M. campbellii* by Hooker in 1855. Were it not for Griffith's untimely death there is little doubt that his *Itinerary Notes* would have been published much earlier than 1847–8, in which event we might now be referring to this fine Magnolia as "*M. griffithii*", a name subsequently given by Hooker in *Flora of British India* 1 : 41 (1872) to a tropical species from Assam and Upper Burma. It would seem that Sir Joseph Hooker was mindful of this when he referred to Griffith's *Posthumous Papers*. A translation of Griffith's latinized description from his *Itinerary Notes* No. 755 p. 153 (1847–8) reads: 'Large tree, at the time of flowering destitute of leaves, with the branchlets green and obliquely annulate, new parts pubescent and with lenticels at length globose, pedicels thick, $\frac{1}{2}$ in. [12 mm] long, glabrate with rings here close together and abbreviated, and there bud-bearing with the buds downwards smaller. The flower, large in diameter, a span (9 in.) [23 cm] wide, with 2 bracts connate, spathaceous, sub-coriaceous, reticulate, on the outside very hispid, pale brown, deciduous.

'Sepals oblong, obovate, palely greenish, fleshy, not easily distinguished from the petals – outspread, reflexed with the petals, white in 2 series – the outer series in the direction of the sepals, the inner series arching over the genital organs forming a globe and giving out a fragrant odour. Stamens indefinite, in many series – lilac-rose, pollen white, spike of carpels elongated – greenish, styles recurved – rose, stigmas fleshy coloured. In woods scarcely below 8,000 ft [2,400 m] Tongsa.' Griffith's drawing of this Magnolia was published in *Icones Plantarum Asiaticarum* 4 : t. 656 (1854.)

In the plate referred to, he depicted an opening flower bud with the furry spathaceous bract splitting equally down both sides to reveal the tips of the tepals, also a partly opened flower with the outer tepals beginning to reflex, and a fully opened flower with the broad outer tepals fully reflexed. There is a marked similarity in the shape of this flower to that of the purple *M. campbellii* subsp. *mollicomata* 'Lanarth'. The author looks upon these two Magnolias as being more closely related to each other than to the pink *M. campbellii*.

The first tree of the white *M. campbellii* to be grown in the Western world was raised from one of three seeds which germinated at Caerhays Castle, Cornwall, after being sent to the late J. C. Williams from Darjeeling in 1926. This original seedling is reported to have almost succumbed following the severe mid December air frosts of 1938, after producing its first flower buds. The worst frost was on the night of 17 December when air temperatures down to 22 °F. (−5·6 ° C.) were general throughout Cornwall, causing widespread damage to trees and shrubs.

According to Johnstone, 'although it contained sufficient sap to develop flower-buds, these withered and dropped from the tree before they were fully open'. One wonders whether this statement was based on personal observations or if it was merely an assumption, which might well have been made fifteen or sixteen years after the event, since his book *Asiatic Magnolias in Cultivation* was not published until 1955. It is contradicted in some notes on this disaster made by the late Charles Williams on 15 October 1949, which make interesting reading: 'J. C. Williams had three seeds from a white Campbellii from India. This was the only one that came up and came into full flower in March 1939 at the time of my father's death. It is very white with a faint line of pink outside the petal down the middle. The flowers were all perfect when out, but the bark was dry. Lady Vyvyan of Trelowarren said to me: "Well, that has survived anyhow." I asked her to feel the bark, but I don't think she quite registered how bad it was. The leaves began to come out, and then the whole thing withered. The cause was frosted sap veins from the previous autumn. We covered the bottom three feet of the stem – a single one – with fern. This was taken off in July, as very feeble white shoots were coming at the bottom of the trunk, which was cut off some four feet up. A bell glass was put on these, and by October 1939 they were healthy, and three were allowed to grow, which in due course got reduced to two by one breaking off. The next ten years these produced very large growths and were held up by cords etc., as they were terribly brittle. When I came back in October 1949 the first flower buds were there quite definitely.'

The author is indebted to Mr. Julian Williams for permission to publish this extract from his late uncle's notes. Although this account was written some ten-and-a-half years after the event, it is most likely that he had retained a vivid recollection of what was a unique occurrence. It would appear that the tree may not have flowered again until after a lapse of eleven years. It was awarded a First Class Certificate by the Royal Horticultural Society on 3 April 1951.

During the winter of 1946–7 one of the coppice-like branches broke away from the base of this mother tree at Caerhays. It was cut into short lengths by the gardeners and these were driven into the ground to support a low wire-netting fence around some near-by beds of seedling camellias. The basal section, some 4 in. (10 cm) in diameter and about 3 ft (91 cm) in length, rooted in the manner of a poplar or willow bough, and made over 10 ft (3 m) of top growth during the next three years. This amazing phenomenon is referred to in the Royal Horticultural Society's *Camellias and Magnolias Conference Report* (1950) on pages 39 and 106. By the autumn of 1969 this Magnolia had grown into a tree of some 35 ft (10·5 m) in height, with a trunk diameter of 22 in. (56 cm) at 3 ft (91 cm) above ground-level.

The tree and its progeny have since proved perfectly hardy and have come through far more severe winters, such as 1962–3, unscathed, apart from damage to open flowers and sometimes to flower buds, when severe frost occurs after they have begun to develop. Because *M. campbellii alba* usually starts to flower several days later than does the pink form it is somewhat less likely to be devastated in this manner.

Mr. Williams writes: 'The seedlings of *M. campbellii alba* (of which 15 to 20 are now flowering at Caerhays) flower here between ten and twelve years from planting out.' This would be at an age of about fifteen years.

He continues: 'I think the White Campbellii and its seedlings are just as hardy – probably a little more so – than the Pink Campbellii. They do flower later than their pink brothers and therefore are more liable to stand up well to winter frosts. Both plants are a little on the brittle side in their wood, but in the case of the White Campbellii this may be due to the fact that they do grow so rapidly.

'Trees of the white Campbellii are readily distinguishable, especially after leaf fall, by their erect trunks and downward-sweeping lower branches.'

The massive flowers of *M. campbellii alba* have an alabastrine texture which has to be seen to be believed. The original tree at Caerhays first flowered when only fourteen years old in 1939. It therefore begins to bloom at a much earlier age than the pink form and this has been proved by second-generation seedlings. One at Trewithen, bearing leaves typical of the Caerhays mother tree, from which it was raised in 1952, first flowered in March 1966 at just over fourteen years of age.

The Caerhays mother tree of *M. campbellii alba* differs in foliage from the pink forms: the leaves measure up to 12 in. (30·5 cm) in length by 6 in. (15 cm) in width, whereas 9 in. (23 cm) by 5 in. (12·5 cm) appears to be the maximum size on other types. However, the main difference is not in the size of the leaves but in the dense silky indumentum completely covering their undersides and petioles, which are light green and not red tinged as is usual on the pink form. The main veins are deeply impressed into the upper surfaces and have a pale, translucent or hyaline appearance when held up to a strong light, as if devoid of colour pigment.

Leaves of some seedlings from the original Caerhays tree measure up to 8 in. (20·5 cm) long by 5 in. (12·5 cm) wide and have reticulate venation and bronze petioles. The undersurfaces are glaucous green and glabrous apart from some hair along the edges of the midribs. It would therefore appear that, as in many other Magnolias, pubescence of the leaves is a variable factor, unless these plants are crosses of hybrids.

The author finds it difficult to reconcile this Magnolia with a close relationship to the type species already described. Attaining florescence as it does in half the time taken by its pink-flowered cousin, it cannot here be argued that such a marked discrepancy in its life cycle is attributable to a different natural distribution (as with subspecies *mollicomata*) for both pink and white forms were introduced from the Sikkim Himalayas.

The flower buds of the white *campbellii* are extraordinarily large, considerably larger than those of the pink form. As spring approaches the three fur-coated perules are progressively split open and shed, owing to the gradual lengthening of the pedicle, which is then exposed as a half-inch of lime green stalk at the base of the bud, now clad only by the spathaceous bract.

Close examination with an illuminated lens reveals patches of fine white woolly down on the peduncle, with collars of short, stiff hairs along the scars left by the perules but none on the pedicle – apart from the collar at its upper extremity, which does not become apparent until the spathaceous bract is shed. The pedicle is dotted with small whitish lenticels, with occasional larger ones which become coated with raised brown corky scabs. These scab-coated lenticels are very large and pronounced on the olive-green internodes beneath the peduncle and also remain prominently raised on the darker-coloured two-year-old shoots.

Returning to the massive flower bud, we see that the spathaceous bract splits down both seams and remains for a time suspended below the flower before being finally shed. It appears to be almost black in contrast to the creamy whiteness of the tepals. These usually number eight or twelve and have a heavier texture than any other precocious Magnolia which the author has examined. They are spoon shaped, 4½ in. by 2½ in. (11·5 by 6 cm) long, with broadly rounded and sometimes emarginate tips. There is a very faint flush of pink towards their base. The stamen filaments are a pale shade of rosy purple and, when the flower begins to fade, the creamy stamens split open to shed whitish pollen. The slender gynoecium is lime green and densely covered with buff-pink stigmas pressed closely along its surface.

Some seedlings from the Caerhays mother plant of *M. campbellii alba* which have begun to flower, not only at Caerhays but in such gardens as Chyverton and Trewithen, have produced immense pale pink blossoms intermediate in colour between the white and pink forms. The author assumes that these seedlings are natural crosses with the pink form which in some seasons would be flowering at the same time and at no great distance and would have already matured its flowers and started to shed its pollen.

Reporting on the Garden at Caerhays in the *Journal of the Cornwall Garden Society* 8 : 13 (1965), Mr. Julian Williams wrote: 'Two plants of these that I put out in 1957 flowered for the first time this year. The flowers were not pure white – one was faintly tinged pink, and one had a faint purple tinge in it, but the flowers were very big indeed. The form of these seedlings is very distinct, as the bottom branches tend to sweep downwards, and from six feet [2 m] they go straight up. We were very pleased here with the size of the flower and the vigour of the plants.'

In a letter to the author Mr. Julian Williams suggests that 'these pink seedlings may be hybrids, the nearest neighbours to the seed parent being *M. sargentiana robusta*, *M. denudata (conspicua)* [= *M. heptapeta*], *M. sprengeri* 'Diva', *M. sargentiana*, *M. campbellii* subsp. *mollicomata* and *M.* × *veitchii* The sequence in which these have flowered this year

(1973) being *campbellii* (pink), *sargentiana robusta*, *sprengeri* 'Diva' (still in flower as I write (15.5.73) after six weeks), *campbellii alba*, *mollicomata*, *sargentiana* (pure), *conspicua* (*denudata*). So it may be dangerous to pin-point pink *campbellii* as the parent. *Veitchii* has a very long flowering span, April 5th to May 20th, but hybrids these seedlings must be if only because of their great vigour.'

Several seedling trees were sent from Caerhays to the Gardens at Windsor Great Park. In April 1973 flowering branches off one of them were exhibited at the Royal Horticultural Society's show under the clonal name 'Windsor Belle' and awarded the Society's coveted First Class Certificate. This Magnolia was later renamed 'Princess Margaret'.

Cytologically *M. campbellii alba* is also hexaploid with 2n = 114 chromosomes.

Downy Magnolia

MAGNOLIA CAMPBELLII subsp. *MOLLICOMATA* (W. W. Smith) Johnstone

M. mollicomata W. W. Smith

W. W. Smith in *Notes from the Royal Botanic Garden, Edinburgh* 12 : 211 (1920)

G. H. Johnstone in *Asiatic Magnolias in Cultivation*: 53–9 (1955)

Mollicomata – covered with soft hairs, referring to the perules which cover the embryo flower buds also the peduncles or flower stalks.

Plate 19

This Magnolia comes to us from western Yunnan and extreme south-eastern Tibet and has been recognized by botanists as the eastern form of *M. campbellii* a name applied in 1855 to the pink type from the Sikkim Himalayas by J. D. Hooker and T. Thomson in *Flora Indica* 1 : 77 (1855). The species *campbellii* has therefore an elongated Sino-Himalayan distribution along which considerable variation occurs, especially between plants from the two ends of the range. Consequently the Magnolia under discussion should be referred to as *M. campbellii* subsp. *mollicomata* or *M. c. mollicomata*. However, for the purpose of this chapter the author has written *M. mollicomata*, partly for brevity and partly to conform with extracts from the writings of earlier authors.

Plant collector George Forrest discovered this Magnolia in the spring of 1904 on the western flank of the Mekong Valley in Yunnan, flowering in colonies in the more open Abies forest among deep snowdrifts at an altitude of 10,000 ft (3,050 m), with a dense undergrowth of cotoneasters, daphnes, dipeltas, viburnums and woodland rhododendrons.

Forrest wrote: 'I shall always remember my first sight of a group of these magnificent Magnolias in full flower! I got within a mile of them, from which distance the masses of pink blossoms showed up distinctly, but surrounded, as the trees were, by heavy snowdrifts ten to twelve feet in depth, fully a week passed before I could secure specimens, by which time the flowers were almost gone.'

At first the herbarium specimens of this Magnolia were much confused with *M. rostrata*, both by Sir William Wright Smith of the Royal Botanic Garden, Edinburgh, and by Forrest, although there is little or no similarity between these two species. How the confusion originated one can only guess. Maybe he accidentally attributed a flowering specimen of *M. mollicomata* to *M. rostrata* when he and Sir William Wright Smith were classifying his collections in the Edinburgh herbarium.

This probability was confirmed by J. E. Dandy in a letter to the author in which he wrote: '*M. mollicomata* as a species is a myth arising from an extraordinary mistake by W. W. Smith. Although he had complete flowering and fruiting specimens of the plant he, for some reason (possibly he was misled by the collector George Forrest), attributed the flowering specimens to *M. rostrata*, with the result that he described *M. rostrata* as a precocious-flowered species and gardeners for many years anxiously waited for their *M. rostrata* to produce a gorgeous display of flowers which never came! Having thus misdisposed of the flowers, Smith was then left with the fruiting specimens of "mollicomata" which, in the absence of flowers (as he thought), he referred to the wrong group (*Rytidospermum*) and described as a new species. If only he had placed the flowering specimens with the right fruiting specimens in the first place he might well have realized that the species was *M. campbellii*. (Farrer who had collected flowering specimens in Upper Burma, had already suggested that they were *M. campbellii*.) Thus, because of

what was really a ridiculous error, the name *M. mollicomata* came into existence, and once it got into gardens with Forrest's seeds it was there to stay, despite all my efforts to replace it by the correct name *M. campbellii*.'

Forrest contributed the third chapter on 'Magnolias of Yunnan' in J. G. Millais's *Magnolias*: 31–40. Here he repeated this unfortunate mistake in confusing the precocious *M. mollicomata* with the much larger-leaved *M. rostrata* which bears its huge creamy-white flowers after the leaves have fully developed. On page 34 he described correctly the leaves and growth of *M. rostrata* and then continued: 'The flowers appear some time before the foliage' and thence proceeded to describe the flowering and habitat of *M. mollicomata* under *M. rostrata*.

Forrest's expeditions were partly sponsored by that great Cornish gardener, John Charles Williams of Caerhays Castle. It would appear that the identification of these two species was confused by Forrest at the source of his collecting. The author is obliged to Mr. F. Julian Williams for the following notes on the collections of herbarium materials and of seed of this Magnolia by George Forrest which further illustrate the early confusion which existed between these two quite dissimilar species.

'The following are the numbers under which it [*M. mollicomata*] was sent home. Until 1924 it was material for the herbarium only. If seed was sent I see no sign that it was fertile and I am doubtful if any was sent before 1924.

12915. Kari Pass, Mekong-Yangtze Divide, tree of 50–60 ft [15 to 18 m] August 1914.

14466. Flowers pink seen in flower 1905 flowering May/June 1917. [This may have been a pink form of *M. rostrata* on account of the late flowering. Author.]

18790. No records.

24214. A plant came here under this number from Mr. Wilding but it turned out to be *rostrata*. Forrest was sure that 24214 was *mollicomata*. The confusion was made worse because two of our big *mollicomatas* are growing under this number.

24118. J. C. W. grew one of this in the Orchid House. It also seems to have got muddled by the collectors with 24255. To add to the confusion Forrest listed 24118 as being *rostrata*. This has since been corrected.

25075. The seed under this number certainly came here in Forrest's parcel No. 131. It was sent either as small plants or in seed form to Maxwell (Sir Herbert?), Kew, Edinburgh and Exbury. This looks as if it was the first sending of *mollicomata* by J. C.

W. to Kew. Kew's records could well be wrong and should probably read 1924 and not 1914.

26393. Collected May 1925 by G. F. There is a note by G. F. "A magnificent species with extremely large flowers, but only *mollicomata* according to Professor Smith [Sir William Wright Smith]. J. C. W. states that a plant under this number was grown at Caerhays but where it is now or which one it is or how or whence it arrived I do not know.

26524. Very fine, may be only *mollicomata* G. F." '

Enquiries at Kew have since revealed that they have a specimen (Entry 292 – 14 No. 129) which was raised from seed received from J. C. Williams of Caerhays on 15 May 1914. The seed had been collected by Forrest in the Tali Range. There is a tree from this raising in the Berberis Dell at Kew. There is also an entry in the Kew Arboretum Book which reads 'Seed (Forrest 24214) from J. C. Williams received January 8th 1925. Entry No. 1–25. This Magnolia flowered for the first time in the Temperate House, Kew, in February-March 1945.' Here was a *M. mollicomata* which took twenty years to attain florescence when grown under glass.

As already mentioned *M. campbellii* takes not less than a quarter of a century to attain sexual maturity, a state usually reached by *M. mollicomata* in ten to twelve years. The author finds it difficult to reconcile two Magnolias with such widely different life-cycles as being but geographical forms of the same species. This applies likewise to *M. campbellii alba* which was introduced from the same area as the pink *M. campbellii*, on the Sikkim Himalayas near Darjeeling, the shorter life-cycle of which cannot be attributed to a vast difference in geographical origin. It would appear that, however important time may be to planters of Magnolias, it is irrelevant to botanists. For instance, supposing that you decided that you would like to plant a young tree of *M. campbellii*, perhaps after seeing a specimen of the beautiful pink form in flower in one of the great gardens now covenanted to the National Trust: according to the botanical classification a nurseryman might supply you with a seedling of the pale eastern *mollicomata* as *M. campbellii*. The subsequent disappointment when it eventually flowered would scarcely be tempered by the years of waiting for it to attain florescence.

The late George Johnstone wrote in *Asiatic Magnolias in Cultivation*: 53 'Although this subspecies, as we have decided to regard it, may not be sufficiently distinct from the Sikkim subspecies of *M. campbellii* to justify separate specific differentiation, the two, nevertheless, are sufficiently distinct to enable the gardener at any time of the year to recognize adult plants of either one of these two Magnolias when he meets with them growing in our gardens. An attempt is made in this chapter to make clear these differences which may not be apparent in the herbarium specimens upon which the botanist must necessarily base his opinion to a large extent.' In his monograph he recorded many differences between his plants of *M. mollicomata* and *M. campbellii*. At each stage he carefully qualified his findings by stressing that they applied only to the relatively few specimens which he was able to scrutinize closely and that these were only representative of trees growing in the extremes of their natural distribution.

Among the more salient differences which he uncovered were:

1. Shorter stipules hanging from the growing shoots in early summer. These stipules are equivalent to bud scales. They are at first green, later becoming so dark as to appear black when mature. On *M. mollicomata* 4½ in. (11·5 cm) long, on *M. campbellii* 6 in. (15 cm).

2. Flower bud size in January much larger on *M. mollicomata*, about 2½ in. (6 cm) compared with 1½ in. (4 cm) for *M. campbellii*.

3. The pronounced difference in the shape of the flower buds which are bullet shaped on *M. mollicomata* and ovoid on *M. campbellii*. In addition there are longitudinal depressions along the same plane as the perule, caused by the developing leaf or leaves which it enshrouds. These channel-like depressions impart a pinched or wasted appearance to the lower halves of the flower buds.

4. Only one seam is apparent on the perules of *M. mollicomata* while flower buds of *M. campbellii* are enshrouded with perules containing two distinctly raised seams down both sides, along which they subsequently split into even halves before hanging briefly upside-down and falling. Johnstone recorded that the pubescence on the peduncle or flower stalk of *M. mollicomata* is restricted to the last two, or sometimes, three internodes and that it can be observed without difficulty throughout the year after the flowers have fallen and less distinctly throughout the second and third years afterwards. The author has recorded a form on which the internodes are glabrous with collars of dense silky hairs on the four nodes below the pedicle.

5. The author considers that the general shape of the flowers is different. Those of *M. mollicomata* are always of a formal cup-and-saucer shape when fully expanded while one often sees flowers on *M. campbellii* which remain more or less cup shaped, the outer tepals failing to reflex to a horizontal position.

The four inner tepals of *M. mollicomata* tend to form a bulbous dome over the centre of the flower, the tepals bulging apart at the base to admit pollen and pollen-bearing insects from more mature flowers. The four inner tepals of *M. campbellii* are usually clasped in the form of a rosebud, eventually opening at the top as the flower matures.

6. The flowers of *M. mollicomata* open much more rapidly than those of *M. campbellii* once the final covering of the spathaceous bract has split longitudinally to reveal the colour of the tepals. A tree showing colour on just two or three of its flower buds one day can burst into full flower within forty-eight hours.

Californian Magnolia breeder, the late D. Todd Gresham, in the *Morris Arboretum Bulletin* 15 : 30 (1964) wrote: 'From the practical gardener's judgement, *M. campbellii* and *M. mollicomata* are so unlike as to rate individual listing and recommendation in nursery lists. The word "recommendation" will appear more often when *M. mollicomata* clones are propagated and grown in direct competition with the undeniable beauty of *M. campbellii*.'

Let us therefore consider the ways whereby *M. mollicomata* differs from *M. campbellii* apart from the latent factor of early sexual maturity already mentioned. D. Todd Gresham wrote: 'Lateness of flowering appears to be sufficiently constant to constitute a characteristic of *M. mollicomata*.

'Within my experience all plants considered to be *M. mollicomata* have been some shade or tint of a cool fuchsia coloring, in contrast to the warmer rose to crimson coloring of *M. campbellii* forms.

'One character which might prove significant if a sufficient number of specimens could be observed, is the coloring of the surface of the stamens. In all plants selected as *M. mollicomata* the introrse surface of the anthers has no color stripe. Viewed from above the stamen boss appears white.' The author has confirmed this on trees which he has examined.

D. Todd Gresham was a professional plant breeder and botanical draughtsman. Some of his Magnolia breeding is described in the chapter on the 'Gresham Hybrids'.

Although no pure white form of *M. mollicomata* has been reported in cultivation, both George Forrest and Reginald Farrer reported seeing them in the wild. One does occasionally come across a tree bearing flowers with a strange ethereal pallor which have so little colouring as to be difficult to describe. Todd Gresham said it was 'a smooth kid-skin white'.

M. mollicomata tends to form an open, spreading, bushy tree, branching freely from almost ground-level and with less ambition to rocket skyward than *M. campbellii*.

In *Asiatic Magnolias in Cultivation* 57 (1955) Johnstone wrote: 'When these notes were originally compiled the presence of pubescence on the flower branchlets was included in the diagnosis for the identification of subsp. *mollicomata* apart from subsp. *campbellii*. Since then, however, the writer's attention has been drawn to a series of specimens recently collected in Bhutan by Mr. Frank Ludlow and Major George Sherriff and now in the Herbarium of the British Museum (Natural History) labelled *M. campbellii*. . . . These sheets show several flowers with well-defined pubescence on the branchlets on which they are carried, not only on the internodes but in some cases on the peduncles as well.'

The author has recently examined the peduncles of three specimen trees of *M. campbellii* referred to earlier as growing in a triangle on a lawn in the National Trust Garden at Lanhydrock, formerly the seat of the Agar-Robartes family, near Bodmin, Cornwall. These apparently originated from seed since they vary somewhat in depth of colouring and date of beginning to flower. All three show traces of hairs on their peduncles. They are said to have originated as seedlings raised from Himalayan seed at Gill's Nursery, Penryn, Cornwall, but the precise area from which the seed was collected is not on record.

A thorough examination of flowers from six different trees of *M. mollicomata* growing at Caerhays was made by the author on 17 April 1970. These were all in about the same stage of development and several differences were observed. In most examples the peduncle was hairy though in one case the hairs were restricted to the nodes while the internodes were glabrous. In three specimens the pedicle was glabrous though in one of these there was a collar of silky hairs below the tepals. The spathaceous bracts had been shed from all but two of the flowers examined but, of these, one was very hairy and had split down both sides while the other had but few hairs and had split down one side only, remaining attached to the pedicle by a basal collar. In every flower examined the stamens were still entire, and had not begun to split laterally and longitudinally to shed their pollen, while the stigmas appeared receptive and in one case withered. In each case the four inner tepals were forced apart to examine the sexual organs. The flowers were kept in water and the stamens did not begin to dehisce until the inner tepals opened. In some cases there was no sign of pollen shedding until the tepals began to drop and the stamens did not ripen fully until all of the tepals had fallen. The same sequence of development was noticed with flowers which developed normally on the trees but it is just possible that this might vary according to season.

Mr. Julian Williams points out that, at Caerhays, the Magnolia under discussion is represented by three distinct types of tree:

1. With a single main trunk. The oldest specimen F24214 is such a tree.

2. With many trunks arising from the bole close to ground-level.

3. Multi-branched and fastigiate, known as the "Poplar Form". Of course the relative date of flowering of any Magnolia is governed to a great extent by the degree of shelter and amount of exposure to sunlight. At Caerhays in a northerly situation near the top lodge, there is a tree of *M. campbellii* subsp. *mollicomata* which flowers a fortnight later than the others.

There is a fine pale-purple form of *M. mollicomata* at Trengwainton near Penzance (*Magnolias and Camellias Conference Report* 1950) and there is also a good coloured form at Caerhays. The Trengwainton specimen has grown into a large arborescent shrub some 30 ft (9 m) high by as much across with a great ramification of branches at ground-level. While an adjacent tree of *M. campbellii* bursts into full bloom in March, the erectly poised flower buds of this tree appear to remain as yet quite dormant and slender until the final perules have been shed, leaving only the spathaceous bracts. Then they suddenly begin to swell until the expanding tepals cause the bracts to split, whereupon the flowers open with remarkable rapidity so that a tree, which shows only bud colour one day, becomes covered with fully opened blossoms some twenty-four hours later.

There are two sizeable specimens of *M. mollicomata* at Kew, both near the Victoria Gate. At Windsor Great Park, *M. mollicomata* has proved disappointing. Mr. T. H. Findlay reporting on 'Magnolias at Windsor' in the *Journal of the Royal Horticultural Society* 88, 2 : 462 (1963) wrote: 'Although flowering at an early age after planting some ten years ago we have not yet flowered a form with good coloured flowers. Ours have always been of poor colour with no real substance. Trees of thirty feet flower freely every year but cause little comment.' What more could be said to emphasize the necessity for vegetative propagation of selected clones by budding or grafting so that one can plant the 'Cox's Orange' of the species and not a tree raised from one of its pips?

Dr. C. E. Simons, Jr., of Edmonds, Washington, reports that the new leaves of *M. mollicomata* are liable to sun scorch in hot June sunshine which causes

them to blacken and curl. He has observed the same damage on 'Eric Walther', the best of the U.S. crosses between *M. campbellii* and *M. mollicomata*, the mother tree of which is growing in the Golden Gate Park at San Francisco. His two plants of this Magnolia were planted out from 3 gal (13·5 l) containers when 4 to 5 ft (1 to 1·5 m) tall, in situations with some protection.

He suggests that *M. mollicomata* is a cool forest tree, perhaps protected from strong sunlight by constant mist in its native habitat while *M. campbellii* is tolerant of maximum sun exposure without damage. Forrest described *M. mollicomata* as a 'plant of the open forests, growing singly or two or three together, and almost always on the west flanks of those ranges where the monsoon rainfall is greatest.'

Cytologically similar to *M. campbellii*, *M. mollicomata* is a hexaploid with 2n = 114 chromosomes.

The Purple Lanarth Magnolia

MAGNOLIA CAMPBELLII subsp. MOLLICOMATA Lanarth Group

SYN. *M. campbellii* subsp. *mollicomata* convar. *williamsiana* Johnstone

G. H. Johnstone in *Asiatic Magnolias in Cultivation*: 61–4 (1955)

Plates 20–3

Continued use of the name *mollicomata* to distinguish Magnolias of the more rapidly maturing Eastern race of *M. campbellii*, of which this Magnolia is a form, has been vetoed by Dandy. However, after very careful consideration, the author remains of the opinion that it is most desirable, from a horticultural point of view, to retain this name as a means of identifying them from *M. campbellii* subsp. *campbellii*.

This remarkable Magnolia was collected by George Forrest in 1924 in open thickets on the

Salween-Kiu Chiang Divide in north-western Yunnan, China, at an altitude of 10,000 to 11,000 ft (3,050 to 3,350 m). Forrest never set eyes on its sensational purple blossoms, for he appended a note 'Only *M. mollicomata* I think. G. F.'

As far as is known only three seedlings were successfully reared from this seed collection under his number F. 25655 which was sometimes referred to as 'the Magnolia with the telephone number'. The three gardens which sustained these three seedlings in cultivation during the long waiting period before they attained florescence were Lanarth and Werrington in Cornwall, and Borde Hill in Sussex. The Werrington tree was the first to flower in 1941 or 1942 (in 1943 according to Johnstone), followed by the Lanarth specimen in 1947. The Borde Hill seedling (Plate 22), planted in a more exposed situation than the two Cornish ones, grew into a rather stunted tree which died without flowering about 1954 but, fortunately, some grafted plants had been raised from it and these have since flowered. Of these three original trees only that at Lanarth has been used extensively as a seed parent. It has now been proved to breed true to type without producing any obvious variation, either in the distinctive form of the leaves or in the remarkable colour and earliness of the flowers.

Several seedlings raised from this sensational Magnolia, and planted out in the garden at Lanarth, have now reached flowering maturity, and it is gratifying to record that the flower colour of those which have reached this stage is almost identical to that of the mother tree. Whereas the original raising from Forrest's seed took nineteen to twenty-three years, this waiting period has been shorter, varying from sixteen to eighteen years, in spite of the part-time shade in which they were planted. Two of these attained florescence in March 1968, the eighteen-year-old tree bearing one solitary flower, while the sixteen-year-old specimen produced some twenty blossoms at its first display.

The Purple Lanarth Magnolia is very distinct from its botanical relatives in many ways apart from its remarkable colour. In growth it is vigorous and erect to the point of being fastigiate, a character more pronounced than the so-called "Poplar Form" of *mollicomata* at Caerhays. The bark is of a light golden-brown colour and the wood is much softer than that of other Magnolias. Our propagator once described it as 'rather like cutting into hard cheese'. The leaves too are distinctive, with deep veining which imparts a rugose or puckered upper surface. Those of the Lanarth tree are oblong obovate, being broader towards the apex than the base and rounded

rather like the base of a cello. Some leaves have a small mucro or drip-tip.

The flower buds are much larger and fatter than those of *mollicomata* with up to four densely woolly internodes in addition to the pedicle, which is very stout and likewise covered with short woolly hairs. If this pedicle is cut through diametrically it is found to have an almost square cross-section with rounded corners while that of related Magnolias similarly treated has been found to be more or less circular.

The growth buds, which are exposed when the perules enshrouding the great flower buds are shed, are covered with silky down. The spathaceous bract, which represents the final covering to the flower bud, is densely hairy and splits down one side only, to hang inverted beneath the opening flower like a dormant bat. When held up to the light it becomes a semi-transparent membrane, coloured bronze pink with a greenish midrib, the entire outer surface being densely coated with pale silky hairs. The spathaceous bracts on most trees of subspecies *mollicomata*, split evenly down both sides of the flower buds (see Johnstone).

The great flowers are upward-facing with twelve to fourteen tepals, the four inner ones remaining in the form of a dome or cone over the gynandrophore while the remainder reflex to form a saucer to produce the cup-and-saucer flower shape which is typical of *mollicomata*. The inner four unfurl later to reveal the stigmatic column and boss of stout purple filaments, tipped with slender creamy-white anthers. Flowers of the Lanarth tree have pale greenish-yellow stigmatic columns with purple stigmas matching the stamen filaments and tepals. Johnstone in *Asiatic Magnolias in Cultivation*: 63 recorded that the stigmatic column in flowers from the Werrington tree of this Magnolia was purple but the immature carpels may have been completely masked by the purple stigmas.

The precise colour of the flowers is difficult to define and seems to vary somewhat according to their age and the light intensity and direction. The earlier-opening buds are, in cool weather, of the most incredible violet-red colour, but this rapidly fades to dark lilac-purple (R.H.S. Colour Chart 031/1). When fully open they are about 9 in. (23 cm) across.

The Lanarth tree is the only one which has been extensively propagated. It has been drawn up by proximity to adjacent trees and has now reached a height of about 70 ft (21·5 m), with a clear trunk for about half its height. At one time it was badly overcrowded which probably caused it to lose its lower branches. A *M. sargentiana* var. *robusta* which grew close by was successfully replanted well clear of the site by the late M. P. Williams. In some years the Purple Lanarth Magnolia has borne heavy crops of fertile fruit cones and all of its seed-raised progeny have been of typical growth and foliage.

The cultivar name 'Lanarth' may be only applied to grafted plants or to those raised by other vegetative means, such as layering, either directly from the mother tree or from its vegetatively propagated descendants. The correct designation for such clonal plants is *M. campbellii* subsp. *mollicomata* 'Lanarth'.

This Purple Lanarth Magnolia has grown much taller than any specimen of *mollicomata* known to the author and its seedling progeny at Lanarth are growing with exceptional vigour. As is usual with these tree Magnolias, the first flowers are at the tips of the topmost shoots and are therefore out of reach for close examination and, even with the help of binoculars, one can only examine the underneath of the flowers. It will be several seasons before flowers are borne low enough for close inspection as the upper branches are too slender and brittle to support an extension ladder, so the only alternatives are to mutilate the tree by removing a whole branch or to shoot down a flower with a ·22 rifle.

Surely this disadvantage is another point in favour of grafted plants, since these usually have a greatly reduced vigour and begin to flower before becoming excessively tall, very soon flowering overall from almost ground-level upward.

A grafted tree of this Magnolia (Plate 23), which was planted in very wet ground at Lanarth, had not exceeded 15 ft (4·5 m) in twenty years, while a tree from the same propagation planted at Trengwainton, has grown into an erect tree some 25 ft (7·5 m) tall with a branch spread of only 8 ft (2·5 m) by 1972. Both of them are well branched and, covered with flowers from ground-level upwards, are a truly incredible sight in late March and April when the eye has been starved of colour by the drabness of winter.

In common with the more pallid Chinese form of *M. campbellii* subsp. *mollicomata*, young grafted plants sent by transpolar flight from London to Seattle in November 1969 suffered badly from an unseasonable heat-wave in late May 1971 when the thermometer in the garden of Dr. C. E. Simons, Jr., at Edmonds, Washington, rose to 94 °F. (34·4 °C.). Plants of the pink Western (Indian) type withstood the heat without damage to their immature foliage, as did *M. sargentiana* var. *robusta*.

Cytologically the same as *M. campbellii*, this Magnolia is a hexaploid with 2n = 114 chromosomes.

Dawson's Magnolia

MAGNOLIA DAWSONIANA Rehder & Wilson

A. Rehder & E. H. Wilson in Sargent, *Plantae Wilsonianae* I : 397 (1913)
J. E. Dandy in *Curtis's Botanical Magazine* 164 : t. 9678–9 (1948)
G. H. Johnstone in *Asiatic Magnolias in Cultivation*: 65–7 (1955)
S. A. Spongberg in *Journal of the Arnold Arboretum* 57, 3 : 289–90 (1976)

Plate 24

This Magnolia was discovered by that great botanical explorer Ernest Henry Wilson in 1908, during his third Chinese expedition (1907–9), which was sponsored by the Arnold Arboretum of Harvard University. He found it in only one locality near Tatsien-lu, now Kanting, eastern Sikang (then in western Szechwan, now Kansu), growing at an altitude between 6,500 and 7,500 ft (1,980 to 2,300 m). The tree which he discovered was in fruit, so he sent back seeds and made a second collection when he returned to the site on his fourth expedition in 1910–11.

(The author has endeavoured to up-date some of the Chinese place-names, of localities where Wilson made his important collections, which led to the introduction of so many hitherto unknown Magnolias. In several instances even the Royal Geographical Society has been unable to verify them. It would appear that much of the area which Wilson visited has never been surveyed in detail and, in consequence, large-scale maps do not exist in the West.)

No flower of this Magnolia had been observed by botanists but in 1913 Wilson, in collaboration with Dr. Alfred Rehder, described it as a new species, naming it in honour of Jackson T. Dawson, first Superintendent of the Arnold Arboretum, at Jamaica Plain, Boston, Massachusetts, and Prof. Sargent's chief assistant in its foundation.

Likewise no trees had been observed during the winter months and they suggested that the leaves might be persistent (i.e. the species could prove to be evergreen), but cultivation has since shown that they are deciduous as in all allied species. The leaves are dark green and glossy with a leathery texture, which no doubt led to this supposition.

M. dawsoniana is likely to be confused only with *M. sargentiana*, for the flowers of these two Magnolias are very similar, apart from the smaller number of tepals which usually is nine, though occasionally ten or eleven, whereas *M. sargentiana* has twelve to fourteen. They are, however, much more freely produced for, when *M. dawsoniana* reaches maturity, it becomes covered with flowers from the topmost branches downwards, especially when growing in an open, sunny situation. It often flowers later than other precocious Magnolias and the flower buds retain their protecting perules for a longer period, often retaining two or three into March whereas, according to Johnstone, *M. sargentiana* tends to shed most of its perules by midwinter, though this course of events may vary from season to season.

M. dawsoniana grows into a dense twiggy tree with slender light-grey branches which become darker with age. It takes some twenty years to flower from seed and the flowers are but sparsely produced at first, always high up and frustratingly out of reach, but each year they tend to be more prolific and spread down the tree.

The original seedlings were raised in the Arnold Arboretum's nursery and, in 1913, they were sent with the rest of Wilson's Magnolias to Léon Chenault's nurseries at Orléans, France. He apparently was, or had, a propagator skilled in grafting Magnolias. Such a factor must have greatly influenced the Arboretum's Director, Prof. Charles Sargent, for it was a very bold step which he took, and fortunately it worked satisfactorily.

Grafted plants were supplied to several of the milder gardens in the British Isles by Chenault in 1919. *M. dawsoniana* is believed to have first flowered at Rowallane, Co. Down, Northern Ireland, in about 1932 or 1933, and at Lanarth, St. Keverne, Cornwall, in 1936. In 1947 the late P. D. Williams reported that the Lanarth tree must have had at least 5,000 flowers, but that it had never been observed to set any seed. Apparently individual trees of *M. dawsoniana* share with many other Magnolias a pronounced incompatibility with their own pollen, or is this phenomenon due to the absence of pollinating beetles at the critical period of anthesis?

Apart from the fact that they are borne freely all over the tree right down to eye-level, the flowers of *M. dawsoniana* are almost impossible to distinguish from *M. sargentiana* when at their best. Johnstone in *Camellias and Magnolias Conference Report* (1950), suggested that *M. sargentiana* might be a natural hybrid of *M. dawsoniana*. *M. sargentiana* has conspicuous, elongated lenticels, while those of *M. dawsoniana* are inconspicuous.

Dr. Stephen Spongberg refers to the manner whereby *M. dawsoniana* differs from *M. sargentiana* 'in the essentially glabrous undersurfaces of its more strongly reticulated leaves, in its flowers with fewer tepals, in its usual shrublike habit, and in the different structure at the base of the inner seed coats . . . the inner black seed coat having a basal pore surrounding a small stalk'.

Johnstone in *Asiatic Magnolias in Cultivation*: 66 described how the branchlets bearing the flower buds bend over until they are almost horizontal as these develop. The spathaceous bract then starts to rupture down one side, but the protruding tepals are prevented from unfolding fully until the bract splits open completely. Thereupon the tepals of the outer whorl begin to open and allow the inner ones to part at their tips to form a funnel exposing the gynoecium, the stigmas of which are, at this stage, receptive to pollination, while the immature stamens are still enclosed in the base of the opening flower. The bract continues to split and eventually falls away, the flower then usually becoming fully pendent, whereupon the eight outer tepals begin to curl back, the inner four remaining furled in a slender cone. Then these reflex likewise before appearing to collapse and hang limply downwards to expose the gynandrophore.

The mature flowers have a rather ragged appearance because the tepals recurve outwards and downwards and this, combined with their horizontal-to-nodding poise, makes them become floppy when they lose their turgidity. They also tend to conceal their coloured backs and display mainly the inner surface which is white, faintly tinted lilac or mauve. The tree is most spectacular when the long slender flower buds begin to show colour as the spathaceous bracts gradually split down their seams to release the tips of the tepals in the manner already described.

In 1971 the largest tree at Caerhays measured 54 ft (15·5 m) with a trunk girth of 5½ ft (1·5 m) at 3 ft (91 cm).

M. dawsoniana was planted at Birr Castle in Co. Offaly, Ireland, by Lord Rosse in 1946 and flowered first there in 1961, attaining a height of over 30 ft (9 m) in twenty years. It is skilfully sited against a background of golden Monterey cypresses (*Cupressus macrocarpa* 'Lutea'). It proved to be a faster grower than either *M. campbellii* or its subspecies *mollicomata*.

There is a considerable number of trees of *M. dawsoniana* in the Gardens at Windsor Great Park. They are conspicuous in the summer on account of their dark-green, leathery leaves and rounded bushy habit when grown in open situations. A seed-raised tree of *M. dawsoniana* first flowered there in 1962, when almost 30 ft (9 m) high with a spread of 20 ft (6 m), while at Newby Hall, near Ripon, Yorkshire, a tree planted in 1952 flowered for the first time in 1971 when more than 20 ft (6 m) tall.

A tree of *M. dawsoniana* in Mr. Nigel Holman's Magnolia collection, at Chyverton near Truro, produced its first flowers in 1967 at the age of twenty-three years. These opened very late in April, the backs of the tepals being a startling bright crimson, the colour showing through to the white upper surfaces. The stamen bosses are deep crimson and the green stigmatic columns have crimson styles. *M. dawsoniana* 'Chyverton' (Plate 24) will be worth travelling a long way to see when it starts to flower more freely in a few years' time, and is likely to be a much-sought-after clone. Unfortunately this crimson colouring has since varied considerably from season to season and is most pronounced in colder weather. The flowers have as many as eleven tepals.

James Gossler of Oregon reported in the *Newsletter of the American Magnolia Society* 4, 2 : 5 (1967) that grafted trees of *M. dawsoniana* started to bloom ten years from the grafting, providing fifteen blossoms when 10 ft (3 m) tall. Another specimen, a few years older, produced 200 blossoms in its second year of flowering. Gossler points out that *M. dawsoniana* is inclined to form several leaders, with crossing side branches which become overcrowded, and some of them are liable to be affected by die-back if the tree is not pruned.

James Gossler's testimony confirms the author's theory that grafted plants not only tend to flower in about half the time taken by those raised from seed, but that they also come quickly into more prolific blooming once they attain florescence.

In common with other members of Section *Yulania*, *M. dawsoniana* is a hexaploid with 2n = 114 chromosomes.

Sargent's Magnolia

MAGNOLIA SARGENTIANA Rehder & Wilson

A. Rehder & E. H. Wilson in Sargent, *Plantae Wilsonianae* I : 398 (1913)

J. G. Millais in *Magnolias*: 215 (1927)

J. E. Dandy in *Curtis's Botanical Magazine* 164 : t. 9678–9 (1948)

G. H. Johnstone in *Asiatic Magnolias in Cultivation*: 69–72 (1955)

S. A. Spongberg in *Journal of the Arnold Arboretum* 57, 3 : 288–9 (1976)

This species forms a tall, erect tree with slender whippy branches, taking many years to reach flowering maturity when raised from seed. Dr. E. H. Wilson discovered and introduced this Magnolia, which grows to a greater size than any other Chinese species.

In a letter to J. G. Millais in *Magnolias*: 217, Wilson gave a fascinating description of his discovery of this species which reads: 'This Magnolia grows to a greater size than any other Chinese Magnolia and is one of the noblest of its family. I have a vivid recollection of seeing, in June 1903 at Yin-Kou, a hamlet 6 miles [9·6 km] west of Wa-shan, a tree of this species which was more than 80 ft [24·4 m] tall, with a trunk 10 ft [25·5 m] in girth 6 ft [2 m] from the ground, and clean for 16 ft [5 m] where the branches commenced. The branches were very numerous, wide spreading, forming a massive head, flattened oval in contour. In 1908 a special journey for the purpose of photographing this tree was undertaken, but it had been cut down. This was the largest specimen I ever met with, but examples 45 to 60 ft [13·5 to 18 m] tall and 6 to 8 ft [2 to 2·5m] in girth are (or were in 1908) fairly common west of Wa-shan.'

It would appear that Wilson never saw this Magnolia in flower for he continued: 'The Chinese informed us that the flowers were rosy-red to rose-pink in colour and about 8 in. [20·5 cm] across. From the size of the peduncles and of the scars left by the fallen sepals and petals there is a good reason to believe that the size of the flowers must be very large; and undoubtedly this Magnolia vies with *M. campbellii*, Hooker & Thomson, in beauty.'

A flowering specimen was collected in 1939 by the Chinese botanist C. L. Sun on Omei Shan, about thirty miles east of Wilson's seed collection.

Mount Omei (Omei Shan) is an enormous outcrop of hard limestone with a flattened top 11,000 ft (3,350 m) above sea level and 9,700 ft (2,950 m) above the surrounding Szechwan countryside. It is about 25 m (40 km) north-east of Wa Shan (or Mount Wa) and near the large city of Kiating. Wilson wrote 'upwards of seventy Buddhist temples and monasteries are to be found on this mountain, with upwards of two thousand priests and acolytes. The whole mountain is, or rather was, church property, and only the land on the lower slopes, suitable for cultivation, has been sold.' The surrounding countryside is relatively densely populated —overall average of 365 persons per square mile (2·5 sq km) increasing to 1,610 in the farmlands.

M. sargentiana flowers somewhat sparsely at first, but in subsequent years the blossoms increase in size, up to 8 in. (20·5 cm) in diameter, as well as in quantity. The tepals average twelve in number, fourteen being exceptional, the inner ones being somewhat longer than those in the outer whorl. The poise of the flowers varies considerably on the same tree, some opening upright, others nodding horizontally and later hanging inverted, to display their full beauty when viewed from below, often subsequently returning to an upright position. The flower colour varies considerably from tree to tree, as it does on *M. sargentiana* var. *robusta*, while the leaves are usually smaller and paler, as well as being rounder and abruptly pointed at the apex, sometimes emarginate. Their undersides are covered with fine greyish pubescence.

The flower buds of *M. sargentiana* are smaller and more ovoid than those of *M. sargentiana* var. *robusta*. The perules are more densely clad with grey-green hairs and have seams down one side only, while those of var. *robusta* have seams down two sides. Soon after opening, the outer strap-like tepals hang downwards, then the inner tepals curl upwards then outwards to reveal the long and slender green stigmatic column surrounded by a fringe of erect, purple-backed stamens. The peduncle is pubescent.

At Caerhays it flowers later than other Magnolias of its type, the original tree having blossoms of a deeper pink than those of *M. sprengeri* 'Diva'.

The flowers most closely resemble those of *M. dawsoniana* except that the tepals of that species are shorter, narrower and fewer in number, usually varying from nine to ten, two less than the average for *M. sargentiana*.

Stand a mature blossom vertically in water, so that the long narrow tepals reflex, and you will see a remarkable likeness to a greatly enlarged pink form of *M. stellata* with but twelve tepals.

Johnstone reported that the flower buds appear to be more susceptible to frost damage than those of similar species and suggested that this is because they tend to shed two of their three hairy perules in autumn, leaving only one to protect the developing bud during winter. By mid January many of the buds have shed their remaining perules, leaving them protected only by their spathaceous bracts, which become tough and are pubescent with grey matted hairs. The fruit cones are stout and elongated with congested, beaked carpels.

M. sargentiana was one of Wilson's discoveries of 1903, and he first collected seed on a subsequent expedition in 1908. It was raised at the Arnold Arboretum in 1909 and named after the Director, Prof. Charles S. Sargent. When it was found that the young trees were not hardy enough to withstand the Boston climate, Sargent sent them all to France to Chenault's nurseries at Orléans. On 3 July 1913, Sargent wrote to Chenault: 'I want to consult you about Wilson's Chinese Magnolias. We have now only a few plants of these, and in their young state, at least, they are not hardy and we have been obliged to take them up in the autumn and keep them in a pit during the winter. . . . What I would like to do would be to send to you this autumn the entire stock of these plants with the understanding that you would propagate them as largely as possible, and then after you have got up a stock of them, return to us a couple of plants of each species, reserving the others for yourself. Some of these plants have been sent to Kew but I don't think that any one else in Europe has them and . . . Kew hasn't the whole collection.'

On 17 November 1913 there is a note to Chenault in Sargent's hand that 'We sent you our whole stock of the new Chinese Magnolias.'

The Arnold Arboretum received a grafted plant of *M. sargentiana* from Chenault in 1915. It is not now known how many seedlings there were of each species from which scions were taken for grafting for subsequent distribution. Other species in the consignment included *M. dawsoniana*, *M. sargentiana* var. *robusta*, *M. sinensis* and *M. wilsonii*. Apparently Chenault decided to distribute some of the Wilson seedling Magnolias before embarking on their propagation for, according to the Kew records (Entry No. 616·13), they received from him on 27 November 1913 one plant each of *M. sargentiana*, *M. sargentiana* var. *robusta* and *M. wilsonii*. Five years later on 29 December 1918 (Entry No. 298·19) is recorded the arrival from Chenault of two plants each (presumably grafted)of *M. dawsoniana*, *M. sargentiana* and *M. nicholsoniana* (*M. sinensis*).

The Arboretum's first distribution of seedlings of Wilson's Chinese Magnolias appears to have been in the autumn of 1911. In the records of the Royal Botanic Gardens, Kew, Entry No. 639·11 reads: 'December 18th 1911. Plants from Arnold Arboretum

1. *Magnolia wilsonii*

2. *Magnolia* sp. nov. 923 – later identified as *M. sargentiana* (died 1917)

3. *Magnolia* sp. nov. 914 – later identified as *M. sargentiana* (died 1917)

Seed of *M. sargentiana* was first collected by Wilson on Mount Wa in 1908 and one of his photographs shows a large specimen growing on the open mountain-side. He recorded that it was not uncommon in thickets and woods. It has been reported westward on the borders of western Szechwan (Mount Omei), in eastern Kansu (Sikang) and north Yunnan at altitudes between 5,300 and 6,600 ft (1,610 and 2,010 m). The herbarium type specimen is his No. 914 from Tsai-erh-ti, some 30 miles (48 km) west of Mount Wa at an altitude of 6,000 ft (1,830 m).

Wilson's third and fourth expeditions to China were sponsored by the Arnold Arboretum of Harvard University. The author is indebted to the Director, Richard A. Howard, for permission to publish the extracts from his predecessor's correspondence with Chenault, also to Miss Stephanie Sutton, then of his staff, who was working on a biography of Charles Sargent.

Today the Orléans nursery, founded by Léon Chenault in 1884, trades under the name Grandes Roseraies du Val de Loire and is the largest producer of roses in France. They no longer grow any of

Wilson's Magnolias nor do they know of any specimen trees in France.

At Caerhays, *M. sargentiana* is usually the last of the great Asian tree Magnolias to come into flower, often as late as the latter half of April. It also has about the deepest-coloured flowers, the backs of the tepals being almost crimson. The largest tree, planted in 1921, was 50 ft (15 m) high in 1966.

Although the perules enclosing the flower buds may be seamed down one side only, those which the author has examined have split into halves and are much less hairy than on most other precocious kinds. One flower examined had the usual twelve tepals plus one tepaloid stamen. This was much longer and broader than the normal stamens which are at first in a tight erect cluster clasping the base of the gynoecium.

The deep colouring on the backs of the tepals shades through to their upper or inner surfaces which are consequently more pink than white. Both pedicle and peduncle appear to be glabrous or devoid of hairs but are found to be downy when examined with a lens. The bark is strongly aromatic.

One wonders if this Magnolia will flower more freely if grafted on to a slow-growing stock and planted in a hot sunny situation; but it should be borne in mind that the tree referred to probably originated as a grafted plant.

In contrast to the late flowering of the Caerhays mother tree referred to, a seedling from it which was planted in the angle of the south-facing front wall of Mr. Nigel Holman's house at Chyverton, Zelah, near Truro, comes into flower very early and has much paler tepals.

Apparently *M. sargentiana* first flowered at Nymans, Sussex, in 1932 and this received an F.C.C. when exhibited at an R.H.S. Show in 1935. It is recorded in W. J. Bean's *Trees & Shrubs Hardy in the British Isles* Ed. 8, 2 : 663 (1973) that, when sending material from this tree to Kew in 1943 James Comber, the garden manager, wrote that it was 'a seedling raised by J. Nix, Esq., from Wilson's seed and given to me when visiting Tilgate'. If this is true the tree, which is growing in the Walled Garden, must be one of the few in this country raised directly from wild seed.

Cytologically *M. sargentiana* is a hexaploid with 2n = 114 chromosomes.

Robust Magnolia

MAGNOLIA SARGENTIANA var.
ROBUSTA Rehder & Wilson

A. Rehder & E. H. Wilson in Sargent, *Plantae
  Wilsonianae* 1 : 399 (1913)
G. H. Johnstone in *Asiatic Magnolias in Cultivation*:
  73–7 (1955)
Plates 25, 26 and 27

Wilson did not see this Magnolia in flower when he
discovered it in woodland and open country on
Mount Wa, in western Szechwan, China, at an
altitude of 7,600 ft (2,310 m). In 1913 it was described
by Rehder and Wilson from a dried foliar and
fruiting herbarium specimen (No. 923a).

Had Rehder and Wilson proposed a specific relationship between *M. sargentiana* and *M. dawsoniana*
it is doubtful whether such a classification would be
disputed for in many ways those two Magnolias have
so much in common that they may be readily confused. But to the plantsman the Magnolia under
consideration here is distinct in many ways from
M. sargentiana of which it is claimed to be but a form.

In correspondence with the author, J. E. Dandy
wrote: 'As to *M. sargentiana*; this was described
from only two or three of Wilson's plants, one of
which was distinguished as var. *robusta*. I have since
seen quite a number of other specimens, from both
W. Szechwan and N. Yunnan, and cannot accept
that this single plant (from which all the cultivated
plants are derived) represents a botanical taxon.
Furthermore the var. *robusta* was found growing in
the same area as typical *M. sargentiana* and I know of
no case where two closely related *Magnolia* taxa
inhabit the same area.'

Concerning the closer similarity of *M. dawsoniana*
and *M. sargentiana* he wrote: 'I confess that I have
never been happy that these should have been
described as separate species. *M. sargentiana*, *M.
sargentiana* 'robusta' and *M. dawsoniana* certainly
form one complex growing in the same area of

west China. As they were all based on only one or
two trees it is difficult to decide whether more than
one species is involved; such a decision could only
be made after studying the total population in the
field – and that is scarcely practicable at present.'

M. sargentiana var. *robusta* grows into a large
arborescent shrub, branching freely from the base
unless forced by early pruning to form a clear trunk.
The smooth bark is of a light yellowish-grey colour
with occasional fissures on older specimens. The
young shoots are greenish yellow ageing to grey. A
mature specimen may attain a height of 40 ft (12 m)
with an even greater spread, but the tree flowers at a
relatively early age from seed (twelve years) and
can be readily restricted if desired, so would-be
planters should not be deterred by the dimensions
given.

The deciduous leaves are tapering and slender,
shortly oblong lanceolate, on adult trees usually
emarginate or notched at the tips and occasionally
acuminate. They average 5½ to 8 in. (14 to 20·5 cm)
in length by 2¼ to 3¼ in. (5·5 to 8 cm) in width at
their widest point, which is two-thirds of their
length from their base. The flower buds are protected by four or five hairy perules which are
gradually shed until only the spathaceous bract
remains to protect the expanding tepals. The flowers
are nodding and precocious, opening well in advance
of the leaves. They are very large, sometimes as much
as 12 in. (30·5 cm) across with twelve to sixteen
broad, overlapping tepals, which are white, flushed
mauve pink, sometimes lilac purple on the outside
and towards their base.

This Magnolia is certainly one of the most spectacular plants which can be grown in the open in our
gardens. The flowers present an informal and almost
ragged appearance because they open in a nodding
position as though bending over through their sheer
weight. Consequently the long tepals form an
asymmetrical shape so that, when the flowers have
fully expanded, one can almost imagine the whole
tree being adorned with clusters of Tibetan prayer
flags. Mature trees sometimes flower so profusely
that they form no flower buds the following season.
From the author's observations this tendency to
biennial flowering is restricted to mature trees and is
not related to weather conditions nor to the amount
of fruit cones produced in the previous summer.

As already mentioned, the introduction to our
gardens was in the form of grafted plants propagated
at Chenault's nursery, Orléans, from seedling trees
sent there from the Arnold Arboretum in 1913. It
was reported to have flowered in France by 1923.
Johnstone recorded that one of the two original

Caerhays trees first flowered in 1931. In his contribution of the chapter on Magnolias in W. Arnold-Forster's *Trees and Shrubs for the Milder Counties* (1948) he wrote: '13.4.31. I was privileged today to see *Magnolia sargentiana robusta* flowering at Caerhays for the first time in this country. I do not hesitate to say that it is the most beautiful of all the Magnolias I have yet seen in flower. The flowers, formed with twelve tepals, are semi-pendulous at the ends of the spreading branches, and in size appear to be about 8 to 12 in. [20·5 to 30·5 cm] in diameter, in colour pale rose-purple shading to pale pink at the tips. Looking up into the blooms, they appear like open parachutes of coloured paper, their beauty accentuated by black scales of unopened or partly opened buds.' Johnstone recorded this impression on returning to his home at Trewithen after a visit to Caerhays at the urgent invitation of J. C. Williams. Sights such as he had just witnessed have since become regular spring spectacles in many other gardens, not only in Cornwall and in other parts of the British Isles but in other countries where such Asian Magnolias can be grown.

It is not known what understocks Chenault used, but this tree apparently took some seventeen years to attain florescence, and the second tree somewhat longer. It would therefore seem likely that they were on a slower-maturing stock of a species which normally takes twenty years or more to flower, since seedlings have since flowered at about twelve years of age.

A comparison made by the author in mid April 1970 between flowers of these two original trees at Caerhays showed sufficient minor differences to indicate that they were not propagated from the same original seedling. Referring to them as Clones A and B respectively, Clone A had twelve large, heavy-textured tepals measuring 6 by 3¼ in. (15 by 8 cm) and the peduncle below the flower was pubescent. The deep lilac-purple stamens were somewhat irregular in length and had not yet splayed out into their mature position prior to shedding their pollen. The stigmas were already receptive.

The flower of Clone B had eleven narrower and less substantial tepals, the inner four averaging 4½ by 2 in. (11·5 by 5 cm). The deep fuchsia-purple stamens were still in a tight erect bunch at the base of the stigmatic column, which had curled, pale-mauve styles in receptive condition, arising from light-green carpels. The bark of both trees is faintly aromatic. The flowers were matured in water and the stamens dehisced to shed their pollen after the tepals had fully expanded.

A detailed examination of a flower of a seed-raised specimen of *M. sargentiana* var. *robusta* showed that the spathaceous bract is a dark-greyish brown and densely covered with long silky indumentum. It splits down one side only.

The twelve heavy-textured tepals have raised midribs running down their backs. The inner four are usually broader and shorter than the eight which are first to reflex. The edges of these four inner tepals reflex outwards, so that they form rigid and sometimes slab-shaped guards around the sexual organs. The long purple-backed stamens are splayed in a hemisphere, from the centre of which protrudes the dark-green column of the gynoecium, swathed with long curling purple styles already in a receptive condition.

In artificial light the surfaces of the tepals glisten, as if they were frozen, or dusted with a very fine artificial powdered glitter of the type used on Christmas decorations.

The short, stout pedicle, or peduncle-node immediately below the flower, is densely covered with adpressed silky hairs which almost mask the elongated white lenticels. The three nodes of the peduncle beneath the foot of the pedicle are also covered with silky indumentum, particularly the topmost one which adjoins the pedicle. The flowers emit a heavy spicy fragrance, especially at night, and the stamens do not dehisce to shed their pollen until after the stigmas have withered and the tepals have fully reflexed.

All the flowers examined from different trees had pubescent peduncles or flower stalks, but the Caerhays Pale Form (Plate 26) appeared unique in being glabrous on the node immediately beneath the tepals. The flower of this form is very beautiful when the tepals reflex to display the large purple boss of the androecium.

Let us now consider the features which distinguish this Magnolia from *M. sargentiana*. Both were discovered by Wilson on Mount Wa in western Szechwan. There appears to have been only one collecting of *M. sargentiana* var. *robusta*, under Wilson's No. 923a, whereas *M. sargentiana* was also found by him 30 miles (48 km) west at Tsai-erh-ti, and later by C. L. Sun on Mount Omei (Omei Shan) in western Szechwan, and by E. E. Maire in northern Yunnan.

	M. sargentiana var. robusta	M. sargentiana
Habit	A spreading bushy tree with stout branches ramifying freely from the base of the bole.	A tall slender tree up to 80 ft (24·5 m) with whippy branches. Trunk smooth, light grey, later yellow-brown, becoming fissured on older specimens.
Young shoots	Stout, apple green turning yellowish brown, and later ash grey.	Slender and darker in colour.
Leaves	Oblong obovate, usually emarginate at apex on adult trees, 5½ to 8 in. (14 to 20·5 cm) long by 2¼ to 3¼ in. (5·5 to 8 cm) wide. Generally longer and narrower than those of M. sargentiana.	Obovate, 6 by 2½ in. (15 by 6 cm) across though sometimes much broader, occasionally emarginate at tip. Smaller and paler green than those of robusta, being rounder and more abruptly pointed at the apex.
Flower buds	Prolifically produced right down to ground-level. Large and curved with inner perules seamed down both sides, four or five in number, shed at intervals from December onwards.	Sparsely produced and usually high up. Smaller and more symmetrically ovoid. Perules densely pubescent, seamed down both sides and shed prematurely, often leaving only the spathaceous bract to protect the embryo flower.
Flowers	Very large and freely produced, 9 to 12 in. (23 to 30·5 cm) across with ten to sixteen broad tepals, without tendency to curl when fully expanded. Poise nodding.	Smaller, with ten to fourteen narrow tepals, up to 8 in. (20·5 cm) in diameter when full expanded. Outer tepals curled. Poise varying from erect to pendent.
Fruit cones	Large, stout, oblong 7 to 8 in. (18 to 20·5 cm). Seeds scarlet about ½ in. (12 mm) long, slightly grooved.	Slender and elongated with congested, beaked carpels 5 in. (12·5 cm) long, red turning purple, usually contorted. Seeds bright orange, usually one per carpel, of unpleasant odour.
Seedlings	Flower at eleven to fifteen years.	Take about twenty-five years to attain florescence.

The author's theory that grafting tends to reduce the vigour of a Magnolia, irrespective of the understock, is borne out by the fact that seed-raised trees of *M. sargentiana* var. *robusta* at Caerhays have grown more vigorously than their grafted parents.

This Magnolia is remarkably wind tolerant for such a large-leaved tree. The heavily textured flowers also stand up to a lot of wind buffeting. There is a fine specimen of this Magnolia growing in an open and elevated situation in Sir Giles Loder's garden at Leonardslee near Horsham in Sussex. Another, at Windsor Great Park, was also quite unaffected by the arctic winter of 1962–3 where it is regarded as one of the best of the tree species. It first flowered there in 1958.

It has been said that there are exceptions to every rule and it may well be that, when botanists of the future have an opportunity to re-examine this Magnolia in its native environment, they may decide that it is a distinct species. One would expect that, had the solitary parent tree of var. *robusta*, from which Wilson collected his seed sample No. 923a, been an unusual form of *M. sargentiana*, as is suggested by Rehder's naming, then a percentage of its progeny would have resembled that type. There is no evidence that this has been the case. At Caerhays there are several trees which have been raised from seed saved from the two original grafted specimens and also many second-generation seedlings. No instance of reversion to the type species *M. sargentiana* has been observed. Mr. F. Julian Williams in 'Notes on the Caerhays Gardens' in the *Journal of the Cornwall Garden Society* 8 : 13 (1965) reported that these seedlings took from eleven to fifteen years to flower.

Several white-flowered seedlings have been raised at Caerhays (Plate 27, *M. sargentiana* var. *robusta alba*). It is probable that at least a proportion of their progeny will resemble them when they attain florescence.

In *Asiatic Magnolias in Cultivation*: 73, Johnstone wrote of *M. sargentiana* var. *robusta*: 'The differing characteristics noted below have led the writer of these notes to the opinion that specific rank should be accorded to this Magnolia, instead of regarding it as no more than a variant of *M. sargentiana*, and thus it appeared in these notes as they were originally written.

'However, although the writer, and several of those who like him have had the advantage of studying cultivated examples of these two Magnolias, are of this opinion, it is not shared by the members of the Botanical Department of the British Museum concerned, at whose insistent representation the Council of the R.H.S. have desired alteration of the text to conform to the classification of Rehder and Wilson.

'The establishment of a new species on such evidence as is available in this case either to those who work on dried specimens, or with living examples growing in our gardens, is not a matter on which either horticulturist or herbarium botanists can afford to be dogmatic, for which reason the author has felt obliged to defer to the wishes of the Council, but he retains his opinion that when a further range of specimens of these two Magnolias is available to us from their native habitat it is likely that the difference between them will be incontrovertibly accepted by both sections as being specific.'

Johnstone's monograph has been long out of print and the author, being in full agreement with what he wrote, makes no apology for quoting him so extensively. This unfortunate difference of opinion between plantsmen and botanists remains and is likely to continue until botanical research becomes possible once more in China.

Cytologically this Magnolia is a hexaploid with 2n = 114 chromosomes.

Sprenger's Magnolia
Mu-pi in Hupeh

MAGNOLIA SPRENGERI Pampanini

Commemorating Carl L. Sprenger (1846–1917), a German nurseryman in the Italian town of Vomero.

R. Pampanini in *Nuovo Giornale Botanico Italiano* 22 : 295 (1915)

G. H. Johnstone in *Asiatic Magnolias in Cultivation*: 79–82 (1955)

It is with considerable trepidation that the author embarks on this chapter, for there has been much confusion among botanists as to the identification and classification of the two or more distinct types of Magnolia which are at present included within this species.

The name *M. sprengeri* was given by the Italian botanist R. Pampanini to a Magnolia of which herbarium material had been collected by the Italian missionary P. C. Silvestri, under his number 4104, in northern Hupeh in 1912 or 1913. The specimen had been collected while in flower and, being precocious, there were no leaves to assist in its further identification and it is not possible to determine the original colour of the dried tepals.

The Magnolias now included under this name were introduced some twelve years earlier (in 1901) by the great botanical explorer Ernest Henry Wilson, who embarked on two expeditions to China for the Surrey nursery firm of J. H. Veitch in 1899 and 1903. Later Wilson was commissioned by the Arnold Arboretum of Harvard University to return to China, where he spent a considerable time collecting herbarium specimens and seeds from 1907 to 1909, returning for a briefer period in 1910.

During his third and fourth expeditions Wilson repeated many of the collections which he had made earlier for Veitch's, who later presented their private herbarium to the Royal Botanic Gardens, Kew, when Sir Harry Veitch decided to sell out and retire in 1913. The Veitch sale at Coombe Wood has been described as an all-time record auction of plants, and included many of Wilson's introductions which were as yet only identified by the collector's numbers. Among these plants were a number of seedling Magnolias (under Wilson's number W 688), as yet unflowered, some of which were acquired by J. C. Williams of Caerhays Castle, Cornwall, some by the Hon. H. D. McLaren (who later became Lord Aberconway) of Bodnant in North Wales, while others went to Kew Gardens. These Magnolias apparently originated from seed collected from Ch'ang-yang Hsien, in moist woods in September 1901.

On returning from his fourth Chinese expedition Dr. Wilson joined the Arnold Arboretum's botanist Dr. A. Rehder in classifying and identifying the material which he had collected and in giving names to what were considered to be new introductions. They erroneously believed one of these Magnolias to be identical with that which had been figured by Keisuke Ito in *Figures and Descriptions of Plants in the Koishikawa Botanical Garden* 1 : t. 10 (1884), showing a flower with only seven fairly broad purple-tinted tepals which had been named *M. obovata* Thunberg, but which had been renamed *M. conspicua* var. *purpurascens* by C. J. Maximowicz in 1872. Later the name *conspicua* was discarded by the botanists in preference to *denudata* (and then to *heptapeta*) for reasons stated under that species, so Rehder and Wilson named the pink Magnolia in this group *M. denudata* var. *purpurascens* and the white one *M. denudata* var. *elongata*. They were apparently unaware that those Magnolias had normally twelve tepals while *M. heptapeta* (*denudata*) has only nine.

Since it has been agreed by Rehder, Stapf, Dandy and Spongberg, that it cannot be determined which of these two distinct forms represents the typical var. *sprengeri*, which was collected by Silvestri in Hupeh, the author has decided to follow Johnstone's designations of *M. sprengeri* var. *diva* for trees with pink flowers and *M. sprengeri* var. *elongata* for those with flowers which are predominantly white. The Caerhays tree thus becomes *M. sprengeri* var. *diva* 'Diva', but is also referred to as *M. sprengeri* 'Diva'.

Goddess Magnolia
MAGNOLIA SPRENGERI DIVA
   Stapf ex Johnstone.
Otto Stapf in *Curtis's Botanical Magazine* 153 : t. 9116 (1927)

G. H. Johnstone in *Asiatic Magnolias in Cultivation*: 83–6 (1955)
SYN. *M. denudata* var. *purpurascens* Rehder & Wilson
   A. Rehder & E. H. Wilson in Sargent, *Plantae Wilsonianae* 1 : 401 (1913) excluding synonym
Plates 28 and 29

One of the seedling Magnolias which had been planted at Caerhays under Veitch's sale label *M. denudata* var. *purpurascens* began to flower about 1925 and specimens were sent by the late J. C. Williams to Kew botanist Dr. Otto Stapf for examination in 1927. Stapf decided to name this beautiful new pink Magnolia *diva*, meaning 'goddess', and had actually completed his text to accompany Plate 9116 for publication in *Curtis's Botanical Magazine* when J. E. Dandy, who was working on a monograph of *Magnolia*, drew his attention to Pampanini's herbarium material of *M. sprengeri*, which had just arrived at Kew on loan from Florence. This consisted of some branches of flower buds and a few open flowers but no leaves. They matched the new Caerhays Magnolia so completely that both botanists agreed that it should be named *M. sprengeri diva*.

This Caerhays Magnolia has an erect trunk, with the older bark at the base deeply fissured. The outer branches are widely spreading and horizontal or pendulous. The flowers are up to 8 in. (20·5 cm) across when fully expanded and are composed of twelve long and narrow tepals 4½ by 1¾ in. (11·5 by 4·5 cm), which have a pronounced tendency to curl at the tips.

The flower buds, which open later than those of most precocious Magnolias, have an unusual poise. Instead of being erect they are borne at the tips of short slender shoots which splay outwards along the branches in opposite directions. The pubescent perules which cover the flower buds have a distinctive greenish-yellow tone, whereas those of other members of this section are almost black with lighter-coloured hairs. These buds assume a nodding poise as the spathaceous bracts split to reveal the coloured tepals.

The flowers likewise are of a distinctive shape. After the spathaceous bract is shed, the tepals on the lower side of the opening bud curl upwards to attain a vertical poise, while those on the higher side reflex horizontally to give many of the flowers an asymmetrical, side-swept appearance.

The tepals are rose carmine outside and white flushed or streaked with pale rose or carmine within. The richer outer surface of the tepals is the predominating colour when the myriads of upward-facing flowers are viewed from below. Late flowers continue to open as the leaves appear but these are usually smaller and much paler in colour.

The stamens have lilac-pink bars down their outer face and they do not dehisce to shed their pollen until the flower is fully mature and the white stigmas have withered on the lime-green carpels of the stigmatic column or gynoecium.

The deciduous leaves begin to unfold as the last of the flowers reach maturity. They are obovate, cuneate at the base, the apex obtuse and extended to a shortly acuminate point. They are of a medium dark green.

Seedlings raised from the Caerhays mother tree have since flowered and many have proved disappointing. One of these, now a sizeable tree at Caerhays, opposite the original plant of *Camellia* × *williamsii* 'Saint Ewe', bears pink flowers with only six tepals which never open out and reflex. This tree might represent a link between *M. sprengeri* and *M. heptapeta* (*denudata*). Other seedlings, however, are possibly improvements on the type with richer-coloured flowers. Under these circumstances and after very careful consideration, the author has decided to refer to the original Caerhays mother tree as a clone under *M. sprengeri* var. *diva* 'Diva' in order to distinguish it and its vegetatively propagated offspring from its seedling progeny. There is a fine pink form of *M. sprengeri* var. *diva*, which was planted by the late J. J. Crossfield, at Embley Park near Romsey, Hants.

At Trengwainton a grafted tree of *M. sprengeri* var. *diva* (Plate 28), which was planted in 1955, had reached a height of 12 ft (3·5 m) by the autumn of 1971, with a branch spread of 25 ft (7·5 m) and had formed flower buds within 3 ft (91 cm) of ground-level.

In the Williams's estate garden at Burncoose, midway between Falmouth and Redruth in Cornwall, there was an interesting variant of this Magnolia. This had a spreading bushy habit with long arching branches and no tendency to become arborescent or tree-like in the manner of the Caerhays tree and its progeny. The leaves of this Magnolia were shorter with rounded tips and pale veins, but it has recently died.

M. sprengeri var. *diva* 'Claret Cup' is another named clone, believed to have originated as a seedling from the original *M. sprengeri* 'Diva' of Caerhays. The 8 in. (20·5 cm) saucer-shaped flowers have twelve (occasionally fourteen) tepals arranged in three series of four (occasionally six in the innermost whorl). These are rosy purple on their outer surfaces and a paler shade fading to white on the inner surfaces as the flowers mature. It received an Award of Merit

on 18 April 1963, when exhibited at an R.H.S. Show in London by Lord Aberconway and the National Trust.

M. sprengeri var. *diva* 'Copeland Court' (Plate 29) is a very good dark form resulting from a seedling presented to the late Bishop Hunkin of Truro by George Johnstone of Trewithen and planted in the Bishop's garden at Lis Escop, Truro. After his death, his successor chose a smaller residence and Lis Escop was purchased by the Copeland family, donated to Truro Cathedral School as a hall of residence and renamed Copeland Court. In 1960 the governors of the school decided to build an additional residential block adjacent to the former bishop's palace. When it was realized that this would involve the spot where the hitherto unflowered Magnolia seedling, then some 15 ft (4·5 m) tall, was growing, the headmaster, Maj. H. M. Mischler, had the foresight to contact the author to see if it could be transplanted. After conference with the head gardener, Mr. Blakey, a narrow trench was dug around the tree with a wide ramp leading down to the base of the root ball. A suitable pit with a similar ramp had been prepared for its replanting and the Magnolia was carefully edged on a steel sledge, which had been designed for moving large boulders during rock-garden construction projects, and towed by tractor to its new site. The operation was successful and, although the transplanting appears to have checked the tree's normal vigour, it probably hurried its initial flowering. Growing in an open situation, it has developed into a small erect tree, which has since produced a second main trunk arising from the base of the original one. The flowers have twelve to fourteen tepals and are much richer in colour than those of the Caerhays parent, being of a deep clear pink, shaded crimson, but it would be necessary to grow a grafted tree of 'Diva' beside it to make a fair and accurate comparison since the flower colour may be due, to some extent, to the open situation which contrasts with the woodland environment of the Caerhays tree. The bark of this cultivar does not always have the spicy odour normally associated with Asian Magnolias.

Suffice to say that, when viewed at the end of a day spent visiting such renowned Magnolia collections as Caerhays, Trewithen and Trengwainton in late March, the vivid colour of this solitary Magnolia created a lasting impression on the author and his companion, plant connoisseur Philip Urlwin-Smith, who had driven down from Ascot for the occasion.

At Caerhays *M. sprengeri* 'Diva' flowers later than *M. campbellii* and appears to be more frost tolerant.

In America it is reported to have withstood winter temperatures down to −18 °F. (−27·8 °C.) without any signs of damage. In the same American garden *M.* × *veitchii* had been killed during several attempts at establishing it, while *M. quinquepeta* 'Gracilis' had been killed to ground-level each winter.

Prof. Joseph C. McDaniel of the University of Illinois contributed an interesting report in the *Newsletter of the American Magnolia Society* 7, 1 : 8 (1970) under the heading 'President's Paragraphs'. He reported that he had achieved a remarkable advancement in flower-bud development on *M. sprengeri* 'Diva' by chip-budding on to a mature specimen of *M.* × *soulangiana*. The buds were inserted at 6 to 7 ft (about 2m) above ground-level in August 1966 and the resulting growths produced flower buds three years later. This substantiates the author's theory, expounded elsewhere in this volume, that understocks are bound to influence the age at which a graft begins to flower.

Mr. Julian Williams writes: 'From the hybridist's point of view *M. sprengeri* 'Diva' makes a good parent – we have several here – 'Caerhays Belle' being the best ('Diva' × *sargentiana robusta*). The flowers of this hybrid are good and the seedlings began to flower early in their lives.'

Cyanide in *M. sprengeri* 'Diva'

In 1971 Frank S. Santamour, Jr., and John S. Treese, both research geneticists at the U.S. National Arboretum at Washington, D. C., reported that, of more than fifteen Magnolia species and hybrids tested, *M. sprengeri* 'Diva' was unique in that it produced hydrocyanic acid (HCN) in its leaves [as a result of autolysis of the tissues].

Their experiments were recorded in the University of Pennsylvania *Morris Arboretum Bulletin* 22 : 58–9 (1971). At that time only a few interspecific hybrids of 'Diva' were available for study, but it was shown that cyanide production was an inheritable factor.

Further tests, recorded in *Newsletter of the American Magnolia Society* 11, 2 : 5 (1975), have established that some hybrids between 'Diva' and other species, at three different ploidy levels, have inherited this HCN–positive character, as shown on the table which follows.

In 1968 W. F. Kosar crossed *M. grandiflora* 'Madison' with 'Diva' pollen and, since both parents have the same chromosome number (2n = 114), a progeny with intermediate characters might have been expected – but all seedlings were virtually indistinguishable from *M. grandiflora*. Now negative HCN reaction from all of these hitherto unflowered seedlings suggests that they are of non-hybrid apomictic origin. One might imagine that mere inheritance of evergreen foliage was an adequate indication but recent investigation has indicated that this is not always a dominant factor.

Results of Cyanide Tests on Interspecific Hybrids Involving *M. sprengeri* 'Diva'

Hybrid Combination (female parent first)	Number tested	HCN positive	HCN negative
★*Buergeria* × 'Diva'	3	2	1
quinquepeta (*liliflora*) × 'Diva'	19	11	8
acuminata × 'Diva'	10	2	8
'Diva' × *heptapeta* (*denudata*)	6	3	3
(× *veitchii* × *heptapeta*) × 'Diva'	10	6	4
grandiflora × 'Diva'	8	0	8

★ (*M. kobus* × *M.* × *loebneri* 'Spring Snow')

Method of Testing

Young leaves were collected in May, cut into small pieces and about 1 gram was placed in a test tube fitted with a ground glass stopper. A strip of Whatman No. 1 filter paper was attached to the underside of the stopper with melted paraffin wax. Just before the test the paper strip was dipped in a sodium picrate solution (259g sodium carbonate and 5g picric acid in 1 litre of distilled water) and allowed to dry for a few minutes.

Five to seven drops of chloroform were then added to the leaf material, the stopper with the treated paper strip was inserted and the tube was placed in an incubator at 30 °C. (86 °F.) Release of HCN from the leaves causes the yellow sodium picrate to turn red. Development of the red-brown colour within twenty-four hours was considered a positive test. Some of the first two hybrids listed produced more HCN than did 'Diva' itself.

Earlier tests involving other species and hybrids of Section *Yulania* had proved negative. These tests cannot be considered a conclusive means of establishing that all hybrids of *M. sprengeri* 'Diva' inherit this strange 'Diva' characteristic.

The putative hybrids which failed the test cannot be assessed until they begin to flower, which entails a wait of several years before this interesting experiment is finalized.

MAGNOLIA SPRENGERI var. ELONGATA (Rehder & Wilson) Stapf

O. Stapf in *Curtis's Botanical Magazine* 153 : t. 9116 (1927)

G. H. Johnstone in *Asiatic Magnolias in Cultivation* 87-9 (1955)

SYN. *M. denudata* var. *elongata* A Rehder & E. H. Wilson in Sargent, *Plantae Wilsonianae* I : 402 (1913)

M. sprengeri var. *elongata* has white flowers which are somewhat like the 'Purple Eye' clone of *M. heptapeta* (*denudata*) apart from the extra whorl of tepals, which number twelve as compared to nine in that species. They are shorter and narrower than those of the pink forms of *M. sprengeri*. The leaves are generally more oblong. It forms a compact and erect tree, with stouter branchlets. According to Johnstone there are two forms of this Magnolia in cultivation, one with pure-white narrow tepals and the other with broader cream-coloured ones of lighter texture, which overlap and reflex when fully open in the manner of *M. stellata*. Flowers of both forms are figured on his Plate 10 facing page 87.

Both forms are growing at Kew Gardens and also at Bodnant, and both types are believed to be at Caerhays. W. J. Bean in *Trees & Shrubs* Ed. 8 suggests that their garden value is about equivalent to that of *M. kobus*, but they flower much later so that their impact is thereby lessened though on this account they may prove more suitable for colder localities.

In the Hillier Arboretum at Jermyns, near Romsey in Hampshire, there are several specimens of 10 ft (3 m) with a neat multistemmed habit, which have flowered profusely for several seasons.

Fig. 13 facing p. 88 in Johnstone, *Asiatic Magnolias in Cultivation* is a reproduction of a photograph of a tree at Bodnant with several erect trunks arising close to the base. This habit of growth has been observed also on trees which are seedlings of *M. sprengeri* var. *diva*.

Dr. Stephen Spongberg in 'Magnoliaceae Hardy in Temperate North America' *Journal of the Arnold Arboretum* 57, 3 : 287 (1976) designates arbitrarily to *M. sprengeri* var. *elongata* plants with white tepals and leaves generally more than twice as long as broad.

Cytologically *M. sprengeri* is a hexaploid with 2n = 114 chromosomes.

Details of Yulania *Magnolias awaiting introduction*

Charming Magnolia

MAGNOLIA AMOENA Cheng

S. S. Chien & W. C. Cheng in 'An Enumeration of Vascular Plants from Chekiang' III in *Contributions from the Biological Laboratory of the Scientific Society of China*: Botany Series 8 : 280, Fig. 28 (1933)

This species was discovered in 1933 by Prof. W. C. Cheng of the University of Nanking, at Yutsien, Western Tienmushan, Chekiang, China, growing in forests at an altitude of 2,500 to 3,500 ft (760 to 1,070 m). It forms a tree 25 to 40 ft (7·6 to 12 m) tall.

According to Philip J. Savage, Jr., in *Newsletter of the American Magnolia Society* 10, 2 : 8 (1974), Yutsien is about midway between and some fifty miles distance from the city of Hangchow and the central peak of Mount Hwang. The type specimen, collected by W. C. Cheng in July 1933 included the fruit. A flowering specimen was collected in April of the following year by S. S. Chien. These were sent to the herbarium of the University of Nanking.

It differs from the Japanese *M. stellata* in its long acuminate leaves and oblanceolate or subspatulate tepals which number nine per flower. These are said to be cup shaped, rose pink in colour and 2½ in. (6 cm) in diameter.

Dandy attributes *M. amoena* to Section *Yulania*. This species is not known in cultivation.

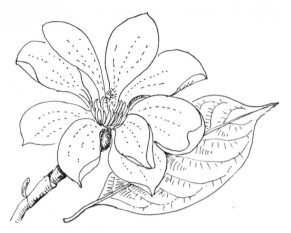

Zen's Magnolia

MAGNOLIA ZENII Cheng

C. P'ie in 'An Enumeration of Vascular Plants from Nanking, II' in *Contributions from the Biological Laboratory of the Scientific Society of China*: Botany Series 9 : 291–3, Fig. 20 (1934)

This species was discovered by Chien P'ie in March 1931 at Mount Paohua, near Nanking, Kiangsu, China, flowering in woods at an altitude of 850 to 1,000 ft (260 to 305 m). It grows into a small tree 15 to 25 ft (4·5 to 7·5 m) tall with glabrous branchlets. A second specimen was collected in leaf in July of the

following year. The leaves are said to resemble those of the Japanese *M. kobus* being oblong obovate, 3 to 6 in. (7·5 to 15 cm) long by 1 to 3 in. (2·5 to 7·5 cm) wide.

The fragrant flowers are 5 in. (12·5 cm) in diameter with nine spatulate tepals 2½ to 3 in. (6 to 7·5 cm) long by 1 to 1½ in. (2·5 to 4 cm) broad, which are purple on the lower half of the outer surface. The fruit cones are cylindrical, 2 to 3 in. (5 to 7·5 cm) long. Cheng's notation, copied from the Harvard Herbarium, reads: 'Related to *M. denudata* [*M. heptapeta*], differs in smaller flowers with subspatulate sepals and petals which are purple on the lower half of the outer surface. It is also related to *M. cylindrica* Wilson, which has oblanceolate-oblong or rarely oblong-obovate leaves with obtuse or acute apex, and with short and straight hairs throughout the whole surface beneath, and has cylindrical fruits with elliptical carpels, and longer (5 to 10 mm) [¼ to ½in.] pedicels. In the shape of its leaves this new species somewhat resembles *M. kobus* of Japan, but differs in the similar sepals and petals of the flower.'

W. C. Cheng dedicated this Magnolia to Director H. C. Zen of the China Foundation for the Promotion of Education and Culture 'whose untiring effort in encouraging biological research is highly appreciated by the workers in this field in China'.

It is not known in cultivation but was believed by Dandy to belong to Section *Yulania*.

SECTION *BUERGERIA* (Siebold & Zuccarini) Dandy

J. E. Dandy in *Camellias and Magnolias Conference Report*: 73 (1950), based on *Buergeria* Siebold & Zuccarini in *Abhandlungen der Mathematisch-physikalischen Classe der Königlich Bayerischen Akademie der Wissenschaften* 4, 2 : 186 (1846)
type species *M. stellata*

The name applied to this section dates back to 1846 when Siebold and Zuccarini described the section type species *M. stellata* as *Buergeria stellata*. The species in this section were transferred to *Magnolia* in 1872 by the Russian botanist Maximowicz who retained the name *Buergeria* for the section in which he classified them. As in section *Yulania* all members are precocious in their flowering and Asian in their origin. They differ, however, in the form of their flowers in which the outer whorl of tepals is reduced in size to form a false 'calyx' which is sometimes shed as the flowers develop.

Included in this section are the three Japanese species *M. kobus*, *M. salicifolia* and *M. stellata*, the

latter now attributed by some botanists to be a multitepalled form of *M. kobus*. In addition we have two Chinese species, *M. biondii*, which does not appear to be in cultivation, and the recently introduced *M. cylindrica* from eastern China. All of these Magnolias have flowers which are predominantly white, though sometimes tinted with rose or purple.

Star Magnolia
Shide-Kobushi in Japan

MAGNOLIA STELLATA (Siebold & Zuccarini) Maximowicz

C. J. Maximowicz in *Bulletin de l'Académie Impériale
des Sciences de St. Pétersbourg* 17 : 419 (1872)

J. D. Hooker in *Curtis's Botanical Magazine* 104 : t.
6370 (1878)

SYNS. *Buergeria stellata* Siebold & Zuccarini (1846)
M. halleana Robinson ex Parsons in *The Garden*
8 : 69 (1875)
M. kobus var. *stellata* B. C. Blackburn in *Amatores
Herbarii* 17 : 1–2 (1955)

Plates 30, 31 and 32

This charming and fragrant Magnolia has been
propagated for generations by the Japanese, who
grew *M. stellata* both as a pot plant to take into their
houses as well as in their gardens, and consequently
called it *Shide-Kobushi* meaning the 'Kobus of
homes'.

Jisaburo Ohwi in his *Flora of Japan* (1965) gives
for *M. stellata* a small natural distribution in the
mountains of southern Honsu (Western Tokaido
District), while another Japanese botanist T. Makino
cited only the woods of Owari and Mikawa, a small
district east of Nagoya in central Japan, where it is
supposed to have been collected by Tschonoski, the
skilled assistant of Maximowicz, in the early 1860s.
My Tokyo correspondent tells me that these localities
are one and the same. Franchet and Savatier said it was
indigenous in woods on Mount Fuji.

According to Dr. Blackburn in *Journal of the New
York Botanical Garden*: 53 (1952) 'Japanese botanists
do not consider *M. stellata* indigenous to their
country, though it is now encountered as a wild
plant in southern Japan.' His informant was Yoshi-
haru Matsumura, former Director of the Nikko
Botanical Garden.

The earliest of the European plant collectors to visit
Japan was P. F. von Siebold, a Bavarian physician,
who founded a nursery at Leyden in Holland for the
express purpose of introducing and propagating
Japanese plants to sell to European connoisseurs. His
efforts must have been severely hampered by the all-
powerful local rulers or Shoguns, who placed almost
impossible obstacles in the way of foreign traders
until 1852, when the American Commodore Perry's
negotiations with the Tokugawa Shogun paved the
way for sweeping changes in the treatment afforded
to them.

Siebold returned to Japan in 1856 and had quantities
of Japanese nursery stock prepared and shipped to
Holland. He was not successful however in his
attempt to introduce *M. stellata*.

Shortly afterwards he was followed by British

plant collectors Robert Fortune, John Gould Veitch
(who sent home *M. quinquepeta* 'Nigra') and Richard
Oldham, Carl Maximowicz collecting for Alexander
II of Russia, and Dr. George Roger Hall of Bristol,
Rhode Island, America. Dr. Hall returned to
America in the winter of 1861 bringing with him a
consignment of plants which included two Magnolias.
He passed these on to the Parsons brothers, nursery-
men of Flushing, Long Island, to propagate and
distribute.

Some years later Samuel Parsons wrote: 'Among
the plants were two Magnolias, one of which we
named *Halleana* after Dr. Hall, the other *Thurberi*
after Dr. Thurber. The former proved a gem, but for
various reasons our propagation of it was small until
1869, when its merits, clearly displayed in large
plants, induced us to extend its cultivation by all
means in our power.' Parsons wrote that the flowers
'when fully opened will often measure 4 inches
[10 cm] in diameter. The individual petals are $\frac{3}{8}$ to $\frac{1}{2}$
in. [9.5 to 12 mm] wide and $1\frac{1}{2}$ to 2 in. [4 to 5 cm]
long.' In 1953 one of Dr. Hall's original plants of
M. stellata was reported to be nearly 16 ft (4.9 m)
tall by as much across. Samuel Parsons's letter,
together with a fine coloured plate of Dr. Hall's
Magnolia, were published by William Robinson in
The Garden 13 (1878). It showed two fully open
flowers bearing thirteen and fifteen tepals respectively

It is reported that Richard Oldham managed to
procure plants of this Magnolia in Nagasaki in 1862,
but apparently they died either in transit or after
they arrived in England. Carl Maximowicz returned to St. Petersburg in 1864 with seventy-two
chests of herbarium specimens, together with
several hundred kinds of seeds and living plants,
among them the Magnolia to which he gave the
name *M. stellata* in 1872. Parson's *M. thurberi* was
later recognized as *M. kobus*.

M. stellata grows slowly into a large, spreading
shrub of dense twiggy growth, studded throughout
the winter with fur-coated flower buds. Late
flowers develop from buds which lack furry coats
and are almost indistinguishable from growth buds.
The flowers have an erect poise, the tepals opening
horizontally and later reflexing downwards. Sometimes two or three flowers occupy the terminal
shoot, sharing a common peduncle. Another unique
character is the number of tepals, which exceeds that
of all other Asian Magnolias. Some are tepaloid
stamens, since stamens are fewer in these multitepalled
blossoms. The leaves are small, narrow and glabrous,
mostly obovate oblong but sometimes oblanceolate.
They average 3 to 4 in. (7.5 to 10 cm) long by $1\frac{1}{2}$
in. (4 cm) in width. The upper surfaces are a dull

green. In England it was first flowered at Veitch's nursery at Coombe Wood in 1878.

It was much grafted by the Japanese on to seedlings of *M. kobus* and it seems likely that the larger specimens originated in this way. Johnstone reported a plant at Inverewe, in north-west Scotland, as being 28 ft (8·5 m) high and 25 ft (7·5 m) across in 1955. The lower-growing and more spreading specimens are likely to have originated from layers, and this could apply to an old plant at Enys, near Penryn in Cornwall, which was 15 ft (4·5 m) high and 20 ft (6 m) across in 1955.

According to Lord Rosse, at Birr Castle in County Offaly, Ireland, a specimen of *M. stellata* planted about 1912 was 9 ft (2·5 m) high by twice as much across in 1964 and this was growing in an alkaline soil (pH 7·7).

M. stellata is remarkably wind tolerant and is probably more adaptable to adverse conditions than any other Magnolia. Its low compact habit and small leaves make it almost impervious to wind fracture but the fully open flowers are as readily bruised by gales as are those of their larger-flowered cousins. Growing as it does into a large dense shrub, sprouting constantly from the base, it has greater powers of regeneration than any other Magnolia. A garden owner, who had a good specimen of *M. stellata* in her garden on the north coast of Cornwall, reported that the plant nearly died during its first summer so that only one horizontal branch remained alive. In the autumn she lifted it, cut away the dead shoots and replanted it with the surviving shoot in a vertical position. The root system apparently adapted itself to the change of plane and the plant flourished thereafter.

It is not known whether any of the older plants in British gardens were propagated from Hall's original introduction into America. Not long afterwards Japanese nurserymen began a brisk export trade to Europe and America, and it was at this time that the world-famous Yokohama Nursery Company came into being. In those days there were no restrictions on plant importations, so any private garden owner could order plants direct from Japan at very low prices.

The tepals of *M. stellata* often have the appearance of having been folded crosswise once or twice, so that they have a zigzag shape when opening to give a curious bursting star effect.

Magnolia stellata AND ITS NAMED CULTIVARS:

M. stellata The type has up to fifteen white twisted strap-like tepals. It is highly scented and has purple stamens.

M. stellata 'Rosea' (Japanese Clone) has fourteen narrow blush-pink tepals fading to white with a false calyx of four brown 'bracts'. Colour deeper on old plants and in dry seasons faintly scented. Stamens carmine at base.

M. stellata 'Rosea' (American Clone) has thirteen tepals flushed lilac pink with outer carmine streaks along midribs. Stamens in a prominent ball-shaped cluster, filaments crimson purple with some flushing extending on to anthers; gynoecium tinted likewise. No scent.

M. stellata 'Rubra' (Plate 31) (probably the Japanese clone 'Keiskii') has darker flowers than 'Rosea' and is described as having crimson-backed tepals fading to deep pink, with a strong, spicy fragrance. The stamens form a compact ball, crimson purple at the base with an upward flush and similar tinting extending on to the gynoecium. Usually a weak grower.

M. stellata 'Norman Gould' is a colchicine-induced polyploid which was raised at Wisley from seed of *M. stellata* which had been treated with colchicine by Dr. Janaki Ammal while she was on the laboratory staff. It is a very compact grower with leaves shorter and broader than is usual for *M. stellata*. The tepals too are broader with a pronounced tendency to reflex their terminal halves downwards to produce quite a distinctive effect.

'Waterlily' is popular in America but the author has discovered that this name was applied to three, or possibly four, different clones of *M. stellata* during the period from 1928 to 1935.

M. stellata 'Waterlily' (Plate 32) According to Donald Wyman in *Arnoldia* 20 : 3–4 (1960), this clone originated prior to 1939 at Greenbrier Farms Inc., Norfolk, Virginia, and was claimed to be a cross of *M. stellata* × *M.* × *soulangiana*. However Paul Vossberg recorded that a thousand seedlings of 'Waterlily' were raised and grown on Long Island and not one showed any traces of such parentage. It is therefore now generally assumed to be pure *M. stellata*. It is of more erect habit than the usual form of that species and the pink buds develop into highly-scented flowers which are slightly larger than the type, with an average of fourteen narrower strap-like tepals flushed along the outside of their midribs with bars of pale pink. The stamens are cream with carmine-tinted bases. Because of conflicting claims concerning the origin and naming of 'Waterlily' the author procured this first-hand account from Edward Levy Bennett, propagator at Greenbrier Farms:

'In 1928 a batch of seed collected from *Magnolia stellata*, growing behind *Magnolia × soulangiana* and adjacent to a fairly large block of *Magnolia liliflora*, were planted. From the seedlings which were produced, in 1931 transplanted, there were approximately 4,000 which came into bloom partially in 1934. One seedling was noticed as having a distinct purplish-pink coloration. The first cuttings were propagated from this plant in 1934 as they bloomed in the early spring. In 1935 Mr. Lyman Tingle (of Tingle Nurseries, Pittsville, Maryland) viewed this plant in full bloom, and he commented that it was distinct from any *M. stellata* or *stellata* clone, with which he was familiar, and concurred in the naming of the same: *Magnolia stellata* 'Waterlily'.

'The contention that it is a cross between *M. stellata* and *M. × soulangiana* is, in all probability, a bit of wishful thinking on someone's part.

'The original seedling is still growing here on Greenbrier Farms. This plant has leaves characteristic of *M. stellata*, heavier than the type and slightly smaller. The blooms arrive approximately 10 days to 2 weeks after the type – (never failing to produce a show from the Norfolk, Richmond and Washington area to the New York area) – which is contrary to *M. stellata* which in two years out of five, blooms so early on the East Coast of the United States, as to suffer severe frost damage to the bloom.

'The bloom of *Magnolia stellata* 'Waterlily' has from 11 to 36 petals (the average being around 18 to 26) – which is considerably more than the type, or any clones of *M. stellata*, with which the writer is familiar. The writer was here at the time the seeds were collected, and planted, and has watched this plant through the last 40–odd years.'

Veteran nurseryman John Vermeulen of Neshanic Station, New Jersey gave the author this account of the origin of *M. stellata* 'Waterlily' when he visited the Vermeulen nursery in September 1970. He said that he acquired three plants of this Magnolia as *M. stellata* 'Rosea', from a plant fancier named Brouwer of Sunken Meadow, Long Island, New York, in the mid to late 1920s. For several years he grew it under that name on his nursery at Westbury, Long Island. Its superior qualities were not fully appreciated until it was compared with plants of *M. stellata* 'Rosea' purchased from Tingle Nurseries, Pittsville, Maryland, several years later. Mr. J. Peter Vermeulen, President of John Vermeulen & Son Inc., says that in the early 1930s at a conference with

Mr. Tingle, John Vermeulen and Mr. L. Manning of a mail-order firm trading as F. W. Kelsey Nursery Co., New York, it was unanimously decided to name the Brouwer plant *M. stellata* 'Waterlily'. It was first listed by John Vermeulen, Nurseryman, Westbury, Long Island, in his wholesale list of lining-out stock for spring 1940, in which it was described as 'A new variety of the star type, clear pink and a full flower with as many as 32 petals. It will bloom about a week later than 'Rosea'.'

From these two thoroughly reliable but conflicting reports one should not rule out the possibility of two very similar seedlings having been raised, and the 'common denominator', Mr. Tingle, having suggested the same name for both of them.

Some while after this account had been drafted the author came across a note which he had scrawled in September 1970 during a visit to the Willowwood Arboretum at Gladstone, New Jersey, recording the dimensions of two specimens labelled *M. stellata* 'Waterlily' – 'Arnold Arboretum 1930'. Imagining that this must be an error, he referred the note to the Arboretum Director, Dr. Benjamin Blackburn, who replied: 'Your notes taken on that too hurried visit to Willowwood seem exactly correct. I do not have any information on the origin of the selection 'Waterlily' but scion wood was sent from the Arnold Arboretum by E. H. Wilson in 1928 and turned over at once to Verkade's Nursery in Wayne, N.J., for grafting. It was arranged that the progeny would be divided between Willowwood and Verkade's, as they were very glad, also, to have a start in any selection praised by Wilson. Of the young plants received by Willowwood in 1930 (possibly 3 or 4), two thriving specimens exist today, and I believe you saw them both.

'I have just measured them again, to make the record more precise. The more rounded plant on the well-drained bank is 14 ft [4·5 m] high and the branch spread is about 12 ft [3·5 m]. The plant in the deep silty loam about 20 ft [6m] from the stream is 25ft [7·5 m] high and 20 ft [6 m] in spread, and entirely of the order of *Magnolia kobus* in branch pattern. Both were planted in these locations in 1930. Their flowers have 34 to 40 petals which are narrower and more delicate than the original form of 'stellata', and of course, considerably more numerous. Sepals are easily noted as the buds open, the thin greenish lanceolate structures, slightly less than ½ in. [13 mm] long, often falling away as the petals expand. These are practically identical with the sepals in typical *M. kobus*, and of course, strong evidence leading to the reduction of *M. stellata* to *M. kobus* f. *stellata*.

'The Verkade share of the grafts has given rise to an extensive progeny, as this family has been very skilled in grafting for many years. I have assumed that other distributions of scions by the Arnold Arboretum resulted in wide distribution of the selection, which is not diminished in beauty, in my estimation, by the gradual color change to pearly white.

'When you were here, we noted its branch pattern being higher than wide, and I believe you commented on the typical growth pattern of 'stellata' being flattened-globose and that old specimens become increasingly wider than their height.'

So now we find that the original *M. stellata* 'Waterlily' came from that maestro of Magnolias Dr. Ernest Henry Wilson as long ago as 1928. Vermeulen lays no claim to having raised the clone which he grows under this name, but he tells us that it has as many as thirty-two tepals, whereas Edward Bennett's testimony describes the raising and selection of a third 'Waterlily' bearing flowers with from eleven to thirty-six tepals compared with thirty-four to forty mentioned by Dr. Blackburn for the Wilson plant. Obviously the only solution to this extraordinary sequence of unintentional use of the same name for three different seedlings of *M. stellata* is to prefix the three clones with the names Greenbrier, Vermeulen and Wilson, until such time as one of the American arboretums, or some enterprising amateur Magnolia enthusiast, secures a plant of each of these three forms of 'Waterlily' and grows them under more or less identical conditions for detailed comparison.

Yet a fourth clone with this name is listed in *Hillier's Manual of Trees and Shrubs* (1972) as *M. stellata* 'Water Lily': 'An outstanding form of Japanese origin, with larger flowers and more numerous petals.' There is no reference to any pink shading so that this clone does not compete in the league for the best pink Star Magnolia.

According to Harold Hillier the *M. stellata* 'Water Lily' which they grow came to them in 1952 in the form of scions from the Kluis nursery which had then transferred or was transferring from Boksoop in Holland to America. Mr. Hillier confirms that this 'Water Lily' is a white-flowered clone and, in this respect, it is distinct from the three other contenders for the name.

With the establishment of the *International Register of Magnolia Cultivar Names* vested with the American Magnolia Society there should be far less likelihood of any duplication, let alone such multiplication, of any cultivar name in future.

M. stellata 'Dawn' This fine pink cultivar was spotted in March 1974 by American magnoliaphile Harold Hopkins of Bethesda, Maryland, flowering in a garden in a residential area through which he chanced to drive. The owner told him that it was established there when she acquired the property ten years earlier and the previous owner said that it had been planted by a Maryland landscaper. In notes on this Magnolia in *Newsletter of the American Magnolia Society* 12, 1 : 28 (1976) Harold Hopkins tells us that Theodore Klein of Yew Dell Nursery, Crestwood, Kentucky, sells a fine pink *M. stellata* which he obtained from Tingle Nursery, Pittsville, Maryland, twenty-five or thirty years ago. My investigations have revealed that Tingle had a say in the naming of both Vermeulen's 'Waterlily' about 1930 and also Greenbrier's 'Waterlily' in 1935 but as neither of these can boast the high tepal number of the Bethesda clone there seems no reason to reject the name on either account.

Harold Hopkins describes the flowers of 'Dawn' as a fairly solid pink on the outside, the pigment darkening the inside to give a slightly translucent effect. The thirty-eight to forty-five closely-packed long, narrow tepals produce a pronounced pompon shape. The flowers hold their colour longest in cool and cloudy weather but as with all coloured forms of *M. stellata* they eventually fade to a pale blush especially when bleached by prolonged sunshine and drying winds.

M. stellata 'Royal Star' This originated as a seedling from Vermeulen's 'Waterlily', at John Vermeulen's old nursery on Long Island in 1947 and it first flowered in 1952, after being transferred as a stunted pot-grown seedling to their new nursery at Neshanic Station, New Jersey. John Vermeulen describes it as being faintly flushed at bud-break, opening to large pure-white flowers with from twenty-five to thirty tepals. Although these are but faintly scented they are much larger than ordinary *M. stellata*. The growth is very robust, the leaves are tough and deeply veined. It flowers freely, and propagates readily from soft-wood cuttings placed under intermittent mist.

The Vermeulen description of this outstanding cultivar reads: 'It was selected in 1955 for its several outstanding qualities. Primary among these are the flower color, size and formation. Each has from 25 to 30 pure white petals, and the entire corolla has an overall spread of from four to six inches. The pistils and stamens are a pretty yellow. Pinkish buds appear around April 5th to 15th, depending on the location and the season. This is about a week or so after the species, and possible blemish by any late spring frosts is therefore often avoided. Flowering lasts about two weeks.

' 'Royal Star' Magnolia has been tested in several cold areas of the North-east. Of particular note are three plantings. There is a plant growing at the home of Herbert Hedstrom, Crystal Lake, Enfield, N.H. (zone 4a, minus 20 to minus 30 degrees F.) [−28·9 ° to −34·4 °C.] which has bloomed each year since it was planted in 1961. Another plant is growing at the home of Mr. Walter Newman, Sardinia, New York (zone 5b), where temperatures to 30 degrees F. below [−34·4 °C.] are experienced. Mr. David Leach has advised us that his plants at Brookville, Pa (zone 5a) experienced 35 degrees below [−37·2 °C.] in the winter of 1962/3, and yet bloomed prolifically that Spring. He is using 'Royal Star' for further breeding work.

'Other attributes of 'Royal Star' are its rate of growth, which is quite rapid and its excellent branching habit. It branches freely and in a short time yields a robust yet compact plant with minimum pruning. The foliage color is a deeper green than the species. It adapts well to most soils and transplants very well.

'It was officially registered in July of 1960 and is not patented.'

M. stellata 'Centennial' This outstanding new cultivar was named by the Arnold Arboretum at Jamaica Plain, Boston, Massachusetts, to mark its centennial year in 1972. 'Centennial' is described as an improved 'Waterlily', the flowers being 5½ in (14 cm) in diameter, with from twenty-eight to thirty-two tepals. It was raised from seed collected in October 1942 from a plant of *M. stellata* 'Rosea' (No. 5186) which had been obtained from Veitch in May 1900. The seed germinated in May 1943. This seedling was selected and planted in front of the Administration Buildings in 1952, not far from the parent plant. The leaves of 'Centennial' have the same stout texture as those of 'Waterlily', which are generally larger, tougher and more obovate than those of the earlier introduction of *M. stellata*, the foliage of which was usually of a papery texture.

The Star Magnolia is, without doubt, the best choice for a small garden, combining as it does a very hardy constitution, a slow and compact growth habit, fragrant flowers liberally produced before the leaves appear even on young plants, and dainty proportioned foliage. It will tolerate annual spur pruning immediately after flowering, where it is necessary to keep it permanently restricted in height and spread. The considerable choice of cultivars now available provides a source of additional interest for the Magnolia connoisseur.

Star Magnolias make excellent large pot plants, which will start flowering in a cool greenhouse in January or February, if kept under glass from late autumn.

Leading exponent of a theory that *M. stellata* is a dwarf multitepalled form of *M. kobus* is Dr. Benjamin Blackburn, Director of Willowwood Arboretum, Gladstone, New Jersey, which is owned by Rutgers, the State University, New Brunswick, New Jersey. Dr. Blackburn first expounded his theory in *Amatores Herbarii* 17 : 1–2 (1955). Two years later he contributed further evidence in an interesting and informative paper entitled 'The Early-Flowering Magnolias of Japan' in *Baileya* 5, 1 : 3–12 (1957). Should Blackburn's suggested re-classification become generally accepted, then all cultivars of this parentage will have to be referred to as forms of *M. kobus*. In the author's opinion this theory has not been conclusively proved, and in this he has been supported by other authorities, notably Prof. Joseph McDaniel and J. E. Dandy.

It has been observed already that the leaves of *M. kobus* are relatively large and often rugulose while those of *M. stellata* are small, narrow and glabrous. Normal flowers of *M. kobus* have only six to nine tepals, spatulate in shape, whereas *M. stellata* has up to fifteen (and in some American clones up to thirty or more) which are invariably strap shaped.

Seedlings of *M. stellata*, from open pollinations, do show a wide variation where flowering specimens of *M. kobus* or *M. salicifolia* are within pollen range and some of the resulting plants attain tree-like dimensions while others remain shrub-like. Their flowers vary considerably too, bearing from six to upwards of thirty tepals, white on most plants, but occasionally pink. It is therefore not surprising that in the Royal Horticultural Society's Garden at Wisley, seed of *M. stellata* treated with colchicine by Janaki Ammal in the early 1950s, has given rise to some very *kobus*-like plants while others are akin to *M. salicifolia*. Named clones among these colchicined seedlings include 'Norman Gould' and 'Janaki Ammal'.

Several large-scale raisings of *M. stellata* seedlings have been recorded in America, such as those mentioned under *M. stellata* 'Waterlily'.

At the Arnold Arboretum in 1970, the author was shown experiments which had been carried out among conifers to investigate the progeny of seeds from cones off "witches'-broom" growths, that curious phenomenon which occurs from time to time on a wide range of trees and shrubs. It had been demonstrated that such seeds not only gave rise to many diminutive plants, similar to ones raised vegetatively from these stunted growths, but also to individuals ranging in stature up to that of seedlings off a normal tree.

These demonstrations have led the author to ponder over the possibility that this might be the key to the origin of *M. stellata*. Might it not have originated perhaps as a witches'-broom, maybe from a hybrid between *M. salicifolia* and *M. kobus*, and long propagated as a garden plant by the Japanese? Such an origin would account for the wide variation in stature reported among seedlings of *M. stellata* from assumed self-pollinations, which have been raised in America and elsewhere. It would also account for the willow-shaped leaves of *M. stellata* which are quite unlike those of *M. kobus*. More especially it would account for the elusive whereabouts of *M. stellata* as a wild plant in Japan.* Both *M. kobus* and *M. salicifolia* share part of their natural ranges in the mountains on the island of Honshu in the Sea of Japan drainage area.

Recorded hybrids of *M. stellata* are described under 'Magnolia Hybrids and Crosses'. These include *M. × loebneri* (*M. kobus* × *M. stellata*), *M. × proctoriana* (*M. salicifolia* × *M. stellata*) and *M.* 'George Henry Kern', an assumed hybrid between *M. stellata* and *M. × soulangiana* which some American authorities

---

* Karl E. Flinck, who grows Magnolias in both Switzerland and in Sweden, sent me this interesting report just after this book had gone to the printers: 'In the autumn of 1976 a seed-collection mission from some Scandinavian arboreta visited one of the two localities for wild *M. stellata* on the main island of Honshu. The place was in the southwestern corner of the island, very warm temperate and the shrubs were growing in a marshy environment like *Myrica gale* in Europe. The shrubs, bordered on rice paddies, were uniform in height (2–3 m) and no tree forms occurred. Altogether there were a few hundred plants . . . I believe that wild *M. stellata* never was introduced into U.S.A. or U.K., but that it always was cultivated plants. This may explain the behaviour of seedlings from those plants, and why in culture the progeny may be transformed. I understand that there are now a few seedlings, from seed collected during the visit mentioned, growing in Sweden. There are also, it is claimed, some at Kalmthout in Belgium, collected a few years ago.'

In *Amatores Herbarii* 20 : 10–14 (1959) K. Inami contributed an article entitled 'Distribution of *Magnolia stellata*'. The text is in Japanese and includes a map.

think might be a hybrid of *M. stellata* 'Rosea' and *M. quinquepeta* 'Nigra'. Such a parentage would classify it under the same group of hybrids as those bred by De Vos and Kosar at the U.S. National Arboretum at Washington, D.C. These too are described under 'Magnolia Hybrids and Crosses'.

Janaki Ammal in *Chromosome Atlas of the World* 2 : 14 (1955) records *M. stellata rubra* as *M. stellata* × *M. quinquepeta* with 2n = 57 chromosomes whereas the norm for *M. stellata* is 2n = 38. *M. stellata rubra* bears little or no resemblance to any of the hybrids of this parentage which have been bred at the U.S. National Arboretum by controlled pollinations.

M. stellata is also reported to have been successfully crossed with *M. heptapeta* by two breeders in America.

In common with other members of Section *Buergeria*, *M. stellata* is cytologically a diploid with 2n = 38 chromosomes.

MAGNOLIA BIONDII Pampanini
Chinese Willow-leaf Magnolia
Hope of Spring Tree in China
R. Pampanini in *Nuovo Giornale Botanico Italiano* 17 : 275 (1910) and in *Bulletino della R. Societa Toscana di Orticultura* 40 : 99 (1915)
SYN. *M. aulacosperma* Rehder & Wilson in Sargent, *Plantae Wilsonianae* 1 : 396 (1913)

This Magnolia was discovered as long ago as 1906 by the Italian missionary and botanist P. C. Silvestri in the central Chinese province of Hupeh, growing at an altitude of about 3,000 ft (915 m) where it is quite a rare tree. It does not appear to have been introduced successfully into cultivation as yet, although it was apparently among Wilson's 1908 introductions to the Arnold Arboretum. J. G. Millais in *Magnolias* (1927) quoted, on page 85, a letter from E. H. Wilson in which he wrote: 'It is the only Magnolia I found in China which I failed to introduce into gardens.'

It may be looked upon as the Chinese counterpart of the Japanese *M. salicifolia* from which it apparently differs in that the flowers are borne on densely pubescent peduncles whereas those of *M. salicifolia* are glabrous. It forms a slender tree with spreading branches, and flowers precociously in the manner of its Japanese cousin.

A flowering specimen collected in Shensi by Abbé Farges was first identified as *M. conspicua* var. *fargesii* but later this was transferred to Wilson's *M. aulacosperma* and later to *M. biondii*. Because Rehder & Wilson did not realize that these were one and the same species they thought it to be very scarce and found only in western Hupeh, but it is now known to have a fairly wide distribution, having been recorded from eastern Szechwan, western Hupeh, western Honan and Shensi. It appears to have a very northerly range for a Chinese Magnolia (about 35 °N.), though not nearly as northerly as the Shen-yang (Mukden) recording by Sowerby for *M. sieboldii* which is about 42 °N.

The leaves are lanceolate and up to 7 in. (18 cm) long by 3 in. (7·5 cm) wide, similar in shape to but considerably larger than those of *M. salicifolia* and with glossy upper surfaces. Specimens collected in Hupeh by Chun, Henry and Wilson have leaves more broadly elliptical than those from Honan and Shensi.

The flower buds are generally larger than those of the Japanese *M. kobus* and the flowers appear to be somewhat larger and borne with a more vertical poise. The six larger tepals are more heavily textured while the three smaller and thinner ones in the outer whorl constitute the false calyx typical of Magnolias in Section *Buergeria*.

The pedicle is described as silky pubescent and the fruits 3 to 5 in. (7·5 to 12·5 cm) long. According to Rehder it also differs from *M. salicifolia* by the seeds which have a deep, broad groove on the ventral side and which are concave at the apex. In *M. salicifolia* and all other allied species the seeds are only slightly grooved or convex on both sides and truncate at the apex. 'This new Magnolia forms a shaggy tree with many rather slender and spreading branches with a wealth of leaves. It is quite rare and the flowers are unknown.'

In 1976 came news from the President of the American Magnolia Society, Prof. J. C. McDaniel, that Dr. Yu-Chen Ting of Boston College was revisiting his birthplace in China and had undertaken to try to locate native Magnolias in Honan Province and endeavour to arrange to have authentic seed and budwood sent to the United States. He reports that he

has visited the Peking Botanical Garden where he found *M. biondii* in cultivation so it may not be long before this species becomes available for planting in gardens in the West.★

M. biondii may be assumed to be a diploid with 2n = 38 chromosomes in common with other members of Section *Buergeria*.

Magnolia with cylindrical young fruits

MAGNOLIA CYLINDRICA Rehder & Wilson

A. Rehder & E. H. Wilson in *Journal of the Arnold Arboretum* 8 : 109 (1927)

S. S. Chien & W. C. Cheng in *Contributions from the Biological Laboratory of the Scientific Society of China*: Botany Series 8 : 281–2 (1933)

This species was discovered by Wilson in 1927 and is to be found over a large area of eastern China from southern Anhwei to northern Fukien. It was not introduced until 1936, when viable seeds reached America from the Lu-Shan Botanical Garden in Kuling, Kinkiang, China. The seeds were reported to have been collected from western Anhwei at an elevation of 4,200 ft (1,280 m). Seeds sent to England failed to germinate but there were successful raisings

---

★ Unfortunately Dr. Ting's visit coincided with the serious earthquake which occurred while he was in Peking and he was forced to abandon most of his plans. Apparently Chinese botanists then had to devote their entire time and resources towards improving food crops with little or no opportunity for such frivolities as Magnolias and rhododendrons. However on 13 September 1977 Dr. Ting phoned Prof. McDaniel to say that he had just returned from a second visit to Honan with both scions and seeds of what was believed to be the true *M. biondii*, the Chinese vernacular name for which he translated

as the "Hope of Spring Tree".

In November 1977, Dr. Spongberg examined the material and confirmed that it was indeed of that species.

It therefore seems reasonable to anticipate an early distribution of this elusive Magnolia. Prof. McDaniel reports that scions which he had received earlier from Germany under *M. biondii* were not of that species (according to Dr. Spongberg) and that two accessions growing in the Canadian Royal Botanical Garden at Hamilton, Ontario, had not been authenticated.

in America whence it was eventually introduced as scions in about 1950. These were grafted by Hillier & Sons, of Winchester. The Lu-Shan Arboretum and Botanical Garden's *Descriptive Catalogue of Chinese Tree Seeds* 1936–7 included '*Magnolia cylindrica*, handsomest small rare deciduous tree, first described by Dr. E. H. Wilson in 1927 and limited supply of seeds becomes available for the first time. Pkt. 40c; 1 oz. $1.00; 2 ozs. $1.80.' The list also offered seed of *M. heptapeta* (as *M. denudata*) and *M. officinalis biloba*, the latter also for the first time. It would seem that this list was intended for American customers and it is known that several were successful in raising seedlings of these Magnolias.

Plants distributed by Hillier's appear to represent two different clones. Most of these Magnolias, some twenty years old in 1970, have developed into spreading bushy plants with almost horizontal branches along which the precocious blossoms arise in candle-like array. Mr. Nigel Holman reports that, at Chyverton, the flower buds have suffered little or no damage from a 10 °F. (−12·2 °C.)ground frost while showing colour when those of *M.* × *soulangiana* were badly damaged. This Magnolia produces a quite sensational display which demands admiration even when seen amid densely-flowered trees of the more colourful and larger-flowered *Yulania* section. A second and more arborescent form, of erect and compact habit, resembles the type seen by the author in a Michigan garden and is referred to later.

The flowers, usually scentless in the daytime, are about 4 in. (10 cm) from base to apex and are composed of nine tepals, the three outermost being much reduced to form a brown, papery, false 'calyx' which persists beneath the six creamy-white floral tepals. These have pink blotches externally at their bases, this colouring becoming more conspicuous during dull weather or when flowering material is cut and kept in subdued light. The flowers retain their cylindrical form and erect poise up to the time of fading. However it was not the shape of the flowers but the form of the immature fruits which prompted Rehder and Wilson to name it *M. cylindrica*.

It is reported to grow into a small tree up to 20 ft (6 m) tall and can be encouraged to develop an arborescent aptitude by gradually shortening and ultimately removing the lower branches. Mr. Nigel Holman has demonstrated this with one of the specimens of *M. cylindrica* which was planted in his garden at Chyverton as a young graft in 1959 and which first flowered in 1965. This Magnolia produced some out-of-season flowers in October 1968. The quite substantial leaves are widely elliptical with a smooth upper surface. Both bark and foliage emit a spicy fragrance of aniseed when bruised or crushed. By autumn 1970 it had attained a height of 13 ft 9 in. (4 m) with a spread of 10 ft (3 m).

The leaves of the specimen in the Kew Herbarium are much smaller and narrower, resembling those of *M. salicifolia*.

M. cylindrica received an Award of Merit from the Royal Horticultural Society in April 1963 when exhibited by the Crown Estate Gardens, Windsor. The flowers have been described as 'resembling *M. kobus* but slightly larger' though in the author's opinion the resemblance, apart from their brown false calyces, is more with *M. heptapeta* (*denudata*) or *M.* × *soulangiana*, indeed one is inclined to wonder whether the Magnolia which we now know as *M. cylindrica* might in fact be a hybrid from it, especially in view of its much larger leaves than those of the Kew Herbarium specimen referred to. This theory is substantiated by Wilson's notes in Rehder and Wilson 'Ligneus Plants of Anhwei', *Journal of the Arnold Arboretum* 8 : 109 (1927) which give the following data on *M. cylindrica*:

'This very distinct new species is well distinguished by its thin narrow prominently reticulated leaves, by its slender petioles and by its cylindrical fruits. It is most closely related to the Japanese *M. salicifolia* Maxim. which has rather larger leaves, usually acuminate and glaucescent on the under-sides, glabrous winter buds and branchlets and a smaller, much less cylindric fruit.

'The flowers of our new species are unknown but they appear before the leaves. The foliage is deciduous and the wood when cut has a spicy fragrance similar to that of *M. salicifolia* Maxim. and *M. kobus* DC.'

Because of its southerly distribution, roughly from latitude 28 ° to 32 ° N., it was naturally assumed that this Magnolia would be of doubtful hardiness, but it has certainly proved tough enough, not only in English gardens, but also in several of the eastern states of North America.

David G. Leach of Brookville, Pennsylvania, reported that he had found *M. cylindrica* completely unharmed at −23 °F. (−30·6 °C.) while Philip J. Savage, Jr., recorded a low of −14 °F. (−25·6 °C.) in his garden at Bloomfield Hills, Michigan, in January 1970, which caused his specimen no harm. He even goes as far as to suggest that the Magnolia now being grown as *M. cylindrica* is likely to have originated in a more northerly habitat than the low mountains south of Hankow, which Rehder and Wilson regarded as its home.

In September 1970 the author went to see Gus Krossa's former garden at Livonia, Michigan, where there are two trees of *M. cylindrica* which he had raised from seed imported from the Lu-Shan Botanical Garden in 1936. Both trees were of erect, compact habit, the larger being some 30 ft (9 m) tall by about half as much in width, a remarkable contrast to the widely spreading habit of the younger grafted specimens in such Cornish gardens as Chyverton, Trewithen and Trengwainton.

The larger tree had two or three small fruit cones but these were out of reach. Gus Krossa, writing from his new home at Saginaw, on the west shore of Lake Huron, told the author that, although they always bloomed profusely, they had not always fruited, and he had never been able to get a seed to germinate, though he had often raised seedlings from his tree of *M. officinalis biloba*. Philip Savage reports that he has raised a seedling from one of the fruit cones and that it produced leaves measuring 10 by 5½ in. (25·5 by 14 cm) during the first growing season.

The few fruit cones which the author has been able to examine have contained only two or three fertile carpels which protruded prominently and contained solitary seeds. The leaves are very similar to those of *M. heptapeta* in both size and shape, about 5½ by 2½ in. (14 by 6 cm). The upper surface is darker and more glossy, with the main veins deeply impressed, while the undersides are glaucous and glabrous. This pronounced affinity to *M. heptapeta* has been referred to earlier in this chapter.

Philip Savage describes Krossa's trees as having 'leaves sub-coriaceous or chartaceous, elliptic, apiculate and glabrescent, with surfaces notably flat and not at all rugulose, (like *kobus*) or reticulate. The petioles, though possibly slender, are quite stiff. There is no odour of anise to the crushed leaves, as in true *M. salicifolia*. The flowers have three papery, small sepals and six petals about 4 in. by 1½ in. [10 by 4 cm], which last about a week and retain their "tulip" shape throughout. They are upright and never nod like *M. kobus* or *M. salicifolia* flowers. Cream white with about as much purple as *M.* 'Alba Superba' at base; they have an attractive sharp scent like 'Bouncing Bet' [*Saponaria*]. Trees are graceful, rather fastigiate. I noticed two fruits this year (1969), which were typical, contorted not cylindric and much like *M. kobus*.'

More recently he has had an opportunity to examine Wilson's herbarium specimens of *M. cylindrica* in the Harvard University Herbarium. He reports that the type appeared to have been collected by Ren-Chang Ching as No. 2949 in 1925, on the Wang Mountains of southern Anhwei. He tells me that 'the two fruit cones from which Rehder named the species are 3 inches [7·5 cm] long and 1 inch

[2·5 cm] in diameter, and notably smooth like breakfast sausages. They look like the sterile cones that hang on *M. acuminata* until midsummer or later.' (These gave rise to the name Cucumber Tree for that species.) Philip Savage described the leaves of the herbarium specimens as 'narrow lanceolate, acute at each end, about 4¾ inches [12 cm] long by 1⅛ inch [3 cm] at widest point and varying greatly in length but not in shape. Some are as small as 2½ inches [6 cm] long. It is described as "Small tree or big shrub to 30 feet [9 m]. Leaves thick, glossy green above. In shaded ravine." Flower buds on specimen are very small and very furry.'

The herbarium specimen described by Prof. Cheng was collected at Suichang, Peimashan, Chekiang by S. Chen under his No. 1236, from a tree 22 ft (6·5 m) tall with smooth whitish-grey bark on 30 April 1933. The specimen is described as 'in young fruits . . . the branchlets are densely yellowish white pubescent. The leaves are oblanceolate-oblong, obtuse or subacute at apex, sparsely shortly pubescent above but soon glabrous, appressed-pubescent beneath, petioles densely yellowish white pubescent. The young fruits are cylindrical, pubescent only at base of carpels. This species is new to Chekiang.'

The author has expressed his doubts as to the authenticity of the Magnolia which is in current distribution as *M. cylindrica* and his reasons are discussed in the Royal Horticultural Society's *Rhododendrons 1975 with Magnolias and Camellias*: 70–2 (1975). Similar doubts have been expressed in other publications (see J. C. McDaniel, ' "*Magnolia cylindrica*", the Chinese Puzzle', in *Newsletter of the American Magnolia Society* 10, 1 : 3–7 (1974)). However Dr. Stephen Spongberg in 'Magnoliaceae Hardy in Temperate North America', *Journal of the Arnold Arboretum* 57, 3 : 290–2 (1976) records that he has made a critical re-examination of the type material both in the herbaria at the Arnold Arboretum and at Kew and has studied also specimens from several sources in cultivation including the original raisings at Gladwyne and Livonia. He agrees that some discrepancies exist, particularly concerning the texture of the leaves, 'a character that has been interpreted to be at variance between the plants in cultivation and the leaves described by Wilson'. His conclusion is that 'the leaves as well as other characters are in agreement. . . .The status of *M. cylindrica* as a distinct species . . . cannot be answered until sufficient material, particularly from China, is available for an assessment of variability.'

According to the late George Johnstone's records the grafted plant of *M. cylindrica* on the south-east lawn at Trewithen was planted in 1952. There is no record of the stock upon which it was grafted, but it appears to have made relatively slow growth for it had reached a height of only 18 ft (5·5 m) when twenty years old. The plant is recorded as having come 'from Hilliers of Winchester who obtained scions from a small nurseryman in Western America who obtained it from Mrs. Henry', (presumably of Gladwyne, Pennsylvania, where her daughter Josephine is now President of the Henry Foundation for Botanical Research). Miss Henry tells me that the Gladwyne records concerning *M. cylindrica* and its distribution have not been catalogued. Brian Mulligan, Director of the University of Washington Arboretum at Seattle, tells me that their plant of *M. cylindrica* came from Fairman Furness of Upper Bank Nurseries, Media, Pennsylvania, in May 1949. It first flowered there ten years later, in March 1959, so it was probably a seedling.

In a letter to Mr. Mulligan, dated 15 December 1958, Mr. Furness wrote: 'The one we have here has flowered now for a number of years. I was quite excited the first spring I saw that it was going to do so, but when it did, I was disappointed. It seemed to me very like *M. kobus*. I do not remember the number of petals, but the size and effect were similar, and from the horticultural point of view it did not seem to offer as much as a good *M. kobus*.

'I got it from Mrs. Norman Henry, who got the seed from the Arboretum at Lu-Shan, China, before the last War. It may not be true, but as I do not know what *M. cylindrica* should look like, I did not know what to expect.'

From the above description it seems that the Magnolia, which Mr. Furness retained, bore flowers inferior to the grafted trees which the author has described from observations made in Cornish gardens. Whatever its ultimate identification the horizontally branched form is a most desirable Magnolia, which carries its vertically-poised blossoms at a low level where their beauty can be observed at close quarters, without one having to gaze upwards towards a bright April sky.

Cytology

Dr. Frank S. Santamour, Jr., now Supervisory Research Geneticist at the U.S. National Arboretum in Washington D.C., carried out a cytological examination of root tips from this Magnolia while he was on the staff of the Morris Arboretum. He recorded that *M. cylindrica* is a diploid with $2n = 38$ chromosomes in common with other species in Section *Buergeria*. He does not recall whether he took root tips from a rooted cutting or from the Arboretum tree. The latter may have been grafted on to *M. kobus* so this count is suspect and requires verification.

It is feasible that the flowers on the parent tree were unsuspectingly pollinated from those on a nearby *M. heptapeta*, in which case one would expect the resulting seeds to give rise to hybrids with chromosome counts midway between diploid ($2n = 38$) and hexaploid ($2n = 114$). They should be tetraploid with $2n = 76$ chromosomes.

Prof. McDaniel suggests that, until this Chinese puzzle has been resolved, it might be wise to refer to them as "*M. cylindrica*".

Kobus Magnolia
Kobushi in Japan

MAGNOLIA KOBUS de Candolle

A. P. de Candolle in *Regni Vegetabilis Systemata Naturale* 1 : 456 (1817)
M. kobus var. *borealis* C. S. Sargent in *Trees & Shrubs* 2 : 57 (1908)
W. J. Bean in *Curtis's Botanical Magazine* 138 : t. 8428 (1912)
G. H. Johnstone in *Asiatic Magnolias in Cultivation*: 92–5 (1955)
Plate 34

The name *Kobus* is the phonetic interpretation of the ancient Japanese *Kobushi* for Magnolias in this group and was used by Engelbert Kaempfer in his *Amoenitatum Exoticarum* 845 (1712).

This Magnolia differs from *M. salicifolia* in the pubescent leaf buds and peduncles or flower stalks and larger obovate leaves 4 to 7 in. (10 to 18 cm) long by 2 to 4½ in. (5 to 11·5 cm) wide which are often considerably puckered or rugulose. It differs from *M. stellata* in the smaller number and larger size of the tepals which are spatulate instead of strap shaped. The flowers of *M. kobus* have three diminutive, evanescent, sepaloid tepals ⅜ to ⅝ in. (1 to 1½ cm) long which are usually shed as the six to nine main tepals expand. These often display a pink flush up their backs or at their bases, those with only six or seven tepals tending to remain vase shaped while flowers with eight or nine tepals seem more likely to open fully to a saucer shape. *M. kobus* forms a large arborescent shrub or small tree of dense twiggy growth, flowering precociously from late February to early April. The bark is grey and fissured and the tree benefits from branch thinning to prevent the formation of competing leaders with intercrossing branches. Care should be taken to avoid suddenly exposing a previously shaded trunk to the heat of the sun since damage from sun scorch has been reported from America following such treatment. It is not surprising that this is a somewhat variable species when one bears in mind its wide natural distribution, not only on the different islands of Japan but also on Cheju Do (Quelpart Island) off southern Korea.

Tab 8428 in *Curtis's Botanical Magazine* shows a flowering branch with young leaves. W. J. Bean explains that the branch figured came from a tree at Kew, then 15 ft (4·5 m) high which usually came into leaf in early April, but in that year (1912) it was retarded for three to four weeks by a long-continued cold spell, so that it did not flower until May, when the leaves developed at the same time as the flowers.

M. kobus was first introduced into British gardens in 1878, since when this Magnolia has achieved a reputation for a long delayed and often inferior florescence, and being shy of flowering once it attains that state.

According to Dr. Benjamin Blackburn, writing in *Baileya* 5, 1 : 3–13 (1957)* on 'Early-flowering Magnolias of Japan', a larger-growing, more vigorous form of *M. kobus* occurs in northern Honshu, and especially on the more northerly island of Hokkaido, where it occasionally attains heights of 80 ft (24·5 m) and over, with trunk diameters of up to 3 ft in. (1 m). 'Although more slender and with darker, more close bark, these trees suggest American Cucumber Trees (*M. acuminata*) in their dominant main trunk. This similarity continues in their conical outline under forest conditions, as well as their habit of expanding into broadly-spreading subjects in open situations. . . . Seeds of the northern Kobus had been sent to the Arnold Arboretum in 1876 by William

---

* *Baileya*, a quarterly journal of horticultural taxonomy published at the Bailey Hortorium of the New York State College of Agriculture, a unit of the State University of New York, at Cornell University, Ithaca, New York.

Smith Clark, first President of the Massachusetts Agricultural College, who was on two years leave to organize an agricultural college in Hokkaido. Plants from Dr. Clark's gift were flowering in the 1890s in Massachusetts, and, in summarizing his notes on the forest trees of Japan, Prof. Sargent designated the northern trees as a natural variety, *M. kobus* var. *borealis*.

'These Hokkaido Magnolias come remarkably true from seed, and young plants can be recognized by their unusual vigor and leaves of thicker texture with more prominently impressed veins. Young plants usually start to flower when they are 4 to 5 m high [13 to 16 ft 6 in.] and in this most vigorous Magnolia these dimensions indicate plants only six or seven years from seed.'

This northern Japanese form, referred to as *M. kobus* var. *borealis*, is considered to be freer flowering and to have larger leaves than the southern *M. kobus* var. *kobus*. Professor Sargent had a magnificent tree of the northern form growing in his garden at Brookline, Massachusetts, which was the subject of an article by Dr. E. H. Wilson in the *Gardeners Chronicle* 3, 73 : 301 (1923) and the accompanying photograph was reproduced in Johnstone's *Asiatic Magnolias in Cultivation*, Fig. 14 facing p. 93. Wilson reported that it had been raised from seed from Sapporo in Hokkaido, North Japan, in 1876 and that it bore its first flowers in April 1899. He stated that it was one of the first of its kind to be raised in America and that it was probably the largest in cultivation at that time. Regrettably it has since given way to a building development.

M. kobus var. *borealis* is now represented at the Arnold Arboretum by a tree which was grafted from the original (No. 15168) in February 1941. In 1970 this tree was some 35 ft (10·6 m) high and being overcrowded by one of two larger specimens labelled *M. acuminata* var. *subcordata* which were growing close behind it. When seen by the author in late September it had only two visible fruit cones whereas many near-by Magnolias were fruiting freely including *M. stellata*, *M. acuminata*, *M. virginiana* and *M. macrophylla*.

In Ohwi's *Flora of Japan*: 468 (1965) the leaves of var. *borealis* are said to be larger, 4 to 6½ in. (10 to 17 cm) long by 2½ to 3¼ in. (6 to 8 cm) wide and the flowers slightly larger, often tinged pink. In addition to Hokkaido it is stated to occur on Honshu, in the north and central parts of the Sea of Japan drainage area. Its native Japanese name is given as *Kita-Kobushi*.

In *Curtis's Botanical Magazine* 138 : t. 8428 W. J. Bean, author of *Trees and Shrubs Hardy in the British Isles*, wrote: 'But besides the lofty form alluded to, which Sargent has treated as a distinct variety, var. *borealis*, there is another form of *M. kobus*, also represented in European collections, which, while it never attains the dimensions of the Sapporo tree, differs from its companion in flowering more freely while still young and in having smaller leaves and more slender twigs.'

A superior Magnolia, at first thought to be of *M. kobus*, originated among a quantity of seedlings, supposed to be of that species, which had been imported from Wada's Nurseries in Japan prior to 1940 and lined out at the University of Washington Arboretum in Seattle. Director Brian Mulligan named it 'Wada's Memory' and described it as having flowers of almost double the usual size and produced in great profusion. It was later thought to be a hybrid under *M.* × *kewensis* or *M.* × *proctoriana*, both of which are absorbed under *M. salicifolia* by Dr. Stephen Spongberg in *Journal of the Arnold Arboretum* 57, 3 : 292–5 (1976).

A large-flowered form of *M. kobus* was described in the *Journal of the Royal Horticultural Society* 91, 4 : 84 (1966) by Capt. Collingwood Ingram of Benenden, Kent, as having flowers as large and shapely as *M. denudata*. It was depicted in a photograph (Fig. 99) which accompanied his notes. On 15 April 1969 an Award of Merit was given by the Royal Horticultural Society to this clone which he exhibited as *M. kobus* 'Nippon'. There is a fine form of *M. kobus* growing against the front of the house in Mr. K. O. Parsons's garden at Penlee, Tregony, near Truro, the flowers having upwards of twelve broad tepals. It is probable that these larger-tepalled forms are of hybrid origin, the obvious pollen parent being *M. salicifolia*, which would bring them under *M.* × *kewensis*, since this is the binomial under which such a hybrid was first published (1957).

Although *M. kobus* is a shy seed bearer when grown as an isolated specimen (a factor common to many other species of Magnolia) the seeds germinate very readily and seedlings have been widely used as understocks for grafting and budding, especially among Japanese nurserymen.

Seed-raised trees of *M. kobus* can prove disappointing but, for those who wish to obtain a good form of the species, some worthwhile clones are now being propagated vegetatively and these should not take as long to attain florescence as the twenty-three years recorded by Dr. E. H. Wilson for the original introduction into America.

There is a large specimen of *M. kobus* in the grounds of Place Manor (Maj. & Mrs. N. Grant-Dalton) at St. Anthony-in-Roseland, at the mouth of the Percuil River, opposite St. Mawes in Cornwall.

In September 1972 it had an estimated height of 32 ft (9·5 m) a maximum branch spread of 54 ft (16·5 m) and a trunk circumference of 5 ft 1 in. (1·5 m) at 3 ft (91 cm) above ground-level.

There is a far larger specimen in the Goldsworth Nursery of Walter C. Slocock Ltd., at Woking in Surrey. Dimensions of this tree which were supplied to the author by Mr. J. A. Slocock in September 1972 were: height 50 ft (15 m), branch spread 36 ft (11 m) with a trunk circumference of 10 ft 3 in. (3 m) at 3 ft (91 cm) above ground-level. There appears to be no record of the date of its planting.

Cytologically *M. kobus* is a diploid with 2n = 38 chromosomes.

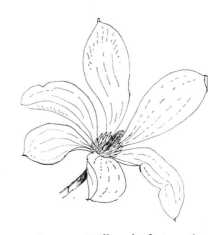

Japanese Willow-leaf Magnolia
Tamu-shiba in Japan

MAGNOLIA SALICIFOLIA (Siebold & Zuccarini) Maximowicz

C. J. Maximowicz in *Bulletin de l'Académie Impériale des Sciences de St. Pétersbourg* 17 : 419 (1872)

SYN. *Buergeria salicifolia* Siebold & Zuccarini (1846)

T. A. Sprague in *Curtis's Botanical Magazine* 139 : t. 8483 (1913)

G. H. Johnstone in *Asiatic Magnolias in Cultivation*: 97–101 (1955)

Stephen Spongberg in *Journal of the Arnold Arboretum* 57, 3 : 292–5 (1976)

Plate 33

This Japanese Magnolia is among the hardiest and easiest to grow and is characterized by its small, narrow, willow-like leaves which usually emit an aroma of aniseed when bruised or crushed though occasionally they smell distinctively of lemon verbena *Aloysia triphylla* (*Lippia citriodora*). A specimen at Kew with this aroma is to be found in the Magnolia collection near the Azalea Garden. It was sent to Kew by the Yokohama Nursery Company of Japan in 1906.

M. salicifolia has a profusion of small, narrow-tepalled flowers, freely produced even on quite young trees, which often start to flower at five to six years from seed while less than 6 ft (2 m) tall.

The very slender and wiry twigs hold their flower buds erect, but they nod over horizontally with the weight of the expanding buds, before opening to small fragrant white flowers in late March or early April. Although the individual flowers tend to be rather floppy and shapeless the general effect is quite sensational.

The flowers consist of two inner whorls of white tepals and an outer whorl of three shorter and thinner ones of a light-green shade, in the form of a false calyx. The filaments of the stamens are blush pink and the gynoecium is green. The flowers attain a diameter of 3 to 4 in. (7·5 to 10 cm) when fully expanded. The peduncles or flower stalks are glabrous or hairless as are the leaf buds. The fruit cones are cylindrical and 2 to 3 in. (5 to 7·5 cm) long.

M. salicifolia has small oblong-lanceolate and narrowly-elliptic leaves, with greyish undersides, well spaced along the shoots and providing a distinctive air of daintiness. They are 3 to 6 in. (7·5 to 15 cm) long by 1 to 2 in. (2·5 to 5 cm) wide.

It differs from *M. kobus* in having glabrous instead of pubescent flower stalks and leaf buds and from *M. stellata* in the smaller number of tepals and in its lanceolate leaves.

M. salicifolia grows into a large erect shrub or small tree with slender twigs and branches and light greyish-brown bark. It is found in the mountains on the Japanese islands of Honshu (mainly in the Sea of Japan drainage area), Shikoku and Kyushu; it also occurs occasionally as far south as central Japan.

Although *M. salicifolia* had been described by Siebold in 1846 it was not successfully introduced to Western gardens until 1892. In October of that year Prof. C. S. Sargent of the Arnold Arboretum and the English nurseryman, James H. Veitch were plant collecting near Aomori, the most northerly city on Japan's main island Honshu, accompanied by Japanese naturalist Tokubuchi, when they harvested a quantity of seed of this species on Mount Hakkoda at altitudes between 2,000 and 3,000 ft (610 and 915 m). In *Forest Flora of Japan* Professor Sargent reported that it was found growing in low wet situations. A month later Sargent was collecting in an area 200 miles (320 km) farther south when he secured more seed from an isolated specimen in the hills below Mount Ontake. Veitch's seeds of *M. salicifolia* from Mount Hakkoda failed to germinate so this species was not successfully introduced into English gardens until 1906.

M. salicifolia is somewhat variable in growth habit and ultimate stature. J. G. Millais in *Magnolias*: 213 described and pictured an erect-growing form of this Magnolia as *M. salicifolia* var. *fastigiata* (facing page 212) growing at Tilgate in Sussex. He also referred to it incorrectly as var. *fasciata* on page 213, while the photograph facing page 214 captioned *M. salicifolia* is surely *M. stellata* since some flowers clearly show fourteen tepals. *M. salicifolia* var. *fastigiata* was probably introduced as a grafted clone from Japan and it is certainly a most desirable Magnolia since it has larger-than-usual flowers and occupies less space. In America there is reported to be a specimen of this form growing in Highland Park, Rochester, New York, which was used as the female parent for attempted crosses with *M. × soulangiana* described later under *M. × slavinii*.

M. salicifolia var. *concolor* has very long, reflexed strap-like tepals numbering seven or eight per flower. The leaves are broader and the shoots stouter than the type and they emit an aroma of aniseed when crushed. It also flowers somewhat later and has a more spreading habit. In 1866 F. A. G. Miquel described a form *concolor* in *Annales Musei Botanici Lugduno-Batavi* 2 : 257–8 which he said was collected by Keiske but he did not record the locality. A tree which grew in J. H. Veitch's Coombe Wood nursery was described in the earlier edition of W. J. Bean's *Trees and Shrubs Hardy in the British Isles* as differing from the typical form in its more spreading habit, its stouter branchlets, larger flowers, broader tepals 1½ in. (4 cm) wide, broader leaves up to 3 in. (7·5 cm) wide, differently scented bark, and in flowering a fortnight or so later. It was subsequently identified by Dr. Sprague of Kew as representing var. *concolor* of Miquel.

Hillier's of Winchester grow a selected cultivar 'Jermyns', described as a slower-growing shrubby form, with broader leaves conspicuously glaucous beneath, and large flowers appearing later than the type. Dr. Spongberg writes '*Magnolia salicifolia* was originally introduced into western horticulture by C. S. Sargent, but it has been questioned whether the plants grown and distributed by the Arnold Arboretum from Sargent's seed collections were typical of *M. salicifolia*. Probably as a result of the skepticism surrounding the original plants and the lack of knowledge of the variability of *M. salicifolia* in nature, several plants of *M. salicifolia* that appeared as seedlings in cultivation were recognized as hybrids, and numerous plants now in cultivation are currently treated as belonging to hybrid groups. In two of the three instances in which putative hybrids were described, it was postulated that other taxa of sect. *Buergeria* were the pollen parents. Thus Rehder described a hybrid between *M. salicifolia* and *M. kobus* var. *stellata* . . . giving the name *M.* × *proctoriana* to the hybrid group (*Journal of the Arnold Arboretum* 20 : 412, 1939), while S. A. Pearce (*Gardeners Chronicle* 3 : 154, 1952) gave the collective name *M.* × *kewensis* to presumed hybrids between *M. salicifolia* and *M. kobus* var. *kobus*. A third hybrid originally assumed to involve *M. salicifolia* as the seed parent and *M.* × *soulangiana* as the pollen parent was named *M.* × *slavinii* Harkness (*National Horticultural Magazine* 33 : 118, 1954). However this hybrid was later (*Morris Arboretum Bulletin* 12 : 19, 1961) reduced to the synonymy of *M.* × *proctoriana*, since its chromosome number, 2n = 38, did not coincide with the number to be expected had *M.* × *soulangiana* 2n = 95, 114, been the pollen parent.'

Dr. Spongberg continues: 'However, a re-examination of the morphology of the three presumed hybrids (including the type specimens of *M.* ×

proctoriana and specimens from the "type" plants of *M.* × *slavinii* and *M.* × *kewensis*) and that of the assumed parental taxa has convinced me that the "hybrids" are easily accommodated within *M. salicifolia*. This conclusion is supported when the variation of *M. salicifolia* in nature is studied in conjunction with the cultivated material. The fact that seedlings of *M. salicifolia* show a degree of variability is undoubtedly correlated to some extent with the fact that the species is self compatible (see J. C. McDaniel, *Newsletter of the American Magnolia Society* 2, 1 : 4 (1965)) and plants grown from self-fertilized seeds should be expected to exhibit variation associated with the expression of recessive traits.'

Dr. Spongberg's work was published just as the text of this book was being completed so that the hitherto hybrid groups referred to are retained among the 'Magnolia Hybrids and Crosses' with references added to draw attention to this theory.

Cytologically *M. salicifolia* is a diploid with 2n = 38 chromosomes.

SECTION *TULIPASTRUM* (Spach) Dandy

J. E. Dandy in *Camellias and Magnolias Conference Report*: 74 (1950); based on *Tulipastrum* Spach, *Histoire Naturelle des Végétaux, Phanérogames* 7 : 481 (1839)

type species *M. acuminata*

This section includes one Asian species, the purple-flowered *M. quinquepeta* (*liliflora*), together with the green-flowered North American species *M. acuminata* and the yellow-flowered *M. cordata* which is now generally recognized as *M. acuminata* var. *subcordata*.

The flowers of these Magnolias appear with their deciduous leaves so that they are never truly precocious, and may develop intermittently over a period of several months.

Section *Tulipastrum* resembles Section *Buergeria* in the reduction of the outer tepals to form false calyces, but differs in the form and colour of the inner ones, which are purple, green or yellow.

An interesting race of hybrids between *M. acuminata* and *M. quinquepeta* was bred in the Brooklyn Botanic Garden, New York, in 1957. One of these has been named 'Evamaria' after Mrs. Evamaria Sperber, who was personally responsible for the hybridizing while she was on the Botanic Garden's staff. This hybrid combination was repeated by Prof. J. C. McDaniel of the University of Illinois, using pollen from a superior form of *M. quinquepeta* on the Klassen

clone of *M. acuminata*. For fuller details of these Magnolia marriages, combining as they do the Eastern and Western members of Section *Tulipastrum*, see under *M.* × *brooklynensis* in the chapter on 'Magnolia Hybrids and Crosses'.

American Cucumber Tree

MAGNOLIA ACUMINATA Linnaeus

M. Catesby in *Flora Caroliniana* 2 (appendix): t. 45, excluding plate 45 (1741)

C. Linnaeus in *Systema Naturae* 10, 2 : 1082 (1759)

A. Michaux in *Flora Boreali-Americana* 1 : 328 (1803)

John Sims in *Curtis's Botanical Magazine* 50 : t. 2427 (1823)

Plates 35, 36 and 37

The apices of the leaves of this Magnolia are *acuminate*, tapering to a point where the blades join the petioles.

The name Cucumber Tree originates from the fruit cones which are green when young and which, with some stretch of the imagination, might be then likened to gherkin cucumbers. These turn dark red on maturity but are usually too sparsely produced to be of much ornament and tend (when unfertilized) to fall soon after they turn colour. They are ovoid to oblong 2½ to 3½ in. (6 to 7·5 cm) long.

M. acuminata was discovered in 1736 by John, the elder Bartram, who sent seed to England where it was raised by that ardent plantsman, Peter Collinson. It first flowered in his London garden at Mill Hill on 20 May 1762. Since then it has proved to be one of the hardiest and fastest growing species, succeeding in northern Europe up to southern Norway. Catesby quoted Bartram as saying that he had seen many in Pennsylvania north of the Susquehannah River, some over 100 ft (30·5 m) tall. He recorded that the wood was tough and of an orange colour.

It is the most widely distributed of the North American species and ranges, from the north shore of Lake Erie in extreme south-eastern Ontario, Canada, to Louisiana, south-east Oklahoma and northern Florida in the United States. Rhind, in his *History of Plants* (1857) said that it was to be found 'along the whole mountainous tract of the Alleghenies' (i.e. from Pennsylvania to North Carolina) while J. E. Dandy, in his 'Survey of the Genus *Magnolia*' gives its range, apart from its intrusion into Canada, as 'extending through the Appalachian and Ozark mountain systems of the eastern United States from New York southwards.'

It is the largest growing of the American deciduous species and second only to *M. grandiflora* as a source of timber. It grows into a large straight-trunked tree from 60 ft (18 m) and up to 90 ft (27·5 m) in height in the Great Smoky Mountains, with trunk diameters from 3 to 5 ft (91 cm to 1·5 m). One of the largest *M. acuminata* trees on record is in the Great Smoky Mountains National Park in Tennessee, with a height of 125 ft (38 m), a spread of 60 ft (18 m) and a trunk circumference of over 18 ft (5·5 m) at 4½ ft (1·3 m).

The largest specimen in the New York area is said to be a tree at Hicks's Nurseries, Westbury, Long Island, with a girth of 12 ft 9 in. (4 m).

At first pyramidal in shape, with dark brown bark, it often becomes spreading when mature. The timber is light and durable and was formerly used by North American Indians for making canoes and wooden bowls. It forms an excellent large shade-tree with a grey trunk and is well worth planting just for the bold effect of the large leaves, which are from 5 to 12 in. (12·5 to 30·5 cm) long, light green and usually slightly downy beneath, acute or pointed towards the apex, hence the botanical name *acuminata*. It is readily raised from seed and has long been used in America as an understock on which to bud or graft other Magnolias.

The fragrant flowers are relatively small and inconspicuous, indeed they may well pass unobserved until they begin to fall, because they are mostly borne high upon the tips of leafy shoots, when the foliage is fully developed in June and July. The nine tepals are usually erect at first, the three outer ones are glaucous green and tend to reflex downwards like a false calyx. The second whorl then becomes outermost and shows greenish-yellow backs, their inner surfaces being milky white overlaid with blue-green shadings. The inner whorl is usually of a clear yellow colour. The tepals usually reflex and become twisted after anthesis. The flowers bear a considerable resemblance to those of the closely related tulip tree (*Liriodendron*), which also is often referred to the Magnolia Family and which further resembles the Magnolias in Section *Tulipastrum* by having a species in both America and Asia.

The flower depicted in 1741 by Mark Catesby on plate 15 in *Flora Caroliniana* does not resemble the Magnolia under discussion here. He qualified it by stating that it was sent to him by one John Clayton of Virginia. Catesby described the flower as '5 ins. [12·5 cm] wide; petals white 12'. The leaves as shown on the plate are likewise out of character being broadly rounded at the apex while the description refers to them as 'Leaves 8″ × 5″ [20·5 × 12·5 cm] ending in a sharp point'. It would appear, therefore, that either the plate became transposed or Linnaeus simply accepted Catesby's latinized description at least as regards the leaves which he recorded as *folio majore acuminato haud albicante*. Linnaeus described them as *folio ovato-oblongis acuminatis* in his *Systema Naturae* 10, 2 : 1082 (1759).

Since writing these notes the author has had an opportunity to refer to John Sims's description and plate of *M. acuminata* in *Curtis's Botanical Magazine* 50 : t. 2427 (1823) which depicts a flower from a tree in the garden of one John Walker, Esq., of Arnos Grove, Southgate. The plate shows a flower with considerable blue shadings towards the outer edges of the six outer tepals while the innermost three are canary yellow. Sims quoted the common name 'Blue Magnolia' and, referring to Catesby's plate 115 in *Flora Caroliniana*, he wrote: 'it appears to us that the flower was made out from one of MAGNOLIA *glauca*, being very unlike that of our plant'. [*M. glauca* was the former name for *M. virginiana*.]

In 1954 the American botanist Dr. James W. Hardin published 'An analysis of variation within *Magnolia acuminata* L.' in the *Journal of the Elisha Mitchell Scientific Society* 70, 2 : 298–312 (1954). After a thorough study of herbarium material Hardin reduced the *acuminata-cordata* complex to three varieties and one form as follows:

'1. *M. acuminata* var. *ozarkensis*. Smallest, most glabrous and darkest-flowered form, found in the Ozarks (Missouri, Arkansas and Oklahoma).
'2. *M. acuminata* var. *acuminata*. The common form with pubescence intermediate between 1 and 3 which may have developed from inter-breeding between them. It is widely distributed over a range from southern Ontario to Louisiana.
'2a. *M. acuminata* var. *acuminata* forma *aurea*, with yellow petals. A form found scattered in the mountains and upper piedmont of the Carolinas, Tennessee, Georgia and possibly Alabama.
'3. *M. acuminata* var. *cordata*. Clearly distinguished by the first-year twigs being pubescent throughout. It is distributed over a relatively narrow range from central North Carolina to Tuscaloosa and Baldwin Counties, Alabama, and Walton County in northwest Florida.'

In September 1970 Philip J. Savage, Jr., took the author to see some fine specimen trees of *M. acuminata* in Woodmere Cemetery, Detroit, several of which have unusually rough, shaggy bark (Plate 35). Prof. J. C. McDaniel has collected similar bark from a tree at Princeton, Illinois.

Among the largest specimens on record in England is the veteran tree at Albury House, Surrey, which was 75 ft (23 m) in 1905 and had added but 10 ft (3 m) to its stature during the next sixty years. Another tree which was planted at Frensham Hall, Shottermill, Surrey, in 1905 was 78 ft (23·5 m) high in 1968.

As might be anticipated with a species of such a wide range of distribution, considerable variation exists. In America several forms of this native tree have been named and propagated including:

'Ludoviciana'   A form from West Feliciana Parish, Louisiana, with broader leaves and larger flowers, having tepals 3½ to 4 in. (9 to 10 cm) long, compared with the normal 2½ to 3 in. (6 to 7·5 cm).
'Variegata'   With leaves attractively blotched golden yellow but tending to revert to the green type.

At Kew there is a large-leaved form known as 'Maxima' which was sent out by the old London nursery firm of Loddiges about 1830.

Prof. J. C. McDaniel of the Department of Horticulture at Illinois University has been carrying out research and hybridizing experiments on this and other North American species and has selected several clones of *M. acuminata* including:

'Dunlap' a late-leafing, early-maturing and probably hardier form. In Illinois its leaves colour yellow before falling.
'Klassen' (Plate 37) a vigorous, self-fertile tree with good-sized flowers of better than usual colour.
'Moyer' a very vigorous tree with large leaves and pendulous branches.
'Philo'   another self-fertile clone growing as a large ninety-year-old tree near Philo, Illinois.

He points out that although trees of *M. acuminata* appear normally to be incompatible to their own pollen and therefore seldom fruit well in isolation, they will, however, set seed if their flowers are pollinated by hand with their own pollen as well as with pollen applied from other trees of the same species.

'Golden Glow' is a yellow-flowered *M. acuminata* which was found in the Smoky Mountains in Sevier County, Tennessee, by Dr. Frank B. Galyon. It is described as being typical in every detail except flower colour 'which is quite yellow after opening'. Apart from the more yellow than usual flowers, 'Golden Glow' tends to flower more freely than ordinary *M. acuminata*, often producing flowers from lateral buds below the terminal ones.

MAGNOLIA ACUMINATA var. SUB-CORDATA (Spach) Dandy
(so named for its sometimes heart-shaped leaves.)

J. E. Dandy in *American Journal of Botany* 51 : 1056 (1964)
SYNS. *M. cordata* A. Michaux in *Flora Boreali-Americana* 1 : 328 (1803)
M. acuminata var. *cordata* C. S. Sargent in *North American Silva* 1 : t. 6 (1891)

Plate 38

This Magnolia was discovered about 1790 by André, the elder Michaux, a French botanist, in the neighbourhood of Augusta, Georgia. In *Flora Boreali-Americana* he described it as growing on sunny slopes in Upper Carolina and Georgia (*in collibris appricis Carolinae superioris et Georgiae*). He sent it to France in 1803. All of the older European specimens are believed to have been propagated from the original introduction, since it was lost sight of in the wild until 1910, when Louis A. Berckmans came across several bushes, only 4 to 6 ft (1 to 2 m) tall, flowering profusely in a dry woodland area some 18 miles (29 km) north of Augusta. It is surprisingly hardy considering its restricted southern range, for Georgia is on the Atlantic coast of America between Florida and South Carolina. It also (as noted earlier) occurs over a narrow range from central North Carolina to Tuscaloosa and Baldwin Counties in western Alabama, and Walton County in north-west Florida.

According to Rehder in *Manual of Cultivated Trees and Shrubs*: 247 (1940) the fruit cones are somewhat smaller and darker red than those of the type. The leaves are usually shorter, broader and more rounded at the apex.

It produces erect, pale-yellow, tulip-shaped flowers about 4 in. (10 cm) across, clustered among its leaves in May and June. Some forms also continue flowering later and in some the flowers are canary yellow. They are faintly though not agreeably scented and the inner tepals sometimes have reddish veins. It is best planted in a sunny situation and is suitable for the smaller garden, usually beginning to flower when quite young at 3 to 4 ft (91 cm to 1·2 m). At Kew a specimen attained a height of only 15 ft (4·5 m) in fifty years, but it should be borne in mind that the poor sandy soil and relatively low rainfall are not ideal growing conditions for Magnolias. Millais described it as a tree 40 to 50 ft (12 to 15·2 m) high, which suggests that he was referring to a more vigorous clone or to *M. acuminata* f. *auera* (Sargent) Hardin.

Sargent in *North American Silva* 1 : t. 6 (1891) and later Hardin (1954) reduced *M. cordata* from specific rank to a form of *M. acuminata* most readily distinguished by the first-year twigs being pubescent throughout. The leaves are, in fact, rarely cordate as the name implies. They are from 3 to 5 in. (7·5 to 12·5 cm) long, comparatively broader and not as pointed as those of *M. acuminata*, and hairy beneath.

This Magnolia is rarely met with in English gardens and might not flower freely in conditions which are ideal for the precocious Asian species and their hybrids, which grow to such magnificent trees in many woodland gardens in the south and west of England. A specimen in the Magnolia Garden at Kew is a large shrub with slender branchlets and the flower buds in winter are very small with furry bracts.

The flowers of *M. acuminata* var. *subcordata* are of the same shade of yellow as those of *M. acuminata* f.

aurea mentioned earlier but, while the latter grows into a large tree, *subcordata* is usually more shrubby than arborescent, at least as regards the form which was originally propagated by grafting. Variety *alabamensis* is a form with greenish flowers and pubescent twigs.

For a long time the largest known tree in America of this rare native yellow-flowered Magnolia was a specimen which had been grafted on to *M. acuminata* in the 1840s, and which had been planted at a farm residence outside Lexington, Kentucky, now incorporated in Woodland Park. It is reported that the graft line on the tree is still visible, and it is believed to be of the same clone which was sent to France by Michaux in 1801 and later brought back to America. It is suggested that this tree was included in a landscape plan drawn by the naturalist Rafinesque, who taught for several years at Transylvania College in Lexington. The actual propagator may have been a Frenchman who had a nursery at Lexington for several years around 1830 to 1840.

It certainly seems remarkable that any tree or shrub, native of such a highly civilized part of the world as North America, could have remained as it were lost or hidden for well over a century, from the date of André Michaux's discovery and recording about 1790 until Berckmans's recording in 1910. André Michaux was assisted by his son François, who succeeded him on his death in 1802. The latinized record cited from *Flora Boreali-Americana* was therefore published posthumously in the following year.

In 1944 American botanist Oliver M. Freeman crossed *M. acuminata* with variety *cordata* and the results are now being evaluated at the United States National Arboretum at Washington, D.C.

According to W. J. Bean's *Trees and Shrubs Hardy in the British Isles*, while either André Michaux or his son was responsible for introducing this Magnolia to France in 1803, there were two earlier introductions to England in 1801. The first was by John Lyon to Loddige's nursery at Hackney, London; the other by plant collector John Fraser, who had his own nursery in Sloane Square, London. This seems to suggest that the first specimens grown in England may have been raised from seed and were not grafted plants of the Michaux clone.

More recently some American botanists have endeavoured to eliminate what has been described as 'the spurious association of "yellow flowers" with the epithet "cordata" ' and refer to the clones with yellow flowers, which have been propagated and distributed since 1801, as 'an *M. acuminata* with yellower than usual flowers and a shrubby or small tree habit'. Both *Hortus III* and the *American Magnolia Check List* will be retaining the old var. *cordata* but whatever botanists may decree it seems logical to perpetuate the André Michaux clone as 'Cordata' to distinguish it from recent rivals which have been selected and named in America.

One of the most promising of these is 'Miss Honeybee', a cultivar registered in 1974 by James Merrill, nurseryman of Painesville, Ohio. It has been classified as *M. acuminata* var. *subcordata* and is said to have larger yellow flowers than the Michaux clone 'Cordata', beginning to open precociously on a more vigorous but equally pubescent plant. The flower buds are reported as being several times greater in volume than those of 'Cordata'.

Cytologically *M. acuminata* and var. *subcordata* are tetraploids with 2n = 76 chromosomes.

Purple Lily-flowered Magnolia
Mu-lan in China
Shi-mokuren or *Tsuneno-mokuren* in Japan

MAGNOLIA QUINQUEPETA (Buc'hoz) Dandy

Adopted from *Lassonia quinquepeta* P. J. Buc'hoz in *Plantes Nouvellement Découvertes* 21 : t. 19 Fig. 2 (1779)

J. E. Dandy in *Journal of Botany* 72 : 103 (1934)

S. A. Spongberg in *Journal of the Arnold Arboretum* 57, 3 : 298 (1976)

SYNS. *M. liliflora* L. A. J. Desrousseaux in Lamarck, *Encyclopédie Méthodique, Botanique* 3 : 675 (1791)

M. purpurea W. Curtis in *Curtis's Botanical Magazine* 11 : t. 390 (1797)

Plate 39

The many synonyms are discussed in chronological sequence in the text. By some authorities the name by which it has been known was spelt *liliiflora* but, after careful consideration, the author has followed the original spelling *liliflora*, which conforms with classical Latin, in which the Romans generally preferred to drop the second 'i'.

According to J. E. Dandy, *M. quinquepeta* (*liliflora*) has no close allies in Asia, and it was his opinion that, despite the contrast in flower colour, the affinities of this species are with the American *M. acuminata*, with which it agrees in both vegetative and floral structure.

This Purple Lily-flowered Magnolia was the first species to be introduced which had coloured flowers. The dark-purple blossoms open from slender pointed buds as the leaves begin to appear and, as they develop, the narrow strap-shaped tepals reflex to reveal their white inner or upper surfaces. It is a comparatively weak grower and this factor, combined with its freedom and prolonged period of flowering, makes it an ideal choice of Magnolia for small gardens and for restricted sites.

M. quinquepeta is hardy on the coastal plain of the south-eastern states of America as far north as New York. At Brooklyn Botanic Gardens it has been reported not to grow vigorously and to be susceptible to winter kill. Further south it occasionally bears fertile fruit cones and several superior seedlings have been given clonal names and propagated vegetatively. Of these 'O' Neill' has very dark green leaves and a compact, bushy habit of growth while 'Reflorescens' has an extended flowering period from March or early April continuing intermittently throughout the summer. It was this clone which was used by William F. Kosar in his contribution to the U.S. National Arboretum's Magnolia breeding programme in 1956.

It is figured under the name *Mu-lan* ("Woody Orchid") in early Chinese Pharmaceutical Natural Histories dating back to the eleventh century. Apparently it was, in ancient times, used as a drug-plant. It was also used as a dwarfing understock for container-grown plants of *M. heptapeta* (*denudata*), which the royal gardeners used to force into flower to provide a long display in the imperial palaces.

Included under this species we have *M. discolor* of Ventenat and De Candolle, *M. purpurea* of Curtis, *M. gracilis* of Andrews and Salisbury together with *M. liliflora* 'Nigra' (*M. × soulangiana* 'Nigra'), the last depicted by Johnstone as *M. liliflora* in Plate 11 of *Asiatic Magnolias in Cultivation* facing page 108.

Gardeners and plant enthusiasts throughout the ages have constantly sought after improved or unusual types of plants both edible and ornamental. This Magnolia has been cultivated for centuries, first in its native China and later in Japan, so it is not surprising that more than one form was introduced into Western gardens.

Let us therefore see how contemporary botanists described and illustrated the different forms of this species about the time of their introduction, before they had become confused in cultivation as they appear to be today. Perhaps it would be best to consider them in the sequence in which they were first recorded by leading botanists of that time.

1. P. J. Buc'hoz in *Plantes Nouvellement Découvertes* 21 : t. 19 Fig. 2 (1779) as *Lassonia quinquepeta*

The plate referred to was obviously based on an original stock picture or artistic representation which Buc'hoz had received from China, for, while the general impression conforms with a flowering branch of the Magnolia which we are investigating, the gynandrophores have been replaced by flattened bosses of stamens, without the protruding stigmatic columns typical of Magnolia flowers. Buc'hoz subsequently fell into such ill repute in the botanical world that a later botanist named the stinking-flowered *Buchosia foetida* after him!

Way back in 1934 Dandy had contributed notes on 'The Identity of *Lassonia* Buc'hoz' in *Journal of Botany* 72 : 101–3 in which he considered that the name *quinquepeta* had been validly published by Buc'hoz and that 'discrepancies in the published descriptions are fully accounted for by defects in the drawings'. Fuller details are given under *M. heptapeta* on p. 82.

The drawings referred to were impressionist Chinese prints which Buc'hoz accepted as being botanically accurate. He counted only five tepals in the purple-flowered Magnolia and therefore named it *M. quinquepeta* whereas it normally has six to twelve plus the three smaller ones in the outer whorl, which represents the false calyx.

It is remarkable that Dandy never adopted the Buc'hoz nomenclature in his subsequent publications. He referred to them only as synonyms in his 'Survey of the Genus *Magnolia*' (1950) also in his 'Revised Survey' (1970) which he prepared for publication in this book. As I mentioned on p. 83, decisions made at the Eleventh International Botanical Congress in Seattle in August 1969 led to the publication of the 1972 *International Code of Botanical Nomenclature*. Article 62 of this 'Seattle Code' reads: 'A legitimate name or epithet must not be rejected merely because it is inappropriate or disagreeable, or because another is preferable or better known, or because it has lost its original meaning.'

In July 1976 Dr. Stephen Spongberg's 'Magno-liaceae Hardy in Temperate North America' was published in *Journal of the Arnold Arboretum* 57, 3 : 250–312. Then in November 1976 Macmillan published *Hortus III* in which the staff of the Bailey Hortorium and numerous collaborators revised and enlarged upon *Hortus II* of 1941. Both of these American publications adopted the Buc'hoz names which Dandy had resurrected in 1934 but which he must have decided subsequently to disregard. It might be said that it had taken over forty years for Dandy's published authentication to soak through the sieve of botanical opinion. As a result two of the most important and popular species of Magnolia became saddled with ridiculous epithets which, with that of Linnaeus's *M. tripetala*, will constitute a trio of botanical inexactitudes which henceforth must be perpetuated for ever.

2. C. P. Thunberg in *Flora Japonica, Magnolia*: 236 7 (1784) as *Magnolia glauca β flore magno, atropurpureo*
2A. 'Botanical Observations of the Flora of Japan' in *Transactions of the Linnean Society*, London 2 : 336 (1794) as *M. obovata*

Unfortunately Thunberg's latinized description is extremely brief and his reference to the leaves being glaucous beneath, reticulate and hairy does not apply to any Magnolia in this group as we know it today.

3. L. A. J. Desrousseaux in Lamarck, *Encyclopédie Méthodique, Botanique* 3 : 675 (1791)
3A. J. Banks in *Icones Selectae Plantarum, quas in Japonia Collegit et Delineavit Engelbertus Kaempfer*: tt. 12–14 (1791)

The Desrousseaux description was based on a re-production by Joseph Banks in the same year, of a drawing by Kaempfer of three Magnolias, now recognized as *M. kobus*, *M. heptapeta* (*denudata*) and *M. quinquepeta* (*liliflora*), in which the plate depicting the Magnolia in question was titled '*Mokkwuren flore albo*'. Unfortunately Banks had made the mistake of interchanging his reproduction of Kaempfer's drawing of *M. heptapeta* (*denudata*) with that of *M. quinquepeta* (*liliflora*). We have therefore to look at Desrousseaux's description of *M. heptapeta* for *M. quinquepeta*.

'The flowers, which are red and terminal, grow singly, are fairly wide open and seem larger than those of *M. glauca. The petals are oval in shape*★,

---

★ The italics are mine.

slightly oblong and display no noticeable veining, at least according to the illustration put out by Mr. Banks. They end in a short point. This shrub grows naturally in Japan.' Clearly Desrousseaux had seen neither live material nor herbarium specimens though it is his description upon which the species is based.

4. W. Curtis in *Curtis's Botanical Magazine* 11 : t. 390 (1797) as *Magnolia purpurea*
    Magnolia floribus hexapetalis, petalis extus purpureis

This brief latinized description throws doubt on the Magnolia depicted as *M. liliflora* in Plate 11 in Johnstone's *Asiatic Magnolias in Cultivation*, which has seven tepals. Curtis, in what appears to be the earliest description recorded direct from a living specimen, stated that his plate was from a small flowering plant about a foot high, supplied by the Countess of Coventry from her London residence. 'It is a native of China, and is reported to have first flowered in the collection of the Duke of Portland, at Bulstrode; is regarded as a greenhouse plant, and most probably will be found hardy enough with a little shelter to bear the cold of our winters'.

He described the flower as being 'about the size of a middling tulip, without scent, cupping somewhat in the same way, rarely fully expanding', adding 'We have since seen much larger plants with proportionate flowers'. This appears to be the earliest description made from personal observations at the time of flowering.

Curtis's Plate 390 depicts a much broader-tepalled flower than that now usually associated with *M. quinquepeta*. He refers to the 'petals six in number, *ovate*, rather fleshy, the three outermost expanding more than the three innermost, all of a purple hue on the outside, base, midrib and veins of a deeper hue, *here and there gashed*' (my italics). This latter detail alone should distinguish the Magnolia to which he referred. This was the first Magnolia to be figured in *Curtis's Botanical Magazine*.

Curtis's description was from a flowering plant the precise size and origin of which he takes pains to record. His reference to the flower having six *ovate* petals corresponds with the Desrousseaux description already quoted. Neither description quite fits the plant now grown as *M. quinquepeta* (*liliflora*) in English gardens.

5. E. P. Ventenat in *Jardin de la Malmaison* 1 : t. 24 (1803) as *Magnolia discolor*

Ventenat's patron was Emperor Napoleon's wife,

Joséphine (Tascher de la Pagerie), who commissioned the artist Redouté to paint the flowers in her famous gardens at La Malmaison near Paris, on which she squandered a vast fortune. Prior to the Revolution his patron had been Marie Antoinette.

Redouté also painted *M. discolor* for Duhamel's *Traité des Arbres et Arbustes* (1804.) Plate No. 66 in Tome 2 shows his painting of Ventenat's *M. discolor*, and who would dare to doubt Redouté's accuracy? The flower depicted is pronouncedly tulip shaped with six broad, obovate tepals, in shape closely resembling those of Curtis's *M. purpurea*, which he ranks as synonymous. Ventenat's text includes more details of the leaves than of the flowers 'which would have every likeness to those of the white lily, if they did not have a purple exterior; each grows at the end of a branch'. He apparently left the finer details to the skill of Redouté's brush.

6. H. Andrews in the *Botanist's Repository*: t. 326 (1803–4) as *Magnolia purpurea*

'*Specific Character*. Magnolia with inversely egg-shaped, flaccid leaves; flowers purple; *petals inversely egg-shaped* and straddling.' (The italics are not in the original text.)

'This fine species of Magnolia is a native of China and Japan, was introduced to us by the late Mr. Slater of Laystonstone, to whom we are so much indebted for the greatest number of beautiful plants which have been imported from thence by any individual. It is a free-growing plant, will resist the severity of our winters, if planted in a warm situation, and is deciduous; but if kept in the conservatory, it retains its leaves the whole year and flowers about June.

'The plant from which our figure was taken is in the magnificent Conservatory of the Right Honourable the Marquis of Blandford, White Knights, near Reading, Berks; and, we believe, the finest specimen of this species of Magnolia in Britain.' (The old estate of White Knights is now the campus of Reading University and the famous collection of Magnolias has long since disappeared.) Andrews's plate shows a flower with six very broad and lax tepals with the tendency to be 'here and there gashed' as described by Curtis.

7. R. A. Salisbury in *Paradisus Londinensis* 2 : t. 87 (1807) as *Magnolia gracilis* (The Slender Magnolia)

'A distinct species from *M. Purpurea* of our gardeners [?gardens] and sent from China some years ago to the Rt. Honble. Charles Greville.

'Flowers without smell, terminating the last years branches when the young leaves are just beginning to appear . . . Petals 6, pale purple with their outside exceedingly dark but the colour gradually vanishing on both sides till the inside at last is almost white, three outer ones about 2 inches [5 cm] long, three inner ones narrower and shorter, obovate-wedge-shaped, obtuse, smooth on both surfaces with a slight dew, of the consistence of soft leather: Nerves deeper coloured.'

The Plate No. 87 from a drawing by W. Hooker was published on 1 November 1807. It shows a smaller and narrower-tepalled flower than that depicted on the earlier plates mentioned.

8. A. P. de Candolle in *Regni Vegetabilis Systema Naturale* 1 : 457 (1817) as *Magnolia obovata* var. *discolor*.

De Candolle described this as having six petals, white inside and purple outside. His brief latinized description and lack of a plate does not help our investigation to any appreciable extent. Yet it was he who listed as a synonym *M. purpurea* Curtis and *M. discolor* Ventenat.

A fuller description of *M. discolor* de Candolle was recorded by Baron Hamelin of Franconville, when he gave a detailed report of the raising of *M.* × *soulangiana* in *Annales de la Société d'Horticulture de Paris* 1 : 90–5 (1827). In a Table of Comparison at the end of the text he compared this new hybrid Magnolia with its parents in full detail. He described *M. discolor* as having six petals rolled one over the other, unequal, *lanceolate and never opening fully*, violet-purple outside, white inside, May to June.

Hamelin's description of *M. discolor* de Candolle sounds more like *M. gracilis* Salisbury. That there were two quite distinct forms or varieties of the Purple Magnolia in circulation at this period had apparently confused contemporary botanists. In reports published by Chevalier Soulange-Bodin in *Annales de l'Institut Royal Horticole de Fromont* 3 : 150–1 (1831) and in 1843, he repeatedly referred to *M. purpurea* as the pollen parent of his Soulangiana hybrids and wrote: 'These attempts [at artificial fertilization] will be repeated until they are successful, for it will be fine to transfer to the large flower of *Magnolia macrophylla* the purple hues of *Magnolia discolor*, as we have done with so much success with regard to *Magnolia yulan* by fertilizing it with pollen of *Magnolia purpurea*.' *M. discolor* must have flowered much later than *M. purpurea*.

9. J. C. Loudon in *Arboretum et Fruticetum Britannicum* 1 : 282 (1838)

Loudon gives as the special characteristics of *M. purpurea*: 'Deciduous. Leaves obovate, acute, reticulately veined; almost smooth. Flowers erect, of 3 sepals and 6 obovate petals; styles very short. Flowering period March, April and May. Introduced 1790.' Loudon quoted three varieties of *M. purpurea* which he copied from De Candolle's *Prodromus* (1824–30) and Don's *Miller's Dictionary* (1837): *M. purpurea denudata* Lamarck, a form flowering before the leaves. *M. purpurea discolor* Ventenat, which was said to be more tender than the species, and '*M. purpurea liliflora* Lamarck, the petals of which are white on both sides'. The reason for this erroneous description has already been laid on Joseph Banks's confused identification of the plates depicting Kaempfer's original drawings, so instead of the above we should read the Desrousseaux description for *M. denudata*, which name Banks had misapplied to Kaempfer's *M. liliflora*. A brief extract translated from Desrousseaux's description has been given earlier. As it was made only from the plate it is not of much significance since we are only really interested in descriptions made from first-hand knowledge of the plants concerned.

Loudon described *M. purpurea* as 'A deciduous shrub, attaining in the gardens about London, the height of from 6 ft to 10 ft [2 to 3 m] in as many years. . . . The stems are numerous, but not much branched; the leaves are large, of a very dark green; and the plant produces a profusion of flowers, which do not expand fully till a day or so before they drop off; and which, unless the weather is warm, do not expand at all, but wither on the plant and disfigure it. The flowers are large, more or less purple (according to the season, but never wholly purple) without, and always white within. The bark, when bruised, has an aromatic odour. . . . About London and Paris it is not only propagated for sale as a flowering shrub, but as a stock for grafting other species on, even of the tree kinds. . . . There is one 20 ft [6 m] high in the garden of the Rev. J. Mitford, at Benwell in Suffolk, which, we believe, is the largest in England.'

Loudon reported that several plants of *M. purpurea* had been raised from seed ripened in this country (presumably under glass) and that such 'plants may exhibit slight shades of difference, as has been the case with certain seedlings raised in the Brentford Nursery, but, as far as we have observed, none of these are worth keeping distinct.'

Loudon's description of *M.* (?*purpurea*) *gracilis* as the slender-growing Purple-flowered Magnolia, more closely resembles *M. quinquepeta* (*liliflora*) as we know it today. 'The only variety which we consider truly distinctive is *M. p. gracilis*, considered as a species by Salisbury and other botanists, but which, we are convinced, is nothing more than a race, or a variety. . . . A somewhat delicate shrub with slender stems and branches, growing rather more erect and fastigiate than *M. purpurea*. The leaves are of the same form, but a little longer, and always of a decidedly paler green. The young leaves are pubescent underneath, as are the young shoots.'

He goes on to describe 'the longer and more slender form of the flower, the points of the petals of which are slightly turned back; while the flower of *M. purpurea* is more cup-shaped and the petals at the points are rather turned inwards. The petals of *M. gracilis* are exteriorly of an entirely dark purple, whereas those of *M. purpurea* melt off into white at their upper extremities. . . . It was brought to England in 1804. The largest plant which we know of is in the conservatory at White Knights, where it forms a narrow bush about 10 ft [3 m] high [in 1838]. . . . It was thought to be a conservatory plant when it was first planted; and it is now much too large to be removed with safety.'

10.   J. G. Millais in *Magnolias*: 133–5 (1927)

Millais described *M. gracilis* as being a very rare hybrid of unknown origin, resembling a smaller form of *M. soulangiana* 'Nigra', but distinct in its flowers, leaves and habit of growth. He described it as having 'curious descending branches that bend upwards at the ends, bearing leaves similar to those of *M. liliflora* but narrower. . . . The flowers are numerous at the ends of new shoots in May, being compressed and upright, the ends of the petals curved outwards . . . petals six, purple outside with a darker purple hue up the centre, inside white.' This description seems to match closely that for *M. discolor* published by Hamelin in his report on *M. × soulangiana* in 1827.

Millais suggested that *M. gracilis* might be a hybrid between *M. liliflora* and *M. stellata* 'since the long narrow shape of the petals suggests this theory'. He likened it to a smaller form of *M. × soulangiana* 'Nigra'.

He described *M. liliflora* as a large, sprawling bush 8 to 12 ft (2·5 to 3·5 m) high and reported having seen a plant in Derbyshire over 20 ft (6 m) high. He said that it was not grown to any extent because of its sprawling habit, adding 'it should be severely pruned and guided into some shape, otherwise it spreads in a drooping mass over a large area'.

11.   A. Rehder *Manual of Cultivated Trees and Shrubs* Ed. 2 : 251 (1940)

Rehder described *M. liliflora* var. *gracilis* as a small shrub with slender branches and narrower leaves and smaller dark purple flowers, introduced from Japan in 1804, giving 1790 as the date of introduction of *M. liliflora*. If he was referring to the same plant as Salisbury (7) his date of introduction seems awry since introduced in 1804 would not have been described three years later as having been 'sent from China some years ago'. The Rt. Hon. Charles Greville, to whom it was sent, was one of the founder members of the Royal Horticultural Society.

Ohwi in *Flora of Japan*: 468 (1965), describes var. *gracilis* as a slender, erect grower with smaller leaves and tepals about ⅛ in. (4 mm) wide, known in Japan as *To-mokuren*.

The Royal Horticultural Society's *Dictionary of Gardening* 2, 3 : 1231–2 (1965) gives the following description for *M. liliflora*: 'Deciduous shrub up to 12 ft [3·5 m] with straggling branches, downy at tips only, buds downy. *Leaves* ovate to obovate, shortly pointed, 4 to 7 in. [10 to 18 cm] long, dark green, slightly hairy above, paler and hairy on veins beneath. *Flowers* bell-shaped, large, purple outside, usually white inside. April to June. *Fruit* oblong.

'Needs wall protection in north. Var. *gracilis* (*M. gracilis* of *Paradisus Londinensis*: 87) is smaller with darker-purple flowers; *nigra* has flowers about 5 in. [12·5 cm] long, dark purple without, paler within, and is perhaps slightly hardier, Japan 1861. SYN. *M. × soulangiana nigra*.'

There is a Magnolia in Mr. Nigel Holman's garden at Chyverton near Truro, which has smaller flowers than *M. quinquepeta* (*liliflora*) 'Nigra', with only six narrow, reflexing tepals which shade from dark purple at their bases to almost pure white at their tips, this colour extending throughout their inner surfaces. This Magnolia appears to correspond with the details of *M. discolor* de Candolle as tabulated by Hamelin in his table of comparison mentioned earlier, but it is not at all like Ventenat's description or Redouté's Plate No. 66.

Quite apart from the obvious differences in tepal shapes and flower forms described by these botanists, and shown in the plates referred to, some of them depicted separate drawings of the gynandrophore, that central column within the flower which bears the stamens and stigmas, together with enlarged drawings of these organs to assist future botanical observations.

When one compares these finer details one finds further differences which might be worth recording here. Redouté's painting (Plate 66) of Ventenat's *M. discolor* de Candolle, depicts an androecium with pointed, flattened stamens, of uneven taper, symmetrically compressed into three ranks which closely clasp the base of a gynoecium of short and conical shape. Andrews's *M. purpurea* (Plate 326) shows an androecium with a loose array of longer stamens of quite a different shape, surmounted by an egg-shaped gynoecium with looser styles. Hooker's drawing of *M. gracilis* in *Paradisus Londinensis* (Plate 87) shows stamens tapering evenly to a point and curving inwards to clasp the base of the gynoecium, which has carpels with conspicuously hooked stigmas.

M. quinquepeta (*liliflora*) is mentioned in the earliest Chinese literature as *Mu-lan* a name which it still bears. It is said to be a native of Chekiang, Fukien and Hupeh. In the Kew Herbarium there is a specimen collected in April 1900 by Wilson in western Hupeh, at an altitude of 1,700 to 2,000 ft (520 to 610 m). There is also a specimen collected in 1910 by Forrest (No. 5539) from the Tien-chin-pu Valley, at 6,000 to 7,000 ft (1,830 to 2,100 m) and described as a bush 6 to 12 ft (2 to 3·5m) high. The flower has pointed tepals which were described as lake crimson, deepest at the base.

Now where does *M. quinquepeta* (*liliflora*) 'Nigra', (so long known as *M.* × *soulangiana nigra*) come into the picture? According to Millais 'There is little doubt that this fine hybrid originated in some Japanese nursery, since John Gould Veitch introduced it from Japan in 1861.' Millais described it as 'A close shrubby bush up to 10 ft [3 m] in height and as much across. In general appearance like *M. liliflora* but more close in habit and better furnished, with leaves which are broader and longer, as well as a darker green in colour. . . . The flowers in bud state are pointed, and when fully developed, 5½ in. [14 mm] across, but many small flowers are put forth as well as large ones and follow one another in succession for two months; colour a rich venous [? vinous] purple, inside whitish.'

What can be said in conclusion? Obviously there were at least three distinct forms of this Magnolia in circulation between the time of the first introduction by Thunberg in 1790 and Loudon's monumental publication of 1838. The fact that at least one French nursery still offers *M. purpurea* and *M. gracilis* seems to indicate that they are sufficiently distinct as garden plants to warrant both being retained some 180 years later.

The importation of the superior cultivar *M.* × *soulangiana* 'Nigra' (latterly known as *M. liliflora* 'Nigra' and now to be referred to as *M. quinquepeta* 'Nigra') from Japan in 1861 probably eclipsed the earlier introductions because of its hardier constitution and larger flowers, usually with seven to nine instead of six tepals.

Prof. McDaniel's article 'Variations within *M. liliflora*' in *Newsletter of the American Magnolia Society* 9, 2 : 20–3 (1973) makes mention of 'fifteen clones, cultivars or varietal forms referable most likely to *M. quinquepeta* (*liliflora*) which were described under *M. obovata*' The Magnolia Check List, then in preparation, listed at that stage thirteen variety or cultivar names not definitely reduced to synonymy under some other species or hybrid. They include, with dates of publication: 'Arborea' (1891), 'Atropurpurea' (1916) (probably = 'Nigra'), 'Borreriana' (1891), 'Darkest Purple' (1949), 'Discolor' (1803) (= *quinquepeta* var. *quinquepeta*), 'Gracilis' (1805) var. *inodora* (1817) var. *liliflora* (1792), 'Nigra' (1883), 'O'Neill' (Plate 39), 'Purpurea' (1797), 'Reflorescens' (c. 1850), 'Trewithen' (1955 illus.). Some of these may be peculiar to the United States though according to McDaniel the clones there in cultivation produce seeds only after cross-pollination, which usually has involved pollen of another species. He suggests that some cultivars now listed could be seedlings originating from back-crosses between *M. quinquepeta* and the various clones of *M.* × *soulangiana*. Somatic mutation is another possible source of new cultivars though none has been documented in *M. quinquepeta*.

Cytologically *M. quinquepeta* is a tetraploid with 2n = 76 chromosomes. Janaki Ammal qualified her tetraploid chromosome count for *M. liliflora* with the suggestion that, since the *Buergeria* Section are diploids with 38 chromosomes, and the *Yulania* Section are hexaploids with 114, it is possible that the specimen which she found to be tetraploid with 76, and so midway between the two, may have arisen as a hybrid between a species of the *Buergeria* and one of the *Yulania* Section, which would account for the sepaloid outer tepals described by Johnstone for his *M. liliflora*. Dr. Wilkinson suggests a more likely explanation in his 'Cytological Considerations' on p. 209.

Manglietia insignis as *Magnolia insignis* K. L. Blume in *Flora Javae* 22–3 (1828)
J. E. Dandy in *Curtis's Botanical Magazine* 173 : t. 443 (1964–5)

The author has added brief notes on *Manglietia* and *Michelia*, the two genera most closely allied to *Magnolia*, since these were included in Dandy's 'Survey' on pp. 36–7.

Manglietia differs technically from *Magnolia* in having four or more ovules or seeds per carpel. The norm for *Magnolia* is two, though occasionally there are three or four in the lower carpels.*

This genus comprises some twenty-five evergreen species and is of mainly tropical distribution, extending across southern China southward to Java. Only the eastern Himalayan representatives are likely to be suitable for consideration as garden plants in our more favoured gardens. Three of these, *M. forrestii*, *M. hookeri* and *M. insignis* were introduced by George Forrest and there are specimens under these three labels at Caerhays. However, when their fruit cones were sent to Dandy in 1968 he ascribed all of them to *M. insignis*, the only one of them which he thinks can be regarded as at all hardy. In his notes on p. 36 he lists two others which may prove hardy in our climate but which have not as yet been introduced. These are *M. szechuanica* and *M. duclouxii*.

All the Manglietias at Caerhays were more or less defoliated by the ten weeks of continuous frosts early in 1963 and they also suffered from varying degrees of die-back afterwards. However, they have since completely recovered. In habit they are erect and compact arborescent shrubs averaging some 25 to 30 ft (7·5 to 9 m) in height in 1972.

Dandy tells us that all species of *Manglietia* show great uniformity in both vegetative and floral structure, a statement which makes one somewhat incredulous of the high praise accorded to *M. insignis* by Nathaniel Wallich when he discovered and described that species in the mountains of Nepal in 1819 and which Dandy quotes on p. 36.

One should, of course, bear in mind that the Manglietias at Caerhays, be they of one or more species, tend to open their relatively small and sparsely-borne flowers at a time when the observer has

become satiated by the earlier and far more sensational displays of the precocious Asian Magnolias.

The natural distribution of *M. insignis* extends from the central Himalayas eastward into western China as far as south-western Hunan and northern Kwangsi, and also northern Vietnam. It was introduced into cultivation from western Yunnan by George Forrest in 1912, while Reginald Farrer sent home seeds from Upper Burma in 1919. The best form growing at Caerhays was raised from seed of Forrest's No. 26506, collected in Upper Burma in 1925.

The habitat of *M. insignis* ranges between altitudes of 3,000 and 11,500 ft (915 to 3,500 m) where it attains dimensions of up to 90 ft (27·5 m) in height. The three species mentioned earlier were introduced into cultivation by Forrest from the same region, on the borders of Yunnan and Upper Burma. They are very similar in foliage and flowers but Dandy points out that *M. insignis* is distinguished in its more elongated gynoecium and fruit cones.

M. insignis is, therefore, an evergreen tree which attains considerable dimensions. The branchlets are glabrous or at first rufous or tawny pubescent at the nodes. The leaves measure up to about 10½ in. (26·5 cm) long by 4 in. (10 cm) wide. They are more or less coriaceous, with glabrous upper surfaces. Their undersurfaces are either glabrous, or rufous pubescent on the midribs, or with scattered minute adpressed hairs. The petioles are up to 1½ in. (4 cm) long, sometimes pubescent and bearing a stipular scar on the lower part, the stipules being adnate to the lower part of the petiole.

The flower buds are ovoid oblong and are at first enclosed in a glabrous spathaceous bract which is inserted on the peduncle at an interval below the flower. The peduncle is stout and glabrous, sometimes at first rufous or tawny pubescent at the scar left by the spathaceous bract. Dandy in *Curtis's Botanical Magazine* 173 : t. 443 (1964–5) described the flowers as being fragrant, with nine to twelve tepals, white to creamy yellow, often more or less tinted with pink or purple, the outer ones with brown. The outer three are oblanceolate to obovate oblong, about 1½ to 3 in. (4 to 7·5 cm) long,

---

* A remarkable abnormality in this respect was noticed on the Hensel tree of *Magnolia virginiana* var. *virginiana* and recorded by Prof. J. C. McDaniel who has shown the author fruit cones bearing three, four and five seeds per carpel.

becoming reflexed; the inner six to nine are erect. The fruit cone is ovoid oblong, about 2½ to 5 in. (6 to 12·5 cm) long and purple red when ripe. Each carpel contains four or more ovules or seeds. Although the Caerhays Manglietias set fruit cones, these fall from the trees soon after they turn red and the carpels are invariably abortive. It seems likely that they require a higher temperature to germinate their pollen or there is an absence of the specialized pollinating insects.

All Manglietias are diploids with 2n = 38 chromosomes.

This large Asian genus comprises some forty-five evergreen species of somewhat similar distribution to *Manglietia* but extending also into Japan. Consequently the majority of them are tropical and therefore outside the scope of this book.

Michelia is distinguished by bearing its flowers in clusters, both terminally and crowded into the axils of its leaves, whereas those of *Manglietia* and *Magnolia* are terminal (i.e. at the tips of the shoots) and usually solitary. Another distinguishing feature of *Michelia* is the stalked gynoecium which, among temperate Magnolias, is peculiar only to *Magnolia nitida*.

MICHELIA DOLTSOPA

J. E. Dandy in *Curtis's Botanical Magazine* 164 : t. 9645 (1943–8)

Best known of the hardier species introduced to date is the Himalayan *Michelia doltsopa* which has a geographical range from Nepal to western Yunnan. Given suitable conditions this vigorous and erect shrub can attain a height of over 25 ft (7·5 m) in twelve years with nearly as great a branch spread. Mature leaves have a deeply reticulate venation on their lustreless sea-green upper surfaces.

In their final stages of development the flower buds are enclosed by spathaceous bracts, densely coated with silky rust-red hairs, which produce a most attractive effect for several weeks before the flowers begin to open.

In a warm April the creamy-white flowers may develop to approximate the size which one associates with *Magnolia heptapeta* (*denudata*) but in average seasons in Cornwall they are somewhat smaller. They exude a delightful fragrance. The topmost branches are often stripped of their leaves by the winter's gales so that the flowers thereon are displayed without being partially hidden by adjacent foliage.

Michelia doltsopa should be planted in a sunny situation to induce it to flower at an early age. In shaded situations it may take many years to attain florescence and then fail to flower excepting after hot dry summers.

The flowers are usually produced with such abandon as to give the effect of a solid mass of blossom with very little intervening space. The brown-velvet peduncles are constricted at their centres and the twelve tepals are of irregular width because of their crowded development.

This species is proving much hardier than anyone had dared to suppose and deserves a trial against a south or west facing wall wherever *Magnolia grandiflora* flourishes.

The Caerhays Michelias were originally identified as *M. excelsa* and *M. floribunda* but both have now been merged botanically under *M. doltsopa*. Mr. Julian Williams recognizes three distinct types: (1) with small, almost yellow flowers, (2) with small white flowers and (3) with very large white flowers.

The hardiest species is probably *M. compressa* from Japan and Taiwan. It has survived for many years at Borde Hill in Sussex and would be worth using for breeding purposes in spite of the smallness of its flowers.

Another species occasionally met with in our mildest gardens is *Michelia figo* which was formerly known as *Magnolia fuscata*, the Port Wine Magnolia or Banana Shrub, both names alluding to the curious aroma from its small brownish-yellow flowers. In fruit *Michelia* differs from *Manglietia* and *Magnolia* in bearing its seeds in free carpels. These are connected in chain-like strands instead of being compressed together in the form of a fruit cone.

All Michelias are diploids with 2n = 38 chromosomes.

MAGNOLIA HYBRIDS AND CROSSES

In this book *hybrids* are considered to be the result of marriages between two accepted botanical species while the term *cross* is used to distinguish the progeny of two variants of the same species. The names of the parents of hybrids are stated *alphabetically*. Where the respective functions of the parents is known, or can be accurately assumed, the male parent(♂) and the female (♀) signs have been added in accordance with the *International Code of Nomenclature of Cultivated Plants* (1969).

At the International Horticultural Congress held in Tel Aviv in March 1970, the authority for the registration of new cultivar names in *Magnolia* was vested in the American Magnolia Society.

For the purpose of this book crosses between *M. campbellii* and its eastern form *M. mollicomata* have been referred to as *M. campbellii* Sidbury-Raffill Group. If considered otherwise all of the progeny of these crosses would have to be listed as cultivars of *M. campbellii* and, while such a classification may satisfy the botanists, it does not fill the requirements of those who propagate, catalogue and sell named cultivars nor the more knowledgeable garden owners who purchase and plant them. The very considerable difference in the age at which they attain florescence is, in itself, sufficient horticultural reason for classifying them separately.

Some American botanists, principally Dr. Benjamin Blackburn, formerly of Drew University, Madison, and latterly of Rutgers, the State University New Jersey, now consider *M. stellata* to be a dwarf multitepalled form of *M. kobus*. Where *M. kobus* is known to be the seed parent, and the offspring bears flowers with numerous tepals, then it is almost certainly *M.* × *loebneri* (*M. kobus* × *M. stellata*), but if this theory becomes generally accepted then the binomial *M.* × *loebneri* would be invalid, since binomials written in this fashion should be used only for interspecific hybrids. Magnolias formerly ranking as cultivars of *M.* × *loebneri* would become cultivars of *M. kobus* (e.g. *M. kobus* 'Merrill', *M. kobus* 'Leonard Messel' etc.) though the original 1930 clone could be referred to as 'Loebneri'. Consequently the classification of hybrids within Section *Buergeria* has become somewhat debatable.

In 1976 Blackburn's taxonomy was adopted by Dr. Stephen Spongberg in 'Magnoliaceae Hardy in Temperate North America' *Journal of the Arnold Arboretum* 57, 3 : 296 (1976).

Ignoring the suggested change in status of *M. stellata*, where *M. kobus* is known to be the seed bearer, a hybrid producing flowers with a normal number of broad tepals is more likely to have *M. salicifolia* as the pollen parent than *M. stellata*, and has therefore been grouped under *M.* × *kewensis* which was the name first recorded for such a hybrid (1957). However, use of this latinized binomial was shunned in America, presumably because if *M. stellata* be regarded as a form of *M. kobus* then the binomial *M.* × *proctoriana* will cover *M.* × *kewensis* (*M. kobus* × *M. salicifolia*) and that name would have to disappear also.

Dr. Spongberg treats both *M.* × *kewensis* and *M.* × *proctoriana* as variants of *M. salicifolia*. In this book the author has maintained, without alteration, his completed text but has added appropriate references to these proposed changes in Magnolia nomenclature.

Taking a really long-term view, one comes to the conclusion that future generations of Magnolia experts, enthusiasts and breeders, will be better served by a nomenclature indicative of the precise origin of a variety or hybrid than by its inheritance of an abbreviated name. It will be far more important to know that a hybrid's parent was *M. stellata* rather than *M. kobus*. The proposed lumped binomials would give no indication whatever.

One views with considerable alarm the tendency, especially noticeable in America, for hybrids to be released solely under clonal names without any latinized binomial to indicate the parentage to either present or future generations of plantsmen. This is apparent with the Freeman Hybrids (*M. grandiflora* × *M. virginiana*) while a much more flagrant example is the recent release and patenting, by no less an authority than the United States Department of Agriculture, of a series of eight girl-named hybrids of *M. quinquepeta* × *M. stellata* without any grex name. Their official descriptions are included under the De Vos and Kosar Hybrids on pp. 151–2.

Hybridizing

So far no hybrids have been bred between species from the two different subgenera (*Magnolia* and *Yulania*) but within a subgenus there appear to be few barriers to hybridization between species of the same or of different sections.

It has been found that each species appears to occupy an exclusive range in the wild so that natural hybridization is precluded. When, however, different species belonging to the same subgenus are brought together in cultivation, hybrids have arisen spontaneously while many more have been produced intentionally and with such ease that several Magnolia breeders have undertaken quite ambitious programmes. This has been done almost entirely in America where experimental breeding, promoted by such horticultural establishments as the United States National Arboretum at Washington, D.C., and the University of Illinois at Urbana, has been recorded and discussed in the *Newsletter of the American Magnolia Society*, so that many of its members have been encouraged to engage in the hybridization of Magnolias.

Apomixis

Sometimes a Magnolia breeder finds that seed produced after a carefully controlled artificial pollination does not produce hybrid seedlings as anticipated, but instead a generation of *apomicts*, which closely resemble the seed parent without a trace of having inherited any genes from the pollen parent.

How does apomixis occur? It has been shown that the female egg cell can be influenced by close proximity to foreign pollen without any sexual union taking place. The female reproductive cells are stimulated to develop embryos without fertilization, so that plants raised from the seed so formed will produce close replicas of the mother plant.

Magnolia breeders must be prepared to accept the fact that some of their apparent successes may turn out to be failures, through apogamous embryos developing into plants which will carry only the morphological characters of the seed parent, or of its combined parents should it already be a hybrid. Such plants will bear none of the characters of the Magnolia whose pollen was used, except where such characters are common to both of them. Apogamy or apomixis may occur regardless of the breeder's skill and the degree of care exercised.

Looking into this remarkable phenomenon more closely, expert geneticists tell us that there are several types of apomixis. In one type an ordinary growth cell, not an egg cell, may be excited to develop as an embryo, through stimulation by the male nucleus from pollen, but without actual physical contact or fusion.

In a second type of apogamy the nucleus in an *unreduced* egg-mother cell is excited to develop into an embryo before the reduction process occurs, thus giving rise to what is termed a diploid embryo. In both of these types of apomixis the pollen nucleus only stimulates the female nucleus, and contributes nothing towards the make-up of the embryo owing to absence of physical union.

In yet a third type of apomixis the *reduced* egg cell, while containing only half the normal number of chromosomes, is excited to embryo development by mere proximity of a male nucleus. Each cell of such an embryo, and later the resulting seedling, will contain only half the number of chromosomes found in the parent and is known as a haploid. Haploids are usually weak in structure and highly sterile, consequently they may vary somewhat from the mother plant in the manner of a false hybrid.

It is necessary, therefore, to scrutinize with a critical eye all seedlings raised from attempted hybridizing, and to be prepared for disappointments which such a phenomenon must inevitably cause.

Apogamy might well account for the unusual fruiting of *M. × wieseneri* at Spetchley Park, Worcester, recorded by Johnstone in *Asiatic Magnolias in Cultivation*: 114 who stated that a nearby plant of *M. sieboldii* likewise set seed freely and frequently produced self-sown seedlings.

A trihybrid is one which has a species as one parent and a hybrid between a second and third species as the other parent so that three species are involved in its genetic make-up.

In the Introduction mention was made of the unusual manner whereby the blooms of most Magnolias are pollinated by flower beetles (*Nitidulidae* sp.) before they open. Such flowers are termed *protogynous*. Since the female organs or stigmas are only receptive while the flowers remain closed, and sometimes for a brief period after opening, during which the stamens have not begun to dehisce and shed their pollen, it seems logical that the earlier blossoms must remain sterile while supplying pollen for insects to transfer on to the receptive stigmas within the unopened flowers. It is also likely that pollen is carried by other insects, or by wind and gravitation from earlier blossoms on to the still-receptive stigmas of the flowers which have just opened.

Conversely one would expect that a Magnolia which opens all its blossoms in one flush must fail to set seed, a condition all too readily attributed to unfavourable climatic conditions after flowering. Such a full flush of flowers is most likely to occur after a very cold and prolonged winter, when the gradual development of flower buds is completely arrested by persisting low temperatures, such as occurred in 1962–3 when the thermometer scarcely rose above freezing point over a period of some ten weeks. Johnstone reported of *M. campbellii* subsp. *mollicomata*: 'It was unaffected by the frost and snow of 1946–47, except that no seed was set that year', which bears out this supposition.

In Knuth's *Handbook of Flower Pollination* 11 : 54 (1906), translated and revised by J. R. Ainsworth-Davis, under 'Magnolia' are two references, the first to *M. heptapata* (as *M. Yulan*) and the second to *M. grandiflora*:

'112. *M. Yulan* Desf. – This species is a native of China. The erect white lily-like blossoms are odorous, and – according to Delpino ("*Ult. Oss.*," *Atti Soc. ital. sc. nat. Milano*) they are protogynous bee flowers. In the first (female) stage of anthesis, the bees that visit them are not able to climb up the smooth petals, nor to free themselves from the short erect carpels occupying the middle of the flower, and therefore remain prisoners till the second (male) stage, in which the anthers dehisce. They are then able to leave the flower and, being dusted with pollen, may transfer this to the stigmas of another flower which is still in the first stage.

'113. *M. grandiflora* L. – This species is indigenous to Florida. According to Delpino (op. cit., pp. 233–5) the white odorous protogynous flowers are visited and pollinated by beetles (*Cetoniae*). During the first stage of anthesis, these insects find, under the three inner petals, which arch over the carpels, a warm nectar-containing shelter,[*] that they only leave when the petals are shed at the time of dehiscence of the anthers. Dusted with pollen they then betake themselves to another flower in the first stage, the mature stigmas of which they necessarily pollinate. Self-pollination is prevented by the pronounced protogyny. Visitors. – *Cetonia aurata* L., and *Oxythyrea funesta* Poda (= *C. stictica* L.)'

Prof. J. C. McDaniel of the Department of Horticulture, University of Illinois, contributed an interesting paper at the International Plant Propagators Society, Eastern Region's thirteenth Annual Meeting in 1963 entitled 'Securing Seed Production in *Magnolia acuminata* and *M. cordata*'. In it he stated 'American Magnolias in general cannot set seed on their earliest flowers of the season. Without exception, their flowers, so far as I have observed, are protogynous. Their pistils are receptive when the flowers first open or shortly before that stage, but do not remain receptive for the day or so longer that it takes a flower to begin to shed its pollen. But later flowers on the same tree, of such species and varieties as are not self-incompatible, can generally receive from their own earlier-opening flowers, pollen carried either by certain beetles, bees and other insects, or even by gravity from flowers higher on the tree.'

A remarkable method of pollen distribution in the tropical West Indian Magnolias was described by Richard A. Howard, then of the New York Botanic Garden and later Director of the Arnold Arboretum, in a paper entitled 'The morphology and systematics of the West Indian Magnoliaceae', *Bulletin of the Torrey Botanical Club* 75, 4 : 335–57 (1948):

'The distinctive character which sets them off as a subsection of the section *Theorhodon* in *Magnolia* is the presence of long, pointed setaceous tips at the apices of the anthers. These are forced against the gynoecium within the flower bud and become firmly embedded in the fleshy tissue, or are caught and held between the carpels so securely that it is almost impossible to extract them.

'When the flower opens the stigmas appear to be receptive and, as the perianth continues to expand, the bases of the stigmas separate from the main axis but are held by their setaceous tips which remain

---

[*] Only the tropical *M. coco* has nectar glands. Author.

embedded in the gynoecium so that they are suspended in a reversed pose exterior to the perianth. They then shed their pollen but at this stage the stigmas have shrunken and are almost dry so that self-pollination is prevented.'

Fertilization does not occur until the pollen grains have germinated on the receptive surfaces of the stigmas and the male nucleus cells have fused with the female egg cells in the ovaries within the carpels. In Magnolias there appears to be a critical temperature for pollen germination and with some temperate Magnolias this could be as high as 70 to 80 °F. (21·1 to 26·7 °C.), an air temperature seldom, if ever, attained in British gardens in April and May. While lower temperatures are apparently adequate for pollen germination on many of the Himalayan species, some of which begin to bloom among deep snow-drifts in their natural environment, one rarely finds fertile fruit cones in British gardens on such Magnolias as *M. stellata*, *M. denudata* and *M. liliflora*, or on any of the American species, some of which produce quite spectacular displays of fruit cones in the eastern states of America, as do the Asian species just mentioned. It is by no means unusual to come across large bushes of *M. stellata* laden with slender, elongated fruit cones in gardens around Boston and New York.

Apparent self-incompatibility, recorded in this volume for a wide range of Magnolia species, is more recently attributed to the absence of pollinating beetles at the brief and critical period of pollen shedding.

Dr. Leonard D. Thien, biologist at Tulane University, New Orleans, Louisiana, in 'Floral Biology of *Magnolia*', *American Journal of Botany* 61 : 1037–45 (1974) records his conclusions after studying the eight species native to south-eastern United States. In his abstract he writes: 'The flowers are protogynous. They are pollinated by several species of beetles that enter buds as well as closed and open flowers to feed on nectar, stigmas, pollen and secretions of the petals. . . . It is suggested that the flowers of *Magnolia* are highly specialized for exclusive pollination by beetles.'

Recent experiments by Prof. J. C. McDaniel, reported in '1974 Observations on *Magnolia acuminata*' in *Newsletter of the American Magnolia Society* 10, 2 : 21 (1974), have shown that hand pollination of flowers on a tree of *M. acuminata*, hitherto considered to be self-incompatible, indicated that it is as compatible to its own pollen as to pollen from the several other clones and hybrids of *M. acuminata* which he applied. All of these gave fully developed fruits with seeds in nearly all carpels, on a tree which, over many years, had been observed to produce only very rare seeds from its thousands of flowers. He had previously assumed that the absence of seed, or very poor seed production, was invariably due to self-incompatibility but he now considers the absence of the right beetles on a tree at the critical time to be the usual cause.

This brings us to wonder whether the inevitable changes in ecology, brought about by human habitation, may have had a deterrent effect on the breeding and distribution of the beetle species responsible, at least as regards Magnolias growing in urban environments.

MAGNOLIA ACUMINATA HYBRIDS

MAGNOLIA ACUMINATA × *MAGNOLIA HEPTAPETA*

The first hybrids of this parentage were bred at the Brooklyn Botanic Garden in 1956 by Evamaria Sperber who also bred, about the same time, the hybrids between *M. acuminata* and *M. quinquepeta*, now referred to as *M.* × *brooklynensis*, of which a select clone bears her name.

A detailed account of the origin, raising, growing on, and flowering of these hybrids was recorded by Dr. Lola Koerting, a plant researcher at the Brooklyn Botanic Gardens Kitchawan Research Station in Ossining, Westchester County, New York, and published in *Newsletter of the American Magnolia Society* 13, 2 : 21–2 (1977). From twelve blooms of *M. acuminata*, which were inoculated with pollen from *M. denudata,* seventy-one seeds developed. The seedlings were transferred to Kitchawan for growing on to adolescence. The first to attain florescence was Number 391 at the age of fifteen years in 1972. By 1977 five further seedlings had produced flowers, all of which were yellow with only slight variations.

In 1976 the as yet unnamed Number 391 was selected for a plant patent. The tree is described as pyramidal in shape and about 6 m tall when 19 years old. At Ossining the flower buds open between the end of April and the beginning of July, the flowering period extending for about two weeks. The flower buds are tinted with green at the base. The flowers, which are comparable in size to *M. heptapeta*, are of a uniform clear yellow when fully open and have a pleasant fragrance. They have six to nine tepals and their shape is intermediate between that of the two parents. The leaf buds begin to open during the peak of flowering. The young leaves are slightly rust coloured and mature to dark green with an obovate shape. They resemble those of the female parent *M. acuminata* as does the tree's habit of growth. About 25 per cent of the soft wood cuttings will root with bottom heat and intermittent mist.

Cytologically these hybrids are pentaploid with $2n = 95$ chromosomes and so are intermediate between the tetraploid *M. acuminata* ($2n = 76$) and the hexaploid *M. denudata* ($2n = 114$).

A series of hybridizing experiments with *M. acuminata* were carried out in 1973, '74, '75 and '76 at the United States National Arboretum at Washington D.C. and reported by research geneticist Dr. Frank S. Santamour, Jr., in *Newsletter of the American Magnolia Society* 12, 1 : 3–9 (1976) 'Our goal in this research was the development of hardy, tree-type cultivars that had a peak blooming period somewhere between early precocious-flowering species and *M. acuminata*, and that expressed the yellow petal color either alone or in combination with other petal pigments.'

The female parents used in these experiments were two isolated *M. acuminata* trees with yellower than average flowers. Anthers were taken from unopened flowers on the pollen parents and allowed to dehisce and shed their pollen on paper spread on a laboratory bench. The pollen was stored in stoppered glass vials in a desiccator over anhydrous calcium chloride at 35·6 °F. (2° C.). Coloured pipe-cleaners were used to transmit the pollen because these held it better than a brush, were colour-coded and disposable.

All tepals and anthers were removed from unopened *M. acuminata* flowers before pollination but they were not then protected from fertilization by stray pollen. The complete isolation of the female trees (more than 100 yds (91·4 m) from the nearest Magnolia of any species or hybrid) was considered a suitable safeguard, apart from the possibility of chance self-pollination. The larger tree had been observed to be highly self-incompatible since the few fruits which it produced were small with mostly one to two seeds. The smaller tree had not matured a single fruit during the three previous years.

The reason for not protecting the flowers immediately after pollination was that past experience had shown that heat build-up within the bags on hot days tended to 'cook' the fleshy gynoecium. In contrast they always bag the hand-pollinated flowers of precocious-flowering magnolias to protect them from freezing or desiccation in erratic March weather.

M. acuminata var. *subcordata* was used as pollen parent in the 'control' cross and yielded an average of 57 seeds per flower pollinated. If the same degree of cross-compatibility had been expressed in the 184 other crosses, 10,488 potentially viable seeds could have been expected but only 67 resulted or 0·64 per cent of the 'control' potential.

The mature fruit cones were harvested in September and allowed to ripen and dehisce on a laboratory bench. The seeds were cleaned and immersed in water to distinguish empty seeds ('floaters') from good seeds ('sinkers'). (Philip J. Savage, Jr., in *Newsletter of the American Magnolia Society* 9, 4 : 7–15 (1973) says that, surprisingly enough some 'floaters' will germinate but flat scale-like seeds should be discarded.) The good seed was sown immediately in flats of a sphagnum-sand mixture in the greenhouse. Seeds that had not germinated by Christmas were removed from the flats and stratified in moist sand for thirty days in a refrigerator, then resown. By these methods a germination rate of over 85 per cent was achieved.

From the results, tabulated in the journal quoted, those successful were:

M. acuminata × *M. heptapeta* (*denudata*) gave 5 good seeds of which 3 germinated.

M. acuminata × *M. sprengeri* 'Diva' gave 28 good seeds of which 22 germinated.

M. acuminata × ('Diva' × *heptapeta*) gave 16 good seeds of which 16 germinated.

M. acuminata × (× *veitchii* × 'Diva') gave 9 good seeds of which 9 germinated.

M. acuminata × (*quinquepeta* × 'Diva') gave 1 good seed of which 1 germinated.

M. acuminata × *M.* × *kewensis* 'Wada's Memory' gave 2 good seeds of which 1 germinated.

M. acuminata × *M.* × *loebneri* 'Merrill' gave 14 good seeds from seven out of eight flowers pollinated.

M. acuminata × *M.* × *loebneri* 'Spring Snow' gave 13 good seeds from seven out of eleven flowers pollinated.

Negative results were reported from pollination by *MMs. grandiflora*, × *veitchii* and several *M.* × *soulangiana* clones.

A main requisite is the accurate determination of true hybridity at an early age to avoid the growing on of all seedlings until they attain florescence. Cytological analyses can be reliable in this series because only *M. liliflora* shares with *M. acuminata* the same number of chromosomes (2n = 76). Morphological comparisons of putative hybrids with seedlings resulting from controlled intraspecific crosses, controlled selfing, and from non-pollination, may be an acceptable alternative.

Another requisite is patience while the trees are growing to a flowering age and then the maturity of judgement to refrain from naming and propagating a mediocre plant merely because it is a hybrid.

MAGNOLIA ACUMINATA × MAGNOLIA QUINQUEPETA, see under *M.* × *brooklynensis*, opposite.

MAGNOLIA 'Ann Rosse'
(*Magnolia heptapeta* ♀ × *Magnolia sargentiana* var. *robusta* ♂)

This fine hybrid originated as a solitary seedling raised from one of two seeds off a specimen of *M. heptapeta* growing at Nymans Gardens at Handcross,

near Haywards Heath, Sussex, in proximity to a tree of *M. sargentiana* var. *robusta* which is assumed to have been the pollen parent. It received an Award of Merit when exhibited by the Countess of Rosse and the National Trust in April 1973 and is described in *Rhododendrons 1974 with Magnolias and Camellias*: 109.

The large, erectly poised, chalice-shaped flowers open to 7 to 8½ in. (18 to 21·5 cm) across with nine long, fluted and pointed tepals. These are white with a rich pink flush, which deepens to red purple towards their bases, where the colour permeates to the inner surfaces to produce flares of pink in the centres of the flowers. The stamen filaments are darker than those of the seed parent. This description has been made after scrutinizing coloured transparencies kindly loaned to the author by Head Gardener Cecil G. Nice.

THE BROOKLYN HYBRIDS

MAGNOLIA × BROOKLYNENSIS
Kalmbacher

Magnolia acuminata × *Magnolia quinquepeta*
G. Kalmbacher in *Newsletter of the American Magnolia Society* 8, 2 : 7–8 (1972); 9, 1 : 12–13 (1973)

These hybrids are of particular botanical interest since they combine the American and Asian members of Section *Tulipastrum*.

They were first bred by Mrs. Evamaria Sperber, while she was on the staff of the Brooklyn Botanic Garden, New York, under the directorship of Dr. G. M. Avery, and the selected clone 'Evamaria' was subsequently named after her. It was the outcome of several hundred hand pollinations; the resulting fruit cones were collected and the seeds cleaned and stratified prior to germination. The unique nature of this particular seedling was discovered when it flowered.

MAGNOLIA × BROOKLYNENSIS
'Evamaria'

(Magnolia acuminata ♀ × Magnolia quinquepeta ♂)

United States Plant Patent 2,820, dated 23 July 1968, stated that this Magnolia attained a height of 15 ft (4·5 m) in ten years, thereby indicating that the hybrid was made about 1957. The bark is described as smooth and grey, with large and conspicuous lenticels, and the young twigs are chocolate brown. Its vigour is considerably in excess of other seedlings of the same parentage which are still being evaluated.

The unopened flower buds are purple, fused with green and yellow shadings, a unique colour among Magnolias. The open flower consists of six broadly rounded tepals in two whorls of three, and the distinctive and unusual colour of the flower is due to the three contrasting shades of magenta rose, suffused with pale orange and yellow. The inner surface of the tepals is pale pink, but this is not obvious, since the flowers do not open widely even at maturity, when they are 3½ in. (9 cm) across and of erect, campanulate form. The stamens are pale yellow and the stigmas are tipped with pale purple. This hybrid is fertile.

Brooklyn is considered to be the northern limit of hardiness for *M. quinquepeta* 'Nigra' in America, where it does not grow vigorously and is susceptible to winter kill. In contrast, this new hybrid grows vigorously and flowers profusely every spring at the Brooklyn Botanic Garden's nursery in northern Westchester County, which is in an unprotected location and exposed to winds. Its flowering period is said to extend for twenty-seven days from 12 May to 9 June, compared with 4 May to 18 May for the male parent, and 12 May to 31 May for the female parent.

Associate Taxonomist Frederick McGourty, Jr., who first drew my attention to these hybrids in 1971 tells me that they have several hundred sibs under evaluation. At the time of patenting, no latinized grex name had been considered for these hybrids but, at the insistence of the author that such a name was most necessary, the Garden's Taxonomist, George Kalmbacher, proposed *M. × brooklynensis* in a letter dated 3 September 1971.

This grex name was validly published by G. Kalmbacher in *Newsletter of the American Magnolia Society* 8, 2 : 7–8 (1972). Prof. J. C. McDaniel, who repeated the Brooklyn hybridizing, described his successes in 'Illinois Clones of *Magnolia × brooklynensis*' in *Newsletter of the American Magnolia Society* 9, 1 : 13–14 (1973). He selected as female parent the self-compatible Klassen clone of *M. acuminata* while the male or pollen parent was the O'Neill clone of *M. quinquepeta* which seems to agree with the plate titled *M. liliflora* 'Trewithen' in Johnstone's *Asiatic Magnolias in Cultivation*, facing p. 108. Reciprocal crosses, made at the same time, failed.

Most of the seedlings raised from the hand-pollinated flowers showed only *M. acuminata* characteristics but two were obvious hybrids. After growing them for three or more years under glass, scions from both seedlings were chip-budded on to *M. × soulangiana*. One seedling flowered for the first time in May 1972 with flowers slightly larger and darker than 'Evamaria', combining the varying shades of yellow, green and purple of the two parents, and this was named and registered as 'Woodsman' in 1974.

Cytologically *M. × brooklynensis* would be expected to show the same four-fold level of ploidy as that shared by both parents (2n = 76).

MAGNOLIA 'Caerhays Surprise'

(Magnolia campbellii subsp. *mollicomata* ♀ × *Magnolia quinquepeta* 'Nigra' ♂)*

Plate 40

This striking and interesting hybrid was first bred in 1959 by head gardener Philip Tregunna in the gardens of Caerhays Castle, by transferring pollen from a mature flower of *M. quinquepeta* 'Nigra' on to the receptive stigmatic surfaces within an unopened flower of *M. campbelli* subsp. *mollicomata*.

Two seedlings resulted from the cross, one of which produced uninteresting pale flowers and subsequently died. The second plant began to flower in 1967.

The author inspected the surviving plant in April 1970 when it carried about a dozen flower buds at the ends of slender branchlets. The more advanced buds were showing tepal colour of a bright reddish violet.

The buds are long and slender and seem to indicate a prolonged flowering season. The plant is of arching habit with slender shoots and reddish-brown bark.

In some seasons the flowers show a pronounced *M. quinquepeta* influence in opening as the leaves develop so that they are not always truly precocious. At maturity they are lilac pink in colour, about 8 in. (20·5 cm) across with nine to twelve narrow tepals, those of the two outer whorls reflexing to a sub-horizontal poise and thereby creating an unusual star-like effect. Both peduncle and pedicle are pubescent.

When exhibited by Mr. F. Julian Williams at the Royal Horticultural Society's show in April 1973 it received an Award of Merit. By then it was 15 ft (4·5 m) high and 12 ft (3·5 m) across. It is described in *Rhododendrons 1974 with Magnolias and Camellias*: 108–9.

In a letter to the author dated 5 October 1970, Japanese plantsman Mr. K. Wada of Hakoneya Nurseries, Yokohama, wrote: 'We have many seedlings of *Magnolia mollicomata* by *soulangiana* [*quinquepeta*] *nigra* and now find they grow very well with us. We cannot grow both *mollicomata* and *campbellii* because of our hot summer but the above mentioned hybrids can grow well. We think these hybrids will become popular in hotter summer climates where *mollicomata* and *campbellii* are not happy.' These hybrids were bred in California by the late D. Todd Gresham, who sent seeds to Mr. Wada.

MAGNOLIA CAMPBELLII × MAGNOLIA SPRENGERI var. ELONGATA

Three trees raised from seed off *M. sprengeri* var. *elongata* were recorded by Head Gardener Cecil G. Nice in the Royal Horticultural Society's *Rhododendrons 1973 with Magnolias and Camellias*: 76 under 'Magnolias at Nymans by Natural Fertilization'. He mentioned that the mother tree was growing close to a mature specimen of *M. campbellii* which is assumed to have been the pollen parent because their leaves resemble those of that species. Mr. Nice tells me that all three of these seedlings began to flower in April 1976 and that a number of flower buds were developing in the autumn of 1977. He hoped to exhibit flowers of the superior seedling at a Royal Horticultural Society Show in 1978.

MAGNOLIA 'Charles Coates'
(*Magnolia sieboldii* × *Magnolia tripetala*)
S. A. Pearce in *Journal of the Royal Horticultural Society* 84 : 426 (1959)
J. R. Seally in *Gardeners Chronicle* 3, 152 : 77 (1962)
W. J. Bean, *Trees and Shrubs Hardy in the British Isles* Ed. 8, 2 : 664 (1973)

In notes on 'Magnolias at Kew' Pearce described this hybrid as being intermediate in habit between the two parents and having fairly large ovate leaves resembling those of *M. tripetala* up to 10 in. (25·5 cm) long by 5 in. (12·5 cm) wide. They tend to be clustered in false whorls at the tips of the branchlets. They are broadly elliptic, with acute apices and cuneate bases.

According to Bean, C. F. Coates found three seedlings of this hybrid in the Azalea Garden at Kew about 1946, so it can be assumed that the best one was selected as the named clone after they had flowered.

'Charles Coates' flowers freely from mid May to mid June, the very fragrant creamy-white blossoms being rather like those of the American *M. tripetala* but with a conspicuous boss of reddish anthers as in the Japanese *M. sieboldii*. The flowers are terminal and erectly poised, saucer shaped, about 4 in. (10 cm) across and fragrant. The three outer tepals are tinged with green and curl inwards soon after they expand, thereby forming the parts of a false calyx. The larger six to eight inner ones are cream and slightly crumpled.

Pearce wrote, 'It is proposed to name this hybrid in honour of C. F. Coates, who was propagator-in-charge of the Arboretum Nursery at Kew for many years and was responsible for the collecting of the self-sown seedlings of both of these hybrid Magnolias.' (His notes included *M.* × *kewensis*.)

It is recorded as having first flowered in 1958 and,

at the date of writing in 1959, the original tree had reached a height of 15 ft (4·5 m) with a spread of 12 ft (3·5 m).

In June 1973 an Award of Merit was conferred on *M.* 'Charles Coates' by the Royal Horticultural Society in recognition of its merits as a hardy flowering tree. It is described in *Rhododendrons 1973 with Magnolias and Camellias* : 108.

Cytologically it is an assumed diploid with 2n = 38 chromosomes in common with both parents.

THE DE VOS AND KOSAR HYBRIDS

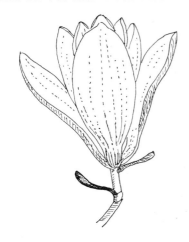

MAGNOLIA QUINQUEPETA × MAGNOLIA STELLATA

SYN. *M. liliflora × M. kobus* var. *stellata*
T. R. Dudley & W. F. Kosar in *Morris Arboretum Bulletin* 19, 2 : 26–9 (1968)

This Magnolia breeding project was carried out at the U.S. National Arboretum at Washington D.C. in 1955 and 1956. The objective was to produce a race of hybrids which would flower later than *M. heptapeta* (*denudata*) and *M. stellata*, thereby lessening the likelihood of frost damage to their flowers.

The programme was initiated by the Arboretum Geneticist Dr. Francis de Vos who successfully fertilized flowers of *M. quinquepeta* 'Nigra' with stored pollen of *M. stellata* 'Rosea'. Unfortunately the precise identity of both parental clones is subject to possible confusion since it is probable that, in the past, the same varietal names have been applied to more than one clone of each of the parent species.

During the following spring the Arboretum Horticulturist William F. Kosar repeated the cross using the same and also different clones of the two parent species.

'The 'Nigra' clone of *M. quinquepeta* which De Vos used for the female parent (as *M. liliflora* 'Nigra') was described as being hardy at Washington D.C. and flowering two or three weeks later than *M. stellata*. The *M. stellata* 'Rosea' clone is described as having been selected primarily for such characters as free flowering, with fragrant multitepalled flowers and of a compact, bushy habit with resistance to mildew. The De Vos hybrids began to flower in 1962.

In addition to the descriptions of both raisings, which were published in the University of Pennsylvania *Morris Arboretum Bulletin*, a leaflet entitled 'Brief Descriptions of New *Magnolia* Selections' was circulated by the Agricultural Research Service, Crops Research Division, of the United States Department of Agriculture, Beltsville, Maryland, details from which have been included in this text.

The four De Vos hybrids which were selected and named after evaluation were:

'Ann' The earliest to flower of this series, commencing about mid April at Washington D.C. Has erect and tapered buds coloured red purple, paler towards the margins and tips of the six to eight broad, acute tepals which remain erect at anthesis and measure 2 to 4 in. (5 to 10 cm) in diameter. The leaves, which average 5 by 3 in. (12·5 by 7·5 cm), are acuminate with deeply impressed veins; texture leathery, margins rippled, petioles rusty tomentose.

'Judy' is the slowest growing of this series and has an erect almost fastigiate habit. The flower buds are erect candle-like and pointed, red purple at the base, paling towards the apex. The inner surface of the ten tepals is creamy white. At anthesis the average flower diameter is 2 to 3 in. (5 to 7·5 cm). The leaves are broadly ovate, averaging 6½ by 3½ in. (16·5 by 9 cm), and glabrous.

'Randy' Has an erect almost columnar habit and is extremely floriferous. The buds are erect and pointed, red purple fading towards the apex. The inner surface of the nine to eleven tepals is white. At anthesis the flowers are 3½ to 5 in. (9 to 12·5 cm) in diameter and have a stellate appearance. They open in late April at Washington D.C.

'Ricki' Also blooms in late April with tousled flowers 4 to 6 in. (10 to 15 cm) which are the largest of the De Vos hybrid selections. The flower buds are erect, long, slender and pointed, red purple at the base and paler towards the apex. The colouring of the inner surface of the ten to fifteen twisted and contorted tepals varies from purple to white.

When William F. Kosar carried out the second stage of the project in 1956 he used pollen saved from the same 'Rosea' clone of *M. stellata* and also from one named 'Waterlily' (which is likewise ambiguous for reasons discussed in the chapter on *M. stellata*). The female parents which he selected were partly the same 'Nigra' clone of *M. quinquepeta* used a year earlier by De Vos and partly the clone 'Reflorescens' which is noted in America for its prolonged flowering.

The four Kosar hybrids which were selected are:

'Betty'   Bred from *M. quinquepeta* 'Nigra' × *M. stellata* 'Rosea' and having pointed red purple flower buds sometimes curved at the apex, opening at Washington D.C. in mid to late April into large flowers up to 8 in. (20·5 cm) across with twelve to eighteen mainly spatulate tepals. The outer surface grades from greyed purple at the base to red purple at the apex. The leaves are broadly ovate 5½ by 3½ in. (14 by 9 cm), reticulate and glabrous, with brown petioles.

'Susan'   was bred from the same parents as 'Betty'. The red-purple flower buds are erect and straight, opening in Washington during the third or fourth week of April. The fragrant flowers have six uniformly deeply-coloured tepals opening to 4 to 6 in. (10 to 15 cm) in diameter at anthesis and retaining the red-purple colouring on both surfaces. A twisting of the tepals imparts a tousled appearance to the flowers. The leaves are ovate, 5½ by 3 in. (14 by 7·5 cm), reticulate and glabrous.

'Jane'   was bred from *M. quinquepeta* 'Reflorescens' × *M. stellata* 'Waterlily' (origin not stated). This is one of the latest to flower, opening in Washington during the first and second weeks in May. The flower buds are erect and slender and uniformly red purple, opening to reveal eight to ten symmetrical broadly obovate to spatulate tepals. The flowers are very fragrant and cup shaped and measure 3½ to 4 in. (9 to 10 cm) at anthesis. The inner surface is white while the outside is red purple. The glossy leaves resemble those of *M. quinquepeta*. They average 6 by 3 in. (15 by 7·5 cm) with petioles brown, tomentose.

'Pinkie'   *M. quinquepeta* 'Reflorescens' × *M. stellata* 'Rosea'. This is the latest-flowering of these hybrids and has the palest flowers. The buds are blunt and stout, red purple at the base and somewhat paler towards the apex and tepal edges. The flowers are cup shaped, 5 to 7 in. (12·5 to 18 cm) in diameter, with nine to twelve broadly obovate to spatulate tepals. The inner surface is white while the outside is pale red purple, approaching pink at maturity. The leaves average 7 in. by 4½ in. (18 by 11·5 cm) and are glabrous.

The author visited the U.S. National Arboretum at Washington D.C. in September 1970 and was shown these Magnolia hybrids by their joint raiser Bill Kosar. Some of the plants were displaying solitary out-of-season blossoms. They had grown into multiple-stemmed, rounded or conical deciduous shrubs 6 to 10 ft (2 to 3 m) tall, of erect growth habit. The flower colours approach the *M. quinquepeta* parental cultivars. This character and number of tepals per flower may vary from year to year, depending upon environmental conditions. Varying degrees of fragrance have been inherited from *M. stellata*. It is claimed that these new cultivars are easily propagated from softwood cuttings. Their erect and compact bushy habit makes them suitable for small gardens, and they are reported to be resistant to the mildew which effects many deciduous Magnolias in that climate.

It is regrettable that no grex name has been registered for these hybrids, whereby their parentage may be readily identified by future generations of garden enthusiasts. In America they are sometimes referred to as 'the eight little girls' but such a title ill befits posterity. Imagine the situation with Magnolia nomenclature today if Soulange-Bodin's hybrids of a century-and-a-half earlier had been distributed under a set of popular Parisienne girls' names, with no suggestion that the various seedlings were even remotely related.

The same course has been adopted by the U.S. National Arboretum with the Freeman Hybrids (*M. grandiflora* × *M. virginiana*).

Cytologically the De Vos and Kosar Hybrids are triploids with 2n = 57 chromosomes, being midway between *M. skellata* (diploid 2n = 38) and *M. quinquepeta* (tetraploid 2n = 76).

MAGNOLIA FRASERI HYBRIDS

A series of hybrids using pollen from *M. fraseri* have been bred by Philip J. Savage, Jr., of Bloomfield Hills, Michigan, who discussed them in *Newsletter of the American Magnolia Society* 12, 1 : 15–16 (1976). He found that the 'earlobes' at the base of the leaves of *M. fraseri* were a very dominant characteristic strongly inherited in the progeny of *M. fraseri* ♂ × *M. tripetala* ♀.

M. fraseri ♂ × *M. hypoleuca* ♀ produced hybrid seedlings morphologically identical to the pollen parent *M. fraseri*, even down to the bright purple colour of the young leaves. He records that the flowers of *M. fraseri* are very resistant to frost and that the colder the spring the more pronounced is the yellow colouring.

M. fraseri ♂ × *M. virginiana* ♀ produced leaves with small 'earlobes' and the telltale purple new growth.

The flowering of these hybrids is awaited with interest.

THE FREEMAN HYBRIDS

MAGNOLIA GRANDIFLORA ♂ × MAGNOLIA VIRGINIANA ♀

O. M. Freeman in *The National Horticultural Magazine* 16, 3 : 161–2 (1937)

W. F. Kosar in *Journal of the Californian Horticultural Society* 23, 1 : 11 (1962)

M. 'Freeman' (Hyland) in the United States Department of Agriculture *Plant Inventory* No. 169 P.I. 277263 (1967)

F. G. Meyer in *Newsletter of the American Magnolia Society* 8, 1 : 7–9 (1971)

Hybrids of this parentage were first bred artificially by Oliver M. Freeman in 1930 while he was attached to the U.S. National Arboretum at Washington, D.C., as Associate Botanist to the Division of Plant Exploration and Introduction of the U.S. Department of Agriculture.

In *The National Horticultural Magazine*, July 1937 (pp. 161–2), a photograph shows a flower of one of these hybrids, together with a very interesting account by the raiser of how they originated. Although *M. virginiana* is a diploid (2n = 38), while *M. grandiflora* is a hexaploid (2n = 114), it was shown, in June 1930, that it was possible to produce hybrids from them.

The mother plant was a large specimen of the Sweet Bay Magnolia (*M. virginiana*) which grew in the grounds of the Department of Agriculture in the Mall at Washington, D.C. It was later transplanted to West Potomac Park, near the Potomac River, but it failed to survive the move.

In each case pollinations were made by forcing open flower buds which would normally have opened naturally within twenty-four hours. The stamens were carefully removed with tweezers, and the stigmas were covered with pollen collected from the fine specimen of *M. grandiflora* growing in Lafayette Park. The flowers, together with their supporting leaves, were then covered with a paper bag fastened to the branch with a paper-clip. After five days the bags were removed and the stigmas were found to be dark brown or black and hardened. Three partly-opened flowers with stigmas tinged brown had likewise been pollinated but these failed to set fruit and soon turned yellow and dropped off.

In the first attempt four flowers were pollinated and seventy-seven seeds resulted. Unfortunately these were sown in ordinary garden soil so that most of them rotted and only five gave rise to strong plants, one of which was accidentally killed after it was planted out.

In June 1931 nine further pollinations were made resulting in the production of 176 seeds. Their pulpy seed coats were removed as soon as they had ripened, and the cleaned seeds were sown in peat moss between layers of cheese-cloth which enabled them to be examined frequently with a minimum of disturbance. Germination began in five weeks and continued for about nine weeks and, as soon as each seed had formed a root tip about half the length of the seed, it was transferred to a small pot containing sandy loam, this transfer being made carefully with tweezers to prevent injury.

The 176 seeds gave rise to 121 plants (126 according to Dr. F. G. Meyer), which were planted out in the Arboretum's nursery in the spring of 1933. Unfortunately no irrigation facilities were available at the time and drought destroyed a number of the seedlings. However, seventy-seven plants survived and four of them began to bloom in 1937 in their sixth year, which indicated that, although all the plants resembled their pollen parent *M. grandiflora*, they inherited this relatively juvenile flowering from their seed parent *M. virginiana*. The flowers were reported to be intermediate in size between the two parents, with a pleasing Sweet Bay fragrance, and of normal appearance with the exception that most of them lacked pollen.

It is of interest that the foliage on all the seedlings was reported to resemble *M. grandiflora*, varying from oblong lanceolate to broadly ovate. None of them had the narrow, somewhat papery-textured leaves of *M. virginiana*, with their conspicuous grey undersurfaces. They inherit the septate pith of the parents.

As might be expected they have proved to be of

variable hardiness. In 1961 two cultivars were named and selected for their relative hardiness and freedom of flowering. 'Freeman' forms an attractive columnar-shaped evergreen shrub, while the second clone, 'Maryland' is of a more spreading habit.

The cultivar 'Griffin' represents a spontaneous hybrid of this group and it was spotted in 1965 by Prof. J. C. McDaniel, growing in City Park, Griffin, Georgia. The leaves are relatively small, acute, thick and glossy. The flowers are large with twelve tepals, borne on long peduncles over a long period. The fruit cones are red and fertile and it roots readily from cuttings.

Several other American Magnolia breeders, including Prof. McDaniel, have since repeated this hybrid and, in 1961, he used pollen from 'Freeman' to make back-crosses on M. virginiana with interesting results. Apparently 'Freeman' is not as sterile as other sibs recorded earlier.

McDaniel considers that because the stigmas of M. virginiana and its variety australis, only remain receptive for about twelve hours, and the stamens do not shed any pollen until the stigmas have become incapable of supporting pollen germination, emasculation of the flowers prior to hand-pollination is unnecessary. Resulting seedlings, which are hybrids (where M. virginiana has been used as the seed parent), can be easily identified by the size and evergreen nature of their leaves, which usually lack the milky undersurface colouring associated with M. virginiana.

A more recent account of these hybrids was published by Frederick G. Meyer, Research Botanist at the U.S. National Arboretum, under the title 'Two New Magnolia Cultivars' in Newsletter of the American Magnolia Society 8, 1 : 7–9 (1971). Meyer stated that fifty-one specimen plants of this hybrid are still growing at the National Arboretum. The terminal vegetative buds are described as slender and silvery puberulent (resembling M. virginiana), while the leaves are thick and leathery (resembling M. grandiflora).

Meyer supplies useful data concerning the two named cultivars. 'Freeman' was originally described in the United States Department of Agriculture Plant Inventory No. 169 (1967) under P.I. 277263. This cultivar was selected primarily for its columnar growth habit. When seen by the author in September 1970, it was some 40 ft (12 m) tall with a branch spread of about 16 ft (5 m). At Washington, D.C., the main flower flush of these hybrids is in May and June with a secondary flush in August. They would be expected to flower later in English gardens. The flowers open to a span of 5 to $5\frac{1}{2}$ in. (12·5 to 14 cm). The cultivar name 'Freeman' was first published by

the National Arboretum's Horticulturist, William F. Kosar, in 'Magnolias Native to North America', Journal of the Californian Horticultural Society 23, 1 : 11 (1962). The first distribution of 'Freeman' was made to arboreta and botanic gardens in the United States in February 1962.

'Maryland' (P.I. 358717) was selected and named primarily because it is relatively easy to propagate from cuttings in intermittent mist. The name was proposed by the Arboretum's Director, Dr. Henry T. Skinner, in 1959, when young plants were sent to nine gardens in England and to one in Italy.

The author was shown the original plant of 'Maryland', which had died back to ground-level several years earlier and had then thrown up a sturdy new growth from the original trunk, some 15 ft (4·5 m) tall. This and the several specimens propagated from it, then from 10 to 15 ft (3 to 4·5 m) high, were of a more spreading growth habit than 'Freeman', with slightly larger flowers.

William F. Kosar told the author that, apparently because of chromosome irregularities, all second generation seedlings which he had raised from these hybrids had exhibited extreme morphological abnormalities in flower structure and were not worthy of retention.

In spite of their maternal M. virginiana parent, the foliage of these Freeman hybrids is indistinguishable from that of M. grandiflora. On our nurseries cutting-raised plants of 'Maryland' have been stood in alphabetical sequence among cultivars of M. grandiflora, where they do not look at all out of place. Nevertheless the author has so far been unable to convince the responsible authorities at the U.S. National Arboretum that an official latinized grex name is long overdue. At present this is governed by Article 17 of the International Code of Nomenclature of Cultivated Plants (1969) which reads: 'A collective epithet in Latin form of an interspecific or intergeneric hybrid must be published with a Latin diagnosis and in combination with a generic name. It is subject to the Botanical Code.' It is the author's opinion that the requirement of a latinized description, to comply with the International Code, is a main deterrent. Perhaps it is time that this clause, which provides for details only comprehensible to the professional botanist, should be modified so that botanical descriptions in a modern language, intelligible to the less gifted reader, and to the researcher, may accompany a latinized grex name at least as regards plants of a hybrid origin.

Cytologically M. grandiflora is a hexaploid with 2n = 114 chromosomes; M. virginiana is a diploid with 2n = 38 chromosomes and M. grandiflora × M.

virginiana hybrids are all tetraploids with 2n = 76 chromosomes according to Dr. Frank S. Santamour, Jr., in his paper entitled 'Cytology of Magnolia Hybrids' *Morris Arboretum Bulletin* 20, 4 : 63–5 (1969). He explains that the hexaploid *M. grandiflora* male parent contributed three times as many chromosomes to the hybrid progeny as did the diploid female parent *M. virginiana*. This resulted in a swamping of *M. virginiana* characteristics and a preponderance of *M. grandiflora* ones, so that all of the hybrids bear a strong resemblance to *M. grandiflora*.

M. GRANDIFLORA × M. QUINQUE-PETA

One of the hybrids bred recently by Dr. Frank Santamour at the U.S. National Arboretum in an endeavour to produce an evergreen Magnolia with coloured flowers. Their flowering is awaited with interest.

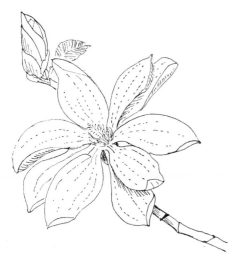

MAGNOLIA 'George Henry Kern'
(assumed *Magnolia* × *soulangiana* × *M. stellata*)

An erect and long-flowering shrub with light-pink flowers opening from rose-coloured buds. The lax strap-shaped tepals of a substantial, velvety texture, are eight to ten in number and develop over an exceptionally long period from April onward. This Magnolia commemorates George Henry Kern, son of the owner of Wyoming Nurseries, Cincinnati, South Ohio, who was killed in France on V.E. Day, 1945.

The author agrees with American authorities who think that this Magnolia might be a hybrid of *M. quinquepeta* 'Nigra' × *M. stellata* 'Rosea'. Such a parentage would bring it into the same grex as the De Vos and Kosar hybrids. Its main attribute is that it flowers on and on and on, starting with *M. heptapeta*, and is still in flower when its foliage is fully matured in July. In 1949 it was covered by an American Plant Patent which restricted free propagation for a period of seventeen years.

Cytologically these hybrids are triploids with 2n = 57 chromosomes. They are sterile and therefore likely to remain as an F1 generation.

Janaki Ammal in *Chromosome Atlas of the World* 2 : 14 (1955) records *M. stellata rubra* as *M. stellata* × *M. quinquepeta* (*liliflora*) with 2n = 57 chromosomes whereas the norm for *M. stellata* is 2n = 38. *M. stellata rubra* bears little or no resemblance to any of the hybrids of this parentage which have been bred at the U.S. National Arboretum by controlled pollinations.

THE GRESHAM HYBRIDS

MAGNOLIA QUINQUEPETA × MAGNOLIA × VEITCHII
MAGNOLIA × SOULANGIANA 'Lennei Alba' × MAGNOLIA × VEITCHII 'Rubra'
MAGNOLIA GLOBOSA Chinese Form × MAGNOLIA WILSONII

D. Todd Gresham in *University of Pennsylvania Morris Arboretum Bulletin* 13 : 47–50 (1962) and 17 : 70–3 (1966)
Journal of the Royal Horticultural Society 89, 8 : 327–32 (1964) 'Deciduous Magnolias of California Origin'

Drury Todd Gresham grew his Magnolias at the 'Hill of Doves', his beautiful home overlooking Santa Cruz Bay and the Monterey Peninsula in California. No doubt his enthusiasm for Magnolia breeding stemmed from his association with the famous plant breeding organization of the Vetterle and Reinelt Hybridizing Garden at Capitola, California, home of the world-renowned Pacific strains of delphiniums and giant polyanthus. In the publications cited he described some of his Magnolia hybridizing experiments, together with some of the resulting seedlings.

He said that he had raised over 3,000 hybrid seedlings. He claimed to have mated practically all known species and varieties in Section *Yulania* and also used their pollen on the best of the Soulangiana Hybrids and an F2 seedling of *M.* × *veitchii*.

In the spring of 1955 he decided to cross *M.* × *veitchii* with *M. quinquepeta* in an attempt to combine the beauty of *M. campbellii*, via its hybrid, with the hardiness of *M. quinquepeta* in what might appear to be an unpromising combination, since *M.* × *veitchii* lacks the elegant cup-and-saucer shape of *M. camp-bellii*.

He referred to his *M.* × *veitchii* parent as an F2 seedling, so one automatically assumes that it was the clone 'Rubra', which had been raised and distributed by Californian nurseryman James C. Clarke of San José. He did not state in his notes in the journals referred to, that the clone of *M. quinquepeta* was 'Nigra', but this is assumed, although he described it as having 'six petals and three sepals' whereas the tepal norm for 'Nigra' is seven or more.

He raised about fifty seedlings of this trihybrid and established them in gallon cans. After screening them for vigour and leaf form, he selected twenty-four plants and planted them out in sets of four. All of them grew vigorously, with foliage and shoots resembling *M.* × *veitchii*.

English Magnolia enthusiasts might imagine that California was a veritable Naboth's vineyard for such a breeding programme, but Todd Gresham described how gophers, those large rat-sized American rodents, acquired a taste for their tangy roots, while birds relished the tepals and foliage of several crosses. Squirrels devoured the gynoecia, as well as the maturing fruit cones, while rabbits ate the tender bark. Slugs and snails laid siege to them at night, devouring their leaves, young bark and tepals. To think that we humble English gardeners grumble at the odd hare, rabbit, mole or slug to say nothing of the constant war against weeds!

M. QUINQUEPETA × *M.* × *VEITCHII*

He described these trihybrids whimsically as 'svelte brunettes' and recorded that the first flower bud appeared in autumn 1960, on a seedling which he had earlier named 'Dark Raiment' because of its very dark coriaceous foliage, which he considered to be rivalled only by *M. dawsoniana*. He also reported that, on the original plant, the lower leaves showed decided autumn colourings, unique in a Magnolia, and that the tree was very vigorous with ascending branches.

He described how the flower buds of 'Dark Raiment' are long and sickle shaped, like those of *M. quinquepeta*, over 5 in. (12·5 cm) in length, and of a deep, glowing red-violet colour. They open to display twelve, slender, 2-in.-wide (5 cm) tepals (4 + 4 + 4) obviously inherited from the *M. campbellii* genes in *M.* × *veitchii*. The eight outer tepals first formed a cup around the inner four which remained erect, clasping the gynoecium. Then these outer ones reflexed downwards to give a graceful and distinctive form to the flower.

—Other outstanding seedlings in this cross, and to which Todd Gresham applied clonal names include:

'Royal Crown' Twelve broad, high-pointed tepals, dark red violet outside, inner surfaces marble white. Flower very large when tepals have fully reflexed (shown in monochrome R.H.S. Fig. 128. M.A.B. Figs. 39, 40 and 41).

'Vin Rouge' Dark wine red with heavy-textured tepals. Young growth glabrous, bronzy red, making it almost worthwhile as a foliage plant.

'Raspberry Ice' Erect *veitchii* form, white flowers, shaded violet blue at the base; twelve tepals compared with only nine in *M.* × *veitchii* (monochrome photograph R.H.S. Fig. 130).

'Peppermint Stick' White with blue-violet base, this colour extending up the centres of the outsides of the very broad rounded tepals. The inner ones remain clasped around the gynandrophore, while the outer ones reflex to a horizontal position to give the flower a very large cup-and-saucer shape and erect poise characteristic of *M. campbellii* (shown in monochrome R.H.S. Fig. 131).

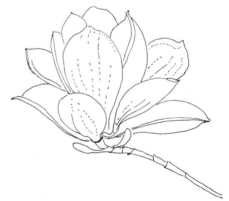

M. × *SOULANGIANA* 'Lennei Alba' × *M.* × *VEITCHII* 'Rubra'

Todd Gresham referred poetically to these three- or

four-fold hybrids as 'Buxom, full-bodied, nordic blondes, their milk-white complexion tastefully enhanced by rouged accents'. He considered that 'they are far more spectacular than the best *soulangiana* white, and compare favourably with good *M. campbellii* and *M. mollicomata* white forms'.

Among these seedlings he selected and named:

'Rouged Alabaster'   Flowers up to 12 in. (30·5 cm) in diameter with nine broad and heavily-textured tepals, up to 6½ in. (16·5 cm) long by 4½ in. (11·4 cm) wide. Lower half of the six outer tepals rose pink, the inner three with deeper shading. Filaments rose red, gynoecium green with straw-coloured stigmas. Peduncle stout and villous with dense grey hairs (R.H.S. Fig. 132 in colour. M.A.B. Fig. 42 in monochrome).

'Crimson Stipple'   Distinguishable from 'Rouged Alabaster' by its unusual pattern of crimson pinpoints (assumed on the backs of the tepals), which create a luminous pink glow against the pure white background.

'Royal Flush'   has the deepest basal colouring of all which Gresham described 'as dark as *M. veitchii* in a vintage year'. Here one again assumes that he was referring to James Clarke's F2 Californian seedling of *M. × veitchii* with the clone name 'Rubra'.

'Spring Rite'   Pure white with rosy basal flush.

'Delicatissima'   A small, compact grower. Flowers white with faint rose-pink basal staining.

'Sulphur Cockatoo'   Has very large white flowers with nine broad tepals, the outer three ultimately reflexing to a horizontal poise. The inner six are stained violet blue, and the whole flower has a warm sunny glow.

M. WILSONII × *M. GLOBOSA*
Chinese Form

This hybrid between two species of Section *Oyama* was first described by Todd Gresham in the University of Pennsylvania *Morris Arboretum Bulletin* 17 : 70–3 (1966). Of vigorous tree-like stature, the young growth resembles that of *M. wilsonii*, with its covering of rufous indumentum, while the mature wood

is fawn-coloured like *M. globosa*, that of *M. wilsonii* being dark tan and later blackish.

The leaves, which are larger and heavier than those of *M. wilsonii* though of similar dark mat-green upper surface, have the midribs and veins on their undersides coated with long, red-gold hairs, as in the Chinese form of *M. globosa*.

The flower is described as a fully-opened cup, 4 in. (10 cm) in diameter, facing almost horizontally to display a green globular gynoecium surmounting a heavy boss of maroon-crimson anthers. The nine tepals are of heavier texture than those of *M. wilsonii*, nearer *M. globosa*. The tepal formation is not characteristic of either parent, resembling that of *M. sieboldii*, but their shape is acute and not obtuse. Flowers in June. This hybrid is reported to be less sun tolerant than *M. wilsonii*. M.A.B. Fig. 65 shows a photograph from a drawing made by Todd Gresham, who was a trained botanical draughtsman.

In *Newsletter of the American Magnolia Society* 4, 2 : 7–8 (1967) he contributed a remarkable article entitled 'Trial by the Royal Family of Magnoliaceae', purporting to be an account of a vivid dream which he had on the night of 23 May 1964 and concerning which he recorded notes when he awoke next morning. This provided an explanation for the dispersal of his remarkable collection of Magnolia hybrids. He claimed that their parentage involved 'the inter- and intra-sectional fusing of the sections *Yulania*; *Buergeria*; *Tulipastrum*; *Rytidospermum*; *Magnoliastrum*; *Oyama* and *Theorhodon*'.

It is sad to relate that Drury Todd Gresham did not survive to see the flowers of all his Magnolia hybrids, for he died on 18 April 1969, at the age of sixty. He was a founder member of the American Magnolia Society and was its first Secretary-Treasurer, an office which he held for many years.

Shortly before his death he had 10,000 of his young seedling Magnolia hybrids transferred to the Tom Dodd Nurseries at Semmes, Alabama, and a further 1,600 larger plants to the Gloster Arboretum at Gloster, Mississippi. He bequeathed his estate to his Alma Mater, the Washington and Lee University, Lexington, Virginia, where the Director of University Development has agreed to a D. Todd Gresham memorial Magnolia planting in the Court of Magnolias on the university campus. (Col. William R. Dodd of Semmes, Alabama, in *Newsletter of the American Magnolia Society* 6, 2 : 7–8 (1969).)

D. Todd Gresham sent the author a set of scions of these hybrids under code numbers in 1968 and the majority of them were successfully bud-grafted. It will, of course, take several years to evaluate their qualities in an English climate, and to raise progeny for distribution.

The full impact of Todd Gresham's Magnolia breeding programme will not be appreciated until his hybrids between the Asian species have attained florescence, and selected seedlings propagated vegetatively for testing under a wide range of climatic conditions. There is little doubt, however, that his name and achievements will join those of Etienne Soulange-Bodin, Peter Veitch and Charles Raffill in the Magnolia Hall of Fame.

M. HEPTAPETA × *M.* × *VEITCHII*

This hybrid was bred at the U.S. National Aboretum at Washington, D.C., in the 1960s. The trees have large white-to-pink flowers. The *M.* × *veitchii* clone was not stated.

THE HIGHDOWN HYBRIDS

MAGNOLIA × *HIGHDOWNENSIS*
(assumed *M. sinensis* × *M. wilsonii*)

J. E. Dandy in *Journal of the Royal Horticultural Society* 75 : 159, Fig. 82 (1950)

SYN. *M. wilsonii* S. A. Spongberg in *Journal of the Arnold Arboretum* 57, 3 : 277–8 (1976)

This Magnolia was first recorded in the garden of Col. F. G. (later Sir Frederic) Stern, which overlies the chalk at Highdown, Goring-by-Sea, Sussex. It had originated as a seedling raised at Caerhays and given to him by the late J. C. Williams. Its origin is discussed at some length by Johnstone under *Magnolia sinensis* in *Asiatic Magnolias in Cultivation* : 121–2.

It is a shrubby Magnolia resembling *M. sinensis* in growth but of more vigorous, spreading habit up to 20 ft (6 m). The leaves are usually more or less pubescent beneath. The fragrant white flowers are somewhat smaller than those of *M. sinensis*, being globular in shape, nodding and attaining a horizontal poise when fully open. It is compared with other Magnolias in Section *Oyama* in the author's Table of Comparisons on pp. 68–9.

Mr. J. D. Bond says that seedlings of *M. wilsonii*, raised in the Gardens at Windsor Great Park, have included plants with leaves identical to those of *M.* × *highdownensis*, but in such a comprehensive collection of Magnolias these may well have been from carpels fertilized by wind or insect-borne pollen off a near-by plant of *M. sinensis*.

Johnstone suggested that *M.* × *highdownensis* was a form of *M. wilsonii* but so far nobody seems to have bothered to resolve this question by performing controlled pollinations between the putative parents. That this Magnolia might have originated in China as a natural hybrid seems possible. Wilson discovered *M. sinensis* in western Szechwan in 1908 and *M. wilsonii* in east Sikang (now Kansu) in 1904. Although these are adjacent provinces, *M. sinensis* has been found in only one locality, but *M. wilsonii* is known to have an extensive range southward into northern Yunnan.

Suffice it to say that there are, in English gardens, many Oyama Magnolias which appear to be intermediates between *M. sinensis* and *M. wilsonii* without having originated from seed off a plant of *M.* × *highdownensis*.

Dr. Stephen A. Spongberg in *Journal of the Arnold Arboretum* 57, 3 : 277 (1976) merged *M.* × *highdownensis* with *M. wilsonii* on the basis that 'all plants of this putative hybrid which I have seen growing in England fall into the range of variation encountered in *M. wilsonii* and are similar to specimens of *M. wilsonii* collected in China. As a result, the name *M.* × *highdownensis* is placed in the synonymy of *M. wilsonii*.'

J. E. Dandy once told the author that he was never quite happy about the hybrid status which he cited for this Magnolia in 1950.

Cytologically as for all members of Section *Oyama* they are diploids with 2n = 38 chromosomes.

MAGNOLIA HYPOLEUCA × *MAGNOLIA TRIPETALA*

Hybrids of this parentage are reported to have occurred spontaneously in the local park in the Czechoslovakian town of Pruhonice, near Prague, by Eng. Vladimir Vasak of the Botanical Institute of the Czechoslovak Academy of Science at Pruhonice. The seed parent tree of *M. hypoleuca* is one of Japanese origin (Shirasawa, Tokyo) which was raised and cultivated in the nurseries of the Czech Dendrological Society between 1910 and 1916 and is now about 55 ft (17 m) tall with a trunk girth of 3 ft (91 cm) at a height of 3¼ ft (1 m). Vasak gives these details in 'Magnolia hypoleuca in Nature and in Cultivation' in *Newsletter of the American Magnolia Society* 9, 1 : 3–6 (1973). He does not give dimensions of the tree of *M. tripetala*.

A similar hybrid of this parentage is recorded by Dr. Stephen Spongberg in *Journal of the Arnold Arboretum* 57, 3 : 272–3 (1976). It originated from seed collected from an Arboretum tree of *M. hypoleuca* which, in turn, had been grown from seed from another tree of that species which had been raised from seed collected in Japan by Prof. C. S. Sargent in 1892. Spongberg describes the hybrid as a large tree upwards of 33 ft (10 m) with the habit and overall resemblance of the *M. hypoleuca* parent (now dead) which was growing in close association with one of *M. tripetala*. It is distinguishable by its more nearly elliptic leaf blades, its flowers being intermediate between those of the two parents and its fruit cones which agree almost exactly with those of *M. tripetala*.

Several writers have referred to a close affinity between those of the two parents and its fruit cones American *M. tripetala* but the latter species bears a much closer likeness to the Chinese *M. officinalis*. It is known that both *M. hypoleuca* and *M. officinalis* have been grown together in China for their timber and it is possible that both of these two very closely related species possess the same medicinal qualities in their bark. It seems reasonable to suppose that they would give rise to hybrids and that such trees, when grown in Japan in association with trees of pure *M. hypoleuca*, would eventually give rise to a race of that species introgressed by genes from *M. officinalis* which could recur as a recessive trait in some future generation and lead to a change in the appearance of the floral characters. If such a tree originated spontaneously from seed collected off *M. hypoleuca* which grew within a short distance of *M. tripetala* it would be naturally assumed to be a hybrid between those species.

When the author compares Marjorie Blamey's paintings of these three species of Magnolia, such a theory is seen to be a reasonable possibility for the floral and foliage characters of *M. officinalis* are midway between those of *M. hypoleuca* and *M. tripetala*. Both have peculiar horseshoe petiolar scars on their branchlets and both have the similar off-white tepals and the same shape of flower.

Spongberg describes the Arnold Arboretum hybrid

as a large tree with the habit of *M. hypoleuca* whereas *M. tripetala* does not grow to any great stature and hybrids between them might be expected to be intermediate in habit of growth; *M. tripetala* does not form an elongated main trunk but produces several limbs which arise close to the base. Unfortunately all three species are diploids with 2n = 38 chromosomes so that cytological investigation (apart from suggesting hybridity in an irregular pairing of the chromosomes at first metaphase of meiosis) could not shed any further light on the question of male parentage in the case under discussion here.

Hybrids of *M. hypoleuca* × *M. fraseri* and of *M. hypoleuca* × *M. macrophylla* have been bred from intentional pollinations by P. J. Savage, Jr., of Bloomfield Hills, Michigan.

MAGNOLIA HYPOLEUCA ♀ × MAGNOLIA VIRGINIANA ♂

Dr. Stephen Spongberg reports that hybrids between *M. hypoleuca* as seed parent and *M. virginiana* as pollen parent, which were bred at the United States National Arboretum, Washington, D.C., by W. F. Kosar in 1956, are almost indistinguishable from *M.* × *thompsoniana* (*M. virginiana* × *M. tripetala*). A selected clone from these plants is expected to be distributed to nurseries for propagation. Their pollen has been found to be highly sterile by Santamour (see *Morris Arboretum Bulletin* 20, 4: 65 (1969)).

M. hypoleuca ♂ × *M. wilsonii* ♀ is a hybrid reported to have been made by Dr. Tor Nitzelius at the botanical garden at Göteborg (Gothenburg), Sweden.

Magnolia 'Iolanthe'

A seedling of *M.* × *soulangiana* 'Lennei' from pollen of *M.* 'Mark Jury' raised at Waitara, on the southwest coast of North Island, New Zealand, by Felix M. Jury. The seedling produced its first flowers in 1970 when only four years old. The blossoms are larger than those of 'Lennei' and of a lighter colour.

THE KEW HYBRIDS

MAGNOLIA × KEWENSIS Pearce
(*M. kobus* ♀ × *M. salicifolia* ♂)

S. A. Pearce in *Gardeners Chronicle* 3, 132 : 154 (1952)
Journal of the Royal Horticultural Society 84 : 426 (1959)
SYN. *M. salicifolia* 'Kewensis' (Pearce) Spongberg
    S. A. Spongberg in *Journal of the Arnold Arboretum* 57, 3 : 294 (1976)

This name was given to a seedling discovered growing close to the foot of a tree of *M. kobus* at the Royal Botanical Gardens at Kew in 1938. It was discovered by C. F. Coates along with the hybrid which now bears his name 'Charles Coates'. It is recorded as having first flowered there in 1957. The leaves are 4 to 5 in. (10 to 12·5 cm) long and the flowers are pure white. It is reported to root readily from cuttings in intermittent mist.

The six main tepals are broader than those of *M. salicifolia*, while the three outer ones form a false 'calyx' as in both the parent species. These are small and of a thin, papery texture with a tendency to turn grey green when they reflex outwards and downwards instead of lying close behind the larger ones or reflexing completely. The stigmatic column is lime green while the stamens and stigmas are creamy yellow. The flowers have a most pleasing and distinctive orange-blossom fragrance, while the bark smells pleasantly of lemon verbena (*Aloysia triphylla*).

M. × kewensis is depicted on Plate 33 in *Rhododendrons and Magnolias*, by Douglas Bartrum (1957). It received an Award of Merit from the Royal Horticultural Society in April 1952. The original tree is growing close to King William's Temple at Kew. Similar seedlings are said to have been growing both at Exbury near Southampton, and at Grayswood Hill, Haslemere, Surrey, in the 1930s.

Another outstanding Magnolia was selected at the Arboretum of the University of Washington, at Seattle, from a number of seedlings of *M. kobus* sent from Japan by Mr. K. Wada of Yokohama. It has been named 'Wada's Memory', an unusual title to apply within the lifetime of its originator. This hybrid bears profusions of fragrant white flowers much larger than those of *M. kobus* (see B. Mulligan in *Arnold Arboretum Bulletin* 22 : 20 (1959)).

Some American Magnolia authorities consider this more likely to be an *M. × proctoriana* hybrid (*M. salicifolia* × *M. stellata*) but such conjecture throws unwarranted doubt on the authenticity of the seed from which it was raised, unless one equates *M. stellata* with *M. kobus*. Mr. Wada informs the author that this Magnolia was sent by him to the Arnold Arboretum before the Second World War (i.e. prior to 1940). He agrees that it 'looks rather like a *salicifolia-kobus* natural hybrid', thus confirming the author's suggestion that it should be classified under *M. × kewensis*.

Dr. Stephen Spongberg in *Journal of the Arnold Arboretum* 57, 3 : 294 (1976) writes: 'The original plant of this putative hybrid and its clonal progeny are now generally known under the cultivar name 'Kewensis'. An alternative designation utilizes the formula *M. salicifolia* × *M. kobus* to cover all progeny of this cross, but if Blackburn's taxonomy (1955, 1957) is adopted concerning *M. kobus* and its varieties, as it is here, the name *M. × proctoriana*, as a collective epithet, covers all hybrids between *M. salicifolia* and *M. kobus*.'

Since Spongberg treats *M. × proctoriana* as easily accommodated within *M. salicifolia* that hybrid grex is likewise repudiated. His reasons are given under *M. salicifolia*.

Cytologically these hybrids (or crosses) are diploids with 2n = 38 chromosomes as for all members of Section *Buergeria*.

THE LOEBNER HYBRIDS OR CROSSES

MAGNOLIA × LOEBNERI Kache
(M. kobus × M. stellata)

P. Kache in *Gartenschönheit* 1 : 20 (1920)
B. Blackburn in *Journal of the New York Botanical Garden* 2, 2 : 43–4 and 53 (1952)
SYN. *M. kobus* var. *loebneri* (Kache) Spongberg
Stephen A. Spongberg in *Journal of the Arnold Arboretum* 57, 3 : 297 (1976)

Plates 32 and 41

In 1920 the new German garden periodical *Gartenschönheit* (Beauty in the Garden) published in its first issue an illustrated article by Paul Kache entitled 'The most beautiful of flowering shrubs in April. Early winter-hardy Magnolias.'

He discussed the respective merits of *M. kobus* and *M. stellata*, the former with its vigorous growth and the second 'which is so generous with its show of blossom that it does not seem to have enough strength left over to make growth'.

Kache continued: 'It lay ready for the ever-searching horticulturist to attempt the masterpiece of associating the fullness of blossom of the one with the vigorous growth of the other. Now that goal has been reached after lengthy, at first unsuccessful, work. For many years Garden Inspector M. Löbner, at present in Bonn but formerly of the Botanical Gardens in Dresden, experimented with countless crosses and fertilizations of *M. stellata* blossoms, until finally success came.'

Kache stated that the first flowering of the new hybrid was in 1917. The flowers of this original hybrid tree had twelve tepals compared with eight for *M. kobus* and eighteen for *M. stellata*. *M. × loebneri* grows into a small slender-branched tree with starry white flowers opening in profusion along its naked branches just as winter gives way to spring. Since then other

Magnolia breeders have followed in Max Löbner's footsteps, thereby adding further members to this useful race of hybrids, which combine cold tolerance with an ability to flourish on almost any type of soil, be it chalk, sand or heavy clay.

In W. J. Bean, *Trees and Shrubs Hardy in the British Isles* Ed. 8, 2 : 657 (1973) is further interesting information to the effect that the original plants were sold in 1923 and it is known that some were purchased by Hillier's of Winchester and five by Wilhelm Kordes nursery at Sparrieshoop in Germany, who reported in 1964 that one of the original plants was then 25 ft (7·5 m) high and 28 ft (8·5 m) across, producing flowers in unbelievable profusion about one week before *M. × soulangiana*. Typical plants have narrowly obovate leaves and flowers with twelve tepals.

'Snowdrift' is a clone selected from the batch of Kache's original seedlings which were sent to Hillier's of Winchester for growing on to flowering age. It has larger flowers than *M. stellata* with about twelve tepals; leaves also a little larger.

In an article by H. G. Hillier and C. R. Lancaster entitled 'Magnolias in the Hillier Gardens and Arboretum' in the Royal Horticultural Society's *Rhododendrons 1975 with Magnolias and Camellias* p. 62, they write 'The growth of typical *M. stellata* is always dense and bushy with crowded branches and this is shown in its various clones. Seed-grown specimens which show unusual vigour and develop strong erect leaders to form a tree are likely to be hybrids with *M. kobus*, a group called *M. × loebneri*. A further distinction is the densely pubescent young shoots of *M. stellata* (even in winter) as against those of *M. × loebneri* which are smooth or near-so (particularly in winter).'

The Loebner hybrids grow into small, slender-branched trees with starry flowers opening along the naked branches before the leaves appear. Most of them can be readily rooted from soft-wood cuttings in intermittent mist and the resulting plants commence to flower at a very early age. All hybrids in this group will flourish in all types of soil, including chalk.

Another controlled hybridization of this parentage is reported to have been made in America about 1930 by Dr. Walter Van Fleet, a professional plant breeder of the United States Department of Agriculture, with *M. kobus borealis* × *M. stellata* 'Rosea', in an attempt to produce a pink-flowered arborescent Magnolia. The dainty pinkish flowers of this hybrid are reported to have up to twelve long strap-like tepals and a good scent.

Then in 1939 Dr. Karl Sax, of the Arnold

Arboretum of Harvard University, contributed M. × *loebneri* 'Merrill', a vigorous clone with fine semi-double white flowers, which he named after the late Dr. E. D. Merrill, its former Director. This clone has been widely listed as 'Dr. Merrill', but the original clone-name of 'Merrill' should be adhered to. It is an outstanding garden plant of compact and erect habit, producing profusions of large white starry flowers in April.

'Spring Snow' (Plate 41) and 'Star Bright' are two other white-flowered American clones; the former has bullate or puckered leaves typical of *M. kobus* while the latter has fine multitepalled flowers and is best described as an arborescent *M. stellata*. Still more so must be 'Ballerina' (Plate 32), a new F2 seedling from 'Spring Snow', which has fragrant flowers with up to thirty-one showy tepals. 'Spring Snow' originated as one of two supposed specimens of *M. stellata*, which was planted in the President's Garden of the University of Illinois at Urbana in 1931. They turned out to be an unmatched pair of Loebner hybrids but their nursery source is not known. The best of these was named 'Spring Snow' by Prof. J. C. McDaniel and has now reached maturity at 30 ft (9 m). At Urbana it flowers from the first week in April, the last spring snowfall often briefly covering the earlier flowers but seldom damaging the good display. It usually continues with diminishing numbers of flowers opening as late as the beginning of May. At Semmes, Mobile County, Alabama, it is reported to begin blooming as early as the first week of January. The fragrant all-white flowers average fifteen tepals 3 in. (7·5 cm) long by 1½ in. (4 cm) wide which reflex somewhat below the horizontal as they mature.

'Ballerina' was selected by Prof. McDaniel in 1968 from seedlings which he raised from 'Spring Snow' in 1960 and planted out on the Horticultural Farm of the University. It has up to thirty tepals, with a pale-pink flush on both surfaces towards their bases, and is more fragrant than 'Spring Snow'. The mother tree was 10 ft (3 m) tall in August 1969.

According to Prof. McDaniel both 'Spring Snow' and its seedling 'Ballerina' are somewhat smaller trees than 'Merrill', but have more tepals in their slightly later flowers with better fragrance than either 'Merrill' or 'Leonard Messel'.

'Willowwood' is yet another American clone, named and selected by Dr. Benjamin Blackburn of Willowwood Arboretum, Gladstone, New Jersey, which is owned by Rutgers, the State University, New Brunswick, New Jersey. Dr. Blackburn, in *Amatores Herbarii* 17 : 1–2 (1955), was the first exponent of the theory that *M. stellata* is a dwarf, multitepalled form of *M. kobus*. He elaborated on this

theory in an interesting and informative paper entitled 'The Early-Flowering Magnolias of Japan' in *Baileya* 5, 1 : 3–13 (1957). Should Blackburn's suggested re-classification become generally accepted, then all hybrids of this parentage will have to be referred to as forms of *M. kobus*. In the author's opinion Blackburn's theory has not been conclusively proved and such a classification would cause considerable confusion within Section *Buergeria*. Several very large-scale raisings of *M. stellata* seedlings have been recorded in America, such as those mentioned under *M. stellata* 'Waterlily'.

Johnstone recorded that seedlings from *M. stellata* raised at Nymans, Handcross, near Haywards Heath in Sussex, by the late head gardener, J. Comber, produced plants of a more arborescent habit than that of the parent plant. From these seedlings originated *M.* 'Leonard Messel', an open branched tree form with fuchsia-purple buds opening to pale lilac-pink flowers and believed to be a cross between *M. kobus* and *M. stellata* 'Rosea'. The flowers consist of eleven or twelve tepals which are creamy white inside with their outer surfaces suffused lilac purple to give a light-pink effect when viewed from a distance. They are star-shaped and expand to 4½ to 5 in. (11·5 to 12·5 cm) across when fully open. They are noticeably more frost resistant than are those of the white-flowered forms, and this clone is sure to be in great demand when it becomes better known. There is a coloured photograph and description of this Magnolia in the *Journal of The Royal Horticultural Society* 94 : 12 (1969).

'Leonard Messel' is the most distinct of these crosses reported to date. It was awarded the coveted First Class Certificate by the Royal Horticultural Society when exhibited by the Countess of Rosse and the National Trust on 15 April 1969. Much confusion will inevitably plague both nurserymen and their customers for the name of 'Leonard Messel' has been bestowed likewise on an outstanding camellia, a hybrid between *C. reticulata* and *C. × williamsii* 'Mary Christian'. One has only to ponder on the confusion which can readily arise between the similarly sounding names Camellia and Magnolia without having the same clonal name in both genera.

Elsewhere plants raised from seed of *M. stellata* 'Rosea' from Capt. Neil McEacharn's garden at the Villa Taranto on Lake Como, Italy, have developed into small trees. One of these seedlings, raised in the Gardens at Windsor Great Park, was named 'Neil McEacharn' in 1952. It is an arborescent form of *M. stellata* 'Rosea' producing the pink-flushed multi-tepalled flowers of the parent with a vigorous tree-like rate of growth of 15 to 18 in. (38 to 46 cm) a year.

It received an Award of Merit from the Royal Horticultural Society in 1968.

Prof. McDaniel, writing in the *Newsletter of the American Magnolia Society* 7, 1 : 2 (1970), stated that it has been demonstrated both in Germany and in the United States, that controlled crosses between typical *M. kobus* and *M. stellata* will give intermediate height seedlings with flowers also intermediate and usually as fertile as either parent. *M.* × *loebneri* forms have also arisen where seeds from open-pollinated flowers of *M. stellata* have been sown, especially where in reasonable proximity to a flowering tree of *M. kobus*. He recorded that his own experience at Urbana, where typical *M. kobus* was not known to have flowered prior to 1969, was for seedlings of *M. stellata* 'Waterlily' and 'Rubra' clones to resemble closely the parent at least in leaf size and rate of growth. From these observations he concludes that pollination by the larger-growing *M. kobus* seems necessary in order to raise *M.* × *loebneri* seedlings from *M. stellata* seeds.

It seems most likely that 'Slavin's Snowy', with its broader-tepalled flowers, resulted from *M. kobus* × *M. salicifolia*, which would bring it into the *M.* × *kewensis* grex. Dr. Wyman of the Arnold Arboretum reported that the flowers of 'Slavin's Snowy' are not as large as those of *M.* × *loebneri* 'Merrill'.

Because of their relatively small leaves the Loebner hybrids, along with *M. salicifolia* and its hybrids, are particularly suitable for providing dappled shade for such subjects as camellias and rhododendrons. Although *M. stellata* is known to have been the seed parent of the original hybrid some of those raised since are known to be seedlings of *M. kobus*.

Dr. Spongberg, having adopted Blackburn's taxonomy for *M. kobus* which treats *M. stellata* as *M. kobus* var. *stellata*, recognizes *M.* × *loebneri* as an intraspecific cross which he renames *M. kobus* var. *loebneri* (Kache) Spongberg.

Cytologically these hybrids (or crosses) are diploids with 2n = 38 chromosomes.

MAGNOLIA MACROPHYLLA ♂ × MAGNOLIA VIRGINIANA ♀

This produced very vigorous progeny with glossy 'king-sized' Sweet Bay leaves 14 in. (35·5 cm) by 4 in. (10 cm). Bred by Philip J. Savage, Jr., of Bloomfield Hills, Michigan, it has not yet attained florescence.

MAGNOLIA 'Mark Jury'
(*M. campbellii* subsp. *mollicomata* Lanarth Group × *M. sargentiana* var. *robusta*)

Raised by Felix M. Jury at Waitara, North Island, New Zealand. It has purple flowers 10 to 11 in. (25·5 to 30 cm) across.

MAGNOLIA 'Michael Rosse'
Plate 42

This Magnolia is believed to have originated as one of a batch of seedlings, supposed to be of *M. campbellii alba*, which were raised at Caerhays. It reached Nymans Gardens at Handcross, Haywards Heath, Sussex, via Hillier's Nurseries at Winchester. It received an Award of Merit at a Royal Horticultural Society Show on 2 April 1968 when exhibited by the Countess of Rosse and the National Trust. The R.H.S. Floral 'B' Committee considered it to be a hybrid of *M. sargentiana* var. *robusta*. By a remarkable coincidence an almost identical Magnolia which, it transpired, had originated in precisely the same way, was exhibited at the same show from the gardens at Windsor Great Park (see *M.* 'Princess Margaret').

The tree is described by Head Gardener Cecil Nice as being fairly erect, with leaves resembling those of *M. campbellii*. There is a very similar Magnolia (Plate 42) growing on the south side of the cottage on our old nursery at Truro which has been given the locality name 'Moresk'. It was purchased from Caerhays prior to 1960 but, unfortunately, no record of its parentage can be found. They would have been bred between 1955 and 1960 (Plate 42).

Since all members of section *Yulania* are hexaploids (2n = 114 chromosomes) cytological investigation would not help to solve the problem. There are probably similar hybrids in the great Magnolia collection at Caerhays which may one day serve as a clue to the parentage of these three named cultivars (see p. 167).

MAGNOLIA 'Orchid'

A seedling of *M. stellata* raised in 1961 by Hillenmeyer's Nursery, Lexington, Kentucky, U.S.A. The tepals are described as a rather uniform red purple, the anthers and stigmas are also coloured. The leaves are said to be more attractive than those of either of the assumed parents, rather resembling *M. sprengeri* 'Diva'. The plant is hardy and free flowering.

Anthocyanin tests carried out on flowers of this

cultivar by Dr. Frank S. Santamour, Jr., and described in the *Morris Arboretum Bulletin* 16 : 46–7 (1965), cast considerable doubt on the assumption that 'Orchid' is the result of hybridization between *M. stellata* and *M. quinquepeta*.

The author saw a specimen plant of 'Orchid' in Phil Savage's garden at Bloomfield Hills, Michigan, in September 1970 and was impressed by the unusually neat, rounded habit and attractive glossy revolute-margined foliage. Savage described the plant and its flowers in *Newsletter of the American Magnolia Society* 9, 2 : 23 (1973), and reported that they have invariably six showy tepals plus the three diminutive ones in the outer whorl. The colour is brighter than *M. quinquepeta* (*liliflora*) 'Nigra', the plant is hardier and resembles *M. quinquepeta* closely in all other respects. It shows no sign of *M. stellata* in its make-up.

MAGNOLIA 'Osaka'

Sarasa-mokuren in Japan

Journal of the Royal Horticultural Society 27 : 20 (1902)
Keisuke Ito in *Figures and Descriptions of Plants in the Koishikawa Botanical Garden* I : Fig. 10 (1884) as *M. obovata* Thunberg

The Cornwall Daffodil and Spring Flower Show held in Truro on 15 April 1902 was honoured by a deputation from the Council of the Royal Horticultural Society, which included the Earl of Ilchester, Member of Council, and the Revd. G. H. Engleheart, an authority on and a breeder of daffodils.

They bestowed an Award of Merit on a Magnolia exhibited by Gauntlett's Nursery of Redruth, Cornwall (and later of Chiddingfold in Surrey), which had been imported from Japan and was labelled 'Osaka'. It was described as having 'large flowers, the petals purple-claret outside and a sort of veined violet-purple on the inside'.

From the Gauntlett description 'magnificent dark purple flowers from May to July, being almost black in the bud and forming a bush about 6 ft [2 m]', it would appear to be a form of *M. quinquepeta* or a hybrid of that species, maybe of the Soulangiana grex.

Today Gauntlett's successors at Chiddingfold are unable to trace this Magnolia so it seems likely that there was only one importation from Japan. This nursery firm had close links with Japanese export nurseries over a long period, and their mammoth illustrated catalogue, with its oriental savour, has now become a collector's edition.

According to Mr. K. Wada, 'Osaka' is the name of the district where the plant originated, and the correct Japanese name for this Magnolia in Japan is said to be 'Sarasa'. Although no trace of it can now be found in English gardens, one wonders if there are any survivors in the older Cornish gardens, also whether it was a hybrid or a variant of *M. quinquepeta*.

It seems possible that it might have been the same as that depicted by the Japanese botanist Keisuke Ito in *Figures and Descriptions of Plants in the Koishikawa Botanical Garden* I : Fig. 10 (1884) under *M. obovata* Thunberg (an early name for *M. quinquepeta* Buc'hoz). The Japanese text has been translated for us in Japan and it tells us that this Magnolia is looked upon as a 'strain' of the species which originated in China and known in Japan as Sarasa-mokuren. The branches and leaves are similar to those of the species but the flowers are somewhat smaller, the eight or nine tepals coloured white with faint violet shadings on their inner surfaces, the outside being reddish purple to white at the tips.

The colour of the flower depicted as Fig. 10 in the copy which the author examined in the Botany Library at the British Museum (Natural History) does not agree with this description, the tepals being of a pale shade of rosy lilac. In addition, the figure numbers, penned in western numerals against the Japanese characters, do not agree with those quoted above, which were given by both of the Japanese translators from Xerox copies sent to them by the author.

The stamens are described as having violet filaments and are compressed vertically into a tight band around the base of a short yellow stigmatic column. The pedicle is long, slender and vase shaped with a prominent collar of stiff hairs around the base. These are absent in the flower depicted on Fig. 10, which follows Fig. 11 in oriental sequence.

This figure represents a very fine form of *M. quinquepeta*. The flower has seven broad violet-backed tepals, quite unlike the colour associated with other purple Magnolias, while their inner surfaces are conspicuously veined and flushed with the same unusual colour. The styles are also purple, as are the tips and edges of the stamens, which are arranged in an erect cylindrical mass around the base of the gynoecium. The base of the short, stout peduncle shows smooth protuberances or scars without any hairs.

In the Harvard Herbarium there is a specimen labelled *M. purpurascens* Makino with the Japanese name 'Sarasa-Mokuren'. It was collected from a cultivated plant at the Kuashiki-Shi, Okayamaken, Honshu, Japan, in April 1952. It is said to resemble *M. heptapeta*. Perhaps 'Sarasa-renge' and 'Sarasa-Mokuren' are one and the same Magnolia. In 1929 Makino suggested that Sarasa-mokuren came within the grex of *M.* × *soulangiana* and in 1937 this was confirmed by the pentaploid chromosome count (2n = 76) recorded by Yasui (see p. 108).

MAGNOLIA 'Paul Cook'

(*M.* × *soulangiana* × *M. sprengeri* 'Diva')

A hybrid bred by Dr. Frank Galyon in Knoxville, Tennessee. The growth is vigorous and winter hardy at Urbana, Illinois. It attains florescence at an earlier age than 'Diva' with 10 in. (25·5 cm) blossoms of a lighter pink.

MAGNOLIA 'Princess Margaret'

This Magnolia originated in precisely the same way as *M.* 'Michael Rosse'. It was exhibited by the Crown Estate Gardens, Windsor, under the name 'Windsor Belle' on 17 April 1973. Two days later it was decided to rename it 'Princess Margaret' under which name the coveted Royal Horticultural Society's First Class Certificate was recorded. The tree was then described as being 20 ft (6 m) high and the date of raising was given as 1957, the seed parent being recorded as *M. campbellii alba* under 'Awards to Magnolias, 1973' in the R.H.S. *Rhododendrons 1974 with Magnolias and Camellias* : 108.

The flowers are described as being up to 11 in. (30 cm) across, each with eleven obovate tepals, red purple outside fading to cream inside. Compared with *M. campbellii* 'Charles Raffill' (*M. campbellii* var. *campbellii* × *M. c.* var. *mollicomata*) 'Princess Margaret' has larger but less rounded tepals of slightly deeper colour.

THE PROCTOR HYBRIDS

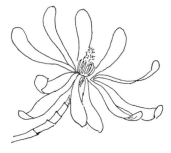

MAGNOLIA × *PROCTORIANA* Rehder
(*M. salicifolia* × *M. stellata*)
A. Rehder in *Journal of the Arnold Arboretum* 20 : 412 (1939)

This hybrid was selected at the Arnold Arboretum in 1928 among seedlings raised from a tree of *M. salicifolia* which was growing in a private arboretum founded in 1900 by T. E. Proctor at Topsfield, Massachusetts. It was grown at Boston under No. 874–28.

Rehder described it as having a tree-like pyramidal habit with slender ascending branches, the leaves smaller, narrower and more pointed than those of *M. salicifolia*. It attains florescence at an earlier age and has flowers more conspicuous than the seed parent, with from six to thirteen tepals, but it does not flower as freely as *M. stellata*.

Plants within this hybrid grex inherit a vigour of growth from *M. salicifolia*, and fragrant multitepalled flowers from *M. stellata*.

Dr. Donald Wyman, in *Arnoldia* 20, 3–4 : 27 (1960), described *M.* × *proctoriana* as having poor blooms and this is substantiated by his Plate 7 showing a comparison of the flowers of Magnolias *kobus*, *stellata*, *loebneri* 'Merrill', *salicifolia* and *M.* × *proctoriana*, with one of *M. denudata* as a yardstick.

If American botanists persist in re-classifying *M. stellata* under *M. kobus*, then hybrids now under *M.* × *kewensis* and *M.* × *loebneri* will become relegated to *M.* × *proctoriana*, as has *M.* × *slavinii* which was formerly acclaimed a hybrid of *M. salicifolia* × *M.* × *soulangiana*.

The late George Johnstone in *Asiatic Magnolias in Cultivation* went out of his way to publish a full description of the latter hybrid as *M.* × *slavinii*, although he avoided doing so for other hybrids as he restricted his text to Asian species. 'This hybrid was raised at Highland Park, Rochester, U.S.A., and is described in the *National Horticultural Magazine* (Journal of the American Horticultural Society Inc.) 33, 2 : 118 (1954). It is named after Mr. Bernard H. Slavin, who has been for many years associated with the Rochester Parks.

'The photographs accompanying the publication mentioned show this Magnolia to be an upright tree with three main stems flowering profusely – it first flowered in 1917 – and the inner tepals, numbering 6 to 9, are $3\frac{1}{4}$ to $3\frac{3}{4}$ in. [8 to 9 cm] long, white with a pink blotch near the base, deepening on the outside at the base of the central vein. A close-up of a flowering branch favours the assumed parentage and shows the hybrid to be a very desirable Magnolia.

'From the article already referred to it seems that several numbered plants of this cross have been preserved and propagated since, B.H.S. No. 85 being selected as the clone for which the cultivar name 'Slavin's Snowy' has been chosen, so that the full name is therefore *M.* × *slavinii* 'Slavin's Snowy'.'

J. E. Dandy pointed out that as *M. salicifolia* is a

diploid (2n = 38), while *M.* × *soulangiana* is generally a tetraploid (2n = 76), a cytological examination would accurately determine the validity of the putative parentage. In 1960 Dr. John Einset, of the Geneva (New York) State Agricultural Experimental Station, made such studies from the root tips of a rooted cutting and found the plant to be diploid (2n = 38). Mr. Bernard Harkness, taxonomist at Highland Park, Rochester, New York, therefore suggested that the cultivar 'Slavin's Snowy' be reassigned to *M.* × *proctoriana*, on the assumption that the pollen parent was another member of Section *Buergeria, Morris Arboretum Bulletin* 12, 2 : 19 (1961). The author is of the opinion that it is of the same parentage as *M.* × *kewensis*.

Dr. Stephen A. Spongberg in *Journal of the Arnold Arboretum* 57, 3 : 294–5 (1976) accommodates *M.* × *kewensis* together with *M.* × *proctoriana* within *M. salicifolia*. 'The conclusion is supported when the variation of *M. salicifolia* in nature is studied in conjunction with the cultivated material. The fact that seedlings of *M. salicifolia* show a degree of variability is undoubtedly correlated to some extent with the fact that the species is self-compatible and plants grown from self-fertilized seeds should be expected to exhibit variation associated with the expression of recessive traits. Support for the non hybrid status of these plants also comes from the cytological condition in plants grown as *M.* × *proctoriana*, (2n = 38) Santamour 1970.'

Dr. Frank S. Santamour, Jr., Research Geneticist at the United States National Arboretum at Washington, D.C., discussed his research into the 'Cytology of Magnolia Hybrids' in the *Morris Arboretum Bulletin* 20, 4 : 63–5 (1969), 21, 4 : 58–61, and 21, 4 : 80–1 (1970). He explains that the pairing of the chromosomes at first metaphase of meiosis may give an indication of genetic similarity. In certain hybrids between *M. kobus* and *M. stellata*, and between *M. stellata* and *M. salicifolia* the chromosomes pair regularly and indicate a close relationship between the parents involved. At meiosis the pairing at metaphase I was regular, with nineteen bivalents being formed. Would the pairing have been irregular had it been a hybrid from two parents of the same level of ploidy? He found that a diploid hybrid showing a remote relationship between parents (*M. hypoleuca* × *M. virginiana*) may show up to six unpaired chromosomes resulting in an abnormal meiosis and high sterility.

Dr. Spongberg treats *M.* × *slavinii* as *M. salicifolia* 'Slavin's Snowy'.

MAGNOLIA QUINQUEPETA × MAGNOLIA SPRENGERI 'Diva'

Hybrids of this parentage, bred by W. F. Kosar at the United States National Aboretum at Washington, D.C., in 1969, were reported as 'now beginning to produce crops of plum coloured flowers' in *American Magnolia Society Newsletter* 13, 1 : 3 (1977).

THE *MAGNOLIA SARGENTIANA* var. *ROBUSTA* HYBRIDS

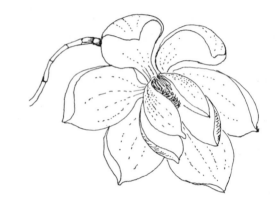

MAGNOLIA SARGENTIANA var. ROBUSTA × MAGNOLIA SPRENGERI 'Diva'

Plate 43

The marriage of these two outstanding Asian Magnolias was performed in the world-famous garden at Caerhays Castle in Cornwall by head gardener Charles Michael in 1951, and the long awaited flowering has upheld the highest hopes of the raisers.

Apparently the first seedling of this parentage to flower took fourteen years to attain florescence, for in *Journal of the Royal Horticultural Society* 91, 7 : 284–5 (1966) Mr. Julian Williams wrote; 'This plant had one flower on it last year and four flowers this. It seems to be the most promising seedling to flower here yet. With its large pink flower it is very distinct, and may before long, demand visits to the garden on its own account.'

The cultivar name 'Caerhays Belle' (Plate 43) has been given to this Magnolia, which produces huge heavily-textured broad-tepalled flowers of light salmon pink in great profusion. The twelve tepals are conspicuously spoon shaped, with flattened, undulating edges, these undulations often extending across the entire surface of the smaller inner ones, the tips of which tend to curve inwards to display the richer colouring along their undersurfaces. The anthers are cream, tipped carmine, and form a spherical mass around the base of the small dark-green gynoecium with its golden stigmas.

The leaves are oval and taper evenly at both ends. After producing its first solitary flower in 1965, and four in the following season, it has flowered regularly with increasing freedom each year since.

MAGNOLIA CAMPBELLI ALBA ♂ × MAGNOLIA SARGENTIANA var. ROBUSTA ♀

This hybrid was also bred at Burncoose from a pollination which Arnold Dance performed in March 1959 on an unopened flower of a tree of *Magnolia sargentiana* var. *robusta* using pollen from a flower of *M. campbelli alba* from Caerhays. This seedling, which germinated in April 1960, developed into a slender, erect tree with the downward sweeping lower branches typical of *M. campbellii alba*. It attained florescence in March 1972 shortly before P. M. Williams died and began to flower freely in 1977. The flower buds are very large and fat – about the size and shape of a goose's egg – opening to reveal the twelve pale lilac-pink tepals which fade to white with pale-lilac tints. The flowers lack the stiff tepal texture and horizontal poise of *M. campbellii alba* and tend to inherit some of the floppiness and sub-horizontal presentation typical of *M. sargentiana* var. *robusta*. (See *Magnolia* 'Michael Rosse' on p. 165.)

MAGNOLIA CAMPBELLI subsp. MOLLI-COMATA × MAGNOLIA SARGENTIANA var. ROBUSTA

Mr. Julian Williams, reporting on this hybrid with his customary reserve, in notes on 'The Garden at Caerhays' in *Journal of the Royal Horticultural Society* 91, 7 : 279–86 (1966), wrote 'There has been no great advantage on either species in this hybrid, but it did flower at a very early age, and this year was the third time it set flower buds and it has fifty flowers on it. I think it is only about twelve years old now.' It was bred in 1951 by the late Charles Williams's head gardener Charles Michael.

There are two seedlings believed to be of this parentage at Chyverton, which Nigel Holman has named 'Buzzard' and 'Hawk'. There is also a good seedling of this hybrid at Burncoose growing close to the hybrid described below, which was raised when the cross was repeated in 1959 by Arnold Dance, head

gardener in the P. M. Williams's estate garden at Burncoose near Redruth in Cornwall.

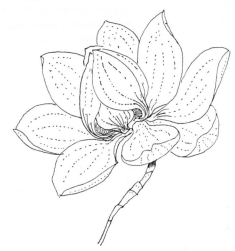

THE SIDBURY-RAFFILL GROUP OF CROSSES

MAGNOLIA CAMPBELLII subsp. CAMP-BELLII × MAGNOLIA CAMPBELLII subsp. MOLLICOMATA

The pink western form of *M. campbellii* (here referred to as subspecies *campbellii*) was introduced from the Sikkim Himalayas about 1870 while the eastern form was discovered in Yunnan by George Forrest in 1904 and was named *mollicomata* in 1920.

As far as the author had been able to ascertain at the time when these notes were first drafted, the earliest successful introduction into English gardens of sub-species *mollicomata* did not take place until 1924. This being the case the first flowering would not have been before 1935 and the first seedlings to be raised from their fruit cones could not have attained florescence before 1946 and probably not earlier than 1950.

These assumptions were based on the extracts from the Caerhays records for *M. mollicomata* which were kindly supplied by Mr. F. Julian Williams in 1967 (see pp. 44–5). Consequently the author saw fit to ignore a rumour that crosses between these two forms of *M. campbellii* had been made in Sir Charles Cave's garden at Sidbury Manor in Devon in the 1930s. However, in 1970 two pieces of fresh evidence came to light.

In May of that year a letter was received from Kew reporting that an entry had been found in their record books to the effect that one of their trees of *mollicomata* (Entry 292 – 14 No. 129) was raised from seed received from J. C. Williams of Caerhays on 15 May 1914, a date ten years earlier than that suggested by the Caerhays records referred to. A tree from this raising survives (December 1977) in the Berberis Dell at Kew.

It should be mentioned here that the only complete copy of J. C. Williams's records was lost when his briefcase was stolen from his railway compartment while he was dining on an express train *en route* from Cornwall to London. This shattering blow was something from which he never completely recovered and it is the reason for the uncertainty of the surviving Caerhays records.

Subsequently the author made a comparison of the paintings of several Magnolias in this group which had been made by Marjorie Blamey, most of which were from material sent to her by the owners or caretakers of various gardens at his request. One of these paintings was of a Magnolia flower sent to her by the Royal Botanic Gardens, Kew, in April 1968 and labelled Kew Clone 72/44 No. 49. Enquiries revealed that this was taken from a grafted tree received from Hillier & Sons of Winchester in exchange for other plant material in 1944. It is to be found growing by the large group of beech trees off Princess Walk.

Mr. Harold Hillier told the author that he remembers visiting Sidbury Manor with his father in the 1930s where they were shown Magnolias of this parentage by the late Sir Charles Cave. The Kew Clone referred to was grafted from a tree which Sir Charles Cave gave to the elder Hillier. In *Hillier's Manual of Trees and Shrubs* (1972) there is an entry referring to this Magnolia under *M. campbellii* 'Sidbury' which reads: 'A medium-sized to large tree of vigorous habit, flowering earlier in life than *M. campbellii*, and equally spectacular in flower. This cross between *M. campbellii* and ssp. *mollicomata* occurred some years prior to 1946 at Sidbury Manor, Devon, the home of the late Sir Charles Cave, Bart. It therefore precedes those made by Charles Raffill at Kew.' It would appear that these crosses were bred by a head gardener named Barton. There are eight such trees at Sidbury which began to flower in 1938 or 1939 about the time of Barton's death.

Correspondence with Sir Charles Cave, son of the previous bearer of the name, in whose lifetime these crosses were made, revealed that no records were kept either by the head gardener who made the cross or by Sir Charles himself. Consequently the author has linked the name of Sidbury with that of Raffill to provide a fitting title for this group of Magnolia crosses.

Charles P. Raffill carried out his Magnolia breeding experiments at the Royal Botanic Gardens, Kew, in the early 1940s. He had a distinct advantage over Peter Veitch in that the mother tree of *M. campbellii* was growing in the protected environment of the Temperate House, where his efforts were not likely to be nullified by a night's frost and where the day temperature was uniformly high enough for pollen grains to ripen and germinate well. He frequently corresponded with the author about his successes and failures, and continually encouraged him to specialize in Magnolias at the Truro Nurseries.

In 1943 he successfully fertilized flowers of *M. campbellii* with pollen from *M. × soulangiana*. The three hybrids of this parentage which the author has examined at Kew, Windsor and Lanarth, are described under the Soulcamp hybrids. They are more shrubby than arborescent, a fact which tends to disprove the suggestion that *M. × veitchii* might be of this parentage.

Then in 1946 Raffill succeeded in crossing *M. campbellii* with pollen from its subspecies *mollicomata*. About 100 seedlings were raised and widely distributed, many without any official records being kept, an omission made excusable by the post-war restrictions which prevailed at the time of their distribution. It seems sad that he did not survive long enough to see any of his hybrids or crosses flower.

Raffill's aim was to raise a Magnolia with flowers of the bright pink of *M. campbellii* and the more graceful poise of *M. mollicomata* with its tendency to open its flowers, cup-and-saucer-wise, a little later when the weather is likely to be more favourable.

As far as is known the first seedling to flower was that at Windsor Great Park in April 1959. This cultivar bears large flowers with the intense pink of *M. campbellii*, overlying an undertone of rosy purple inherited from *mollicomata*, and it was named 'Charles Raffill' after the raiser.

Planted in 1948, when it was two years old, it began to flower at thirteen years of age in 1959. In that year it received a Preliminary Commendation from the Royal Horticultural Society, followed by an Award of Merit in 1963 – this after the coldest winter of the century speaks well for its hardiness. In 1966 it received the coveted First Class Certificate, the Royal Horticultural Society's highest award. When seventeen years old this tree had attained a height of 40 ft (12 m) with a spread of 20 ft (6 m). It is remarkable that trees raised from its cuttings at Windsor have taken as long to attain florescence as did the original seedling.

It should be borne in mind that only plants propagated directly or indirectly from cuttings, layers, buds or grafts, off the Windsor tree or its vegetatively-propagated progeny, are entitled to the clonal name

'Charles Raffill'. Unfortunately in some quarters this name seems to have become loosely applied to these crosses, and even to F2 seedlings of unknown flower potential.

Because this grex or group of Magnolias resulted from the marriage of two botanically accepted sub-species, they are called 'crosses', the term 'hybrids' being reserved for marriages between distinct species.

In his own copy of Millais's *Magnolias*, which he left to his successor at Kew, S. A. Pearce, C. P. Raffill wrote:

'*M. campbellii* × *mollicomata*. This cross was made by the writer C. P. Raffill in 1946 in the Temperate House at Kew and about 100 plants of it were raised and distributed to British Gardens in 1948 and 1949. I propose the name for this cross to be *M. kewensis*. C. P. Raffill 18.1.1950.' (For various reasons discussed in this chapter Raffill's proposed name, '*M.* × *kewensis*', could not be applied legitimately to this group of crosses and, in 1952, it was given to *M. kobus* × *M. salicifolia*.)

In April 1959 Sir Eric Savill sent two flowers to Kew from the Windsor tree of this cross. These were examined by Kew botanist J. R. Seally who wrote:

'*Magnolia campbellii* × *mollicomata*. Two flowers from plant at Windsor which they received from Kew, i.e. one of Raffill's crosses.

'Large flower, intensely coloured like *campbellii* but actual colour of *mollicomata*; perules intermediate in colour between near black of *campbellii* and greenish-brown of *mollicomata*; peduncle and internodes glab-rous as in *campbellii* (*mollicomata* parent very shaggy).

'I suggest the plant be named *Magnolia campbellii* cultivar 'Charles Raffill'. It is plainly a cultivar, and I do not see how botanical nomenclature can be stretched to accommodate it.

'The species already comprises:

1. *M. campbellii* subsp. *campbellii* var *campbellii*.
2. *M. campbellii* subsp. *campbellii* var *alba*.
3. *M. campbellii* subsp. *mollicomata* var *mollicomata*.
4. *M. campbellii* subsp. *mollicomata* var *williamsiana*.

'All these came from wild-collected seeds in contra-distinction to 'Charles Raffill' which is of garden origin. J.R.S. 10/4/59.

'Material from Lord Rosse via R.H.S. 30/3/60 said to be a seedling of Raffill's *M. mollicomata* × *M. campbellii* has flowers light magenta as in *M. molli-comata* but peduncles glabrous and perules a little darker as in *M. campbellii*. It does not agree in colour with the Windsor plant.'

Raffill sent one of his seedlings to the famous Cor-nish garden of Caerhays in the original distribution where, judging from the situation afforded to it, its flowering potential was underrated for, in close proximity to native beech trees, it soon became drawn upwards by inadequate light and shed most of its lower branches. However when it at last began to flower it caused quite a sensation. It was exhibited at the R.H.S. Show on 4 March 1967 by Mr. F. Julian Williams, who aptly named it 'Kew's Surprise', and it too was awarded the Society's First Class Certifi-cate. The flowers are very large, with rose-crimson tepals fading to white on their upper surfaces, with pink veins, and shading to deep pink at the edges. The flower examined had twelve tepals, eight large ones in the two outer whorls with four smaller ones broadly cupped around the gynandrophore, to give a flower shape like *mollicomata* rather than *campbellii*. The Council of the Royal Horticultural Society, at their meeting in November 1967, awarded the Reginald Cory Memorial Cup to the Royal Botanic Gardens, Kew, for this Magnolia. A similar award had been made in 1966 in respect of 'Charles Raffill'.

In February 1969 the author received a copy of an extract from the Kew Mailing List giving addresses to which many of these Magnolia seedlings had been distributed between September 1948 and April 1949, and a questionnaire was sent to each of the recipients named in an endeavour to draw up a record of the progress of the Magnolias, with details of their flowers. A little later the Royal Horticultural Society also contacted these gardens and invited anyone who had a tree of these Raffill Magnolias to send a flower and an opening bud to the Society's Show on 18 March. Unfortunately the preceding weather was most unkind, so that the only blooms were those off three trees in different Cornish gardens, which had been collected by the author.

M. campbellii takes twenty-five years or more to reach flowering and sexual maturity from seed, while its subspecies *M. mollicomata* takes only half this time. It is interesting to observe how this big discrepancy in florescence has been inherited by their offspring. Of the twenty-five addresses extracted from the Kew Mailing List, the author sent questionnaires to eighteen in February 1969. Flowers from the trees in the remaining eight gardens had already been seen. These included 'Charles Raffill' (No. 205) at Windsor, a good seedling (No. 154) at Wakehurst Place, No. 158 at the Royal Horticultural Society's Garden at Wisley, together with those in Cornish gardens: No. 109 at Caerhays ('Kew's Surprise'), No. 159 at Trewithen, Grampound Road, No. 54 at Lanarth, St. Keverne, and No. 222 at Copeland Court, Truro, as well as unrecorded trees at Trengwainton, Penzance, and Antony House, Torpoint. Twelve replies were received from the questionnaire, which was con-sidered a reasonably good response, bearing in mind that some properties had changed hands, or had different head gardeners since the distribution twenty years earlier. By now the surviving trees were twenty-two years old, and the only specimen which had not flowered was Kew No. 166 growing in Mr. C. J. Marchant's Keeper's Hill Nursery at Stapehill, near Wimborne, Dorset, which had then reached a height of 30 ft (9 m). This one might well prove to be an apomict (a phenomenon explained elsewhere in this book p. 144), and it will be interesting to see if it closely resembles *M. campbellii* in its flowers, as seems indicated by its prolonged adolescence.

In contrast, we know that Kew No. 205 had first flowered in the Royal Gardens at Windsor Park in 1959, at thirteen years of age, but the next earliest recordings reported to date are No. 167 in Capt. Collingwood Ingram's garden at The Grange, Benenden, Kent, in 1965 at nineteen years, followed by the Caerhays tree 'Kew's Surprise' (No. 109) in 1966 at twenty. The Trengwainton tree has pale-pink flowers with narrow, pointed tepals and hairy peduncles. The flowers open about a week later than an adjacent *M. campbellii*. More recently similar crosses have been raised in California where a selected seedling has been named 'Eric Walther'.

Flowering maturity at twenty years of age appears to be about the average with these seedling crosses, and this tends to indicate that prolonged adolescence of the species *campbellii* is a dominant character, since its subspecies *mollicomata* normally begins to flower as early as ten years from seed, as is recorded on p. 53 of *Asiatic Magnolias in Cultivation* by G. H. Johnstone.

These marriages between the eastern and western forms have added to the *campbellii* tribe of Magnolias an extensive new strain of hardy, precocious-flowered varieties, all of which bear large, elegantly-poised, upward-facing blossoms of pronounced cup-and-saucer shape, and of considerable variation in tepal shape and colour. The true significance of this Magnolia breeding may not be fully appreciated for several decades.

MAGNOLIA × SOULANGIANA
(*M. heptapeta* × *M. quinquepeta*)
J. F. E. Hamelin in *Annales de la Société d'Horticulture de Paris* 1 : 90–5 (1827)
E. Soulange-Bodin in *Annales de l'Institut Royal Horticole de Fromont* 3 : 150 (1831) and 6 : 46 (1843)
Plate 44

These hybrids are the most popular and best known race of Magnolias at the present time and have remained so now for well over a century. Indeed it is not at present possible to foresee them being readily rivalled. Combining as they do the sterling qualities of hardiness with freedom of flowering – precociously all along their bare branches before the leaves appear – these are the type of Magnolia which the gardening amateur knows and wants. Ideal for the beginner because not only are they easily cultivated and tolerant of a wide range of soils and environments, but they include a considerable variation in colour and growth habit. They will grow in all but the driest and chalkiest of soils, are extremely cold tolerant while dormant and will withstand more wind than any other precocious-flowered type with the possible exception of the Star Magnolia (*M. stellata*). Over the years they have proved to be tolerant of city environments and able to withstand heat, dust, grime and atmospheric pollution, combined with complete neglect.

The type plant *M. × soulangiana* has erect creamy-white tepals tinted either purple or pink at the base. That there are two distinct forms is explained later in this chapter, with evidence that Soulange-Bodin raised and sold several generations of hybrid seedlings.

Consequently the named cultivars are very numerous but many of them are not sufficiently distinct to be worthy of special mention here. Among those still in general circulation – varieties which have stood the searching test of time – are these:

'Alba' ('Alba Superba')   Generally considered the best white opening earlier than the type. It is an erect grower with fragrant creamy-white flowers. There is usually a trace of purple at the base of the outer tepals. Van Houtte, Ghent, 1867.

'Alexandrina' (see also 'Norbertii')   Is of erect growth with long raking branches. The white, purple-tinted flowers are borne in great profusion and open to a deep saucer shape. Cels, Paris, 1831.

'Amabilis'   Large fragrant flowers, almost pure white. Habit like that of *M. heptapeta*. Baumann, Bolwheiler, Alsace, France, 1865. The name has also been used for two other clones.

'André Leroy'   Deep red purple outside, not quite as dark as 'Lennei'. Leroy, Angers, France, 1892.

'Brozzonii'   A later-flowering white clone, sometimes with lime-green shading on the outer tepals which are faintly suffused with carmine, the inner ones being shaded carmine down their backs. The flower buds are sharply pointed but open wide, usually over a considerable period to give a good succession of flowers. R.H.S. First Class Certificate (1929). A second generation seedling probably raised in the garden of Camillo Brozzoni at Brescia, Italy.

'Burgundy'   A seedling of recent introduction which may have originated in New Zealand. Very floriferous with large deep-purple flowers. Precise origin unknown. Believed to be a seedling of 'Picture'. Clarke, San Jose, California, 1943.

'Grace McDade'   Very large, predominantly white flowers with slight purple shading. Believed to be a seedling of 'Lennei', it was named and introduced by Clint McDade of Semmes, Alabama; it is reported to be a prolific seed bearer in the southern United States. About a fortnight later than the type clone.

'Lennei'   One of the finest and toughest of these hybrid Magnolias, the flowers resemble immense rosy-purple tulips, white within. April to June with late flowers in September. Growth vigorous and spreading. R.H.S. First Class Certificate (1863). A second generation seedling believed to have been raised by G. Manetti of Monza, Italy, circa 1840. A septaploid with 2n = 133 chromosomes (Santamour 1970). The mystery surrounding the origin of this Magnolia is discussed later in this chapter (Plate 44).

'Lennei Alba'   A distinct second or third generation seedling bearing large ivory-white goblets which closely resemble those of *M. heptapeta*, but with shorter outer tepals. Froebel, Zurich, Switzerland. 1905.

'Lennei Hybrid'   see 'Lilenny' p. 189.

'Lombardy Rose'   Resembles 'Lennei' but is somewhat paler. It appears to have originated in northern Italy about the same time as 'Lennei' and may be either a seedling from it or of the same raising, circa 1850. 6·5 ploid with 2n = 123 chromosomes (Santamour 1970).

'Norbertii'   Slightly fragrant goblet-shaped flowers about 4 in. (10 cm) across when open, each with nine narrow tepals, white with a faint purple flush, in three whorls of three. Somewhat less vigorous and slightly earlier than the very similar 'Alexandrina' which has larger flowers. In 1915 Pampanini listed this as a synonym for 'Alexandrina' adding that it was raised in Montrouge near Paris by Cels who listed it in his 1835 catalogue (he also listed a *M. norbertiana* as a distinct variety). There appear to be two distinct clones with this name. One is more erect with darker shadings on the outside of the flowers. The form at Grayswood Hill, Surrey has flowers resembling 'Alba Superba'. R.H.S. Award of Merit (1960).

'Picture' ('Wada's Picture')   A very vigorous and erect Japanese hybrid with rounded leaves resembling those of 'Lennei'. Commencing to bloom when only 2 or 3 ft (61 to 91 cm) tall, the large reddish-purple buds open to huge heavily textured flowers, white within and fading to rosy pink without. The tepals maintain their stately horizontal poise without becoming floppy. An outstanding and easily grown arborescent hybrid suitable for the smaller garden. The origin is discussed later in this chapter. ± 7·5 ploid with ± 143 chromosomes (Wilkinson 1970). Wada, Yokohama, Japan. About 1925.

'Rustica Rubra'   Large, faintly scented pear-shaped flowers expanding to goblet shape about 5 to 6 in. (12·5 to 15 cm) across, Magnolia purple outside and milky white within, composed of six broad tepals partially enclosed by three small 'petaloid' segments. Somewhat earlier than 'Lennei' which the flowers closely resemble, apart from their lighter texture and redder hue. Growth vigorous and erect. Because it roots readily from cuttings in intermittent mist and forms a stout erect stem this clone makes an excellent understock upon which to bud or graft the more difficult Magnolias. R.H.S. Award of Merit (1960) as 'Rubra'. An irregular polyploid with 2n = 156 chromosomes (Kew 1968). Boskoop, Holland. 1893.

'Soulangiana Nigra'   See under *M. quinquepeta* 'Nigra' on p. 135.

'Speciosa'   This resembles a smaller edition of the

type clone with somewhat paler flowers. They are white, tinged purple on the outside. Growth erect, late flowering. Cels, Paris, 1825.

'Sundew' Bears very large white fragrant flowers up to 10 in. (25·5 cm) in diameter and flushed pink at the base. It has been suggested that this may be another seedling of 'Picture'. Sometimes shaded orange pink. Pickard, Canterbury, England, 1968.

'Verbanica' A cultivar with well-shaped flowers flushed rich pink; looked upon in America as one of the hardiest of the Soulangiana hybrids on account of its lateness. Leroy, Angers, France, 1873.

Cytologically the M. × soulangiana hybrids should be pentaploid (2n = 95) since M. heptapeta is hexaploid (2n = 114) and M. quinquepeta is tetraploid (2n = 76). Several higher ploidy levels have been observed and these are discussed by Dr. John Wilkinson in his chapter on 'Cytological Considerations'.

It is interesting to observe that most of the second and third generation seedlings, which have been named and introduced, have larger flowers than those of the first generation. Assumed second generation seedlings include 'Brozzonii', 'Lennei' and 'Lennei Alba' while assumed third generation raisings include 'Burgundy', 'Grace McDade' and 'Sundew'.

Probably a large proportion of these raisings produced average-sized flowers, not sufficiently distinct from the original race of hybrids, so that only improved ones have been named and recorded.

Now let us look farther afield, and we find hybrids of assumed Soulangiana parentage, which originated long ago in Japan or possibly China. These include 'Picture' and possibly 'Sarasa', 'Osaka' and maybe the controversial M. denudata purpurascens which Keisuke Ito figured in 1884 as M. obovata Thunberg (see under M. 'Osaka'). It would not be surprising if there were others awaiting 'discovery' in some sacrosanct oriental garden. T. Makino in Journal of Japanese Botany 6, 4 : 8 (1929) suggested that the Magnolia depicted by Ito was a hybrid between M. heptapeta (denudata) (2n = 114 chromosomes) and M. quinquepeta (liliflora) (2n = 76), which brings it within the grex of M. × soulangiana. In 1937 Japanese geneticist Yasui reported the chromosome number to be pentaploid (2n = 95), tending to confirm this treatment.

The Soulangiana Hybrid Complex

Etienne Soulange-Bodin was a cavalry officer in the French Army, who, after Napoleon's final defeat at Waterloo in 1815, forsook the destructive craft of war for the creative art of horticulture.

In 1819 he wrote in the Gardener's Magazine (edited in London by J. C. Loudon): 'It is to this that I cheerfully devote the remainder of my life. It must be confessed that for the last thirty years great obstacles have presented themselves to the simple care which the earth demands. I shall not retrace the sad picture of the past – alike by the beaters and the beaten, the statues of Flora and Pomona were quickly thrown down and substituted by that of Bellona. The Germans have encamped in my garden. I have encamped in the gardens of the Germans; and it was with sword in hand that I visited the botanical collection of Schönbrunn (Vienna), Schauenburg (near Minden), Stuttgart and Petrowski (Moscow). I have said of others as they have said of me: Barbarus per segetes! [Literally 'a foreigner passing through standing corn'.] It had doubtless been better for both parties to have stayed at home and planted their cabbages. We are returned there, and the rising taste for gardening becomes one of the most agreeable guarantees of the repose of the world.'

Soulange-Bodin founded the Royal Institute of Horticulture, Fromont, at Ris, near Paris, and became its first Director. By 1837 he had attained such eminence in French horticultural circles that L'Abbé Lorenzo Berlèse saw fit to dedicate a monograph on camellias to him in these terms: 'Soulange-Bodin, Secretary-General of the Royal Society of Horticulture in Paris: member of many learned societies and Chevalier of many Orders; to you, founder of the most esteemed Horticultural Establishment in France; to you, who grow in your huge greenhouse at Fromont the most precious offerings of Nature; to you, who by your writings, your learning and your example have established such a powerful precedent to the progress of Horticulture; to you, I dedicate this essay.'

Soulange-Bodin's name is perpetuated by the race of hardy Magnolia hybrids which he raised at Fromont from about 1820 onwards. The first mention of Magnolia × soulangiana appeared in the Transactions of the Linnean Society of Paris (1827), the text of which is translated as follows: 'By the crossing of a Magnolia yulan, grown from seed with the pollen of a Magnolia discolor, the Fromont gardens have witnessed the birth, growth and establishment, among the varied specimens to be admired there, of a new hybrid which is remarkable for its tree-like habit, its handsome foliage and above all for its wide spreading brilliant flowers in which the purest white is tinged with a purplish hue. My worthy colleagues have named this beautiful species Magnolia soulangiana.' Note the original spelling and small 's'. The same spelling but with a capital 'S' was used by Lindley in the first English description in the Botanical Register 14 : t. 1164 (1828) which was accompanied by a drawing made at Young's Nursery at Epsom.

In the *Annales de la Société d'Horticulture de Paris* 1 : 90–5 (1827) a fully detailed description was contributed by Baron Hamelin of Franconville and dated 12 September 1827. Here is a translation of the introductory paragraph: 'In 1826 M. Soulange-Bodin, from a seed from *Magnolia yulan*, DC, fertilized by *Magnolia obovata* var *discolor*, DC, obtained a magnificent hybrid, which the Linnean Society of Paris has named *Magnolia soulangiana*.'

It should be pointed out here that the date 1826 apparently referred to the initial flowering of the particular hybrid seedling which Soulange-Bodin had selected to perpetuate his name.

The DC citation refers to the French botanist A. P. de Candolle, whose classification of *Magnolia* in *Regni Vegetabilis Systema Naturale* 1 : 456–7 (1817) included: *Magnolia obovata* β = var. *discolor* = *purpurea* in *Curtis's Botanical Magazine* 11 : t. 390 (1797) = *M. discolor* Ventenat in *Jardin de la Malmaison*: 1 : t. 24 (1803).

It is of interest that Hamelin gives *M. discolor* de Candolle as the pollen parent of the cross, but Soulange-Bodin repeatedly stated that it was *M. purpurea* and not *M. discolor* and that, in disagreement with De Candolle, he regarded these as distinct species. This is made abundantly clear in a report which he published in the *Annales de L'Institut Royal Horticole de Fromont* 3 : 150–1 (1831) entitled 'Beau Phénomène de Fructification, *Magnolia macrophylla – Magnolia yulan*'.

In this paper there is an important reference to the breeding of the Soulangiana hybrids. After giving a detailed description of seed production on a sixteen-year-old tree of *M. macrophylla*, which he said had fruited at the age of fourteen years, Soulange-Bodin gave an interesting account which has been translated as follows: 'This precious harvest would have been greater if many cones had not been sacrificed at the time of flowering in attempts at *artificial fertilization*★ which did not succeed. These attempts will be repeated until they are successful, for it will be fine to transfer to the huge flower of *Magnolia macrophylla* the purple hues of *Magnolia discolor*, as we have done with so much success with regard to *Magnolia yulan* by fertilizing it with pollen of *Magnolia purpurea*. The mingling of this new introduction with the finest glistening white flowering type will one day produce in our shrubberies an effect which one can readily imagine.'

From this we see that not only did Soulange-Bodin regard *M. discolor* as being distinct from *M. purpurea* but he definitely states that his hybrids were achieved by artificial fertilization. However Loudon, in his

★ My italics.

Arboretum et Fruticetum Britannicum 1 : 278 (1838) tended to belittle Soulange-Bodin's accomplishment. In his description he mis-spells the hybrid *M. Soulangeana* (as compared with Hamelin's modern-looking *M. soulangiana*) stating it was raised at Fromont, near Paris, from the seeds of *M. conspicua* (here Loudon uses a more modern naming compared with Soulange-Bodin's *M. yulan*) 'which stood near one of *M. purpurea* in front of the chateau of M. Soulange-Bodin; the flowers of the former of which had been accidentally fecundated by the pollen of the latter'. Loudon's work runs into eight volumes, each of some 500 pages, of which Volume 1 devotes some twenty-five pages to Magnolias. The first four volumes are of letterpress with occasional illustrations, while the last four are of plates.

Though the two earliest descriptions distinctly stated that the male or pollen parent of these hybrids was *M. discolor* it is clear that Soulange-Bodin looked upon this as a variety distinct from *M. purpurea* which he insisted that he used for this purpose. He also stated that his hybridizing was carried out deliberately and artificially and that the transfer of pollen was not left to either insects or wind as suggested by Loudon.

Seventeen years later, in 1843, Etienne Soulange-Bodin published a further report in the *Annales de L'Institut Royal Horticole de Fromont* 6 : 46–8 (1843), entitled 'Nouvelles Variétés de *Magnolia soulangiana*'. From this is translated the following extract: 'I take advantage of this opportunity to inform lovers of beautiful plants that, having obtained new hybrid varieties of *Magnolia yulan* fertilized with pollen from *Magnolia purpurea*, I found that these began to flower with me last year [1842] and allowed me to determine distinguishing characteristics in some preliminary descriptions which the poor flowering season of last spring did not permit me to check or to extend. As a result, nevertheless, of this initial work, out of eighty plants procured from seed artificially fertilized, I have already obtained and been able to verify eight varieties quite distinct from one another by their habit, the shape of their leaves and the shape and shade of their flowers. Although all of them more or less resemble *Magnolia soulangiana*, these varieties are all tree-like and of a vigorous growth more pronounced than that of their parents.

'Thus it will soon be possible to propagate all these varieties, and others which I can count around the mother tree *Magnolia yulan*, and to procure thus and successively, in the finest race of ornamental shrubs all the shades of purple, more or less pronounced, produced by the hybridization, mingled with the pure whiteness of *Magnolia yulan*.'

Later authorities, including Johnstone, have given

M. discolor de Candolle as a synonym of *M. liliflora* Desrousseaux, but Hamelin's Table of Comparison contains two important details which makes *M. discolor* distinct from *M. liliflora* as described by Johnstone. The main difference is in the number of 'petals'. Johnstone gives *M. liliflora* three or four 'sepals' and six, often seven 'petals' arranged in two whorls, but Hamelin's Table of Comparison states that *M. discolor* has 'six unequal petals rolled one over the other'. It does not differentiate between 'sepals' and 'petals' as does Johnstone and gives *M. yulan* (= *M. conspicua*) as having 'nine unequal petals in three rings' and the same for *M.* × *soulangiana*.

Another difference is with the colours of the inside of the 'petals'. Johnstone describes those of *M. liliflora* as being 'dark rosy purple on the outer side and within white, more or less heavily stained with rose-purple, especially towards the base and along the veins', while those of Hamelin's *M. discolor* are described as being 'of a pure white within, violet outside, this colour extended as far as the edges of the petals'. *M. liliflora* Desrousseaux now gives way to *M. quinquepeta* Buc'hoz.

Baron Jacques Felix Emmanuel Hamelin had been a Rear-Admiral in the French Navy and was senior second-in-command of the Baudin scientific expedition to New Zealand and the South Seas, from 1800 to 1802, in the ships *Géographe* and *Naturaliste*. In 1827 he was living in retirement in Paris and became one of the founder members of the Horticultural Society of Paris. Although this sounds like a rival organization to Soulange-Bodin's Royal Institute of Horticulture at Fromont, perhaps they were complementary in the manner of the Royal Horticultural Society and the Royal Botanic Gardens at Kew in British horticultural circles. The Baudin expedition had no connection with Soulange-Bodin whose name, though pronounced the same, is spelt differently.

Hamelin was apparently an experienced botanist, for the paper which he contributed also contained details of *Amaryllis* hybrids raised by Count Melazzo of Palermo, *Daphne* hybrids by one Fion of Paris, and *Crinum* hybrids by the Hon. the Revd. W. Herbert of London. It would appear that Fion, being a nurseryman, did not even merit an initial in front of his name in such illustrious company!

The entire stock of Soulange-Bodin's first batch of hybrid Magnolias is said to have been purchased for a large sum by a London firm of nurserymen. In 1834 he wrote in his Society's Journal: 'Mr. Loudon reports in the *Gardener's Magazine* that *Magnolia soulangiana* has produced, throughout April this year, the most beautiful effect in the Vauxhall nursery belonging to Messrs. Chandler & Sons, where it is

trained against a wall exposed to the west. Growth which it has made also in Brown's nursery at Slough inclines us, says he, to strongly recommend this variety, distinguished by three equally valuable characters: the first, it begins to flower later than *Conspicua*, *Purpurea* or *Gracilis*, the second, being of a sweeter fragrance, more agreeable and more pronounced than the latter species, and the third, being tougher than any of them.' He then proceeded to relate how another generation of Soulangiana hybrids had begun to flower and were being selected and recorded in advance of propagation.

In the sixteen or seventeen years which had elapsed since the original raisings began to flower he had probably raised several other series of hybrid seedlings from successive artificial fertilizations and doubtless these met with a ready demand from various Continental nurserymen and later gave rise to a spate of additional names. The Belgian nurseries of Louis Van Houtte were among the Magnolia specialists who supplied nurseries in England, France and Italy, and did much to popularize such well-known Soulangiana varieties as 'Alba Superba', 'Alexandrina' and later, 'Lennei'.

The author is of the opinion that the clone of *M.* × *soulangiana* generally grown today as the type plant differs from the original descriptions and earliest plates. The flower depicted as *M. yulan* var. *soulangiana* on Plate 1164 of Lindley's *Botanical Register*: 14 : t. 1164 (1828) has very broad tepals which are rounded at their tips, while Hamelin's detailed description already referred to says: 'Corolla composed of nine petals arranged in three rows; they are very fleshy and have a sweet scent. The three exterior, narrower than the middle ones, are oval and spear-shaped, broad near their tip. . . . *The three intermediate ones are the largest, they are spathulate, broad and blunt at the apex.*★ . . . The three interior petals are smaller, *rounded at the tip.*'★

Other contemporary botanists did not all agree on the shape of the tepals of this new hybrid which leads one to suspect that some of their observations were made from different seedlings of the same series of hybrids.

Among those who described, or depicted in their plates, a flower with blunt tepals were John Lindley in his *Botanical Register* 14 : t. 1164 (1828) (from a plant growing in Young's nursery at Epsom), Dumont de Courset in *Botaniste Cultivateur* and R. Sweet in his *British Flower Garden* 3 : 260 (1827–9).

Among those who depicted flowers with pointed tepals were Redouté in *Choix des plus belles fleurs*

★ My italics.

(1827) and Michel in *Du Hamel* 2, 224 : t. 66b (1828).

That there are at least two distinct forms of *M.* × *soulangiana*, apart from its numerous named cultivars, was first pointed out to the author during a visit from Australian Magnolia specialist Cyril H. Isaac of Noble Park, Victoria. The last edition of his Nursery Trade List (printed on his retirement in February 1969) depicts *M. soulangiana* 'Pink Form' in a colour plate on the back cover. This he says, is the Magnolia grown as *M.* × *soulangiana* at Kew. Having admired the fine plants of this Magnolia in the Kew collection the author was much impressed by the rosy-red shading on the outside of the buds and the warmth of the pink undertone on the open tepals, which are broader and blunter in shape, thereby conforming closely with Lindley's plate referred to earlier. They seemed much more attractive than the purple-tinted, pointed-tepalled form in general circulation in English gardens and nurseries at the present time in which the buds and flowers are but faintly tinted with mauve.

It is likely that there will always be a considerable amount of speculation concerning the true make-up of these hybrids for, although Etienne Soulange-Bodin declared his pollen parent to be *M. purpurea*, this, in itself, might well have been an old Japanese or Chinese hybrid between *M. heptapeta* (*denudata*) and *M. quinquepeta* (*liliflora*).

The manner in which the Chinese Yu-lan Magnolia (*M. heptapeta*) was cultivated for hundreds of years in the palace and temple gardens of China, and later in Japan, to such an extent that wild plants became relatively scarce while the cultivated trees became improved by constant selection, has been discussed in the appropriate chapter. It is very likely that the rarer Purple Chinese Magnolia (*M. quinquepeta*) had been introduced into Japan from the Yangtze River area during a period of friendly co-existence and reciprocal trading such as that which prevailed during the T'ang dynasty (A.D. 618–906).

Japanese gardeners would have planted this new acquisition to contrast with their white-flowered trees of *M. heptapeta* and it would not have been long before natural cross-pollination took place even were we to be so naïve as to imagine that diligent gardeners of that era did not, in fact, forestall the pollen-carrying flower beetles.

It seems likely therefore that Magnolia hybrids of the same parentage as that claimed for the Soulangiana grex or group were being grown in China and Japan long before *M. heptapeta* (as *M. yulan*) was introduced into the Western world by Sir Joseph Banks in 1789 or 1790.

M. 'Picture' is probably such a hybrid. It was discovered by Mr. Koichiro Wada, a Japanese plantsman of international repute, whose Hakoneya Nursery Company at Yokohama carries on a considerable export trade with nurseries in England and America. He tells me that he first noticed it in the garden of Kaga Castle in Kanazawa, capital of Ishikawa province, in about 1930. He immediately recognized it as an outstanding hybrid and persuaded a local nurseryman to propagate it for him by approach grafting. Two plants were successfully grafted by this method and sent to Mr. Wada who described it thus: 'A hybrid of *Magnolia conspicua* [*heptapeta*] and *M. soulangiana* 'Nigra' [*quinquepeta*] having a hybrid vigour, being stronger and sturdier in growth than either of the parents, with larger leaves and thicker stems and larger flowers of more substance. It flowers at the same time as *M. conspicua* with huge blooms, vinous purple on the outside and pure white inside. Moreover it flowers at a young age, when it is two or three years old.' The flowers of *M.* 'Picture' are sometimes as much as 14 in. (35·5 cm) across and, under some conditions, the colouring is quite a clear pink without any trace of carmine or purple.

It should be borne in mind that, since the earliest published description of hybrids between *M. heptapeta* and *M. quinquepeta* were those of Soulange-Bodin's *M.* × *soulangiana*, all earlier raisings of similar parentage, as well as future ones, must bear this grex or group name. In conformity with the *International Code of Nomenclature of Cultivated Plants* this old Japanese hybrid was correctly styled by Mr. Wada as *M.* × *soulangiana* 'Picture' on the assumption that it is of similar parentage. More recently, however, he has had cause to doubt its origin, for in 1968 he reported: '*Magnolia* 'Picture' is most interesting to us because some of its open-pollinated seedlings have bloomed huge milky-white flowers flatly open, twelve inches across, recalling those of *M. campbellii alba*. But we have no plant of *M. campbellii* or *M. campbellii alba*. The only Magnolia plants we have in that Numazu nursery are *denudata*, *kobus*, *salicifolia*, *stellata* and 'Picture', and no more. We now come to doubt its parentage and all its seedlings bloom as early as *M.* 'Picture'.'

In 1969 he added: 'We find that *Magnolia denudata* has invariably nine-petal flowers as had its supposed hybrid *Magnolia* 'Picture'. Seedlings of *Magnolia* 'Picture' have given us many interesting plants. One has soft pink flowers of huge size and great substance, looking like a *campbellii* hybrid. We have petal counts ranging from five to eleven on flowers opening on the same branch of this Magnolia.'

The suggestion that there is a second and very similar Magnolia masquerading under this name is confirmed by Magnolia specialist Amos A. Pickard of Canterbury, who has been a major importer of this fine hybrid since its introduction. He tells the author that the second, and slightly inferior form, differs from the original in having thinner shoots, a slightly different poise to its flower buds and slightly smaller flowers of paler colouring, with a distinctive lemon fragrance 'whereas those of the true "Picture" smell of violets'.

Mr. Wada disagrees about the existence of two forms so that the second one may have originated either as an unsuspected mutation or branch-sport on 'Picture' in one of the big oriental Magnolia nurseries, or it was sent out as a near substitute by another exporter. In view of the difference in fragrance referred to by Mr. Pickard, the latter probability is the more likely one.

In March 1969 the Royal Horticultural Society gave an Award of Merit to Magnolia 'Picture' when exhibited by L. R. Russell, Ltd., Richmond Nurseries, Windlesham, Surrey, but this was subsequently withdrawn when the responsible committee debated that, as the plant had been forced under glass, the flowers might not have possessed their normal colouring. The author suspects that this decision might well have been influenced by knowledge of the paler form referred to.

Mr. Pickard reports that he has flowered several seedlings of 'Picture'. Most of them have large goblet-shaped flowers of white or pink while one produces very long and erect buds 'just like a stick of rock'. opening to display long, narrow tepals. Mr. Wada has selected and named some of his seedlings of 'Picture' including 'Superba', a very strong grower with huge goblet-shaped flowers after the style of 'Lennei', and 'White Giant' with immense milky-white flowers opening wide like those of *M. grandiflora*.

Another old Japanese Magnolia is the cultivar formerly known as *M. × soulangiana* 'Nigra', later as *M. liliflora* 'Nigra' and now as *M. quinquepeta* 'Nigra'.

The true *M. quinquepeta* is somewhat of an enigma and the author is of the opinion that the plant grown and described by Johnstone as *M. liliflora* is in fact the cultivar under discussion. According to Millais: 'The exact origin of this handsome and long-flowering Magnolia is unknown, although one parent is undoubtedly *M. liliflora*. The other may be *M. denudata* var. *purpurascens*, the purple variety of Yulan (from China) which occurs in a few Japanese gardens, for it is difficult to believe that so dark-flowered a hybrid could have originated from true

M. denudata and *M. liliflora* since the flowers and leaves are much darker than is likely to be produced from such parents. There is little doubt that this fine hybrid originated from some Japanese Nursery, since John Gould Veitch introduced it from Japan in 1861.'

However Mr. Wada reports that: '*M. soulangiana* 'Nigra' seems to be a species from China because it sets seed and it comes true from seeds with very minor variations in the colour of flower. No seedlings have come out with the habit like Soulangiana. From this it would appear that this Magnolia is not a hybrid between *M. denudata* [*heptapeta*] and *M. liliflora* [*quinquepeta*] but either a separate species or a geographical form of *M. quinquepeta*.'

Nevertheless there is good reason to suppose that Soulange-Bodin's *M. purpurea* was, in fact, not pure *M. quinquepeta* but a Japanese-bred hybrid of *M. heptapeta* × *M. quinquepeta* so that what Soulange-Bodin achieved was a series of crosses between an unsuspected hybrid and his *M. heptapeta* (*denudata*) (= *conspicua* = *yulan*). Such a cross would produce a race of hybrids with greater *heptapeta* influence than *quinquepeta* and this is suggested as the reason why the majority of them show but slight traces of purple pigmentation in their flowers.

Only two Soulangiana hybrids have deeply-coloured flowers, and, curiously enough, neither of these was raised at Fromont and both were second- or third-generation seedlings. The first is the sensational 'Lennei' which originated in northern Italy and was at one time known as "Lombardy Hybrid". The large tulip-shaped flowers are rich rosy purple outside and white within, beginning to open in April and continuing into May, with occasional late flowers in September and October.

The leaves of 'Lennei' are almost identical in shape with those of Wada's 'Picture', mostly being almost circular in outline with blunt tips. 'Lennei Alba' is not a white sport of the original as one might suppose but a distinct seedling. According to Dr. Dorsman, Director of the Dutch Horticultural Experimental Station for Nurseries at Boskoop, it was raised in Froebel's Nursery at Zurich in 1905, and was propagated and introduced by Keesen's of Aalsmeer, Holland in 1930. It bears large, white goblet-shaped flowers which resemble those of 'Lennei' in shape and substance, but the foliage resembles that of Soulange-Bodin's hybrids.

The second dark-flowered Soulangiana hybrid of Continental origin is 'Rustica Rubra' which is said to have originated in Belgium as a chance seedling from 'Lennei' which would make it a third generation Soulangiana hybrid. This vigorous Magnolia forms a tall bush with straggling branches. The large flowers are cup-shaped and of a rich rosy-red colour, brighter than that of 'Lennei'. The leaves are almost oval with sharply pointed tips. On vigorous plants it is advisable to shorten the long, straggling side shoots on both of these varieties in July to induce bushy growth and the formation of flower spurs.

The flowers of 'Rustica Rubra' are almost identical to those of 'Lennei' in colour and shape, but the tepals of 'Lennei' have a much heavier texture and in most seasons they begin to open somewhat later than those of 'Rustica Rubra'. 'Lennei' can also be distinguished from 'Rustica Rubra' by the shape of its leaves, most of which are almost circular with a short, rounded tip at the apex.

In a letter dated 8 December 1949, the late Charles Raffill, then Assistant Curator at the Royal Botanic Gardens, Kew, wrote to the author: 'As you know *M. soulangiana* has given us a very fine set of forms when self-pollinated, and has even given us flowers which were larger and finer than the hybrid parent – I refer to the large-flowered 'Lennei'. I have a fine specimen of this form (a derivative of *M. soulangiana*) in my garden at my official residence here and it regularly fruits and it must be all self-pollinated as I have no Magnolia near it which flowers when *M. Lennei* does. . . . I have never seen any seedling flower of self-pollinated *M. Lennei* but we have a few at Kew now several years old.'

There is a veteran specimen of 'Lennei' in the Magnolia collection which was 30 ft (9 m) across and about 10 ft (3 m) high in 1970.

MAGNOLIA × SOULANGIANA 'Lennei'
A. Topf in *Gartenflora* 1 : 244, 86 (1852)
SYN. *M. lenneana* Topf
Plate 44

A possible origin of *Magnolia* 'Lennei'

According to French botanist Charles Lemaire in *Illustration Horticole* 1, t. 37 (1854), this fine hybrid Magnolia 'was raised in the beautiful garden of Joseph Salvi of Vicenza [Italy], who handed over the entire ownership of it to nurseryman Alfred Topf of Erfurt [Prussia], who named it after Lenné, a most distinguished contemporary German botanist'. Peter Joseph Lenné (1789–1866) was at one time director of the Botanical Garden at Potsdam. *Illustration Horticole* was then being edited and published by Ambroise Verschaffelt following the death of his father André in 1850. They are better known in connection with

their *Nouvelle Iconographie des Camellias* which Ambroise continued to edit and publish until 1860.

Lemaire stated that Topf had put this Magnolia on the market two or three years previously, which would make the date of introduction about 1850. But he says he saw it flowering in the Verschaffelt garden in Paris in 1853, so it seems fairly certain that the transaction between Salvi and Topf took place several years before 1850, because a young grafted plant or layer of this hybrid would be unlikely to flower until it was four or five years of age. J. G. Millais in *Magnolias* gives 1850 as the year in which Topf procured it from Italy as does Dr. A. Henry in *Trees and Shrubs of Great Britain and Ireland* 6 : 1596 (1912).

One cannot help wondering on what terms such a fine acquisition changed hands and what price was charged for the earlier distribution by Topf. Lemaire wrote: 'The fact that our plant is a hybrid surely cannot be in doubt? But is it the product of a cross-pollination performed by a human hand, or by insects (or the wind?). We do not know, and whatever may be the case, it is, we readily repeat, a superb acquisition for our gardens, where it has nothing to dread from our winters. It survived the winter of 1853–4 without suffering in the slightest from its excessive severity.'

Professor Pampanini of Florence was a distinguished Italian botanist and an authority on Magnolias. He contributed a paper entitled 'Le Magnolie' in *Bulletino della R. Societa Toscana di Orticultura* 41 : 40–1 (1916). Concerning *M.* 'Lennei' he wrote: 'It is uncertain whether the origin of this hybrid is natural or artificial and not even its source is certain: from Vicenza or from Lombardy according to some, from Florence according to others. It was raised in 1850 or 1851 in the garden belonging to a Giuseppe Salvi, a professional horticulturist in Vicenza (or otherwise to Count Giuseppe Salvi, a keen amateur horticulturist in Florence). Some specimens were distributed under the name *Magnolia* 'Maometto' which persisted in some lists as *Magnolia Mahometi* or *Mahoneti*. Anyway Salvi sold the plant to Topf, horticulturist in Erfurt, probably in 1859, who introduced it as his own novelty, with the name *Magnolia Yulan* var. *Lenné*, in honour of Lenné, a famed horticulturist in Bonn and general superintendent of the Royal Prussian Gardens (b. 1789–d. 1866).

'It should be named *Magnolia mahometi*, but I think it best to maintain the name *Magnolia lennei*, which was the one regularly printed and is everywhere known.

'Also the identity of the plant was sometimes confused. C. Koch believed '*M. lennei*' was nothing but *Magnolia amabilis* (*Magnolia denudata* var. *amabilis*); and it was also confounded with *M. campbellii* under which name it was cultivated in Pallanza (Lake Maggiore).

'This magnificent Magnolia blossoms freely and its blossoms often last until October – var. *roseagrandiflora* Hort. Flowers pink, very large.'

The author is indebted to Dr. Carlo Stucchi of Cuggiano, near Milan, for kindly supplying this translation of Pampanini's notes and also for his persistent efforts to unearth details of Salvi and Maonetti in the botanical libraries and archives in Italy.

While Pampanini in 1916 was able to contribute several details unknown to Lemaire in 1854 his suggestion that 'Lennei' was raised in 1850 or 1851 must be incorrect for the reasons already mentioned. The actual date of raising must have been at least ten years earlier. Also it is most unlikely that this Magnolia was raised by Count Giuseppe Salvi of Florence, since the contemporary report of Charles Lemaire definitely stated that it was raised by Salvi of Vicence (Vicenza). It would be far more likely for a travelling Prussian nurseryman to locate such a find in an Italian nursery, which he might well have reason to visit in the normal course of business, than in a private garden in a foreign country to which he would not have normal access.

Now let us search farther. Under *Magnolia conspicua Soulangeana*, Loudon reported in his *Arboretum et Fruticetum Britannicum* 1 : 279 (1838) that 'The plants raised from seed of *M. c. Soulangeana* at Fromont may be productive of something new, as may those raised by Mr. Curtis at Glazenwood [near Coggeshall, Essex], and by Mr. Ward at White Knights [near Reading]. *If Signor Manetti succeeds in raising plants from the seeds of M. c. Soulangeana, which have ripened at Monza, he also may introduce some new varieties.*'*

In his notes on the 'Trees and Shrubs of Italy' (p. 168) Loudon wrote: 'we are informed by Signor Manetti, the director of the Viceregal Garden at Monza . . . "In the List of Contributors (p. 19) appears the name Giuseppe Manetti, C.M.H.S. Monza."'

Thus it was Loudon who supplied the long-sought clue to the probable origin of *Magnolia* 'Lennei', which had been known in Italy until 1850 as 'Lombardy Hybrid', 'Mahometi', 'Mahoneti' and 'Maometto'.

It seems reasonable to suppose that the Italian surname Manetti became confused with 'Mahoneti',

'Mahometi' and 'Maometto', also that it would have been indiscreet for Signor Giuseppe Manetti, as Director of the Viceregal Garden at Monza, to have disposed of this Magnolia seedling in his own name.

It is a matter for conjecture how and where Salvi fits into the picture, but it seems likely that he acted either as Manetti's agent or as an intermediary in the disposal of this fine new Magnolia to Topf, who took it to his Prussian nursery at Erfurt and introduced it under an entirely new name which bore no relationship either to himself or to the hybrid's origin.

M. 'Lennei', was still being listed as *M. Mahoneti* in the nursery catalogue of Fratelli Sgaravatti, of Saonara, near Padova, in 1884.

Magnolias listed by Giuseppe Manetti

In *Catalogus Plantarum Horti Regii Modoetiensis* (*Monza*) *ad annum* 1825 (1826) are listed:

MAGNOLIA
acuminata
auriculata
fuscata
fuscata annonaefolia
glauca
grandiflora
grandiflora elliptica
grandiflora lanceolata
macrophylla
obovata
obovata discolor
pumila
pyramidata
umbrella
Yulan

In *Catalogus Plantarum Caesari Regii Horti prope Modiciam ad annum* 1842, p. 61:

MAGNOLIA
conspicua
conspicua Alexandrina A. B.
conspicua Morteri Hort.
conspicua Norbertii Hort.
conspicua Soulangiana A. B.
conspicua speciosa A. B.
conspicua triumphans Hort.
purpurea Curt.
gracilis A.B.
pygmaea Casoretti Hort.*

---

* My italics

* The abbreviated citations which follow the names in the 1842 list are A.B. referring to *Arboretum et Fruticetum Britannicum* Curt. probably referring to *Curtis's Botanical Magazine* Hort. hortulanorum – of garden origin.

Supplement I 1843/4, p. 23 lists:

MAGNOLIA *fuscata* Andr. *longifolia* H. Modoet.
glauca L. *flore pleno* Hort.
glauca Thompsoniana Hort.
glauca grandiflora L. *aucubaefolia* Hort.
glauca Hartwicus Hort. (hybrids)

There is no further mention of Magnolias in Supplement II to 1845 (spring) or in Supplement III to 1845 (autumn).

THE SOULCAMP HYBRIDS

MAGNOLIA CAMPBELLII ♂ × MAGNOLIA × SOULANGIANA ♀

A race of trihybrids bred at Kew in 1943 by the late Charles P. Raffill and there labelled *Magnolia × raffillii*. This grex is quite distinct from his race of crosses between *M. campbellii* and its eastern (Chinese) subspecies *mollicomata* described on pp. 161–70 under *M. campbellii* Sidbury-Raffill Group. In the absence of a published grex name with a Latin diagnosis for the hybrids under consideration here, the author has coined the name Soulcamp which combines the identity of its two parents.

Although it has been said and written that no worthwhile seedlings of this hybrid have been reported to date, there is, at Lanarth in Cornwall, a fine Magnolia believed to be of this parentage which attained the height of some 15 ft (4·5 m) at twenty-five years of age, but by nature it is a tall shrub rather than a tree, with slender, somewhat pendulous branches. The leaves are of moderate size, 6½ by 3¼ in. (16·5 by 8 cm), with nine pairs of main veins, tapering abruptly at each end and with a tendency to ripple along their margins. The flowers are goblet shaped with four narrow papery 'bracts', in the form of false calyces, drooping from their bases in the manner of *M. × soulangiana* 'Lennei'. Similar 'bracts' are to be found around the opening growth buds.

After shedding their perules, prior to opening, the flower buds are enclosed in spathaceous bracts which are densely coated with grey silky hairs. They split evenly into halves and are often retained beneath the flowers after the tepals have fully expanded. They provide an attractive contrast to the carmine-tinted backs of the eight broad, spoon-shaped tepals which are conspicuously recurved along their edges. Their upper surfaces are white with a pink flush extending along the main veins and deepening towards their bases.

The androecium is composed of a loose array of incurving stamens, with crimson filaments and creamy-white anthers. The gynoecium is dark green with creamy-white stigmas.

The heavy, spicy fragrance of the flowers is quite distinct, being somewhat reminiscent of grenadilla or passion fruit. It is a charming and graceful Magnolia.

There is a plant of this grex in the Magnolia Garden at Kew labelled *M. × raffillii* (No. 59) which by 1970 had grown into a small spreading tree some 15 to 18 ft (4·5 to 5·5 m) tall by 24 ft (7·5 m) spread with stouter branches and longer lanceolate leaves up to 8½ by 2¾ in. (21·5 by 7 cm) with nineteen pairs of veins. This specimen produces flowers which fail to develop normally. The plant at Windsor is more arborescent and has been reported to produce insignificant white flowers.

As with the seedlings of his cross between *M. campbellii* and its subspecies *mollicomata*, Raffill disposed of most of these hybrids privately, without any official records being kept. The author would like to hear from anyone who knows where they are to be found.

In his copy of Millais's *Magnolias*, which he presented to his successor S. A. Pearce prior to his death, Raffill wrote on page 203:

'M. × Raffillii (Campbell of Kew) = *M. soulangeana × campbellii*. Raised in 1946 by C. P. Raffill on an emasculated plant of *M. soulangeana*. Seeds germinated in May 1947.'

It would appear that the name *M. × raffillii* was proposed by W. M. Campbell, who was at that time Curator at Kew. Raffill's note was probably written on 18 January 1950 at the same time as the note on

M. campbellii × *mollicomata*, referred to in the chapter on the Sidbury-Raffill crosses. The spelling *soulangeana* was that in general use at the time.

In 1959 Kew botanist J. R. Seally recorded these notes about these hybrids:

'*Magnolia* × *raffillii*. *M. soulangeana* × *M. campbellii* cross made at Kew by C. P. Raffill (who seems to have sent it out under the name *M.* × *raffillii*). Very few plants raised. One at Kew has upright habit of growth but not yet flowered (April 1959).

'A plant in flower at Lanarth had habit of *soulangeana* and flowers very much like that sp. I could not see *campbellii* in it, but did not have material for close examination at Kew. S. A. Pearce also saw the plant and came to the same conclusion (independently).'

The name *M.* × *raffillii* has never been validly published. Following a discussion with the author concerning these hybrids in 1969, Dandy arranged for a cytological study to be carried out at Kew.

Cytology

M. campbellii is a hexaploid with 2n = 114 chromosomes.

M. × *soulangiana** ranges from triploid 2n = 57 chromosomes to octoploid 2n = 152 or irregular polyploid 2n = 156.

Soulcamp Hybrids (*M. campbellii* × *M.* × *soulangiana*)

Lanarth Tree 2n = ± 95 chromosomes (Wilkinson 1972).

Kew Tree (No 59) 2n = ± 106 chromosomes (Kew 1969)

---

* It is not known which cultivar of *M.* × *soulangiana* Raffill used as a pollen parent. The flowers of the Lanarth tree suggest 'Lennei' which has been pronounced to be a septaploid with 2n = 133 chromosomes (Santamour, 1970) or 'Rustica Rubra' with 2n = 156 chromosomes (Kew 1969).

Thompson's Magnolia

MAGNOLIA × THOMPSONIANA
(Loudon) C. de Vos

(*M. tripetala* × *M. virginiana*)

C. de Vos in *Nederlandsche Flora & pomona: Pomologische vereeniging* 131: t. 43 (1876)

SYNS. *M. glauca major* Sims (1820)

M. glauca Thompsoniana Loudon (1838)

John Sims in *Curtis's Botanical Magazine* t. : 2164 (1820) as *M. glauca* var. *major*

Plates 45 and 46

This little-known hybrid Magnolia originated in 1808 in the nursery of Archibald Thompson at Mile End, London, among seedlings of *M. virginiana* (*glauca*). This was probably the first hybrid Magnolia to be raised in the Western world, preceding by several years the Soulangiana hybrids raised in France by Soulange-Bodin in his garden at Fromont near Paris.

M. virginiana, the American Sweet or Swamp Bay, the first Magnolia to be grown in England, had been introduced as early as 1688 while *M. tripetala*, the Umbrella Magnolia, was introduced in 1752 and was first flowered in England at Mill Hill near Hendon, Middlesex, by wealthy mercer and botanist Peter Collinson, who was also the first to flower *M. acuminata*. It is possible that Thompson grew both of the parent species, though it seems unlikely that the hybrid was raised from seed off one of his own plants of *M. virginiana*, since neither species normally sets seed in our climate. At the Royal Botanic Gardens, Kew, there are several plants of *M. virginiana* in close proximity which are not of the same clone, yet which have not been known to set seed. It appears that a higher temperature is necessary at flowering time to germinate the pollen of this species.

It therefore seems reasonably certain that *M. × thompsoniana* is a natural hybrid, which originated from imported seed, since Thompson assumed that this larger-leaved seedling was merely a form of *M. virginiana* (*glauca*). Thus it was described in 1820 by Dr. John Sims in *Curtis's Botanical Magazine* as 'Thomson's New Swamp Magnolia' (having misspelt Thompson's name); a large form of *M. glauca* to which he gave the varietal name *major*.

For many years the parentage of Thompson's Magnolia gave rise to conflicting conjecture by leading botanists. While in 1838 J. C. Loudon in *Arboretum et Fruticetum Britannicum* 1 : 267 described it as *M. glauca* var. *thompsoniana*, half-a-century later Sargent expressed the prevailing opinion that it was in fact a natural hybrid between *M. tripetala* and *M. virginiana* (*glauca*), by which time the Dutch botanist, C. de Vos, had already bestowed upon it the name by which it has since become generally known. However in 1895 Nicholson, in the *Gardeners Chronicle*, differed by suggesting that it was probably a hybrid between *M. virginiana* and *M. fraseri*. Recently, in the mid 1960s, Prof. J. C. McDaniel in America has proved its putative parentage by repeating the cross, using several different forms of *M. virginiana* as female parents, but about this there are more details later.

While the flowers of *M. tripetala* emit a somewhat unpleasant odour, those of Thompson's hybrid are delightfully fragrant. The plant is virtually evergreen in mild localities, and produces flowers three times larger than those of *M. virginiana* with an attractive primrose shading on the outer tepals of its high-pointed flower buds.

The three outer tepals, in the form of a false calyx, are narrower and of a papery texture, fading from a greenish white to rusty brown, and persisting in a reflexed position as in *M. tripetala*, instead of falling away as in *M. virginiana*. The inner nine tepals are in three ranks, each diminishing in size. The leaves are somewhat similar to those of *M. virginiana* but larger, glossy green above and glaucous beneath. On young plants they may approach the size of those of *M. tripetala*, measuring up to 10 in. (25·5 cm) long by 5 in. (12·5 cm) wide but they are smaller on the flowering branches. In shape they are more obovate than elliptical, slightly acuminate and narrowed towards the base.

The veteran tree at the Garden House, Saltwood, Kent, no longer survives. Millais in *Magnolias*: 237 described this specimen as being 20 ft (6 m) high and 30 ft (9 m) across. It may well have been one of Thompson's original propagations of his hybrid.

M. × thompsoniana should be winter hardy in most parts of the British Isles. In America it is reported to tolerate winters down to −25 °F. (−31·7 °C.) at Brookville, Pennsylvania, but it has sometimes failed to survive in the milder winters around Philadelphia. It is assumed that this winter tenderness must be due to the *M. virginiana* parent having originated from a less hardy strain of this wide-ranging species, probably from a southern area, where plants did not have to adapt themselves to very cold winters. *M. virginiana* ranges from northern Massachusetts to southern Florida and east Texas. It was introduced into England some 120 years before Thompson's raising.

Plate 45 is from a photograph taken by the author at the end of June 1967 of a fine specimen growing in the garden of the late the Hon. Mrs. Bertram Bell on Fota Island, Co. Cork. It had at that time been flowering since April and continued to open a succession of flower buds for several weeks.

So far as is known no further hybrid of this parentage has occurred naturally, nor had been made artificially before 1960, when Prof. Joseph McDaniel, of the University of Illinois Agricultural Experiment Station, Urbana, set out to breed a new *M. × thompsoniana* by using northern forms of *M. virginiana* as seed parents and also making reciprocal cross-pollinations whenever the flowering of the two parent species overlapped. *M. tripetala* usually flowers before *M. virginiana*.

Although he has failed so far to secure fertilization of flowers of *M. tripetala* with pollen from *M. virginiana*, he has raised several new *M. × thompsoniana* seedlings resulting from *M. virginiana* pollinated by *M. tripetala*, and these are now undergoing trials.

These new clones have been multiplied by bud-grafting, and also from cuttings under intermittent mist. The first one flowered in 1965 as a graft on *M. tripetala*. The second one flowered in May and June 1966, after a frost on 10 May had killed most of the new foliage and flower buds on trees of *M. tripetala*. These two new clones have only minor differences. Both closely resemble the original hybrid, with fragrant flowers larger than *M. virginiana* but smaller than *M. tripetala*. Like *M. virginiana* they have three well-defined 'sepals' enclosing eight white 'petals', whereas Dr. John Sims's description of Thompson's hybrid, in *Curtis's Botanical Magazine* (1820), gives the flowers three sepals and nine petals. *M. tripetala*, and other American Magnolias generally, have six to nine 'petals' although eight-'petalled' flowers do occur.

Prof. McDaniel has made an interesting record of the flower life of his hybrids. Like *M. tripetala* they open for the first time in late afternoon, then close for the night to reopen permanently on the second day to shed their pollen. He also tells us that they vary in colour and odour, the 'Urbana' clone (Plate 46) having the best scent, with less yellow colouring in its flowers than another hybrid from a different *M. virginiana* seed parent, and that two of his clones were undamaged when exposed to −14 °F. (−25·6 °C.) temperatures during the 1962/3 winter at Urbana, Illinois. A detailed description of the re-creation of this hybrid was published in *Illinois Research*: 8–9 (1966).

It is hoped that his 'Urbana' clone of *M. × thompsoniana* will shortly become available to Magnolia enthusiasts in other parts of the world, not only to enable them to compare the old with the new, but to permit those who garden in colder climes the option of planting a hardier hybrid, which can be relied upon to produce a long succession of fragrant blossoms on a plant unlikely to grow too large for the smaller modern garden. Plant it near a terrace or garden seat where its enchanting fragrance can be appreciated at leisure.

Dr. Spongberg draws attention to the incompletely septate pith of branchlets of *M. × thompsoniana* which contrasts with the distinctly and completely septate pith of *M. virginiana* and which should aid in distinguishing these two Magnolias at any season of the year.

M. × thompsoniana has been proved to be almost, if not completely, sterile. In 1965 Dr. Frank S. Santamour, Jr., of the University of Pennsylvania, carried out cytological investigations on this hybrid, subsidized by a grant from the American Philosophical Society. Detailed reports on his findings were printed in the *Morris Arboretum Bulletin* 16 : 63–4 (1965) and 17 : 29–30 (1966), which is published by the University of Pennsylvania and which is now recognized as the official organ for the publication of Magnolia information in America. He reported that 'the haploid chromosome number of the hybrid was n = 19, as in both parents, thus eliminating the possibility that hybridization had been effected originally by a diploid gamete'. Santamour found that only 1·2 per cent of the pollen grains shed by *M. × thompsoniana* appeared to be normal, and suggested that similar abnormalities probably occur likewise in the formation of the egg cells. The pollen norm of the putative parents averaged 97 per cent for *M. virginiana* and 89 per cent for *M. tripetala*.

Santamour also carried out a series of bio-chemical studies on several different Magnolias to investigate anthocyanins in the flowers and fruits and leucoanthocyanins in the leaves. Concerning *M. × thompsoniana*, and its putative parents, he reported of the

flowers 'while the filaments of *tripetala* are brightly coloured, there was no pigmentation in the single hybrid specimen that was observed'. In tests for leucoanthocyanin in the leaves, *M. virginiana* showed negative while *M. × thompsoniana* gave positive reactions which could not have been inherited from *M. virginiana*.

Leucoanthocyanins are colourless compounds which are structurally related to the anthocyanin pigments responsible for almost total pigmentation to the intensely pink fruit cones of *M. tripetala*. Since *M. × thompsoniana* is almost completely sterile, and has not hitherto been known to set seed, it has not been possible so far to evaluate its fruit cones. It may well be, however, that when different clones of McDaniel's re-created hybrids and Thompson's original are brought together, with or without the proximity of one or both of their parents, a small quantity of fruits may set which will enable similar investigations to be made and recorded.

Apart from grafting, *M. × thompsoniana* can be propagated from layers or by cuttings in intermittent mist. Any ungainly branches should be shortened in July or August to induce bushy growth. Combining as it does the qualities of hardiness, fragrance and long flowering, it is surprising that propagation of this hybrid seems to have been almost completely neglected by British nurseries. It appears to have become obscured by the introduction of the precocious-flowered Soulangiana hybrids which followed in the 1830s, the flowers of which are so vulnerable to the vagaries of our springs.

Cytologically *M. × thompsoniana* is a diploid with 2n = 38 chromosomes.

MAGNOLIA 'Treve Holman'

This originated among a batch of hybrids which the author purchased from Caerhays about 1960 and which were lined out on our Truro nurseries under the label *M. sargentiana × mollicomata*. However the first part of the name later became almost indecipherable in our wet climate and was erroneously overprinted *M. soulangiana × mollicomata* under which name one of the plants was sold in the spring of 1964 to Mr. Nigel Holman of Chyverton near Truro.

In the Royal Horticultural Society's *Rhododendrons 1973 with Magnolias and Camellias*, Nigel Holman contributed an interesting account of 'Asiatic Magnolias in a Cornish Garden' which he concluded with a description of this Magnolia. He recorded that it had turned out to be the fastest grower among the many Magnolias planted at Chyverton, growing to 30 ft (9 m) by 1973. It flowered for the first time in April of that year when it turned out to be one of the finest he had ever seen. He named it to commemorate his father who was responsible for much of the planting over the thirty years during which he gardened at Chyverton. He describes the flowers as deep rose pink with red-purple shading while their shape is the elegant cup and saucer typical of *M. campbellii* subsp. *mollicomata*.

THE VEITCH MAGNOLIA HYBRIDS

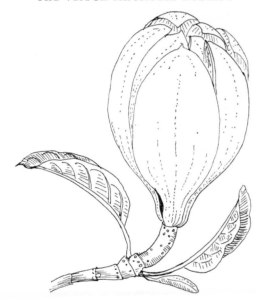

MAGNOLIA × VEITCHII Bean
(*M. campbellii* ♀ × *M. heptapeta* (*denudata*) ♂)
W. J. Bean in *Journal of the Royal Horticultural Society* 46 : 321 (1921) and in *Trees & Shrubs Hardy in the British Isles* Ed. 2, 3 : 226 (1936)

Plate 47

Peter C. M. Veitch, nurseryman of Exeter, was the first successful British Magnolia breeder, commencing his attempts almost a century after Soulange-Bodin. It is of course possible that others had tried and failed.

His success in hybridizing *M. campbellii* with pollen from *M. heptapeta* (*conspicua*) in 1907 was the only result from a series of attempts to cross this Queen of Magnolias with pollen from several others, including *M. stellata* and *M. × soulangiana*. Indeed it has been suggested that the flower form and poise of *M. × veitchii* more closely resembles that of *M. × soulangiana* than *M. heptapeta*, and one might even

wonder if any error of recording could have crept in. Against this is the extremely rapid and vigorous growth of *M. × veitchii* and the quite different results of Raffill's successful hybridizing of *M. campbellii* with *M. × soulangiana*. Peter Veitch had the reward of seeing the results of his Magnolia breeding attain florescence, a pleasure which was denied Charles Raffill of Kew, the next successful British Magnolia breeder some forty years later, who died several years before any of his Magnolia crosses and hybrids reached flowering maturity.

The late W. T. Andrews, Nursery Manager at Veitch's until his retirement, recorded his personal recollection of the history of *M. × veitchii*. He wrote to the author: 'I sometimes wonder if a mistake was made in labelling the seed pod *M. campbellii × denudata*, for without a doubt *M. soulangiana* was being used at the same time to fertilize flowers of *M. campbellii*. Wrong labels do get put on plants and I just wonder if this happened with the only pod to set fertile seeds. I sometimes think that I can see in *M. × veitchii* a strong resemblance to *M. soulangiana* both in the shape and its way of producing flowers along the stems, whereas both the *said* parents flower mostly singly at the ends of leading, or short side-shoots. . . . I wonder, am I adding confusion to a long-accepted fact in suggesting this error. I wonder am I, but perhaps it would be as well to go more fully into this by comparing living flowers, or perhaps photographs. I once suggested to the late Mr. Veitch that there could have been a mistake, but I decided that it might be wiser not to continue with my argument.'

W. T. Andrews, who spent his entire working life with Veitch's, had recorded in his own words the actual circumstances of the raising and propagation of this hybrid: 'Early in the present century the late Mr. Peter Veitch used pollen from *Magnolia denudata* and other kinds to pollinate flowers of *Magnolia campbellii*. His object in trying to make these crosses was to raise a hybrid as beautiful as its parents, more hardy, and that would flower in a reasonable time. Of all the flowers of *Magnolia campbellii* pollinated only one seed pod developed; this contained six seeds, and it had been labelled *campbellii × denudata*. These seeds were sown, and all germinated. When large enough to handle each plant was numbered, one to six, and in time planted out in a sheltered part of his nursery garden, there to grow till flowers were produced. Within fifteen years all six seedlings had flowered, but none had the colour or poise of *Magnolia campbellii* and in this respect Mr. Veitch must have been disappointed, for the growth of all six plants was decidedly that of *M. campbellii*.

'Seedling Number Three was the first to flower, it being the best of the six was eventually named 'Veitchii'. Number Six was the next to flower, and at the time was thought to be identical with Number Three. Both plants were layered, and, unfortunately the first batch of layers to be released to the public were taken from the two plants. The following year the mistake was discovered and propagation from Number Six was discontinued for many years. Magnolia seedlings One, Two, Four and Five were considered to be no improvement on existing varieties and as such were destroyed.

'Our plants of *Magnolia* × *veitchii* (seedling Number 6) are, and always have been raised from layers taken from the original plant, or from other plants resulting from such layers. Several buyers have told me that their plants have flowered within seven years of planting, this rather suggests that I may have grounds for saying that I think layered plants can be expected to flower sooner than if raised from seeds. Magnolia Number Six was in disgrace with us for a long time, but eventually we named it *M.* × *veitchii* var. 'Isca'. It is a delightful flowering tree, flowering about five days earlier than *M.* × *veitchii* and, judging from the original tree, it is wider and perhaps not as tall growing as *M.* × *veitchii*.

'*Magnolia* × *veitchii* 'Isca' soon reaches maturity and then produces numerous satiny-white flowers along somewhat flat-growing branches.' The author has noticed that the young shoots of *M.* × *veitchii* are bright olive green in winter, while those of var. 'Isca' have a brownish sheen.

The pink *M.* × *veitchii* was awarded a First Class Certificate on 22 March 1921, and a full description with a figure of the bloom is given in the *Journal of the Royal Horticultural Society* 46 : 321 (1921) (pages 321, 322 and facing page 336). It was given the cultivar name 'Peter Veitch' in 1970 (Plate 47).

In *Trees and Shrubs Hardy in the British Isles* Ed. 2, 3 : 226 (1936) W. J. Bean disagrees with Andrews's statement that *M. campbellii* was the seed parent, by describing *M.* × *veitchii* thus: 'A hybrid between *M. campbellii* and *M. conspicua* (*denudata*), raised by the late Mr. Peter C. M. Veitch of the Royal Nurseries, Exeter, who made the cross in 1907, the seed-bearer being *M. conspicua*.' The report in the *Journal of the Royal Horticultural Society* appears to have been written by the same author.

W. T. Andrews first joined Veitch's as a boy in 1913, and, after serving in the Armed Forces during the First World War, he rejoined the staff in 1920. He distinctly remembered being told by Sam Radley, who probably carried out the hybridizing, that the mother plant was *M. campbellii*, which flowered

freely in Veitch's old nursery at New North Road but which did not normally set seed. He was told how the largest and best seed pod was knocked off the tree by the general foreman, who was digging up some kind of plant growing beneath its branches, and that this mishap was covered up at the time by saying that it had fallen off naturally.

A tree of *M.* × *veitchii*, planted at Caerhays in 1921, had attained a height of 80 ft (24·5 m) by 1967, and is unrivalled in the amount of flowers it produces every season. Its one drawback is the extremely brittle nature of its branches, which is more pronounced than with any other Magnolia. Unlike *M. campbellii* the flowers are not chalice shaped, nor exclusively terminal, but are borne all along the branches in the manner of *M.* × *soulangiana*. *M.* × *veitchii* first flowered in 1917 having reached flowering maturity in ten years from seed.

The late C. P. Raffill of Kew wrote to the author in December 1949 to say that the 'rose' form of *M.* × *veitchii* often fruited freely at Kew 'but this last Spring we removed all the seed vessels as soon as the flowers were over as the seeds do not produce the coloured form. Years ago we raised a batch of our own seedlings of the 'rose' form and they all came into flower when about fourteen or fifteen years of age, and all were white. So we gave it up as a bad job as they were poor forms.' This experience proves the impropriety of raising and selling seedlings of hybrid Magnolias under their seed parent's name, as has been done on some nurseries in the past. At Caerhays it is nearly always sterile so that it loses no energy or vigour in maturing unwanted fruit-cones.

There is a fine tree of the pink form of *M.* × *veitchii* in the Valley Garden at Antony House, near Torpoint, Cornwall, the flowers of which can be viewed at eye-level from the opposite slope. On the bank above the pool is a second, somewhat stunted, bushy specimen which is reputed to have come from Japan in the 1930s. This is quite possible, since Japanese Magnolia growers would probably have imported this hybrid soon after its release by the raisers. It provides yet another example of the manner in which these vast tree Magnolias can be restricted in vigour by grafting. All of the Veitch distribution was of layers so that the very vigorous specimens would be on their own roots.

A worthwhile seedling of *M.* × *veitchii* was catalogued in 1969 by veteran Australian Magnolia expert Mr. Cyril H. Isaac, who in recent years has done much to popularize these plants in Australia, after perfecting a method of propagation from softwood cuttings at his Nursery at Noble Park, Victoria. This seedling was included in a list which he sent to the author in April 1969, on the cover of which he had written 'This is my "Swan Song".' It went to the printer only a few days before the nursery was sold early in February. 'I will carry on my interest in the industry and will be looking for outstanding new plants to import wherever I travel and don't propose to add the word "retired" to my vocabulary.'

Mr. Isaac also wrote: 'I imported two plants of *Magnolia* × *veitchii* 'Rubra' from the J. Clarke Nursery Co., of San Jose, California in 1964 and they have been quite rewarding. They have grown strongly and cuttings have rooted readily apart from flowering in their second year. The flower is quite different to anything else, it opens a bit better than 'Veitchii' which has always impressed me most as a bud, and the colour is wine red of a different hue to any other and much deeper than the 'Pink Form' of *soulangiana*.'

With this letter he enclosed leaves off his stock of the original *M.* × *veitchii* and the Californian *M.* × *veitchii* 'Rubra' and these were identical in size and shape.

James S. Clarke, Nurseryman of San Jose, California, writes: '*Magnolia veitchii* 'Rubra' was a chance seedling from seed gathered from our own tree. A number of seeds were gathered and grown on. This one tree was the only one that was a great deal different from the parent. It is very dark coloured but otherwise the growth, habit, foliage, etc., are the same or very similar to the original plant.' He added that he had very few Magnolias left and was discontinuing their propagation.

To summarize let us review the correct nomenclature of these hybrids. Hitherto the name *M.* × *veitchii* has seemed adequate but, as there are now at least three worthwhile clones, the original type plant should be styled *M.* × *veitchii* 'Peter Veitch' and its white counterpart *M.* × *veitchii* 'Isca', while Clarke's California seedling has been described under *M.* × *veitchii* 'Rubra', but should be written as *M.* × 'Veitchii Rubra' since the pollen parent is not known.

Whichever way the original hybrids were raised the outstanding difference between *M.* × *veitchii* and *M. campbellii* is that the flowers are erect and chalice shaped with a pronounced fragrance of bluebells (*Endymion non-scriptus*). They lack the wide 'saucers' which are formed by the outer tepals reflexing horizontally, which often contribute such an elegant poise to the flowers of *M. campbellii* and its subspecies *mollicomata*.

The pink cultivar 'Peter Veitch' (Plate 47) is the best known form of this hybrid. The fragrant flowers open precociously at the ends of short spurs. The nine pink tepals, 6 in. (15 cm) long, are obovate and broadly rounded near the apex, tapering towards the base. The flowers are vertically poised and inverted pear shaped. It is a very vigorous, large-leaved tree, the leaves measuring up to 12 in. (30·5 cm) in length by 6 in. (15 cm) in width, in shape obovate, generally rounded at the base and terminated by an abrupt point at the apex. They are purplish when young, turning to dark green at maturity, the midribs, main veins and petioles covered with grey indumentum.

The tree's habit resembles *M. campbellii*, the rapid growth and large leaves combining to make the tree vulnerable to serious gale damage, especially when the foliage is weighed down by driving rain.

It seems remarkable that trees raised from layers should take so long to attain florescence. The original seedlings took some ten years, while W. T. Andrews reported that trees raised from layers have taken seven years after purchase (at which time they would have been not less than three years from the date of layering and more likely four or five years). In a similar manner, trees raised at Windsor from cuttings of 'Charles Raffill' have taken as long to flower as did the original seedling.

By contrast, Cyril Isaac has referred to cutting-raised plants of *M.* 'Veitchii Rubra' flowering in their second year. This might apply to cuttings taken from the higher part of the tree and they may have been influenced by climate and by his unusual treatment. He told the author that his cutting benches under glass were never shaded and that instead of intermittent mist he had quite coarse irrigation jets actuated by a valve which was triggered open when water evaporated from a plate at the end of a balanced and pivoted horizontal rod.

Wiesener's Magnolia (pronounced Vézner)
Watson's Magnolia
Gyokusui and *Ukesaki Oyamarenge* in Japan
MAGNOLIA × *WIESENERI* E.-A. Carrière
(*M. hypoleuca* × *M. sieboldii*)

(SYNS. *M. obovata* × *M. parviflora*)

E.-A. Carrière in *Revue Horticole* 62 : 406–7 (1890)
    excluding reference to white filaments.

S. A. Spongberg in *Journal of the Arnold Arboretum* 57,
    3 : 272 (1976)

SYN. *M.* × *watsonii* J. D. Hooker in *Curtis's Botanical
    Magazine* 117 : t. 7157 (1891)

Plate 48

Shortly after this manuscript had been delivered to
the printers the author decided to adopt (without
alterations to this text) Dr. Stephen Spongberg's
reversion to the Carrière citation *M.* × *wieseneri*
(1890) although the description 'with white filaments'
is at variance with those of Hooker's *M.* × *watsonii*
(1891) which has been the name generally accepted
for the past eighty-seven years. This change in
nomenclature, regrettable as it may be, conforms with
the rule of priority in publication laid down by the
International Code of Botanical Nomenclature.

Dr. Spongberg details the features whereby *M.* ×
wieseneri is distinguished from *M. hypoleuca*: in the
bushy habit of growth, the smaller leaves with fewer
lateral veins, in the pubescent young branchlets and
in the smaller tepals.

The original importation of this oriental hybrid
into England was of a flowering specimen, which
had featured in the Japanese Court at the International
Paris Expo in 1889, whence it was acquired for the
Royal Botanic Gardens, Kew, and named by J. D.

Hooker (later Sir Joseph Hooker) after Mr. W.
Watson, the Assistant Curator. One wonders if
Watson had a hand in procuring this fine acquisition
from the Paris Exhibition, though Hooker justified
his citation by adding 'to whose skill and care the
Botanical Magazine is indebted for the flowering of so
many of the interesting plants depicted in its plates'.

Hooker proceeded to describe the new introduction with the inbred caution of the systematic
botanist: 'It is with considerable hesitation that I
propose the subject of this plate as a new species of
Magnolia, considering how imperfectly described
are the Chinese and Japanese members of the genus.
That it is not *M. parviflora* is obvious, as the size of the
flower implies. . . . *M. Watsoni* is much nearer *M.
hypoleuca* . . . which is a larger plant with robust
branches, large oblong leaves, densely pruinose and
thinly hairy beneath, and more or less biennial in
duration.' It is now generally accepted as a hybrid
between these species.

In his description Hooker omitted the most
important difference between his *M.* × *watsonii* (as it
is now correctly spelt) and *M. sieboldii* (*parviflora*),
that is the upward-facing poise of the flowers, which
it inherits from *M. hypoleuca* and which distinguishes
it from all species of Section *Oyama*, to which *M.
sieboldii* belongs. It is termed an intersectional hybrid
since *M. hypoleuca* (*obovata*) belongs to Section
Rytidospermum.

M. hypoleuca (*obovata*), a Japanese species closely
resembling the Chinese *M. officinalis*, had been
introduced in 1878, and it would appear that Hooker's
reference to its 'more or less biennial' foliage was
made from observations of a tree growing in the
Temperate House at Kew, since it sheds its leaves at
the first frost when grown in the open.

As far as is known, the putative parentage of this
hybrid Magnolia remains to be proven, as has been
accomplished by Prof. McDaniel of Illinois with
M. × *thompsoniana*.

M. × *wieseneri* grows into a small bushy tree with
long gangling branches arising from a short basal
trunk. These are best shortened occasionally to
restrict their spread. The leathery obovate leaves,
measuring 6 to 8 in. (15 to 20·5 cm) and sometimes
10 in. (25·5 cm) in length, are bright green above with
deeply impressed yellow veins. The undersides are
glaucous and slightly hairy and the margins somewhat waved. They are blunt at the apex and taper
towards their half- to one-inch stalks or petioles. The
young stems are green while those of *M. hypoleuca*
are reddish brown, and of *M. sieboldii* glabrous to
light brown.

The upward-facing flowers of *M.* × *wieseneri* are

about twice the size of those of *M. sieboldii*, opening from spherical white buds which develop to the size of golf balls. The open flowers maintain their globular shape, with six to nine ivory-white concave inner tepals and three outer sepaloid ones which become tinted pink or mauve outside as the flowers mature.

The gynandrophore differs considerably from *M. sieboldii* (*parviflora*) in which the red stamens predominate and are surmounted by a central brushlike cluster of stigmas. In *M. × wieseneri* the rosy-crimson stamens form two-inch rosettes in the centres of the flower cups, surmounted by the lime-green columns of the pistils. Hooker described the scent of the flowers as a powerful odour of *Calycanthus*, but Millais in *Magnolias*: 245–7 says they are 'highly scented like pineapples'.

The photograph was taken by the author in Mrs. G. R. Browne's garden on Garinish Island by Parknasilla on the Kenmare River, County Kerry, on 19 June 1967 (Plate 48). It seems older specimens tend to produce flowers with up to twelve tepals while younger ones more usually have eight or nine.

Its precise origin is not on record, but that dedicated Japanese plantsman Mr. K. Wada reports that, in Japan, *M. × wieseneri* was formerly called *Gyokusui* which is believed to be a very old name, while in some provinces it became known as *Ukesaki Oyamarenge* meaning 'upward-facing flowered *Magnolia parviflora*' a name believed to have originated among Japanese nurserymen.

This natural hybrid fuses the good qualities of the two putative parents in a flowering plant of great beauty. Young plants often begin to flower about the beginning of June when only 1 or 2 ft (30·5 or 61 cm) high, and older specimens continue to open successive groups of flowers until mid July or even later. It received an Award of Merit from the Royal Horticultural Society in 1917.

Because of its late flowering *M. × wieseneri* might prove a suitable Magnolia for colder localities where the precocious spring-flowering species and their hybrids would be unsatisfactory. Its branch habit would make it an easy subject for espalier training against a sunny wall. It seldom sets seed and no description of its progeny is on record.

In *Asiatic Magnolias in Cultivation*: 33, mention is made of a tree of *M. × wieseneri* at Spetchley Park, Worcester, which ripened seed regularly. The author would be interested to hear from anyone who has observed the flowering of any of its progeny. He is of the opinion that more than one clone of this hybrid is in existence and that they differ only in minor details. In one the flower buds appear to be spherical throughout their development, and the slender creamy-buff stamens with their rosy-crimson filaments are surmounted by the pale green stigmatic column.

In another form the fat-pointed buds are shaped like those of water-lilies (*Nymphaea* species), enshrouded by the outer tepals which are stained bronze pink and green. These open to reveal eight almost circular, concave, white inner tepals. In this form the pale-green stigmatic column is shorter and stouter with conspicuously hooked orange-yellow styles. The deep rose stamens are at first clustered tightly around the base of the column, later opening flat to display a band of short, deep-crimson filaments or stalks supporting the long buff-pink stamens which fade considerably as the flower matures. The white tepals then usually fade to parchment before falling.

Yet a third form would appear to have been introduced into France at precisely the same time as that which was displayed at the Paris Expo in 1889. It was part of an exhibition which was staged at the Trocadero in Paris by a Japanese horticulturist named M. Tokada, and it was likewise labelled *M. parviflora*. As such it was purchased by M. Wiesener, a landowner at Fontenay-aux-Roses (Seine). It was described by E.-A. Carrière in *Revue Horticole* 62 : 406–7 (1890) as *M. Wieseneri* thus: 'A dwarf shrub, branching, bushy, glabrous throughout. Cuticle of the buds smooth, glaucescent, golden green and slightly velvety. Leaves oval-oblong, certainly entire, fairly thick, deciduous, borne on a strong cylindrical petiole, the largest reaching up to 18 and even 20 cms [7 and 8 in.] in length and 8–10 cms [3 to 4 in.] in breadth, glaucescent green. Flowers strongly scented, upright, growing singly. Calyx of three sepals, pure white, as is also the corolla, which is composed of eight petals, these being oval, generously rounded and not spreading when the shrub comes into flower. Stamens very numerous *with white filaments** inserted at the base of the central, conical ovary. The *M. Wieseneri* flowers from the end of May. The blooms have a strong, penetrating scent but it is also delicate and pleasant.'

A. Pucci in *Bulletino della R. Societa Toscana di Orticultura* 6 : 162 (1907) described this Magnolia as a 'dwarf, bushy shrub with oval-oblong, glaucescent leaves and solitary, erect, pure-white flowers'. He referred to Wiesener as a 'grower' whereas Carrière said he was a landowner. Pucci said that it featured at the Paris Exhibition in 1889, which apparently

---

* The italics are mine.

included the Trocadero display mentioned by Carrière.

Carrière's description is a little at variance with Hooker's *M.* × *watsonii*. Because it often begins to flower when only 1 or 2 ft (30·5 or 61 cm) high it could well be mistaken for a 'dwarf shrub', but the main difference between *M.* × *watsonii* and *M. wieseneri* is in the colour of the filaments which Carrière recorded as white. Could this therefore be a variant of the same hybrid?

Efforts made by the author over the past ten years to trace further information about *M.* × *wieseneri* in French horticultural circles have so far proved fruitless, so it seems probable that Wiesener's purchase from Tokada eventually perished without being propagated. During these investigations Dandy suggested that the author was endeavouring to become a 'name-changer' when, in fact, the implications of the rule of priority of publication were not under consideration. It was apparent that Dandy had resolved to resist any attempt at name-changing in *Magnolia*.

In *Curtis's Botanical Magazine*: t. 7157 (1891) the two flowers shown vary considerably from those of either form referred to. The gynoecia are very large, prominent and brush shaped, lime green in colour with slightly hooked or recurved styles, while the boss of the stamens is predominantly yellow with a relatively small and irregular zone of crimson purple formed by their filaments. The tepals too have quite a wide area of their tips and margins recurved. It would almost seem that this corresponds more with Carrière's description, unless this flower condition occurs after blooms have been cut and kept in water. The flowers shown have eight white tepals and four rose-tinted sepaloid ones.

Hooker described the stamens as 'very numerous, in many series, recurved, forming a broad ring round and incumbent on the petals, about one-third of the latter in length, filaments blood-red, as long as the linear, dirty reddish-yellow anthers. Pistil an oblong mass of closely imbricating lanceolate carpels narrowed into slightly recurved styles, and terminating a very stout columnar stipes; stigmas linear, decurrent on the inner face of the style.'

Mr. K. Wada writes from Yokohama: 'A nurseryman friend tells us that, when he raised seedlings from open-pollinated seeds of *Magnolia parviflora*, he has found different-looking rogues among the batch.' This seems to suggest that this hybrid may occur naturally from time to time where the two parents are grown in close proximity.

Concerning frost tolerance, Mr. Geoffrey Gorer reported that the flower buds of *M.* × *watsonii* in his garden at Sunte House, Haywards Heath, Sussex were damaged by a late May frost in 1969. In June 1969 he supplied this description: 'The primary buds on my *Magnolia* × *watsonii* are spherical, but elongate to a waterlily shape about a week before flowering. The secondary buds reach a waterlily shape much earlier – say a couple of weeks before flowering. The stamens seem to be of two colours, a dark crimson round the pistil, and a paler red, fading to straw colour further out.'

In September of that year of a prolonged summer, which lasted from the end of May right up to November 6, he wrote: 'You may be interested to know that my *M.* × *watsonii* has put on quite a good show of flowers this month, after the extraordinarily dry and warm summer. It has half-a-dozen flowers out at the moment. This has not happened in any previous season, to my recollection.'

In notes entitled 'Magnolias at Nymans by Natural Fertilization', in the Royal Horticultural Society's *Rhododendrons 1973*, Head Gardener Cecil G. Nice recorded a selected seedling of *M. sieboldii* 'which was as if it were a reproduction of the glorious *Magnolia watsonii* . . . now twenty feet high'. Mr. Nice has since confirmed that it bears upward-facing flowers so there seems little doubt that his identification is correct.

From America comes a comparison of hardiness. At North Manchester, Indiana, *M.* × *wieseneri* and *M.* × *thompsoniana* repeatedly withstood temperatures down to o °F. (−17·8 °C.) with occasional lows down to −18 °F. and −20 °F. (−27·8 °C. and −28·9 °C.), conditions which proved too severe for *M.* × *veitchii*, which, in two trials, perished at midsummer when trying to recover from the previous winter's damage.

In J. E. Dandy's 'Review of the Genus *Magnolia*' mention is made of evidence that *M.* × *wieseneri* had been introduced into America (again as *M. parviflora*) before 1883. This evidence consists of a coloured plate of a Magnolia published by G. Nicholson in *The Garden* 24 : 508, t. 417 (1883) as *M. parviflora*, from an oil sketch sent by Mr. S. B. Parsons of Flushing, Long Island. This is likely to have been from a plant imported from Japan as much as ten years before its appearance at the Paris Expo in 1889.

By a strange coincidence, *M.* × *wieseneri* was also figured in 1883 by Japanese botanist Keisuke Ito in *Figures and Descriptions of Plants in the Koishikawa Botanical Garden* 1 : t. 13 (1883) as '*M. hypoleuca*, Sieb. et Zucc.', the caption in the volume in the Botanical Library of the British Museum (Natural History) having been corrected: 'This is *M. watsonii* Hook. f., not *M. hypoleuca*.' The leaves are certainly like *M.* × *wieseneri* as we now know it, but the androecium is shown as an upward curved collar of rosy-red stamens, closely resembling *M. hypoleuca*, though the gynoecium is almost cylindrical, with prominently hooked or recurved stigmas, tinted rosy at their tips. The tepals appear to be eleven in number and incurved, with a certain amount of undulation along their margins.

This Magnolia has proved completely hardy in the Philadelphia area and flourishes in the Arboretum of the Barnes Foundation at Merion, Pennsylvania. Established plants in Michigan are unharmed by −20 °F. (−28·9 °C.). It was however one of only two out of thirty-odd Magnolia species and hybrids killed in the abnormally cold winter of 1963 in David Leach's collection at Brookville, Pennsylvania.

In 'Magnoliaceae Hardy in Temperate North America', *Journal of the Arnold Arboretum* 57, 3 : 272 (1976) Dr. Stephen Spongberg gives priority to the name *M.* × *wieseneri* for this hybrid. Did he either overlook the error in Carrière's description or assume that there was also a clone with white filaments?

He tells me that the herbarium specimens which he has examined as *M.* × *wieseneri* give no indication as to the colour of the filaments and presumably he is correct in reasoning that, even if there are or were two or more clones of this hybrid, priority of publication of a grex name must be attributed to Carrière who published *M. wieseneri* on 1 September 1890 while the Hooker publication of *M. watsonii* is dated 1 February 1891.

Cytologically a diploid with 2n = 38 chromosomes as for both parent species.

MAGNOLIA HEPTAPETA (DENUDATA) ♂ × MAGNOLIA STELLATA 'Waterlily' ♀

This hybrid has been newly reported on good authority from the States as being 'unquestionable', because it resembles its pollen parent *M. heptapeta* in growth. No doubt its first flowering will be eagerly awaited by its raiser. I do not know which of the several *M. stellata* clones named 'Waterlily' was the seed parent.

At the U.S. National Arboretum, Washington D.C., William F. Kosar was successful in crossing *M. sprengeri* 'Diva' with *M. heptapeta*.

Otto Spring of Okmulgee, Oklahoma, has bred some interesting seedlings by crossing *M. quinquepeta* 'Nigra' with *M.* × *soulangiana* 'Rustica Rubra', three of which have been registered under the cultivar names 'Dark Splendor', 'Orchid Beauty' and 'Red Beauty'.

MAGNOLIA QUINQUEPETA × MAGNOLIA × SOULANGIANA 'Lennei'

According to Mr. A. A. Pickard of Canterbury, Kent, who has named this hybrid 'Lilenny', it was raised many years ago by a nursery in Alabama. He says that it resembles *M. quinquepeta* (*liliflora*) in growth and foliage but the flowers are larger and the tepals are a satin pink outside, shading to white on their upper or inner sufaces. He says that he doubts whether it has any 'Lennei' in its make-up. Apparently it is similar in many ways to the De Vos and Kosar hybrids but he finds it a better doer on his heavy Canterbury clay.

MAGNOLIA GRANDIFLORA × MAGNOLIA GUATEMALENSIS

Prof. J. C. McDaniel reported having made this cross when he visited Guatemala in July 1964. At Tactic he collected fertile seeds of *M. guatemalensis*, also flowers, from which he later transferred pollen on to those of a tree of *M. grandiflora* growing in Guatemala City. He also collected herbarium specimens and scion material from trees of *M. guatemalensis* growing at both Tactic and Cobán. A grafted plant of this species, which flowered under glass at the U.S. National Arboretum, Washington, D.C., was used by W. F. Kosar to pollinate flowers on *M. virginiana* var. *virginiana* from which several vigorous hybrids are reported.

Prof. McDaniel reports that *M. guatemalensis* seedlings had passed safely through winters at Lafayette, Louisiana, and Tampa, Florida. This species often has showy reddened stipules and new leaves. His account was published in the *Newsletter of the American Magnolia Society* 5, 1 : 2–3 (1968).

Soils

Most Magnolias seem to prefer a fairly heavy neutral-to-acid loam and a rainfall of 30 in. (762 mm) or more per annum. That they will tolerate drier soils and lower rainfalls has been demonstrated at the Royal Botanic Gardens, Kew, at the Royal Horticultural Society's Garden at Wisley, and at the Gardens at Windsor Great Park. In such areas they do best on sites shaded for part of the day and sheltered as much as possible from drying winds. The Japanese, and probably some of the Chinese species, together with those from North America, are probably more tolerant of summer heat and drought than those from the Himalayas. Once fully established they will survive prolonged periods of drought.

No Magnolia likes stagnant water or too high a water table (i.e. a waterlogged subsoil) nor do they like heavy clay or compacted soils unless these are amply aerated by a liberal admixture of decomposed vegetation preferably containing a proportion of sharp grit. That they will tolerate waterlogged conditions, at least during winter dormancy, has been demonstrated at Lanarth where there are numbers of trees growing on the old croquet lawn, the original drains having become blocked so that the whole area becomes waterlogged in winter.

In some English gardens which are open to the public the root areas of flowering Magnolias are roped off in wet seasons to prevent soil compacting by persons anxious to take close-up photographs of the flowers.

The majority of Magnolias will grow on alkaline soils if provided with adequate reserves of humus, but the range of species and hybrids which will tolerate chalky soils is somewhat restricted. Probably the best material to incorporate with alkaline soil is an acid granulated peat, preferably the black kind recommended for rhododendrons. Avoid applications of composted garden refuse from an alkaline plot and any which has been treated with an alkaline accelerator. Also avoid using bonfire ash (invariably alkaline), and leaf-mould from trees growing on alkaline land. Chlorosis, a yellowing of the foliage on certain calcifuge plants, may be caused either by the presence of excess amounts of lime or of potash. An excess of lime can cause chlorosis of Magnolia leaves and lime also accelerates the depletion of humus in the soil; this is because lime aids bacterial activity and this, in turn, breaks down the complex carbon compounds in humus. An excess of potash

may do so in two ways: it might result in salinity and also aggravate magnesium deficiency. Conversely very low potash levels can induce chlorosis in Magnolias. Indeed it is safe to say that very low potash levels can cause chlorosis in most plants. Magnolias growing in dry situations should have an abundant supply of potash because the surface 6 to 8 in. (15 to 20·5 cm) may get very dry and the roots will have to depend on potash reserves from soil below the surface layer. Magnolias growing in sandy soils, and which have displayed chlorosis, might benefit from a dressing of 4 oz per sq yd (133 g per sq m) of sulphate of potash applied in late autumn; this would allow some down-wash during the winter months.

Wood-ash should not be applied as a top dressing because of its alkaline nature. Burnt vegetable matter is very alkaline and this you can see for yourself if you drop a small quantity of cigarette ash into some indicator solution – it will turn it blue immediately.

Chlorosis induced by soil conditions should not be confused with the pallor normal for the young leaves of many Magnolias. The young leaves of M. × loebneri 'Leonard Messel' are usually of pale chlorotic appearance, becoming gradually greener as the summer advances. Similar leaf conditions are to be observed on other Magnolias, notably on several of the Soulangiana hybrids.

To rectify chlorosis and the soil conditions which cause it, apply only lime-free materials such as leaf-mould from trees on neutral-to-acid soils, acid peat, bracken, or well-composted chicken manure – in preference to farmyard manure – either when preparing the ground for planting or as a surface mulch during the growing season. Avoid using lime when making compost – substitute with a layer of peat or soil, and apply sulphate of ammonia as an accelerator. The pH of the soil can be gradually lowered with frequent light applications of sulphate of ammonia at 2 oz per sq yd (66 g per sq m), at intervals of fourteen days during the growing season and copiously watered in. Should the soil be dry, irrigate the area before applying the fertilizer, and keep the crystals off the foliage or they may cause burning. Discontinue this treatment about the end of August to avoid encouraging, into October, soft growth which may not withstand severe frosts.

There is no evidence that any species of Magnolia is calciphobe (i.e. completely intolerant of lime). The main problem with chalky soils is the speed with which applications of bulky organic materials –

humus suppliers – are dissipated by bacterial activity which is accelerated by lime. There is also the problem of essential trace elements being present only in insoluble forms and therefore unavailable to plant life. Modern chemistry has provided a material to overcome the shortage of soluble iron salts, but the effect is usually transient and further applications are necessary at regular intervals.

Sequestrene, a chelated iron compound, has the property of releasing iron and other essential minerals 'locked' in the soil by an excess of lime. Used according to the manufacturer's instructions it can be of great help in resuscitating chlorotic foliaged plants. Foliar feeds probably present the simplest way to rectify chlorosis and excellent results are reported following their use on Magnolias growing on chalk.

In his lecture to the Royal Horticulture Society on 'A Cold Chalk Garden' (July 1966) the Hon. Lewis Palmer said: 'There are very few Magnolias which will stand our soil. As far as I know there are only five, *grandiflora*, *kobus* and the three closely related species *wilsonii*, *sinensis* and *highdownensis*'. One would expect that the wide range of *M. kobus* derivatives could be added to this list, also *M. sieboldii*.

Harold Hillier in *Manual of Trees and Shrubs* (1972) writes: 'Magnolias are very tolerant of heavy clay soils and atmospheric pollution. The most lime tolerant are *M.M. acuminata*, *cordata*, *delavayi*, × *highdownensis*, *kobus*, × *loebneri* and *wilsonii*', and he describes *M. grandiflora* as 'lime tolerant if given a good depth of rich loam'.

Siting

Ideal situations are those which afford maximum wind shelter though it is surprising what exposure even the larger-flowered kinds can tolerate. When planting in proximity to other trees try to select a site with overhead clearance and without too much root competition. Coloured flowers are darker and retain their colour better in part shade. For example *M.* × *loebneri* 'Leonard Messel' is at its best when it flowers during a sunless period or in a shaded situation. When grown in the open it loses much of its colour when warm sunny weather coincides with its flowering season.

Magnolias are remarkably wind-tolerant considering the large size of the leaves of many of the tree species. Unfortunately their branches are somewhat brittle so that they are prone to the effects of freak wind gusts, especially while the leaves and branches are weighed down by heavy rain. Trees growing in sheltered situation, or those drawn up through proximity to taller trees, are more prone to such damage than those growing in open situations, where adaptation to environment brings about the development of shorter and stouter branches and sometimes smaller-than-usual leaves.

Planting

Liberal quantities of peat, leaf-mould, well-rotted animal manure, or similar bulky decomposed organic material, or a combination of two or more, may be thoroughly incorporated in the top-soil over an area of 5 to 6 sq. ft (1·5 to 2 sq. m) prior to planting. Where the soil is lacking in essential plant nutrients this dressing may be supplemented with several handfuls of a compound fertilizer (such as John Innes Base). A surface mulch of similar organic materials may be added after planting, to retain soil moisture and feed the surface roots. Unless the planting sites have been prepared in advance, plantings delayed until late spring should have only minimal site preparation, to avoid loosening and drying out the surrounding soil. At all times deep planting should be avoided because Magnolias are surface rooting.

Magnolias may be planted from November to May. Container-grown plants can be planted out during the summer months if reasonable care is taken to saturate thoroughly and avoid any disturbance of their root balls, and to keep them adequately irrigated during dry weather until fully established.

Magnolias grown in the open ground are usually lifted and burlapped by nurserymen to retain a quantity of the soil around their roots though this is by no means essential. They may be either planted as received and the hessian wrapping allowed to decompose in the soil, or this may be removed and the roots carefully spread out. Whichever method is adopted remember that Magnolias are surface rooting and that over-deep planting may lead to failure through root suffocation.

Quite large specimen Magnolias can be transplanted if adequate care is taken. The author has frequently transplanted trees of 12 to 15 ft (3·5 to 4·5 m) with considerable success, where adequate overhead irrigation was provided from May to September to encourage the formation of new leaves especially at the tops of the trees. Where no such facilities are available it is advisable to remove all weaker growths completely and to shorten all remaining side branches back to within a few inches (centimetres) of the main stems, the leaders of which should be considerably shortened also. These severe measures are particularly advisable where the transplanting is left until April or May, though Magnolia specialist Mr. A. Pickard of Canterbury advocates severe pruning for all Magnolias prior to replanting. Philip Urlwin-Smith has successfully transferred quite large specimens from Cornwall to his garden at Ascot without having to resort to pruning but he has used regular overhead irrigation.

If stakes or canes are required to provide initial support for the tree, it is advisable to drive these in during the process of planting, while the roots are still visible so that these are not damaged.

Magnolias on sandy soils

For guidance on growing Magnolias in conditions far less favourable than those to be found in the great estate gardens of Cornwall one cannot do better than make enquiries at the Crown Estate Gardens at Windsor Great Park which can boast as comprehensive a collection as is to be found anywhere apart from Caerhays.

It would appear that Magnolia plantings were begun at Windsor in the late 1930s with such iron-clads as *M. stellata*, *M. acuminata*, *M. kobus* and a selection of cultivars of *M. × soulangiana*. The four species of Section *Oyama* were planted in 1939, namely *M. sieboldii*, *M. sinensis* and *M. wilsonii* together with the more tender Chinese form of *M. globosa* (var. *tsarongensis*) which has survived though often crippled by late frosts.

After a lapse during the war years Magnolia plantings were resumed in 1947 so that today the gardens contain an almost complete range of the temperate species together with a good selection of hybrids. The gardens are on poor sand and gravel with a low rainfall of only 22 in. (56 cm).

John Bond, Keeper of the Gardens, has kindly supplied details of the planting procedures which have been developed over the years by Sir Eric Savill and Mr. T. H. Findlay.

Because of the abnormally dry soil conditions which exist during periods of drought, the preparation of planting sites needs to be extensive and thorough, and lack of summer rain has to be overcome by regular and copious overhead irrigations.

Two methods of site preparation have been practised. When preparing for an isolated Magnolia on a grassed area the 'pot' method is used. This consists of skimming off the herbage over a circle 5 to 6 ft (1·5 to 2 m) across and excavating the top-soil to a depth of 18 in. (46 cm). The sub-soil is then loosened and liberal quantities of well-rotted animal manure and good leaf-mould are mixed with the excavated material before back-filling.

As might be expected the occupant of such a site will eventually develop roots which will extend beyond the bounds of the prepared 'pot' and then its rate of growth will slow down through a reduction in soil moisture and nutrients.

Consequently better results are evident where larger beds have been prepared and liberally dressed with well-rooted farmyard manure and leaf-mould so that the trees have a more uniform medium throughout their root-runs. Every three years or so these beds are heavily mulched with a fifty-fifty mixture of the same materials.

Wherever possible such extensive preparations as those described should be carried out in the autumn and winter for early spring planting, after the loosened ground has been settled by the action of rain and frost. It is better to incorporate such bulky materials with the soil as evenly as possible than to place a layer in the pit bottom where it will tend to act like a sponge during periods of drought and absorb moisture from the sub-soil, while preventing the normal rise of capillary moisture towards the surface.

Materials used for mulching – the form of surface dressing employed to reduce loss of soil moisture from the surface through the action of sun and wind – are best applied well in advance of drying conditions. A mulch of dry material is likely to act as an absorbent and thereby defeat its purpose. Tan bark has become a popular mulching material. It has the advantages of being clean to handle and easy to apply. It is less absorbent than peat and it does not cake or tend to repel moisture when in a desiccated condition. Frozen soil conditions provide an excellent opportunity for wheeling, tipping and spreading such bulky materials without risk of causing soil compaction with a resulting loss of essential aeration.

Recommended Treatment of Imported Magnolias

Readers contemplating an importation of Magnolias from another country or state, where regulations insist that all traces of soil be washed from their roots as phytosanitary precaution, may appreciate some advice on how to treat such plants on arrival. The soil has to be washed off prior to phytosanitary examination on the nursery.

After being hosed clean the plants are placed in polythene bags to drain off without being allowed to become dry. They are then packed individually with the roots tightly enclosed in polythene bags of damp sawdust which should be washed off on arrival.

1. *Immerse plants in a bath of water* for several hours to remove traces of insecticidal dip or phytosanitary fumigation and to correct the drying effects of export preparation and transit period.

2. Plant into the SMALLEST available containers, ones *barely adequate to accommodate the roots* are best. *Oversize containers may induce failures* in re-establishing for reasons not clearly understood.

3. Use a lime-free neutral-to-acid compost where available. A loam-based preparation has a wider range of water and nutritional tolerance than a soil-less type.

4. Avoid burying roots too deeply in the containers.

5. Firm the compost well around perimeter of containers before watering.

6. Support with canes where necessary.

7. Place in a cool, sheltered environment and protect from extremes of sunlight and temperature. If under glass, avoid temperatures above 65 °F. (19 °C.) and below 25 °F. (−3·9 °C.). Mild freezing will not harm them prior to bud-break.

8. Delay planting out until plants show signs of re-growth and protect from late frosts. Smaller plants should be kept in their containers until the following October or later. Ensure that they are adequately irrigated during dry spells until the end of the first summer.

Cultivation

It is probable that more newly-planted Magnolias are killed by 'over-gardening' than from neglect. By 'over-gardening' I mean over-deep cultivation such as that caused by the use of a hand-fork to remove weeds close to the roots. On no account should Magnolias be dug around to remove weeds since such treatment loosens and damages their surface roots and is likely to prove fatal if indulged in during the spring and summer.

Magnolias will usually tolerate complete neglect but in areas of high rainfall small plants may have their foliage severely damaged by slugs and snails especially where there is a dense coverage of weeds or long grass. Generally speaking the less after-care they receive the better, apart from adequate irrigation during periods of prolonged drought during the first summer after planting. Cultivations should be restricted to very shallow hoeings to check weed growth around the plants. This may also be controlled by careful applications of an approved non-residual herbicide such as Paraquat, taking great care to keep it away from the foliage. Such chemical

weed control, and also mulching with a few inches of tan bark or moist peat or similar non-alkaline material, avoids the inevitable loss of soil moisture associated with hoeing.

Fertilizers for Magnolias

Where the soil is known to be of low fertility I am in favour of applying light dressings of a good balanced fertilizer, about a handful per sq yd (sq m), distributed evenly over the planting site and repeated with the seasonal mulches or simply scattered over the surface in March or April. In areas of low rainfall this would be better applied in January or February. It should be borne in mind that the majority of the feeding roots are beneath the drip-line of the outer branches and not close to the base of the bush or tree. Remember too that Magnolias are surface rooting so on no account should the ground be dug over beneath their branches.

Most woody plants have comparatively low nutrient requirements so that no improvement in growth rate is likely after fertilizers have been applied to soils which have no pronounced nutrient deficiencies. Because of this some Magnolia growers have become convinced that their plants are incapable of assimilating fertilizers. The fact remains that Magnolia roots, like those of many other plants, are highly selective and only able to absorb their normal requirements.

Some gardeners have a pronounced phobia for all fertilizers which are not completely organic – that is of animal or vegetable origin. They therefore trust only bone-meal or hoof-and-horn, ignoring the fact that both are rich in calcium and neither contains any potash. Above all their great bugbear is sulphate of ammonia, long derived from coal, which originated in the world's primeval forests, and latterly from oil. Used sparingly and at regular intervals, sulphate of ammonia is, as already mentioned, an effective means of reducing soil alkalinity. It is best applied during wet weather so that it becomes rapidly diluted. If used late in the growing season it tends to delay the ripening of the new shoots and these may suffer damage from early autumn frosts. Excessive applications would be likely to cause leaf-burn so it should only be used with caution.

My personal choice of fertilizer is I.C.I.'s organic-based 'Garden Plus' which is available at most garden shops in a wide range of package sizes. Whatever fertilizer is used it is a good idea to mix some into any bulky organic material which is available for mulching.

Cold tolerance

Writing in the *Newsletter of the American Magnolia Society* 3 : 1, 6 (1966) Fred Lape, Director of the George Landis Arboretum at Esperance, New York, an area subjected to winter lows down to −20 °F. (−28·9 °C.), reported that the only Magnolias which had proved completely hardy were *M. acuminata, M. kobus,* and *M. stellata* in all its forms, together with the Loebner hybrids (*M. kobus* × *M. stellata*).

He also referred to the killing effect of prolonged droughts which he suggested might be connected indirectly with these severe winters. It stands to reason that considerable desiccation of plant tissues must occur during periods of deep freeze, and if such conditions are followed closely by inadequate spring or summer rainfall, then failures are more likely to occur. He recommends mulching all Magnolias heavily early in the summer. The author advocates mulching in spring, before signs of any curtailment of rainfall, and to use only wet material for the mulch so that it does not proceed to absorb moisture from the surface upon which it is laid.

There is good reason to apply such surface dressings on top of any snow covering so that the material will absorb and retain some of the moisture when thawing begins.

Comparative Winter Hardiness in Magnolias

Some interesting comparisons in winter hardiness following the winter of 1962–3, which (as in Europe) was the coldest in modern times, were reported in *Newsletter of the American Magnolia Society* 9, 4 : 3–4 (1973) by David G. Leach, President of the American Horticultural Society. David Leach is a professional plant breeder with nurseries and trial grounds at Brookville, Pennsylvania, in the foothills of the Allegheny Mountains, an area sometimes described by TV weathermen as 'the iceberg of Pennsylvania' on account of its notably low temperatures. Winter temperature of −15 to −20°F. (−26·1 to −28·9 °C.) are commonplace but in early 1963 the thermometer went down to −35 °F. (−37.2 °C). His list contains some thirty species, cultivars and hybrids including:

NO INJURY	SLIGHT INJURY	MODERATE INJURY	SEVERE INJURY	KILLED
M. acuminata	*M. acuminata* var. *subcordata* (100% bud loss)	*M.* × *soulangiana* 'Brozzonii'	*M. heptapeta* ★× *M. sargentiana* var. *robusta*	*M. sieboldii*
M. fraseri		*M.* × *soulangiana* 'Grace McDade'		*M.* × *wieseneri*★ (*watsonii*)
M. 'George Henry Kern'	*M. cylindrica*		*M.* × *soulangiana* 'Lennei'	
M. kobus var. *borealis*	*M. hypoleuca* (tips killed)		*M.* × *soulangiana* 'Liliput'	
M. macrophylla (a second specimen was considerably injured)	*M. kobus* var. *nana compacta*		*M.* × *soulangiana* 'Rustica Rubra'	
M. salicifolia (a second plant was severely injured)	*M. quinquepeta*★ 'Nigra' *M.* × *loebneri*		*M. virginiana* (probably from a more southerly source than 'Henry Hicks')	
M. stellata including cvs. 'Royal Star' and 'Water Lily'	*M.* × *soulangiana* 'Alexandrina' *M.* × *soulangiana* 'Verbanica' (60% of flower buds killed) *M. stellata* 'Rubra' *M. tripetala* *M. virginiana* var. *australis* 'Henry Hicks'			

★ The names of these Magnolias have been up-dated by the author.

Irrigation

Where watering becomes advisable this should be prolonged and copious. The garden sprinkler usually needs to be left in one place for several hours before the water penetrates to root level. This form of overall watering encourages weed seed germination while a hose left to trickle at the foot of a plant for an hour or two applies water economically where required. You can finish off by spraying the foliage, but avoid wetting the leaves in hot sunshine when the roots are dry, since leaf scorch may result.

Forcing

Magnolia flower buds may be forced to open in February or March by placing either the plants, or cut material in water, in a temperature of 75 to 80 °F. (23·9 to 26·7 °C.) until they open. Coloured forms will display deeper colouring if kept in the dark or away from direct daylight. Opening of the more advanced buds may be delayed by wrapping them in thick cloth or foam rubber, held in place by rubber bands. Flowers so treated will open almost immediately after release.

Pruning

Magnolias require no routine pruning but may be pruned, if desired, in the same manner as other trees and shrubs. Complete removal of all but the stronger shoots is sound pre-planting practice. At the same time any over-long shoots may be shortened as may those growing in unsuitable directions since this basic pruning may well reflect on the future shape of the tree or shrub.

Where a Magnolia is to be grown as a specimen tree, a temporary stake or stout cane, not less than 6 ft (2 m) in length, should be driven into the ground before planting in order to avoid root damage. The main stem should be positioned close to the stake and then be tied to it to ensure maximum support. If necessary the plant's main growth impulse can be diverted to this leader by removing the tips of the side branches or by pruning them even more severely and pinching out the tips of any competing growths, which may subsequently arise in July and August.

Sometimes a newly planted specimen fails to make any growth during the first growing season. This usually happens when a prolonged drought occurs before it has a chance to re-root and it is then advisable to prune severely in the manner of a rose bush while it is dormant in the following winter.

Newly planted tree species may be cut down to ground-level after one growing season if a straight-stemmed trunk is required but it must be borne in mind that the young shoots which arise in the spring are very susceptible to damage by late frosts and slugs. In colder climates the wisest adage is 'Prune in June', referring of course to gardens in the northern hemisphere. Over-vigorous new shoots may be shortened in late July.

If the foliage of a newly-planted evergreen Magnolia such as *M. grandiflora* shows signs of drying out, by turning brown from the top of the plant downwards, then immediate and drastic pruning may be necessary to save it, even to the extent of shortening all growths to within an inch or two of the main stem or stems. The plant should then be kept copiously watered during dry weather and a water-saturated mulch or surface dressing spread over its root-run to retain moisture and keep the roots cool. It may be worthwhile enclosing the retained portion in a polythene bag with a few vent holes until growth recommences. Regular overhead watering would be also beneficial. Removal of at least half of the mature leaves is a pre-transplanting recommendation for rooted layers of *M. grandiflora* and *M. delavayi*.

Where it becomes necessary to restrict a Magnolia by pruning drastically, the best time to perform this operation is immediately after flowering with deciduous kinds, and in early spring with evergreen ones. Larger branches requiring the use of a saw should have the bark surrounding the cut neatly bevelled with a sharp knife before being painted over with an approved fungicidal wound dressing such as Arbrex. In the absence of a specialized dressing, thick paint will probably suffice, but is not generally to be recommended. Sometimes the scar will burgeon forth with adventitious shoots the following spring. These should be either rubbed off when 1 in. (2·5 cm) or so long, or gradually thinned until one or more replacement growths have been selected for retention. Even shrubby Magnolias may be encouraged to become tree-like by gradually removing the lower branches and by supporting the main shoot with a stake to form a leader. Removal of quite large branches at flowering or fruiting season, either for indoor decoration or exhibition, has no harmful effect on the tree or shrub. It is a good way of making use of crowded or over-crossing branches.

Some deciduous tree Magnolias have a pronounced tendency to produce secondary leaders. These usually arise from the upper sides of horizontal lower branches and grow vertically through the branch system towards the top of the tree. It seems advisable to remove these at an early age in order to maintain an open-branched growth pattern, otherwise they are likely to cause a certain amount of die-back where they smother weaker side shoots with their larger leaves and greater vigour. The cause of these so-called 'water-shoots' can be only surmised. It could be that our climate is wetter and cooler in summer than that to which these trees have become adapted in their native environment or perhaps our soils are richer and deeper. It is also possible that our longer summer day-length, due to our more northerly latitude, may affect their growth pattern.

Where a strong basal shoot arises on young trees growing on their own roots the original growth may be cut away in March or April to give way to the stronger replacement. Some Magnolias tend to produce long gangling branches and it may become desirable to shorten these especially where space is limited. The best times to perform this operation are immediately after flowering, or in July or August. At both seasons the plant is in active growth so that the wounds heal over rapidly and subsequent growth has time to ripen before the winter.

Root Pruning

A method of root pruning has been suggested by Australian Magnolia grower, Cyril H. Isaac, as a means of restricting the growth of the larger tree types and reducing the time taken for a tree to begin flowering. He recommends that a circle be marked out 3 or 4 ft (about 1 m) from the trunk. A sharp spade is then forced down to its full depth to sever all roots in its path. Then, missing a spade's width, repeat the operation and so on right around the tree. For obvious reasons this operation would be safer if performed in the autumn or winter than after the plant has started into growth, when it might suffer too great a setback through root severance at a critical period in its growth impulse. Mr. Isaac also advocates a repetition of this operation during the following dormant season in order to sever those roots not pruned in the first instance. In practice it might prove difficult to perform this second operation with much accuracy. At the Strybing Arboretum, San Francisco, tree Magnolias have been made to flower at an earlier age by keeping them severely root-bound in containers (see p. 87).

Propagation

As with most other woody plants two different types of propagation or reproduction are possible. The first is from seed – the result of sexual contributions from one or two parents. Whether such seed has resulted from pollination and subsequent fertilization of the ovules by the plant's own pollen, or that from a neighbouring Magnolia, is a matter for conjecture unless the seed is from an isolated plant or where controlled hand-pollinations have been carried out in the manner discussed under Magnolia breeding.

Provided that the parent plant is a true species and not a hybrid, then the progeny from self-fertilization, or from pollination by another Magnolia of the same species, will turn out true to type within the range of variability of that particular species. Many of them, therefore, will differ somewhat from the seed parent in such inherited characters as vigour, growth habit, leaf size, flower colour (where this is a variable) and the age at which they attain flowering maturity or florescence.

The second of the two types of propagation mentioned is termed asexual or vegetative, since it results from the rooting of cuttings or layers, or from the grafting or budding of vegetative material from the parent on to another Magnolia referred to as the understock. The resulting Magnolia will have all main characters identical to those of the parent, the only variable being vigour, which might be influenced initially or permanently by the understock on which it has been budded or grafted. This second type of propagation is discussed later in this chapter.

Seeds

Generally only a small percentage of fruit cones of Magnolia develop perfectly in English gardens. This is particularly so with the precocious-flowering species and hybrids, and may be associated with the effect of weather on early insect activity and the susceptibility of Magnolia blossoms to frost damage.

Among summer-flowering Magnolias *M. sinensis* and other members of the *Oyama* Section, are usually prolific seed bearers. Perhaps this is partly due to the nodding or pendent poise of the flowers which must provide protection for visiting insects.

On the other hand the evergreen species which flower in the summer are notoriously rare at setting seed in English gardens. Here we never see fertile fruit cones on *M. grandiflora*, nor on *M. delavayi*. Perhaps they need a hotter and drier climate for their reproductive processes and this theory is substantiated by the freedom with which I have observed *M. grandiflora* and *M. virginiana* develop fertile fruit cones in the hotter summers of the eastern states of America and the same may apply to *M. stellata*, *M. tripetala* and other deciduous ones which I have seen fruiting there.

Mention is made elsewhere in this book of the apparent incompatibility of some Magnolias to their own pollen. In addition many of them appear to require a higher temperature at flowering time than that which normally prevails in the British Isles in order to germinate their pollen once it reaches the receptive stigmatic surfaces within the unopened flowers, for their protogynous nature ensures that the earlier blooms are sterile. The transfer of pollen from these earlier flowers on to the receptive stigmas of unopened secondary blossoms is generally ascribed to the activity of tiny flower beetles. In some seasons these are probably not active so early in the year, while in some localities they may be entirely absent, and it seems likely that both gravitation and wind may sometimes act as alternative agents for pollen dissemination.

Plants raised from seed generally take longer to attain flowering age than those raised vegetatively, and there is often a considerable variation even between seedlings raised from seed borne within the same carpel. There is always the risk that, having taken many years to attain flowering age, a seed-raised Magnolia turns out to be inferior to its parent, whereas plants propagated vegetatively will produce leaves and flowers which are identical to the mother plant.

In Cornwall it has been observed that the large-flowered Asian species, such as *M. campbellii* subsp. *mollicomata* and *M. sargentiana robusta* do not usually bud profusely while bearing heavy crops of fruit-cones. There appears to be a definite tendency for Asian Magnolias raised from seed to produce flowers of inferior size and colour during their first few flowering seasons. Mr. F. Julian Williams of Caerhays said, in his 1966 lecture to the Royal Horticultural Society: 'We have often here been disappointed in the flowers of new Magnolias for the first few years of their flowering. It seems that they take some time to settle down to flower properly. This is especially true of *sprengeri diva* and *mollicomata* seedlings. There is one *mollicomata* at Caerhays that has consistently caused vexation over the past seven years and, in fact, only shortage of staff has prevented it from being hewn down. But this year it flowered as freely and with flowers as good in quality as those of the old plants.'

The author recalls a similar instance at Trewithen, while being shown around the garden one March afternoon in 1956 by the late George Johnstone, shortly after publication of his wonderful monograph *Asiatic Magnolias in Cultivation*. Halting his battery-powered wheel chair opposite a fifteen-foot tree of *M. campbellii* subsp. *mollicomata*, which was displaying its first few flowers, he commented that it was not good enough for the prominent situation it occupied at the end of the main walk, and would have to be grubbed out.

I promptly asked him if I could have the tree, provided that I supplied the labour to lift it, and this was immediately agreed upon. But the weather during the subsequent weeks was abnormally wet, so that the ground became waterlogged and vehicle access across the adjacent field for loading the tree became impossible, even if labour could have been spared from our nurseries on one of the few fine days during the critical period for lifting. So the operation was postponed until the following spring when, lo and behold, the tree redeemed its lost prestige by producing finer flowers than its parent, and the owner very wisely decided to retain it in his collection and to give me a different and much taller tree instead.

This was successfully transplanted after cutting away all branches to the bare trunk, the top of which was also severely shortened. I think it most essential to prune severely large specimens which are transplanted in the spring, unless provision can be made for almost constant overhead irrigation during dry weather, until they come into full growth.

There is a tree of *M. campbellii*, growing in a sunny situation at Caerhays, which was raised from seed in 1926 and had not produced a single blossom by 1971, a lapse of forty-five years. By September 1970 the short, silvery-barked trunk of this tree had a girth of over 4 ft (1·2 m), the branches radiating widely from about 6 ft (2 m) above ground-level.

Seedlings raised from Magnolias of hybrid origin should normally show a considerable variation, but where they appear to be more or less identical to the mother plant they are probably *apomicts*, the product of *parthenogenesis*, originating from seeds produced without fertilization of the ovules. Apomicts are more obvious if they occur after controlled artificial pollinations have been carried out, when it is reasonably certain that only introduced pollen of known origin reaches the stigmas of the seed parent. Seedlings resulting from such attempted artificial fertilizations, which show only the characters of the mother plant, are almost certainly apomicts. This phenomenon is not uncommon among plants: it results in progeny resembling the mother plant, as in vegetative propagation. The several possible causes of *apogamy* are discussed under 'Magnolia Hybrids and Crosses' on p. 144.

It is advisable to harvest Magnolia seed as soon as the carpels on the fruit cones begin to split longitudinally to reveal the bright orange, scarlet or crimson seeds. Delay in harvesting may result in rapid losses to squirrels and other seed-eating rodents and birds. Usually the seeds hang for a while suspended from the carpels by fine thread-like appendages before falling to the ground; there they provide diet attractive to mice and other seed-eating mammals and birds. The freshly gathered fruit cones should be placed in trays out of reach of mice to allow them to ripen. When the cones have started to decompose the seeds should be extracted from the carpels and their fleshy coverings removed.

Then place the cleaned seeds in a glass of water and remove those which float. If seed is scarce these 'floaters' may be carefully checked and only the flat, scale-like ones discarded. The cleaned seeds may then be sown immediately, buried about $\frac{1}{2}$ in. (13 mm) in pots or shallow trays of well-drained seed compost. These require to be protected from mice and treated as described later. Any which do not germinate by midwinter may be retrieved and washed before placing in a small polythene or plastic bag, carefully labelled, and stored until March in the bottom of a domestic refrigerator where the temperature is normally 35 to 40 °F. (1·7 to 4·4 °C.).

Alternatively the cleaned or uncleaned seeds may be stored immediately in small polythene bags and kept in the lower section of a domestic refrigerator for about 100 days, at the end of which period they should be taken out and sown. They are still attractive to mice and will require protection until after germination. Seed so treated will usually germinate evenly and rapidly and deterioration of viability is much less than when stored without chilling.

The seeds may be sown $\frac{1}{2}$ in. (13 mm) deep, either singly in tiny pots, or 1 in. (2·5 cm) apart in seed trays of suitable compost, and watered-in with a fine rose. They should then be placed in a propagating frame with bottom heat, or covered over with sheets of glass or polythene after being placed over a source of artificial heat. Shading is beneficial and, once germination begins, it is advisable to wipe off moisture condensation from the inside of the glass each morning, and expose the seedlings gradually to more intense daylight to prevent them becoming drawn up and spindly. When germinated in trays the seedlings will have to be carefully lifted and potted into 2$\frac{1}{2}$ in. (6 cm) diameter pots when 1 or 2 in. (2·5 to 5 cm) high. They should be kept under glass and shaded for a few days until they recover from transplanting. Maintain a high humidity without over-watering the young plants.

If it is not possible to clean and treat the seeds soon after harvesting they may be stored in a refrigerator without removing the fleshy coating until February and then sown immediately after cleaning. Magnolia seeds tend to lose their viability after six months of storage in normal conditions. Sometimes germination is delayed for over a year from the date of sowing, but rapid germination is usually assured by vernalizing the seed for about 100 days at 35 to 40 °F. (1·7 to 4·4 °C.) in the manner described.

An example of delayed germination has been recorded at Kew with 200 seeds of *M. wilsonii* which, after remaining dormant for two years, then proved to be highly fertile.

Now let us follow briefly the development of the young seedling Magnolia from the time of its transfer from the seed tray or flat into a 2$\frac{1}{2}$ or 3 in. (6 or 7·5 cm) diameter pot. The seedlings' roots are soft and fragile so care must be taken to avoid tearing or bruising during this first potting operation. The compost must be light with a liberal proportion of moss peat or similar organic material. Avoid excessive firming as this will tend to retard growth.

Water sparingly at first, using a fine rose or intermittent mist, and shade the seedlings from intense sunlight for a week or two until growth commences. Even now they will prefer diffused or dappled light and a moist atmosphere. The foliage may scorch if the plants are watered overhead in bright sunlight once the roots have become too dry.

At all stages slugs, snails and wood-lice must be effectively controlled. They are very fond of young Magnolia leaves and find such moist environments much to their liking. Most pellet forms of slug bait seem to lose their effect rapidly under glass. The modern slug controls containing methiocarb are extremely economical and highly effective in use. Wood-lice hide by day and are controlled by pouring boiling water into their hiding places.

When the seedlings have attained a height of 6 in. (15 cm) or more they may be transferred to a cold frame to harden off; there the pots should be plunged in moist moss peat to avoid rapid fluctuations in soil moisture. If, however, there is adequate space for them under glass and they still have several months of the growing season ahead, they may be transferred to 4 or 4$\frac{1}{2}$ in. (10 to 11·5 cm) diameter pots, with somewhat firmer compost consolidation and kept in the same environment until the end of October, by which time some of them may have reached a foot or more in height.

It is possible to grow Magnolias successfully in quite a wide range of composts and containers, but in my experience they seem to prefer a soil-based one such as John Innes No. 2. While many growers, both amateur and professional, prefer one of the soil-less preparations, I do not think that these provide a sufficient range of tolerance in moisture retention and trace element supply to suit Magnolias. They are inclined to dry out rapidly and then become resistant to water absorption, often with fatal results. Also when used for potting taller specimens the plants tend to topple over easily, which leads to rapid drying out if not quickly rectified.

Magnolia seedlings may be planted out in a well-prepared bed for their second and third growing seasons. A sheltered site in partial shade is preferable to one which is fully exposed to prolonged sunlight and drying winds. Spring planting is recommended because the plants are then about to come into active growth and soil conditions are more likely to be ideal – that is not too wet and not too dry. Plant them about 9 in. (23 cm) apart in rows 12 in. (30·5 cm) apart taking care not to bury the root balls too deeply. Keep weeds under control by shallow hoeings taking care not to damage the fleshy roots, or by hand-weeding, and irrigate thoroughly during prolonged spells of dry weather.

The seedlings should put on a further foot or more of new growth during their second growing season. They may be left in the beds for a further year, repotted, or lined out in nursery rows for growing on. It is advisable to let them grow for four or five years before planting them out in their final quarters, by which time they should have attained a height of 4 to 5 ft (1·2 to 1·5 m) or more.

Some Magnolias begin to flower at a relatively early age from seed, but the majority require from ten to fifteen years and some over twenty years. It is for this reason that preference is usually given to plants raised vegetatively, from cuttings, layers, buds or grafts, since these represent horticultural prolongations of the selected tree or clone from which they were originally taken. In England the earliest recorded Magnolia cultivar is probably *M. grandiflora* 'Exmouth' (about 1720). Plants of this clone are still being propagated, although the original tree has long since perished (1794).

Vegetative Propagation

This entails the removal of a portion of the parent plant and inducing it to grow, either by forming its own roots, or by budding or grafting it on to another Magnolia. The resulting plant will have all the main characters of the parent with the possible exception of vigour, which may be controlled to some extent by the rootstock in the case of budded or grafted plants.

The four methods of vegetative propagation are: 1. Cuttings; 2. Layering; 3. Grafting; 4. Budding. Let us discuss each of these in turn.

1. Cuttings

Magnolias do not normally root from dormant hardwood cuttings, but they can be rooted from soft or half-ripe cuttings in the summer, if their rather exacting requirements are met. Where intermittent mist and adequate bottom heat are available, the softer the cuttings the more likely they are to root quickly. The amateur propagator, unable to fulfil the most exacting conditions and constant attention which these require, may be better advised to use half-ripe shoots. The precise state of growth indicated by 'half-ripe' is not easy to define, but it soon becomes recognizable to the propagator. Early batches of soft cuttings may be secured from plants established in containers which are transferred to a heated greenhouse in January or February to induce early growth. Usually two successive batches of soft cuttings may be taken from such stock plants, which are then returned to a sheltered standing ground as soon as the risk of a late spring frost has passed. They need to be kept fed and watered regularly throughout the summer to build up their stamina for their next forcing period the following season.

Material from Magnolias growing in the open is usually in suitable condition from late June to the middle of August. The earlier that cuttings can be rooted the better, since late propagations tend to perish during the first winter after having formed roots, though such losses are reduced where they are rooted in containers so that they may be transferred to a cold frame without any root disturbance, or where they can receive artificial warmth and light to compensate for shortening days and colder weather.

The cuttings are normally made without a heel of the old wood, indeed some propagators prefer to make the basal cuts internodal (i.e. midway between the leaves) rather than nodal, but in my experience there is no advantage in so doing. They may have from three to six leaves prior to the removal of the lower two or more to allow for insertion into the rooting medium.

While some expert propagators claim to shun the use of synthetic rooting hormones to induce rooting, I am in favour of dipping the freshly cut bases of the cuttings into a proprietary powder, of the grade recommended for soft cuttings, prior to insertion into the rooting medium. They should be watered-in with Captan fungicide immediately after insertion

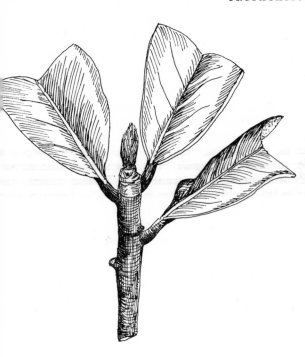

and this treatment should be repeated at fortnightly intervals. Dipping the cuttings into the solution prior to insertion appears to inhibit rooting.

The rooting medium may be pure sharp sand, or a mixture of moss peat and sand. Some growers use Vermiculite instead of sand, and I have noticed that American nurserymen now make extensive use of Perlite. Both are expanded inorganic materials, the former being derived from a micaceous mineral and the latter from a glassy rock of volcanic origin. They have the great advantage over sand in being relatively weightless, thus saving time and energy where large-scale propagation is entailed.

The propagation bench should have bottom heat supplied either by under-bench hot-water pipes, hot air ducts, or by electric soil-heating cables embedded in the drainage layer, to provide a constant temperature of 70 to 75 °F. (21 to 24 °C.) within the rooting medium.

The cuttings will require a constantly high humidity so that an intermittent mist unit is virtually essential, since every effort should be made, from the moment of removal from the stock plant, to prevent wilting. Larger-leaved Magnolias may have their leaves shortened by as much as half to reduce transpiration and prevent overcrowding on the cutting bench. A regular inspection should be made to remove all decaying leaves or dead cuttings, which might harbour a fungus capable of spreading on to live tissues. Slugs should be rigorously controlled with

methiocarb or they will wreak havoc with the cuttings. Those which shed their leaves often root afterwards, and then tend to remain dormant until the following spring.

Some Magnolias will root more readily than others, and probably none is impossible to propagate this way. The larger-leaved species present the biggest problem, though most of these could be persuaded, by judicious pruning, to form adventitious side shoots with relatively small leaves, which would be more suitable material for propagation.

Root initiation can be ascertained by periodic testing of the cuttings. As soon as good clusters of roots have emerged from their bases, they may be lifted and potted in the manner already described for seedlings, the size of pot selected being only just large enough to accommodate the young roots. Sometimes Magnolia cuttings form a basal callus with no sign of rooting and the amateur propagator is at a loss to know what to do with them. If they are left to their own resources they may ultimately die, but if parts of the callus are pared away with a sharp knife or razor-blade and the exposed surface dipped into a rooting hormone powder or liquid prior to replanting, there is every likelihood that the cutting will proceed to form a healthy root system.

I have seen cuttings of *M. × soulangiana* grow into plants over a foot high by early September, but more frequently they tend to consolidate their root development and delay further branch growth until the following season. The growing-on method is precisely the same as that advocated for seed-raised plants. They will usually tend to make slower and bushier growth than seedlings and will usually begin flowering at a much earlier age.

M. quinquepeta 'Nigra' has been reported to root from hardwood cuttings in a cold frame and it is quite possible that some other Magnolias will do likewise, but the resulting plants would probably take much longer to start into active growth than those raised from soft or half-ripe cuttings. Half-ripe or dormant Magnolia cuttings, which have been successfully rooted in cold frames or similar structures, are best left undisturbed for two years before they are lifted and potted, since earlier disturbance is often fatal. During this prolonged wait they must be kept free of slugs and weed competition and they will benefit considerably from a top-dressing of peat combined with a good compound fertilizer such as John Innes Base. In my experience Magnolias respond to fertilizers in the same manner as other woody plants, but if the soil is already adequately endowed with nitrogen, potash and phophates, then no noticeable improvement may result.

Some interesting notes entitled 'Propagation of Magnolia 'Freeman'' were contributed by Alfred J. Fordham, Propagator at the Arnold Arboretum, Harvard University, in *Newsletter of the American Magnolia Society* 8, 2 : 6 (1972) which reads: 'At the Arnold Arboretum we shut down our misting equipment during fall and winter and propagate either under polyethylene plastic or on open greenhouse benches. Cuttings of broad leaved evergreens such as Rhododendrons, Ilex, Kalmia, Pieris, etc., propagate well under polyethylene. Magnolia 'Freeman' also roots easily when handled in this manner. Cuttings about 8 inches [20·5 cm] long are taken in October or November before they are exposed to low temperature injury. A deep 1½ inch [4 cm] long wound is made at the base of the cuttings through the rind and into part of the wood. Shallow wounds can be unsatisfactory for they frequently heal over, leading to what is essentially an unwounded cutting. Next the cuttings are treated with a root-inducing substance. Various materials have proven satisfactory. Therefore, it seems practical to treat with the one simplest to use. This comprises a powder formulation of 8 mg of IBA in a gram of talc with the fungicide Thiram added at the rate of 15%. After treatment the cuttings are placed under polyethylene plastic in a rooting medium consisting of equal parts sand and Perlite with bottom heat at 75 °F. [24 °C]. In 10 to 12 weeks sufficient roots will have developed so the cuttings can be moved on. No dormancy is involved and plants about 18 to 20 inches [46 to 51 cm] tall can be expected after the first growing season.'

Perhaps it should be pointed out that this method refers to propagation within a greenhouse, the polyethylene (which resembles clear polythene) being used for additional coverage close to the tops of the cuttings.

2. Layering

There is no doubt that this method constitutes the oldest form of vegetative propagation for types of woody plants which do not root spontaneously from branches which have been inserted or driven into the ground (though such a phenomenon is on record for a Magnolia and is described in this book under *M. campbellii alba*).

At a very early date civilized man would have learned how to imitate nature by burying portions of the lower branches of trees and shrubs to induce the formation of roots. He would also have discovered that roots arose more readily where the buried sections of branches were cracked or scarred, and

this would have encouraged him to wound them intentionally at the lowest point of burial. There is good reason to believe that Chinese gardeners were the first to layer Magnolias over 1,000 years ago.

The layering of Magnolias has been extensively practised in nurseries, especially in Holland and Belgium, ever since the introduction of the Soulangiana hybrids in the 1830s, and it still continues. The professional method differs considerably from that of the amateur, who pegs or weighs down the tip of a low branch in an endeavour to persuade it to root. In the Boskoop nurseries the mother plants or stool bushes (on their own roots) are set out in plots of very heavily manured peaty soil at about 9 ft (2·7 cm) centres, sometimes in tight triple clusters. They are kept meticulously clear of weeds and are mounded in January with cow manure overlaid with leaf-mould.

The long whippy young shoots which develop are arched outward and downward in August or September, so that portions of them may be buried to induce root formation while the tips are bent upward, supported with bamboo canes. The stool bed method of layering was much used on the Veitch nursery at Coombe Wood in Surrey.

It is usually advisable to leave layers undisturbed for two years, during which time the control of weeds and slugs can present quite a costly problem. The rooted branches may be severed from the parent plant in the autumn but lifting may be postponed until late winter or early spring. It is always advisable to pot the layers and start them off under glass, where regular watering and a humid atmosphere will prevent the disastrous losses which can occur among field-planted layers during a spring drought.

The late W. T. Andrews, former manager of Veitch's Nurseries, Exeter, wrote: 'You will know of my reasoning that a layer taken from a mature tree could be expected to flower many years before one raised from seed, and, providing the parent is a good type, size and colour of the flower is a certainty, but plants raised from seed could, after waiting a very long time to flower, be very disappointing. We raised a good many plants from layers, but have never kept them long enough in the nursery to prove my reasoning to be correct or otherwise. At least one disadvantage of raising plants by layers is, it takes two years before new roots have formed, and meanwhile the layered shoots make a lot of topgrowth, and even with gradual severence from the parent plant, many layers fail to make good.'

He wrote that layered plants of their *M. × veitchii* often flowered within seven years of leaving the nursery, which puts the probable time from date of layering at ten years, if we allow one season for a layer to develop an independent root system in the nursery after severance from the mother tree.

A Veitch layer of *M. campbellii*, planted at Chyverton in 1953 when 3½ to 4 ft (about 1 m) high, did not begin to flower until 1967, when it produced its first two blossoms. In 1968 it increased its flower production to twenty-six blossoms, by which time it had attained a height of 25 ft (7·5 m). Again, assuming that the layer was not less than three years old when it left the nursery, the actual age at which it began to bloom was seventeen against an average of twenty-five years for a tree of this species raised from seed.

Sometimes it is desirable to layer a Magnolia which has no branches close to the ground. It then becomes necessary to introduce the rooting medium wherever a suitable branch happens to be growing. Extensive scaffoldings, to support boxes and tubs of soil, were erected around the trunks of some of the early introductions of *M. grandiflora* for the purpose of layering the higher branches and, in the days before the advent of garden hoses, some laborious water carrying must have been necessary to prevent them drying out in hot or windy weather. The Chinese practised this form of propagation more than 1,000 years ago and it became known in various parts of the world as *Chinese layerage, pot layerage, circumpostion, marcottage* and *gootee*, Hartman and Kester, *Plant Propagation* 406 (1961).

Aerial layering revived in popularity with the advent of polythene (polyethylene) film in the 1950s. It was widely used as a wrapping material to retain the moisture of sphagnum moss, with which the stems were girdled after slitting or ringing them at the points where root formation was desired. It was found difficult to prevent the moss becoming waterlogged in our wet and windy climate, so that root initials, produced in late autumn, often rotted before the spring.

It is doubtful whether the layering of Magnolias could be an economic proposition today unless the soil, climate and environment were ideal. Prices of five guineas were quoted for layered plants of the Exmouth Magnolia (*M. grandiflora*) in about 1760, while the gardener responsible for the operation received half a guinea. This seems to have been a very fair reward when one ponders what a guinea would have bought in those far-off days.

3. *Grafting*

This may be carried out from about mid August up to the time of growth commencement in May, pro-

vided a supply of suitable pot-established understocks is available, at any rate for the period between mid August and November. From then onward it is possible to bench-graft bare-rooted understocks which are much easier to handle and require less space in the propagating house than those which are in pots.

Better results are obtained from stocks which have become hardwooded, that is with brown bark towards the base of the main stem. This contains a thick layer of cambium, those actively dividing cells responsible for callusing and healing.

The same applies to the scions. Better results are from short woody spurs, which are closely ringed with petiolar scars, than from strong young shoots of the current season's growth, such as one would select for grafting apple trees. With late summer grafting it is usual to reduce the leaves on the scions to half their length to check transpiration.

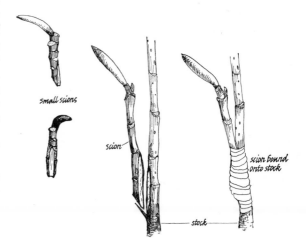

The stocks are side-grafted about 6 in. (15 cm) above root level without being headed back. There are several methods of cutting the scion to fit a complementary incision on the understock. Care should be taken to avoid exposing the pith so no attempt should be made to form an evenly-matched union diametrically or to try cleft or saddle grafting. If possible both edges of the cut surface on the scion should match those on the understock. It is advisable to seal the graft with molten paraffin wax (candle grease) or one of the proprietary grafting preparations before or after binding, since any moisture intrusion between the cut surfaces will lead to failure.

Immediately after waxing, the August-grafted stocks must be transferred to a propagating frame with bottom heat, preferably situated within the propagating house. They should be laid over on their sides with the scions uppermost to take advantage of the tendency of sap to flow to the highest point and also to allow the frame lights to be closed over the plants. The pots are usually covered over with moist peat to prevent the roots drying out and to help maintain a humid atmosphere. The plants require regular syringing combined with judicious shading and ventilating in an endeavour to prevent the leaves on the scions from wilting. Moisture condensation on the inside of the glass must be wiped off each morning to prevent dripping on to the scions. If the leaves wilt and shrivel without falling from the scion the graft has failed, whereas a normal shedding of the leaves is a good sign.

After a few weeks the ventilation is gradually increased, and shading dispensed with, until the lights may be raised, the pots stood upright, and failures removed for regrafting.

The late W. T. Andrews, for many years manager of the well known nursery firm of Robert Veitch and Sons, Exeter, Devon, was formerly their propagator and, over the years, he successfully grafted a considerable number of *M. campbellii*. Here he gives an account of his method and of what became of the mother tree when the firm transferred their nursery from near the centre of Exeter to the outskirts at Alphington.

'When I was a young man, I was fairly successful in grafting *Magnolia campbellii* on to stocks of *M. obovata* [now *M. hypoleuca*]. I found that stocks grown in small pots would become hard wooded, and that these were best suited for my purpose. About mid-August I would select short growths with a few rings at the base of the grafts to be, and when cutting I was careful not to cut into the pith of either the graft or the stock. At no time was I able to flood the market with plants produced by this method of propagation, but results were encouraging.

'On moving our nursery from New North Road, Exeter, to the village of Alphington, the question arose what to do with our thirty-foot-tall mother tree of *Magnolia campbellii*, and, after a good many debates on the subject, we finally decided that it would not survive the move. Soon after our decision against moving the tree, a gentleman from Ireland (I cannot remember his name) suggested that we give him the tree on the understanding that he paid us for lifting and loading on to a lorry he would send from Ireland. This was agreed. During the autumn of 1928/9 we heavily pruned the tree, dug a trench around and as far as possible under the tree, boxed it, and, on the arrival of the lorry, and the new owner of the tree, hauled it out of the hole and

on to the carefully placed lorry; no small undertaking this, but it was successfully done without damage to the tree, or ball of earth so important to its survival. For a short time the lorry driver and his mate were loath to leave with their perilous load, but after a little talk moved off. I believe there had to be considerable lopping of branches to enable the tree to pass under low bridges and along narrow roads. In spite of severe treatment the tree lived, and in a short time put on new growths. The cost of preparing and loading the tree amounted to £100, so by the time it reached its destination it must have cost a fairly large sum of money.

'Our Irish friend was a keen collector of rare trees and shrubs, and I have been told that his garden was most interesting. Unfortunately he died before he was able to see the full beauty of our gift to him. On his death, the estate was broken up, and his collection of unusual trees and shrubs was destroyed to make room for new development.'

Inarching or Grafting by Approach is a method occasionally adopted where other methods are either impracticable or have failed. It is usually performed while both the understock and the mother plant are in active growth. The understock should be established in a pot or larger container so that it may be conveniently placed for the operation. The intended points of union having been decided upon, thin slices of bark are removed from each surface, the cuts carefully matched, then bound fairly tightly together and sealed with wax. After a few weeks the ties should be loosened or renewed to allow for the expansion which accompanies callusing.

The understock must be kept well watered during dry weather and, when the union has been accomplished, all unwanted portions may be cut away gradually. The point of severance from the mother plant must be several inches (centimetres) below the union so that a sizeable snag remains to be pruned away, some time after the scion has started into growth, nurtured by the root system of the understock. The final severence is usually best delayed until the end of the following growing season, about the time of normal leaf fall. The grafted portion should be adequately supported with a cane or stake and any long branches shortened to reduce initial demands upon the resources of the understock and to encourage vigorous growth the following summer.

Understocks for Grafting: the type of Magnolia used as understocks does not appear to be important, as far as results are concerned, provided they are well ripened or hardwooded at the base where the grafting operation has to be performed. This usually pertains to three- or four-year seedlings or cutting-raised plants.

It is, of course, advisable to graft tree forms on to understocks of similar ultimate stature, but there is no evidence, though some surmise, that closely related stocks and scions might lead a more harmonious existence than where a Magnolia of one section is grafted or budded upon the roots of another more distantly related species.

In practice it has been observed that the two Japanese species *M. kobus* and *M. hypoleuca* provide good understocks, while *M. acuminata* is favoured in America. These three species tend to produce stout bark-covered stems on three-year seedlings whereas Himalayan Magnolias usually take a year longer. In Cornwall *M. sargentiana* var. *robusta* provides a reliable source of understocks. Understocks which have been grown in relatively poor soil in an open situation usually produce better results than those which are over vigorous. Clearly the ultimate choice depends upon the availability of suitable seedlings, rather than the species which they represent, and this, in turn, is reflected on which species are regular seed producers, unless a reliable source of imported seed or nursery-grown understocks can be found.

The late Charles S. Sargent, founder-director of the Arnold Arboretum at Boston, once wrote that *M. virginiana* did better on *M. acuminata* than on its own roots. There is a considerable planting of *M. virginiana* at the Arboretum between the administration building and the public roadway, just inside the main entrance to the gardens. When I saw them one hot afternoon in late September 1970 they were aglow with scarlet-seeded fruit-cones, but I do not recollect mention of any being grafted plants, when I searched through the Magnolia section of the Arboretum's records.

Bud-grafting or *Chip-budding* is an adaptation of budding which is more akin to grafting. It has the advantage over budding and stem-grafting in that it may be practised at almost any time of the year, as and when propagating material becomes available.

This technique has been developed in America over several decades by fruit- and nut-tree propagators. It is particularly useful for propagating hardwood material, when the bark is tight and when growth conditions are unsuitable for orthodox 'T'-budding. There is probably no closed season for this type of propagation provided any understocks, chip-budded in late autumn or winter, can be placed under glass to avoid the lifting of buds by severe freezing.

In chip-budding the scion is reduced to a small piece of wood containing only one bud. First a chip of bark is removed from a smooth section between two nodes near the base of the stock and then replaced with a matching scion containing a dormant growth bud from the mother plant. Both chips are cut out in the same manner. The scion is cut into just below the bud, cutting downwards through the wood at an angle of about 45°, taking care not to cut into the central pith. The second cut is started about $\frac{1}{2}$ in. (13 cm) above the bud and goes inward and downward to meet the first cut.

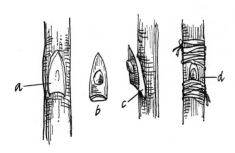

With a little practice on some less valuable material it soon becomes possible to make well-matched cuts, so that good close fits are obtained when the chip buds are transferred to the corresponding excisions on the understocks. The 'transplanted' buds should be tied in and either waxed over or covered with a polythene wrap for about three weeks, or waxed before being tied in, but the binding should be severed before constriction occurs. Ordinary paraffin wax (candle grease) is readily available and excellent for use in all kinds of grafting; it should be heated to a liquid condition and applied with a brush. As with other methods of side-grafting the stock is not cut back until a successful union is completed.

To achieve rapid callusing, transfer the bud-grafted stocks to a humid atmosphere at 70 to 80 °F. (21 to 27 °C.) for two to three weeks. On a small scale this might be achieved by laying them on their sides in a box with the scion buds uppermost and covering them completely with moist peat or sawdust. The box should then be placed where it can heat up to the desired temperature already mentioned. On removal any new shoots which may have sprouted from the understocks should be rubbed off.

Autumn and winter-budded stocks are not headed back until the spring while spring-budded ones are headed back as soon as a good union has been established. In either case any shoots arising subsequently from the understocks should be rubbed out as soon as they appear.

The University of Illinois at Urbana has published a leaflet on 'Chip-Budding'. Prof. J. C. McDaniel of the University's Horticultural Department tells me that he prefers to chip-bud in August or September, leaving a portion of the leaf blade attached to the petiole, and to overwrap the tied-in bud-piece with polythene film. To date this method has proved somewhat disappointing here, possibly because our August–September temperatures are much lower than those experienced in the eastern States. We have had good results from the brief 'sweat-box' treatment advised for later propagations.

Prof. McDaniel spent his early years on state research and experimental work in the fruit- and nut-growing industry in America and has had considerable experience with this type of propagation for a varied range of woody plants. He showed me many examples of his craft when I visited Urbana in September 1970. In one instance, on a farm several miles from Urbana, he had literally 'farmed out' some buds of rare Asian Magnolias by inserting them on to strong water-shoots springing, about 10 ft (3 m) up, from the trunk of a veteran *M. acuminata*. In another instance he had formed his own Magnolia 'bank' by chip-budding quite a number of new acquisitions on to a sizeable *M.* × *soulangiana*, with the idea of maintaining a supply of propagating material for future use.

4. Budding

Magnolias are extensively propagated by budding in the open field by growers in Japan and South Korea, in a manner similar to that practised for large-scale rose production in other parts of the world. Seeds of *M. kobus* are drilled about 3 in. (7·5 cm) apart in rows 6 to 9 in. (15 to 23 cm) apart. Dormant growth buds are cut from half-ripened shoots off the mother trees and the leaf blades removed before the buds are inserted into vertical 'T' cuts on the north sides of the stems of two-year seedlings, during warm weather at the end of September. The buds are wrapped with polythene strips and banked up with soil to prevent sun scorch. If the petiole has been shed by autumn the bud has taken, if it dries and shrivels the bud has failed to take. In the following March the stocks are headed back to a point close to the successful unions before the 'buds' begin to swell. Growths of 3 to 4 ft (91 to 120 cm) or more during the first season are not unusual. The ground is kept at a very high peak of fertility and the summers are very hot – too hot, I am told, for some of the Himalayan Magnolias such as *M. campbellii*.

Attempts to imitate this process on our own nurseries have resulted in complete failure even when the understocks were bedded out under glass. I am of the opinion that the much higher temperature and sunnier climate is a controlling factor.

An early account of some successful propagations of Magnolias by budding was contributed by Gerald Mundey in an article in the *Journal of the Royal Horticultural Society* 77, 12 (1952). Mundey used seedlings of *M. kobus* and *M. salicifolia* as understocks after establishing them in 4½ in. (11·5 cm) pots. He recorded no instances of incompatibility between these stocks and a considerable range of bud material. He found that it was important to avoid wetting the binding of the 'eyes' and to keep the budded stocks well ventilated until the petioles were shed, after which he cut the ties and renewed them.

Mundey discussed the considerable time taken for his Magnolia propagations to reach flowering maturity and suggested that a required carbon/nitrogen ratio had to be reached before flower bud initiation could occur.

Pests and Diseases of Magnolias

Pests which attack Magnolias are fortunately few indeed but it should be stressed here that the author's experience relates mainly to the milder parts of the British Isles.

Their aromatic sap appears to be unpalatable to most animals and insects, although rabbits and hares might be tempted to test the bark and young shoots when their normal diet is buried by frozen snow.

Moles and occasionally field-mice and ants, have been known to jeopardize recently-planted Magnolias by burrowing beneath their roots and thereby loosening and drying out the soil. Moles might well be attracted by earthworms which would be taking advantage of the moist decayed vegetation supplied by the mulch, which should be a routine post-planting procedure. It is therefore sound practice, during dry spells, occasionally to consolidate the soil around their roots, since this may tend to become loose and spongy, especially where bulky organic materials such as leaf-mould, peat or composted refuse have been dug in prior to planting. It is a good idea to water copiously the compacted area prior to raking over with loose soil or mulching material

Fortunately the rapidly spreading grey squirrel, which strips the bark from the upper branches of so many of our woodland trees, does not appear to relish the aromatic bark of Magnolias.

In some Cornish gardens long-tailed tits have been observed attacking the opening buds of *M. campbellii*, presumably in search of nectar. But in this they must be disappointed for, with the exception of the tropical *M. coco*, Magnolia flowers have no nectar glands, but some of the floral organs contain sugary secretions.

Damage to the foliage of young plants may be caused by slugs and snails which can be readily controlled by a small sprinkle of methiocarb. Several nocturnal insects are likely to perforate or eat the margins of the leaves and the precise pest is generally difficult to establish. Vine weevil beetles, earwigs and even wood-lice are suspect in English gardens and may be controlled by sprinkling an insecticidal powder on the foliage, the main stems, and around the bases of the plants. In some gardens the buds of *M. sieboldii* are perforated by weevils.

While in America I was shown an isolated attack of the giant Magnolia scale, an insect so large in comparison the forms met with in this country, that it could be readily destroyed by crushing. I have not come across scale insects on Magnolias here though they can become a pest on camellias both in the open and under glass and, as they appear to be vulnerable to insecticides only during the brief mobile periods of their life cycle, they need carefully planned and consistent control measures.

It is probable that mealy-bug would attack Magnolias grown perpetually under glass. A simple method of control is to dab paraffin or methylated spirits on to the mealy covering beneath which the insects are hidden.

A beetle, which normally restricts its attention to coniferous trees, has caused considerable damage to a grafted specimen of the Purple Lanarth Magnolia at Trewithen, by depositing its eggs in the soft aromatic bark which is peculiar to this particular group of *M. campbellii*. The larvae burrow into the cambium layer which they proceed to destroy, either by exuding some toxic liquid, or by introducing a disease organism in the manner of the beetle which is responsible for the spread of Dutch Elm Disease. The first sign of damage was the discharge of a black juice from the bark which had begun to separate from the wood. A similar occurrence close to ground-level, which was noticed several years earlier, had been ascribed to a form of canker, but laboratory tests had subsequently proved negative. Head gardener Michael Taylor had carefully excised the area of dead bark, and painted the exposed wood with Arbrex wound dressing.

The fresh attack was much more extensive, extending from eye-level upward, and he noticed that tiny well-spaced shot-holes had penetrated the bark and outer layer of the wood. The entire bark and cambium tissues within the attacked area had been killed and within some of the tiny larvae tunnels were live larvae which were sent away for

identification. They were later named as *Trypodendron lineatum* (Olivier). A careful search has failed to reveal similar damage to any other tree in this extensive collection of Magnolias.

Greenhouse red spider (*Tetranychus telarius*) can cause considerable damage to the leaves, especially of deciduous Magnolias, where grown under glass. The symptoms are a discoloration of the leaves which assume an unhealthy sulphur-yellow colour, sometimes with tiny rust-red spots. The responsible insects are microscopic and operate entirely on the undersurfaces of the leaves, where they are largely protected and concealed by fine web-like coverings which they manufacture, as they feed by sucking the sap from the leaf veins. Only the adults are red, the younger spiders ranging from cream to yellow and orange according to age. They are visible only with the aid of a lens.

Because of the extent of their natural protections it is very difficult to eradicate them by spraying, though the modern systemic insecticides can be extremely effective. Where fumigation is feasible a smoke generator or electrically heated fumigator is recommended.

Diseases affecting Magnolias are far fewer than the pests. Die-back of shoots and branches can be attributed generally to a natural overcrowding of the branches, combined with the relatively large size of most Magnolia leaves, which mask the light from competing growths close beneath them. Secondary fungal organisms soon prey upon these overcrowded growths and may resemble a primary infection.

Leaf Spot, sometimes spreading over the surface of isolated leaves in more-or-less concentric rings, has been attributed to the common Grey Mould fungus (*Botrytis cinerea*), also *Phyllosticta* species. Although primarily a saprophytic organism, in some cases it behaves as a pathogen, particularly if it gains entry through an area of mechanical cell damage such as that caused by a hailstone. It is only likely to become apparent in humid climates and does not normally require treatment, though the removal of infected leaves is good hygiene. The dithiocarbamate sprays such as Zineb are now the routine control of such organisms.

Cankers, occasionally met with in Magnolias, are generally attributed to infection by *Phomopsis* species, but there is conflicting evidence as to whether it is primary or whether it follows mechanical damage. These problems rarely occur where the basic requirements of fertile, not-too-alkaline soil, adequate drainage and suitable climatic conditions prevail.

Magnolia Chromosome Counts

In Magnolias the base or X chromosome number is 19.

Some are *diploid* (two fold) with 2n = 38 chromosomes in their somatic cells.

Others are:

triploid (three fold) with 2n = 57 chromosomes.
tetraploid (four fold) with 2n = 76 chromosomes.
pentaploid (five fold) with 2n = 95 chromosomes.
hexaploid (six fold) with 2n = 114 chromosomes.
heptaploid (seven fold) with 2n = 133 chromosomes.
octoploid (eight fold) with 2n = 152 chromosomes.

A few exhibit odd levels of ploidy.

A *haploid* contains only half the number of chromosomes found in the parent.

SPECIES	SECTION	COUNT
*acuminata	Tulipastrum	2n = 76
*ashei see macrophylla		
campbellii	Yulania	2n = 114
*cordata see acuminata		
cylindrica	Buergeria	2n = 38
dawsoniana	Yulania	2n = 114
delavayi	Gwillimia	2n = 38
denudata see heptapeta		
*fraseri	Rytidospermum	2n = 38
globosa	Oyama	2n = 38
*grandiflora	Theorhodon	2n = 114

SPECIES	SECTION	COUNT
heptapeta (denudata)	Yulania	2n = 114
hypoleuca (obovata)	Rytidospermum	2n = 38
kobus	Buergeria	2n = 38
liliflora see quinquepeta		
*macrophylla (including ashei)	Rytidospermum	2n = 38
mollicomata (campbellii)	Yulania	2n = 114
nitida	Gynopodium	2n = 38
obovata see hypoleuca		
officinalis	Rytidospermum	2n = 38
parviflora see sieboldii		
*pyramidata	Rytidospermum	2n = 38
quinquepeta (liliflora)	Tulipastrum	2n = 76
rostrata	Rytidospermum	2n = 38
salicifolia	Buergeria	2n = 38
sargentiana	Yulania	2n = 114
sargentiana var. robusta	Yulania	2n = 114
*schiediana	Theorhodon	2n = 114
sieboldii	Oyama	2n = 38
sinensis	Oyama	2n = 38
sprengeri	Yulania	2n = 114
stellata	Buergeria	2n = 38
*tripetala	Rytidospermum	2n = 38
*virginiana	Magnoliastrum	2n = 38
wilsonii	Oyama	2n = 38

(* Denotes American species, the others are Asian in origin)

MAGNOLIA CHROMOSOMES
as seen at cell division (× 1500)
by Dr. John Wilkinson
(OPPOSITE)

1. *M.* × *soulangiana.* A typical tetraploid with 2n = 76 chromosomes
2. *M. quinquepeta* 'Nigra' showing a diploid chromosome count (2n = 38)
3. *M. quinquepeta* 'Nigra' showing a triploid chromosome count (2n = 57)
4. *M. quinquepeta* 'Nigra' showing a tetraploid chromosome count (2n = 76)

N.B. Drawings 2, 3 and 4 show different levels of ploidy observed in the same plant of *M. quinquepeta* 'Nigra'.

CYTOLOGICAL CONSIDERATIONS

Contributed by Dr. John Wilkinson Ph.D., F.L.S., lately Senior Lecturer in Biological Sciences,
University of Exeter

As with the great majority of dicotyledons, especially the taxonomically more primitive tree groups, the chromosomes of *Magnoliaceae* are relatively small in size, while their number in each nucleus tends to be large. In the first place, whereas most flowering plants have a base chromosome number between 7 and 12, that for this family is exceptionally high, namely 19. This particular number is but rarely found in other families of flowering plants, other notable examples being the willows and poplars (*Salicaceae*). Again, comparatively few Magnolias are merely diploids, with 38 chromosomes in their normal vegetative (somatic) cells; the majority appear to be tetraploids, with 76 chromosomes, or hexaploids, with 114, while not a few exhibit odd degrees of polyploidy, being for example pentaploid with 5×19 chromosomes. Indeed, some appear to exhibit higher orders of polyploidy than hexaploid, for septaploids and octoploids have already been reported within the Soulangiana complex (Santamour).

Thus, critical study of Magnolia chromosomes, even in connection with so fundamental a matter as their number, requires a certain amount of technical sophistication, specialized equipment and patience. Certain current investigators appear to rely exclusively for their chromosome counts upon the maturing pollen mother-cells. These are pressed out from anthers at a particular stage of development, assessed by trial and error, fixed and stained in suitable fluids (e.g. aceto-carmine), then examined under a high power of the microscope ($\times 500$ or even $\times 1000$ magnification). An obvious disadvantage here is that anthesis (anther development) occurs for a very limited period during each season, so that the available time for the collection of material is necessarily short. Again, the pattern of chromosome behaviour, especially as it involves the pairing of homologous chromosomes within the nuclei of the dividing reproductive cells, is more complicated than is the case in nuclei within ordinary vegetative tissue, so that there is here more likelihood of error than if one observed the nuclear divisions (mitosis) which appear in normal somatic cell-multiplication in, for example, actively dividing root tips.

Traditionally, somatic chromosome numbers have usually been studied in growing organs such as these, fixed *in situ* in carefully balanced fluid mixtures which yield a clear and life-like 'fixation image', then stained in dyes which pick out chromosomes and other nuclear contents. In procedures widely employed up to about 1940, fixed root tips, after a fairly lengthy process involving dehydration and infiltration leading to embedding in wax, were finely sectioned upon a microtome. The sections, of thickness of from 12 to 15 *thousandths* of a millimetre, were then affixed to slides, and stained after removal of the wax. This technique, though capable of beautiful results, was tedious and time-consuming, and became superseded by 'smear' methods in which the fixed root tips were macerated (i.e. the walls binding individual cells were broken down) and stained in a fluid such as acetic acid saturated with a powerful dye, carmine; the tips were then spread out upon a slide under a very thin cover-glass, whereupon dividing nuclei exhibiting chromosomes in a suitable stage for counting could readily be obtained by the trained investigator. This method obviously depends upon the availability of actively elongating root tips and, while many plants (e.g. willows) can readily be induced to produce roots from cuttings, some genera are notoriously difficult in this respect. Oaks and Magnolias are examples of the latter category.

In consequence, the writer decided to employ a method developed during the past decade in which the tips of young unfolding leaves or growths buds were employed as the source of dividing cells. Leaf-tips of growing leaves, rich in meristematic zones (containing actively dividing somatic cells), were collected on warm, humid days when extension of the tips was at its maximum, which proved to be from approximately mid morning to mid afternoon. About $\frac{1}{8}$ in. (3 mm) from each tip was removed

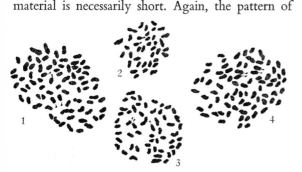

with forceps and placed without delay into phials of freshly mixed fixing fluid consisting of 3 parts of absolute ethyl alcohol to 1 part of propionic acid (an organic acid higher in the fatty series than acetic) saturated with ferric acetate. Each phial or fixing tube contained about 5 ccs (ml) of freshly mixed fixative, and could accept up to ten tips from the specimen plant, whereupon the tube was carefully corked to prevent evaporation and then labelled. The fixed leaf-tips can be conveniently stored in the tubes of fixing fluid for several weeks if kept cool, and up to six months if chilled at 2 to 4 °C. (35·5 to 39 °F.) without deterioration of the 'fixation images' within the cells.

'Squash' preparations were made by immersing each leaf-tip in a macerating/staining fluid consisting of 9 drops of concentrated aceto-carmine to 1 drop of normal hydrochloric acid contained in a watch-glass, which was then cautiously warmed over the flame of a spirit lamp until a stream of bubbles appeared from the leaf-tip. This was cooled in fresh aceto-carmine for twenty minutes, mounted in a drop of the same fluid on a slide, covered with a thin cover-slip, then pressed out into a thin layer by applying a firm rounding pressure via the stub-end of a matchstick. If required for immediate study the preparations were temporarily sealed by running nail-varnish around the edges of the cover-slip; when permanent preparations were required the cover-slips were allowed to separate from the slides by immersion overnight in absolute alcohol, then the smears were mounted afresh in a proprietary fluid, Euparal. The 'temporary' preparations usually gave the clearest pictures of dividing chromosomes, as some shrinkage inevitably accompanied their subjection to the more drastic effects of the fluids used to make the preparations permanent.

Chromosome counts were made on the microscope from selected nuclei at metaphase of the somatic division under $\frac{1}{2}$ in. (2 mm) oil immersion objective, by means of a *camera lucida*. This is an attachment which, by means of a reflecting prism, superimposes the observer's paper and pencil over the image of the 'plate' of chromosomes as seen in the field of the microscope, so that the position of each chromosome in the somatic metaphase plate can be recorded as a dot or a line.

There is nothing unusual about the shapes and sizes of the chromosomes in the range of Magnolia cultivars under investigation. The chromosomes are cylindrical, with rounded ends, and possess regions of constriction where the width is a little less than normal. These regions are generally regarded as the positions of attachment of the so-called spindle-fibres, which are thought to be involved in the process whereby longitudinally split daughter-chromosomes separate from one another during the division of the nucleus (somatic mitosis). Each individual chromosome has a width of about one-quarter to one-third of a micron (1μ, i.e. one micron, one-thousandth part of a millimetre), and the chromosomes are mostly between 1 and 2μ in length. Thus, each chromosome is roughly the same size as a typical rod-shaped bacterium. Many plants and animals have chromosomes of this order of size; this is seen for example in the chromosomes of willows and poplars (Wilkinson, *Salix, Populus,* 1944), *Cymbidium* orchids, and in fact in many mammals including Man.

It is the base number (19) of chromosomes in *Magnolia* which is somewhat uncommon, being higher than the average. Most plants have a gametic (haploid) number between 7 and 12, so that the somatic (body-cell) number is 14 to 24. This applies to normal diploid species; polyploids, which occur in nature, and which appear with particular frequency under cultivation, have multiples of these numbers as their chromosome counts, and tetraploid strains are probably the commonest, though of course hexaploids and higher polyploids are quite well known.

The 19-base is found in willows and poplars (*Salicaceae*) and some of the most primitive naturally occurring willow species such as the purple osier, and the creeping willow of the sand-dunes, are diploids with 38 somatic chromosomes. The same seems to be true of the primitive Magnolias in the wild.

Plant breeders have often made crosses which yielded new and desirable forms from wild diploid and tetraploid species or strains but the resulting triploids usually turn out to be highly sterile; however, further types derived from these, by design or even by spontaneous occurrence (e.g. the famous *Primula* × *kewensis*) have resulted in the establishment of higher polyploids, such as pentaploids or hexaploids, or even types with odd chromosome complements such as have been reported for the *soulangiana* complex in Magnolia. It would seem that the complicated range of segregates in the complex known as *soulangiana* has mostly arisen from the chance crossing and back-crossing which has occurred for several centuries, first in the Far East and later in Europe.

During recent decades the producers of new strains, both of crop plants and of horticultural varieties, have employed methods more sophisticated than hybridization and subsequent selection, as, for example, by irradiation and treatment with various drugs like colchicine, which may readily modify the chromosome number and in the future there will doubtless be much scope for this type of treatment in the case of *Magnolia*. The entire or even partial doubling of the chromosome complement in strains of odd polyploid number such as triploids or pentaploids is often accompanied by greatly increased fertility observable in the resultant types, and manoeuvrings in this direction on the part of breeders will greatly extend the potential range of desirable cultivars for the future.

The assemblage of strains of hybrid origin designated as *soulangiana*, reputedly derived since 1820 from a not-quite-completely sterile natural cross between *heptapeta* and *quinquepeta* grown by Soulange-Bodin at Fromont, near Paris, is of particular interest to the cytologist. Whitaker (1933) first reported certain cultivars as tetraploid (2n = 76), while Janaki Ammal (1953) counted 'several varieties' as pentaploids (2n = 95) and noted one in particular, 'Lennei', as being hexaploid with 2n = 114 chromosomes. Further investigation by Santamour (1970) has demonstrated even higher orders of polyploidy than these for some of the *soulangiana* cultivars; thus, 'Lennei' and 'Grace McDade' were found to be septaploid (2n = 133) while another, 'Lombardy Rose' was, remarkably, intermediate between a hexaploid and a septaploid and was described by him as '6·5 ploid' (2n = 123). One octoploid cultivar was also reported.

The present writer has recorded various *soulangiana* types as being (i) triploid, this specimen, from the Hatherly garden at the University of Exeter, was probably closely related to the original sterile first-generation hybrid between *heptapeta* and *quinquepeta*; (ii) tetraploid, in the case of well-established specimens in Treseder's Nursery at Truro (drawing 1); (iii) pentaploid, a specimen from Lanarth, thus verifying one of Janaki Ammal's findings; (iv) hexaploid, a specimen of 'Rustica Rubra' from Chyverton[*]; and, finally, (v) specimens of 'Picture', from established plants (hexaploid), and from more recent imports from Japan which appear to be septaploid or even octoploid.

It will be appreciated that examination of complements possessing high numbers of very small chromosomes must necessarily involve a greater margin of possible error. The specimens of 'Picture' were large and vigorous, exhibiting the kind of luxuriance often associated with higher polyploid cultivars. A septaploid form could obviously have arisen from the fusion of a triploid gamete from *heptapeta* with an unreduced gamete (tetraploid) from some such type as *quinquepeta*.

Finally, the results obtained from a very long-established specimen of *quinquepeta* 'Nigra' growing in the garden of a hotel in Truro, may well have special significance when taken in conjunction with the facts just reported. The specimen in question, having a dark-purple flower and a variously crinkled leaf reminiscent of 'toadskin' varieties in other cultivated plants, displayed an inconstant number of chromosomes as seen in different regions of the preparations obtained by leaf-tip smear methods. The counts varied from diploid through triploid to tetraploid (drawings 2–4) and included also odd numbers of chromosomes which could not be related to any particular degree of ploidy. It seemed to the writer that this specimen might well have been chimerical in origin, thus possibly incorporating in its structure tissue-layers from the various ancestral forms that preceded it; it must at the same time be recalled that for thirty years it has been realized that some cultivated plants (e.g. wheats) occasionally show some variability of chromosome number within a given individual. Thus, though it is generally true that the number of chromosomes in all the somatic nuclei of a given organism is constant, this cannot be taken as a rigid and unchangeable law. We must therefore conclude that if a single specimen of a long-established *soulangiana* type can undergo such variability within its tissues, it is not surprising that cultivars such as 'Picture', evidently of rather high polyploid constitution, and also some which Santamour has reported, appear to be so variable in their chromosome make-up.

References

JANAKI AMMAL, E. K., 1953, 'The Race History of Magnolias', *Indian Journal of Genetics and Plant Breeding* 12 : 82–92

SANTAMOUR, F, S., JR., 1970, 'Cytology of Magnolia Hybrids 11', *Morris Arboretum Bulletin* 21, 3 : 58–61

WHITAKER, T. W., 1933, 'Chromosome Number and Relationship in the Magnoliales', *Journal of the Arnold Arboretum* 14 : 376–85

WILKINSON, J., 1944, 'The Cytology of *Salix* in Relation to its Taxonomy', *Annals of Botany* 8 : 269–84

---

[*] A chromosome count of ± 156 has been made from 'Rustica Rubra' at Kew. (Author)

A.G.M.   Award of Garden Merit
A.M.   Award of Merit
B.C.   Botanical Certificate
C.C.   Cultural Commendation
F.C.C.   First Class Certificate
P.C.   Preliminary Commendation

Magnolia:

'Ann Rosse' (assumed *heptapeta* × *sargentiana* var. *robusta*) A.M. (Nymans 1973)

'Caerhays Surprise' (*campbellii* subsp. *mollicomata* × *quinquepeta* 'Nigra') A.M. (F. J. Williams 1973)

campbellii F.C.C. (Gumbleton, R. Veitch 1903)

campbellii alba F.C.C. (C. Williams 1951)

campbellii 'Betty Jessel'
   A.M. (Jessel 1972)
   F.C.C. (Jessel 1975)

campbellii 'Charles Raffill'
   P.C. (Windsor 1959)
   A.M. (Windsor 1963)
   F.C.C. (Windsor 1966)

campbellii 'Kew's Surprise' F.C.C. (F. J. Williams 1967)

campbellii subsp. *mollicomata* see *mollicomata*

'Charles Coates' (*sieboldii* × *tripetala*)
   P.C. (Kew 1962)
   A.M. (Windsor 1973)

conspicua see *heptapeta*

cylindrica A.M. (Windsor 1963)

dawsoniana A.M. (M. P. Williams 1939)

dawsoniana 'Chyverton' A.M. (N. T. Holman 1974)

delavayi
   F.C.C. (J. Veitch 1913)

denudata see *heptapeta*

fraseri A.M. (S. Clarke 1948)

globosa A.M. (Stair 1931)

grandiflora 'Exmouth' A.G.M. (1969)

grandiflora 'Goliath'
   A.M. (Preston 1931)
   F.C.C. (Roberts 1951)
   A.G.M. (1969)

heptapeta
   A.G.M. (1936)
   F.C.C. (1968)
   A.M. as *M. heptapeta* Veitch's var. (= 'Purple Eye') (S. Clarke 1926)

× *highdownensis* (assumed *sinensis* × *wilsonii*)
   A.M. (Stern 1937)

hypoleuca (*obovata*) F.C.C. (J. Veitch 1893)

× *kewensis* (*kobus* × *salicifolia*)
   A.M. (Kew 1952)

kobus
   A.G.M. (1936)
   A.M. (Aberconway 1942)

kobus borealis A.M. (Price 1948)

kobus 'Nippon' A.M. (Collingwood Ingram 1969)

liliflora 'Nigra' (× *soulangiana* 'Nigra') see *quinquepeta*

× *loebneri* (*kobus* × *stellata*) A.G.M. (1969)

× *loebneri* 'Leonard Messel'
   P.C. (Nymans 1954)
   A.M. (Nymans 1955)
   F.C.C. (Nymans 1969)

× *loebneri* 'Neil McEacharn'
   P.C. (Windsor 1966)
   A. M. (Windsor 1967)

macrophylla F.C.C. (J. Veitch 1900)

'Michael Rosse' A.M. (Nymans 1968)

mollicomata F.C.C.(Aberconway 1939)

mollicomata 'Mary Williams' A.M. (C. Williams 1954)

mollicomata 'Lanarth' F.C.C. (M. P. Williams 1947)

nitida A.M. (F. J. Williams 1966)

obovata see *hypoleuca*

officinalis Pink Form A.M. (Windsor 1971) [Subject to verification of name, probably a form of *M. hypoleuca*]

'Osaka' A.M. (Gauntlett 1902)

'Princess Margaret' F.C.C. (Windsor 1973)

quinquepeta (*liliflora*) 'Nigra'
   A.M. (Cuthbert 1907)
   A.G.M. (1969)

rostrata B.C. (Bolitho 1938)
   A.M. (Hillier 1974)

salicifolia
   A.M. (Rothschild 1927)
   A.G.M. (1941)
   F.C.C. (Windsor 1962)

sargentiana F.C.C. (Messel 1935)

sargentiana var. *robusta* F.C.C. (Aberconway 1947)

sieboldii (*parviflora*)
   F.C.C. (J. Veitch 1894)
   A.G.M. (1935)

sinensis
  A.M. (Bodnant 1927)
  F.C.C. (R. Veitch 1931)
  A.G.M. (1969)
× soulangiana (heptapeta × quinquepeta) A.G.M.
  (1932)
× soulangiana 'Alba Superba' A.G.M. (1969)
× soulangiana 'Brozzonii'
  F.C.C. (Rothschild 1929)
  A.G.M. (1969)
× soulangiana 'Lennei'
  F.C.C. (Paul 1863)
  A.G.M. (1969)
× soulangiana
'Norbetii' A.M. (Pilkington 1960)
× soulangiana 'Picture' A.M. (Russell 1969)
× soulangiana 'Rustica Rubra' ('Rubra')
  A.M. (Pilkington 1960)
  A.G.M. (1969)
sprengeri A.M. (Aberconway 1942 and 1947)
sprengeri 'Claret Cup' A.M. (Aberconway 1963)

sprengeri 'Diva' C.C. (Upcher 1964)
sprengeri var. elongata A.M. (Aberconway 1955)
sprengeri 'Wakehurst' A.M. (Price 1948)
stellata
  F.C.C. (J. Veitch 1878)
  A.G.M. (1923)
stellata 'Norman Gould' F.C.C. (Wisley 1967)
stellata 'Rosea' A.M. (J. Veitch 1893)
stellata 'Rubra' A.M. (Notcutt 1948)
× thompsoniana (tripetala × virginiana) A.M.
  (Thomas 1958)
× veitchii (campbellii × heptapeta) 'Peter Veitch'
  F.C.C. (R. Veitch 1921)
× watsonii see × wieseneri
× wieseneri (× watsonii) (hypoleuca × sieboldii)
  A.M. (Allgrove 1917)
wilsonii
  A.M. (Clarke 1930)
  A.M. (Loder 1932)
  P.C. (Windsor 1965)
  F.C.C. (Simmons 1971)

This list is intended as a rough guide to gardens where there are collections of Magnolias and which are likely to be open to the public during Magnolia blossom time. In most cases there is either an admission charge or a collection for a specified charity.

The author apologizes for including several gardens with noteworthy Magnolias which may have no official open-days. He apologizes also to the owners of gardens with good Magnolias which may not have been included. For easy reference the counties and the nearest towns are listed in alphabetical order.

England

AVON *Bristol* Algars Manor, Iron Acton. (J. Naish, Esq.)

BERKSHIRE *Windsor* The Savill and The Valley Gardens, Windsor Great Park. (Crown Estate Commissioners)

CORNWALL *Bodmin* Lanhydrock. (The National Trust)

Falmouth Glendurgan, Mawnan Smith. (The National Trust)

Penwarne, Mawnan Smith. (J. M. Williams, Esq.)

Launceston Werrington Park. (A. M. Williams, Esq.)

Penzance Trengwainton. (The National Trust)

Trewidden. (Executors of the late Mrs. Charles Williams)

St. Austell Caerhays Castle, Gorran. (F. J. Williams, Esq.)

St. Keverne Lanarth. (Mr. & Mrs. Paul Tylor)

Torpoint Antony House. (The National Trust)

Truro Chyverton, Zelah. (N. T. Holman, Esq.)

Trelissick Gardens. (The National Trust)

Trewithen, Grampound Road. (Mrs G. H. Johnstone)

CUMBRIA *Grange-over-Sands* Holker Hall, Cark-in-Cartmel. (Richard Cavendish, Esq.)

DERBYSHIRE *Duffield* Hazelbrow, Hazelwood Road. (Sir Max Bemrose)

DEVON *Barnstaple* Marwood Hill, Marwood. (Dr. J. A. Smart)

Budleigh Salterton Lee Ford, Knowle. (B. M. Lindsay-Fynn, Esq.)

Dawlish Stonelands Gardens. (Mr. & Mrs. Gerald Moore)

Exeter Castle Drogo, Drewsteignton. (The National Trust)

Killerton Gardens. (The National Trust)

Salcombe Sharpitor Gardens and Overbecks Museum. (The National Trust)

Sidmouth Sidbury Manor. (Sir Charles Cave, Bt.)

Totnes Dartington Hall. (The Dartington Hall Trustees)

Yelverton The Garden House, Buckland Monachroum. (L. S. Fortescue, Esq.)

DORSET *Dorchester* Hyde Crook, Frampton. (Maj. & Mrs. P. Birley)

ESSEX *Dunmow* Hill Pasture, Broxted. (J. G. Scott Marshall, Esq., and Mr. & Mrs. J. Wyand Brooks)

GLOUCESTERSHIRE *Chipping Campden* Hidcote Manor Gardens. (The National Trust)

Kiftsgate Court, Mickleton. (Mr. & Mrs. J. A. F. Binny)

HAMPSHIRE *Basingstoke* Herriard Park. (J. Loveys Jervoise, Esq.)

Romsey Embley Park.

Southampton Exbury Gardens, Exbury. (E. L. de Rothschild, Esq.)

Winchester Jermyns, Ampfield, near Romsey. (Hants C.C.)

KENT *Cranbrook* The Grange, Benenden. (Capt. Collingwood Ingram)

Lamberhurst Court Lodge. (William Morland, Esq.)

Westerham Crockham House. (Gerald Williams, Esq.)

LEICESTERSHIRE *Loughborough* Long Close, Woodhouse Eaves. (Mr. & Mrs. G. W. Johnson)

LONDON *Brentford* Syon Park. (His Grace the Duke of Northumberland)

Chiswick 91, Park Road, W.4. (Mr. & Mrs. Phillip May)

NORTHAMPTONSHIRE *Northampton* Maidwell Hall School.

SALOP *Market Drayton* Elds Wood, Blackbrook. (Willoughbridge Garden Trust)

Hodnet Hall, Hodnet. (A. E. H. Heber Percy, Esq.)

SOMERSET *Crewkerne* Wayford Manor. (Robin L. Goffe, Esq.)

SUFFOLK *Bury St. Edmunds* Ickworth. (The National Trust)

SURREY *Dorking* The Wilderness, Holmbury St. Mary. (Mrs. Louis Reynolds)

Godalming Hascombe Court. (Mr. & Mrs. C. C. Jacobs)

Richmond Royal Botanic Gardens, Kew. (Ministry of Agriculture, Fisheries and Food)

Ripley Wisley Garden. (The Royal Horticultural Society)

WEST SUSSEX *Ardingly* The Gardens, Wakehurst Place. (Royal Botanic Gardens, Kew)

East Grinstead Gravetye Manor Hotel. (Gravetye Manor Hotel, Ltd.)

Handcross Nymans Gardens. (The National Trust)

Haywards Heath Borde Hill Garden, Ltd. (R. Stephenson Clarke, Esq.)

Horsham Leonardslee. (Sir Giles Loder, Bt.)

South Lodge. (Miss E. Goodman)

WILTSHIRE *Bradford on Avon* Innwoods. (H. Whitehead, Esq.)

Corsham Corsham Court. (Lord Methuen, R.A.)

NORTH YORKSHIRE *Ripon* Newby Hall. (R. E. J. Compton, Esq.)

WEST YORKSHIRE *Wakefield* Nostell Priory Grounds, Nostell. (The National Trust)

Ireland

CO. CORK Fota Island

CO. DOWN Rowallane, Saintfield.

CO. OFFALY Birr Castle. (Lord Rosse)

Wales

GWYNEDD *Llanfairpwll* Plas Newydd. (The National Trust)

Tal-y-Cafn Bodnant. (The National Trust)

SOUTH GLAMORGAN *Cardiff* Bute Park, Castle Grounds. (Cardiff Parks Dept.)

Cefnon Parc, Capel Gwilym Road, Llanishen. (Cardiff Parks Dept.)

Scotland

LOTHIAN *Edinburgh* Royal Botanic Garden. (Dept. of Agriculture and Fisheries for

STRATHCLYDE *Helensburgh* Glenarn, Rhu. (J. F. A. Gibson, Esq.)

Isle of Arran Brodick Castle, Brodick. (The National Trust for Scotland)

Isle of Colonsay Kiloran. (Lord Strathcona)

SOME BRITISH NURSERIES WHICH SPECIALIZE IN MAGNOLIAS

CHANNEL ISLANDS Caledonia Nurseries, Guernsey

CORNWALL Treseders' Nurseries (Truro), Ltd.

DEVON Robert Veitch & Sons, Ltd., Alphington, Exeter

GWYNEDD Bodnant Garden Nursery, Tal-y-Cafn

HAMPSHIRE Hillier & Sons, Winchester

KENT Pickard's Magnolia Gardens, Stodmarsh Road, Canterbury

SOMERSET John Scott & Co., Royal Nurseries, Merriot, Crewkerne

SUFFOLK Notcutt Nurseries, Ltd., Woodbridge

SURREY L. R. Russell, Ltd., Richmond Nurseries, Windlesham

Walter C. Slocock, Ltd., Goldsworth Nursery, Woking

Waterers' Nurseries & Garden Centres, Bagshot

WEST SUSSEX F. Toynbee, Ltd., Croftway Nurseries, Yapton Road, Barnham, Bognor Regis

(N) = Nursery   (W) = Wholesale only

ALABAMA *Mobile* 36609 Dr. John A. Smith, 3961 Cottage Hill Road

Semmes 36575 (N) Tom Dodd Nurseries, U.S. Highway 98

ARKANSAS *Calion* 71724 Mr. Carl R. Amason, P.O. Box 164

CALIFORNIA *Arcadia* CA 91006 Los Angeles State and County Arboretum, 301 North Baldwin Avenue

Auburn CA 95603 (N) Mr. Edward Hetzer, Little Lake Nursery, Rte. 2, Box 2503–E

Fort Bragg CA 95437 Dr. Paul Bowman, 160 Brandon Way

San Francisco CA 94122 Strybing Arboretum Society, Ninth Avenue and Lincoln Way

San Marino CA 91108 H. E. Huntington Library

Saratoga CA 95070 Saratoga Horticultural Foundation, P.O. Box 308

FLORIDA *Liberty County* Torreya State Park

Tallahassee FL 32303 (N) Mr. Charles E. Salter, 2206 Durward Ride

GEORGIA *LaGrange* 30241 Mrs. Alice Callaway, Box 400

Pine Mountains 31822 Callaway Gardens

ILLINOIS *Glencoe* 60022 Botanic Garden of the Chicago Horticultural Society, 775 Dundee Road

Urbana 61801 Mount Hope Cemetery (large *M. heptapeta*)

University of Illinois, Department of Horticulture

Woodlawn Cemetery (*M. tripetala* 'Woodlawn')

KENTUCKY *Crestwood* 40014 (N) Yew-Dell Nursery

Lexington 40500 (N) Hillenmeyer's Nursery

LOUISIANA *Opelousas* 70570 (N) Mr. Kenneth G. Durio, Jr., Louisiana Nursery, Old Sunset Road, Rte. 1 Box 43

MARYLAND *Kingsville* 21087 (N) Kingsville Nurseries (the late H. J. Hohman)

MASSACHUSETTS *Boston* 02130 Arnold Arboretum of Harvard University, Jamaica Plain

MICHIGAN *Bloomfield Hills* 48013 Mr. Philip J. Savage, Jr., 2150 Woodward Avenue

Detroit Westcroft Gardens

Woodmere Cemetery. (Several large *M. acuminata* trees)

MINNESOTA *Chaska* 55318 Minnesota Landscape Arboretum, 3675 Arboretum Drive

MISSISSIPPI *Gloster* 39638 Gloster Arboretum

MISSOURI *Saint Louis* 63110 Missouri Botanical Garden, 2345 Tower Grove Avenue

NEW JERSEY *Gladstone* 07935 Willowwood, Arboretum of Rutgers University. Hacklebarney Road

Marlboro 67746 (N) Kluis Nursery, Ryan Road

Neshanic Station 08853 (W) John Vermeulen & Son, Inc.

NEW YORK *Brooklyn* 11225 Brooklyn Botanic Garden, 1000 Washington Avenue

Esperance 12066 George Landis Arboretum

(*Long Island*) Planting Fields Arboretum, Oyster Bay 11771

Millbrook 12545 The Cary Arboretum

Ossining 10562 Kitchawan Research Station of Brooklyn Botanic Garden, 712 Kitchawan Road, Rte. 134

Rochester 14620 Highland Park, Monroe County Park System

OHIO *Cincinnati* 42532 Spring Grove Cemetery, 4521 Spring Grove Avenue (Several trees of *M. grandiflora*)

North Madison 44057 Mr. David Goheen Leach, 1894 Hubbard Road

Painesville 44077 (W) Merrill's Nursery, 870 Madison Avenue

Strongsville 44136 Gardenview Horticultural Park, 16711 Pearl Road

OREGON *Canby* 97013 (N) Mrs. Roy L. Burden, 23230 S. Highway 99E

Salem 97304 (N) Iufer Landscape Co., 3995 12th Street, S.E.

Springfield 97477 (N) Gossler Farms Nursery, 1200 Weaver Road

OKLAHOMA *Okmulgee* 74447 Mr. Otto Spring

PENNSYLVANIA *Gladwyne* 19035 Gardens of the Henry Foundation for Botanical Research

Merion Station 19066 Arboretum of the Barnes Foundation, Merion

Kennett Square 19348 Longwood Gardens, Kennett Square, Chester County

Philadelphia 19118 Morris Arboretum of the University of Pennsylvania, 9414 Meadowbank Avenue

Swarthmore 19081 Arthur H. Scott Horticultural Foundation, Swarthmore College

TENNESSEE Great Smoky Mountains National Park, Gatlinburg 37738
1816 Tanager Lane

Nashville 37205 Tennessee Botanical Gardens and Fine Arts Center, Cheekwood

Winchester 37393 (W) Tennessee Valley Nurseries

TEXAS *Conroe* 77302 (N) Lowrey Nursery, 2323 Sleepy Hollow Road

VIRGINIA *Chesapeake* 23320 (W) Greenbrier Farms Inc. Nurseries, 412 Thrasher Road

Lexington 24450 Washington and Lee University

WASHINGTON, D.C. 20002 U.S. National Arboretum, 34th and R Streets, N.E.

WASHINGTON (State) *Seattle* 98195 Washington Park Arboretum (formerly University of Washington), Aboretum Office XD–10

WISCONSIN *Hales Corner* 53130 Milwaukee Park Commission, Boerner Botanical Gardens, 5879 S. 92nd Street, Hales Corner

The Secretary of the American Magnolia Society is: Mr. Richard B. Figlar, 14876 Pheasant Hill Court, Chesterfield, Missouri, 63017, U.S.A.

WHERE TO SEE MAGNOLIAS IN OTHER COUNTRIES

AUSTRALIA (N) Mr. W. J. Simpson, 'Wayside', 602 Nepean Hwy, Frankston, Victoria 3199

BELGIUM: Kalmthout Arboretum, Kalmthout 2180

CANADA Royal Botanical Gardens, Box 399 Station A, Hamilton, Ontario L8N 3H8
(N) Ocean Park Nurseries, 2124 Stevenson Road, White Rock, British Columbia
(N) Sheridan Nurseries, Ltd., 116 Winston Churchill Boulevard, Oakville, Ontario

NETHERLANDS Herman J. Grootendorst, 'Acadia', Burg, Colynstraat 106, Boskoop

NEW ZEALAND (N) Oswald Blumhardt, No. 9 R.D., Whangarei
(NW) Duncan & Davies, Ltd., P.O. Box 340, New Plymouth, Taranki

SWEDEN Karl Evert Flinck, Bjuv
Dr. Tor Nitzelius, Fladalt, S–31010 Vaxtorp

SWITZERLAND Sir Peter Smithers, CH–6911, Vico Marcote
Dr. P. van Veen, Villa Iris, 6574 Vira Gambarogno

These bibliographical citations date back to the earliest publication extant which depicts a Magnolia, the mediaeval Chinese Reclassified Pharmaceutical Natural Histories of Thang Sheng-Wei of 1083 and 1108.

From the New World the earliest reference is to the Mexican *Talauma mexicana* – a close relative to *Magnolia* – in the translation into Spanish of an Aztec Herbal by Martinus de la Cruz (1552). This was followed by the delayed publication, in 1651, of the works of Francisco Hernandez, which he compiled in Mexico between 1570 and 1575 and which included a plate depicting the tropical *Magnolia dealbata* under the Mexican name *Eloxochitl*.

Notes: 1. In some cases the author's date is a year or two prior to that of publicatios.
2. Italic figures at the end of each entry are the page references for this book.

AMASON, C. R. (1975) An old southern manner of growing *Magnolia grandiflora*. *Newsletter of the American Magnolia Society*. 11, 2 : 22. *74*

ANON. (1849) *Société Nantaise d'Horticulture et Recherche*. [History of *M. grandiflora* 'La Maillardière'.] 131–46. *73–4*

— (1902) The Cornwall Daffodil and Spring Flower Show. *Journal of the Royal Horticultural Society*. [*M.* 'Osaka' A.M.] 27 : 20. *164*

— (1969) *Ibid*. [Description and colour plate of *M.* × *loebneri* 'Leonard Messel'.] 94 : 12. *162*

ANDREWS, H. (1803–4) *The Botanist's Repository*. *M. purpurea*. t. 326. *132, 135*

ARNOLD-FORSTER, W. (1948) Magnolias by G. H. Johnstone. *Shrubs for the Milder Counties*. 228–48. *90, 105*

AUSTIN, O. L. (1962) The Magnolia Warbler. *Birds of the World*. 285 *6*

BAILEY, L. H. (1919) *Cyclopedia of Horticulture*. *44*

BAILEY, L. H. & BAILEY, E. Z. (1941) A Concise Dictionary of Plants Cultivated in the United States and Canada. *Hortus Second*. *131*

BANKS, J. (1791) *Icones Selectae Plantarum, quas in Japonia Collegit et Delineavit Engelbertus Kaempfer*. [Kaempfer's plates of *M. kobus, M. heptapeta* and *M. quinquepeta*, the latter two transposed.] tt. 12–14. *83, 131*

BARTRAM, W. (1791) *Travels through South and North Carolina*. *M. fraseri*. 338–9. *58, 59*

BARTRUM, D. (1957) *Rhododendrons and Magnolias*. [Part II Magnolias: 104–70.] *160*

BEAN, W. J. (1912) *Curtis's Botanical Magazine*. *M. kobus*. 138 : t. 8428. *122*

— (1921) *M.* × *veitchii*. *Journal of the Royal Horticultural Society*. 46 : 321–3, Fig. facing p. 336. *183, 184*

— (1925) *Trees and Shrubs Hardy in the British Isles*. Ed. 4, *Magnolia*. 2 : 65–76. *84, 125*

— (1933) *Ibid*. [*M. sinensis*] Ed. 1, 3 : 225. *70*

— (1936) *Ibid*. [*M.* × *veitchii*.] Ed. 2, 3 : 226. *183, 184*

— (1973) *Ibid*. Ed. 8 (Sir George Taylor, ed.), 2 : *Magnolia*: 641–75, Figs 86–94; *Manglietia*: 719–20; *Michelia*: 737–8. *47, 70, 103, 111, 125, 129, 150, 161*

BLACKBURN, B. C. (1952) A Promising Hybrid Magnolia. *Journal of the New York Botanical Garden*. 2, 2 : 43–4 and 53, t. 1. *113, 161*

— (1955) A question about Shidekobushi: a re-examination of *Magnolia stellata* Maxim. *Amatores Herbarii*. 17 : 1–2. *38, 113, 117, 162*

— (1957) The Early-Flowering Magnolias of Japan. *Baileya*. 5, 1 : 3–13. *117, 123, 162*

BLUME, K. L. (1828) *Flora Javae*. [*Manglietia insignis* as *Magnolia insignis*.] 22–3. *36, 137*

BROWN, G. E. (1973) *Royal Botanic Gardens* [Kew] *Newsletter*. [*M. campbellii*.] 60 : 4–5. *88*

BUC'HOZ, P. J. (1776) *Collection Précieuse*. [Plate of *M. heptapeta* without a botanical name.] 1 : t. 4. *82*

— (1779) *Plantes Nouvellement Découvertes*. [*Lassonia heptapeta* and *L. quinquepeta*.] 21 : t. 19, Figs 1 and 2. *39, 81, 82, 130, 131*

— (1785) *Le Grand Jardin de l'Univers*. [Coloured plate of *Lassonia heptapeta*.] t. 131. *82*

CANDOLLE, A. P. DE. (1817) *Magnolia. Regni Vegetabilis Systema Naturale*. *Magnolia*. 1 : 449–560. *29, 47, 122, 133, 173*

— (1824–30) *Prodromus*. *Magnolia* 1 : 80. *31, 43*

CARRIÈRE, E. -A. (1890) *M. Wieseneri*, *Revue Horticole*. 62 : 406–7. *186, 187*

CATESBY, M. (1741) *Flora Caroliniana*. 1. *M. virginiana*: t. 39. *14, 43*

Ibid. 2 (appendix). *M. grandiflora*: t. 61. *71*

M. tripetala: t. 80. *55*

M. acuminata: t. 45 (excluding Pl. 45). *126, 127*

— (1771) *The Natural History of Carolina, Florida and the Bahama Islands*. *14*

CHIEN, S. S. & CHENG, W. C. (1933) Chekiang Plants. Contributions from the Biological Laboratory of the Scientific Society of China. Botany Series 8.

M. amoena. 9 : 280, Fig. 28. *111*

M. cylindrica. 9 : 281–2. *119*

M. officinalis var. *biloba*. 9 : 282. *52*

CIBOT, P. M. (1778) Le Yu-lan. *Mémoires concernant l'Histoire, les Sciences . . . de Chinois, par les Missionaires de Pe-kin*. 3 : 441–3. *81*

COURSET, D. DE. (1828) *Botaniste Cultivateur*. [Plate of *M.* × *soulangiana*.] *174*

CRUZ, M. DE LA. (1552) *The Badianus Manuscript*. [An Aztec Herbal translated into Spanish by Martinus de la

Cruz. Later translated into Latin by J. Badianus (*Codex Barberini* 241).] English translation, with introduction and annotation, by E. W. Emmart (1940).   11

CURTIS, W. (1775) *Flora Londinensis.* 1.   *xiii*

— (1787) *Curtis's Botanical Magazine.* 1.   *xiii*

— (1797) *Ibid. M. quinquepeta* as *M. purpurea.* 11 : t. 390.
                                                            130, 132, 173

DANDY, J. E. (1927) Key to the Species in J. G. Millais's *Magnolias.* [Name mis-spelt Dendy.] 41–53.   25

— (1930) *Curtis's Botanical Magazine. M. tsarongensis.* 159 : sub t. 9467.   65

— (1934) The identity of *Lassonia* Buc'hoz. *Journal of Botany.* 72 : 101–3.   *39, 81, 82, 130, 131*

— (1936) *Curtis's Botanical Magazine. M. globosa.* 159 : sub t. 9467.   *62, 65*

— (1943–8) *Ibid. Michelia doltsopa.* 164 : t. 9645.   *139*

— (1948) *Ibid. M. dawsoniana, M. sargentiana.* 164 : t. 9678–9.   *99, 101*

— (1948) *Ibid. Magnolia* section *Gynopodium, M. nitida* and Section *Maingola.* 165 : sub t. 16.   *32, 33, 79*

— (1950) The Highdown Magnolia. *Journal of the Royal Horticultural Society.* 75 : 159–61, Fig. 52.   *33, 81, 158*

— (1950) A survey of the genus *Magnolia* together with *Manglietia* and *Michelia. Camellias and Magnolias Conference Report.* (Royal Horticultural Society.) 64–81.
xv, 7, 15, 25, 29, 33, 34, 35, 40, 44, 81, 83, 112, 126, 127, 131, 188

— (1964) *Magnolia acuminata* var. *subcordata* (Spach) Dandy. *American Journal of Botany.* 51 : 1056.   *128*

— (1964–5) *Curtis's Botanical Magazine. Manglietia insignis.* 173 : t. 443.   *137*

    Ibid. Magnolia virginiana. 173 : t. 457.   *43, 46*

— (1971) The Classification of *Magnoliaceae. Newsletter of the American Magnolia Society.* 8, 1 : 3–6.   26

— (1973) *Magnolia hypoleuca. Baileya.* 19, 1 : 44.   *49, 50*

— (1973) *Magnolia hypoleuca. Newsletter of the American Magnolia Society.* 9, 4 : 4–5.   *50*

DESFONTAINES, R. L. (1809) *Histoires des Arbres et des Abrisseaux. M. heptapeta* as *M. yulan.* 2 : 6.   81

DESROUSSEAUX, L. A. J. (1791) Lamarck, *Encyclopédie Méthodique, Botanique.* Magnolier 3 : 671–5.
                                    55, 81, 82, 85, 130, 131

DIELS, L. (1900) *Botanische Jahrbücher für Systematik Pflanzengeschichte und Pflanzengeographie. Magnolia.* 29 : 321–2.
                                                            51, 52

DODD, W. R. (1969) Obituary, Drury Todd Gresham. *Newsletter of the American Magnolia Society.* 6, 2 : 7–8. *157*

DON. (1811) *Don's Miller's Gardener's Dictionary. Magnolia pyramidata.* 1 : 83.   *59, 133*

DUDLEY, T. R. & KOSAR, W. F. (1968) Eight new *Magnolia* cultivars. *Morris Arboretum Bulletin.* 19, 2 : 26–9. *151*

DUHAMEL. (1804) *M. heptepata* as *M. discolor. Traité des Arbres et des Arbustes.* 66 : t. 2.   *132*

EARNSHAW, D. P. (1976) Bud Orientation in the Genus *Magnolia. Newletter of the American Magnolia Society.* 12, 1 : 13.   8

EGOLF, R. L. (1966) Observations on Deciduous Magnolias

in Florida. *The American Horticultural Magazine.* 45, 4 : 388–92.   *59, 62*

— (1967) Two Rare American Magnolias. *Newsletter of the American Magnolia Society.* [*M. macrophylla* var. *ashei* and *M. pyramidata.*] 4, 1 : 6.   *59, 62*

FERNALD, M. L. (1950) *Gray's New Manual of Botany.* Ed. 8. *M. virginiana* var. *australis:* 49.   45

FINDLAY, T. H. (1963) Tree Magnolias at Windsor. *Journal of the Royal Horticultural Society.* 88, 2 : 462. *97, 193*

FINET, A. & GAGNEPAIN, F. (1906) *Mémoires publiés par la Société Botanique de France.* 1, 4 : Magnoliacées : 23–54, *M. parviflora* var. *wilsonii:* 39.   67

FLINCK, K. E. (1973) Magnolias in my Garden in Sweden. *Newsletter of the American Magnolia Society.* 9, 2 : 3–8.
                                                            64, 118

FOGG, J. M. JR. (1961) The Temperate American Magnolias. *Morris Arboretum Bulletin.* [An informative and well-illustrated treatise.] 12, 4 : 51–8.   57

— (1976) *Magnolia* × *watsonii* in the Philadelphia area. *Newsletter of the American Magnolia Society:* 12, 1 : 12. *189*

FOGG, J. M., JR. & MCDANIEL, J. C. (1975) *Check List of the Cultivated Magnolias,* American Horticultural Society, Plant Data Center, Mount Vernon, Va.   *130*

FORDHAM, A. J. (1972) Propagation of *Magnolia* 'Freeman'. *Newsletter of the American Magnolia Society.* 8, 2 : 6. *202*

FORREST, G. (1927) Magnolias of Yunnan in J. G. Millais's *Magnolias.* 31–40.   *84, 94*

FRANCHET, A. R. (1889) *Plantae Delavayanae. M. delavayi.* 33 : 9, 10.   *47*

FREEMAN, O. M. (1937) A new Magnolia hybrid. *The National Horticultural Magazine.* [*M. grandiflora* × *M. virginiana.*] 16, 3 : 161–2.   *153*

— (1951) New Magnolia Hybrids. *Ibid.* [Crosses within *M. acuminata.*] 30 : 132–5.   *14, 129*

GOSSLER, J. (1967) Impressions of *Magnolia dawsoniana. Newsletter of the American Magnolia Society.* 4, 2 : 5. *101*

GRESHAM, D. T. (1962) Decidous Magnolias of Californian Origin. *Morris Arboretum Bulletin.* 13 : 47–50. *M. quinquepeta* × *M.* × *veitchii* 'Rubra'.   *156*
    M. × *soulangiana* 'Lennei Alba' × *M.* × *veitchii* 'Rubra'.
                                                            157

— (1964) An Appreciation of *Magnolia campbellii* subsp. *mollicomata. Ibid.* 15 : 30.   *96*

— (1964) Deciduous Magnolias of Californian Origin. *Journal of the Royal Horticultural Society.* 89, 8 : 327–32.
                                                            155–8

— (1966) *Magnolia wilsonii* × *Magnolia globosa* Chinese Form. *Morris Arboretum Bulletin.* 17 : 70–3.   *153*

— (1967) Trial by the Royal Family of *Magnoliaceae. Newsletter of the American Magnolia Society.* 4, 2 : 7–8. *157*

GRIFFITH, W. (1848) *Itinerary Notes,* published as *Posthumous Papers.* [Plate of *Magnolia campbellii alba* with description in Latin.] 2, 153 : 755.   *86, 90, 91*

— (1854) *Icones Plantarum Asiaticarum.* [Drawing and description of *M. campbellii alba.*] 4 : t. 656.   *86, 90, 91*

HAMELIN, J. F. E. (1827) Hybrides Nouvelles. *Annales de la Société d'Horticulture de Paris.* [*M.* × *soulangiana.*] 1 : 90–5.
                                                                        133, 170, 173

— (1827) *Bulletin de la Société Linnéenne de Paris.* [Brief report on raising of *M.* × *soulangiana.*] 5 : 73.   *172*

HARDIN, J. W. (1954) An analysis of variation within *Magnolia acuminata* L. *Journal of the Elisha Mitchell Scientific Society.* 70, 2 : 298–312.   *128*

HARKNESS, B. (1954) A New Hybrid Magnolia. *National Horticultural Magazine.* [*M.* × *slavinii.*] 33, 2 : 118–20.
                                                                        126, 165, 166

— (1961) Magnolia Notes from Rochester. *Magnolia slavinii* reduced to synonymy. *Morris Arboretum Bulletin.* 12, 2 : 19.
                                                                        126, 166

HARTMAN, H. T. & KESTER, D. E. (1961) *Plant Propagation.* Ed. 3. Chinese or Pot Layerage: 406, Chip Budding: 448, Figs 13–14.   *203*

HARTWEG. (1825) *Hortus Carlsruhanus.* [*M. virginiana* as *M. glauca.*] 171.   *43*

HEADLAM, A. W. (1974) Magnolias in Melbourne. *Rhododendrons 1974 with Magnolias and Camellias.* 82–8.   *8, 90*

HENRY, A. (1912) *Trees and Shrubs of Great Britain and Ireland.* [*M.* 'Lennei'.] 6 : 1596.   *177*

HERKLOTS, G. A. C. (1964) Flowers of the Valley of Nepal. *Journal of the Royal Horticultural Society.* 89 : 294–300.   *87*

HERNANDEZ, F. (1651) *Nova Plantarum Historia Mexicana.* [Plate and earliest Western description of a Magnolia: *M. dealbata* under *Eloxochitl.*] 376.   *10, 31*

— (1790) *Francisci Hernandi medici atque historici Philippi II Hisp. et Indiar. regis et totius novi orbis, archiatri opera, cum edita, tum inedita.* [The published and unpublished works of Francisco Hernandez, doctor and historian of Philip II, King of Spain and the Indies and of the whole new world.]
                                                                        11

— (1959) Historia Natural de Nueva España. [Universidad Nacional de Mexico.] *Del Eloxochitl.* 1 : 368 capitulo 37.   *11*

HILLIER & SONS. (1972) *Manual of Trees and Shrubs.* Magnolia. 178–85.   *66, 116, 168, 192*

HILLER, H. G. & LANCASTER, C. R. (1975) Magnolias in the Hillier Gardens and Arboretum. *Rhododendrons 1975 with Magnolias and Camellias.* 61–9.   *161*

HOLMAN, N. T. (1973) Asiatic Magnolias in a Cornish Garden. *Rhododendrons 1973 with Magnolias and Camellias.* 67–75.   *182*

HOOKER, J. D. (1855) *Illustrations of Himalayan Plants.* [Colour plate of *M. campbellii.*] tt. 4, 5.   *86*

— (1878) *M. stellata. Curtis's Botanical Magazine.* 104 : t. 6370.   *113*

— (1885) *M. campbellii. Ibid.* 111 : t. 6793.   *85, 86*

— (1891) *M.* × *wieseneri* as *M. watsonii. Ibid.* 117 : t. 7157.
                                                                        51, 186–8

— (1895) *M. sieboldii* as *M. parviflora. Ibid.* 121 : t. 7411.
                                                                        63, 64

HOOKER, J. D. & THOMSON, T. (1855) *Flora Indica.* 1. *M. campbellii:* 78, *M. globosa:* 77.   *65, 85, 93*

—— (1872) *Flora of British India.* 1. *M. campbellii* : 41.   *91*

HOPKINS, H. (1976) 'Dawn', a good pink *Magnolia stellata. Newsletter of the American Magnolia Society,* 12, 1 : 28.   *116*

Hortus Third. (1976) A Concise Dictionary of Plants Culti-
vated in the United States and Canada. Staff of the L. H. Bailey Hortorium [and selected collaborators], Cornell University, Ithaca, New York. [The text was sent to the printers shortly before the publication of Dr. Spongberg's *Magnoliaceae Hardy in Temperate North America* so that it does not take into account many of the changes in nomenclature which he advocates.] *Magnolia:* 694–7.   *38, 130, 131*

HOWARD, R. A. (1948) The Morphology and Systematics of the West Indian Magnoliaceae. *Bulletin of the Torrey Botanical Club.* 75, 4 : 335–57.   *145*

HUTCHINSON, J. (1964) *Families of Flowering Plants.* Ed. 1. Magnoliaceae. 50–7.   *26*

— (1973) *Ibid.* Ed. 3. Magnoliaceae 154–6.   *3*

INAMI, K. (1959) Distribution of *Magnolia stellata* Maxim. *Amatores Herbarii.* [Text in Japanese includes map.] 20 : 10–14.   *118*

INGRAM, C. (1966) *Journal of the Royal Horticultural Society.* 91, 4 : 84.   *124*

INTERNATIONAL ASSOCIATION FOR PLANT TAXONOMY, THE. (1972) *International Code of Botanical Nomenclature* adopted by the Eleventh International Botanical Congress, Seattle, August 1969. [Referred to as the 'Seattle Code'. Text in English, French and German. 426 pp. English section 1–79.]   *17, 40, 50, 63, 83, 131, 186*

INTERNATIONAL BUREAU FOR PLANT TAXONOMY, THE. (1969) *International Code of Nomenclature of Cultivated Plants.* [Text in English. 32 pp.]   *17, 25, 143, 154, 175*

ITO, K. (1884) *Figures and Descriptions of Plants in the Koishikawa Botanical Garden,* Tokyo. 1. [The figure numbers are those quoted in translations from two independent Japanese sources. Those in brackets are the interpretations pencilled on the copy in the Botany Library, British Museum (Natural History).]

 Magnolia obovata Thunberg [= *M. quinquepeta* Buc'hoz]. Fig. 9 (7). A strain of *Magnolia obovata* Thunberg as Sarasa Mokuren [recently identified as *M.* × *soulangiana* 'Sarasa']. Fig. 10 (8).   *108, 164*

 Magnolia parviflora Siebold & Zuccarini. [= *M. sieboldii* Koch: the flower has twenty-two tepals (= cv. 'Kwanso'). The norm is nine.] Fig. 11 (13).   *64*

 Magnolia hypoleuca Siebold & Zuccarini [now identified *M.* × *wieseneri* Carrière]. Fig. 13 (15).   *188*

JANAKI AMMAL, E. K. (1952) The race history of Magnolias. *Indian Journal of Genetics and Plant Breeding.* 12 : 82–92.   *211*

— (1955) *Chromosome Atlas of the World.* 2 : 14.
                                                                        118, 135, 155

JOHNSTONE, G. H. (1948) Magnolias in Arnold-Forster's *Shrubs for the Milder Counties:* 228–48.   *89, 90, 105*

— (1953) *Magnolia ashei. Journal of the Royal Horticultural Society.* 78 : 288–9. Fig. 90.   *62*

— (1955) *Asiatic Magnolias in Cultivation.* [A standard reference to the Asian species, with detailed notes on cultivation and taxonomy. This monumental work, so well written and beautifully illustrated, was my original inspiration to compile this more comprehensive work including the temperate American species and details of the many hybrids and crosses recorded to date.]

*xvi, 47, 53, 54, 64, 65, 70, 85, 86, 88, 91,
93, 95–101, 104, 107, 108, 111, 122–4, 130,
132, 144, 158, 162, 165, 170, 174, 187*

KACHE, P. (1920) The most beautiful of flowering shrubs in April: Early winter-hardy Magnolias. *Gartenschönheit.* [The earliest published account of the breeding of *M. × loebneri* by Max Löbner; title translated from the German text.] 1 : 20. 161

KAEMPFER, E. (1712) *M. heptapeta* as Mokkwuren flore albo, *M. kobus* as Kobus and Side Kobusi, *M. quinquepeta* as Mokkwuren flore lilio-narcissi rubento. *Amoenitatum Exoticarum*: 845. 83, 122

KALMBACHER, G. (1972) *Magnolia × brooklynensis* 'Evamaria'. *Newsletter of the American Magnolia Society.* 8, 2 : 7–8. 148, 149

— (1973) More on *Magnolia × brooklynensis* 'Evamaria'. *Ibid.* 9, 1 : 12–13. 148

KINGDON-WARD, F. (1927) *Journal of the Royal Horticultural Society.* [*M. campbellii alba.*] 52 : 16. 87

— (1960) *Pilgrimage for Plants*: [*M. campbellii alba*] 44. 90

KNUTH, P. E. V. W. (1898–1905) *Handbook of Flower Pollination.* Based on H. Müller's *The Fertilization of Flowers by Insects.* Translated and revised by J. R. Ainsworth-Davis (1906). [*M. heptapeta* (as *M. yulan*) and *M. grandiflora.*] II : 54. 145

KOCH, C. H. E. (1853) *Hortus Dendrologicus. Magnoliaceae*: 3–6. 63

KOERTING, L. (1977) A Tree Born in Brooklyn. *Newsletter of the American Magnolia Society.* [Detailed description of seedling No. 391 of the yellow-flowered *M. acuminata × M. heptapeta.*] 13, 2 : 21–2. 147

KOIDZUMI, G. (1926) *The Botanical Magazine of the Tokyo Botanical Society.* [*M. sieboldii* as *M. verecunda.*] 40 : 339. 63

KORT, A. (1905) *Revue de l'Horticulture Belge.* [*M. × wieseneri* under *Magnolia Watsoni* et *Oyama.*] 31 : 258–9. 63

KOSAR, W. F. (1962) Magnolias Native to North America. *Journal of the Californian Horticultural Society.* [Includes the first publication of *M.* 'Freeman' p. 11.] 23, 1 : 2–12. 153, 154

KOSLOFF, I. V. (1950) Notes on Plants collected by Mr. Arthur de Carle Sowerby in Eastern China. *Notes de Botanique Chinoise.* [Includes references to *M. sieboldii* in southern Kirin.] 64

KROSSA, G. F. (1964) Two Rare Magnolias in Michigan, *The American Horticultural Magazine.* [*M. cylindrica* and *M. officinalis biloba.*] 114–16. 121

LAPE, F. (1966) Hardy Magnolia Clones needed for the North. *Newsletter of the American Magnolia Society.* [Compares the relative hardiness of the hardiest species and hybrids growing at the George Landis Arboretum, Esperance, New York.] 3, 1 : 6. 195

LEACH, D. G. (1973) The Winter of '63. *Ibid.* [Notes on the comparative winter hardiness of Magnolias at Brookville, Pennsylvania.] 9, 4 : 3–4. 195

LEMAIRE, C. (1854) *Magnolia* de Lenné (Hybride). *Illustration Horticole*: 1, Pl. 37. 177

LEPPIK, E. E. (1975) Morphogenic Stagnation in the Evolution of Magnolia Flowers. *Phytomorphology.* 25, 4 : 451–64. 2

LI, H. L. (1959) *The Garden Flowers of China.* Magnolias. 145–7. 9, 53, 82

LINDLEY, J. (1828) *Botanical Register.* [*M. × soulangiana* as *M. yulan* var. *soulangiana.*] 14 : t. 1164. 172, 174

LINNAEUS, C. (1737) *Genera Plantarum. Magnolia.* 62 : 456. 1

— (1753) *Species Plantarum.* 1. Magnolia : 535–6. 1, 29, 43

— (1754) *Genera Plantarum.* Ed. 5. Magnolia : 240. 1, 29

— (1756, 1759) *Flora Monspeliensis* [based on Magnol's *Botanicum Monspeliense*]. 1

— (1759) *Systema Naturae.* Magnolia 10, 2 : 1082. 43, 55, 71, 126

— (1763) *Species Plantarum.* 2, 1. Magnolia : 756. 55

LOUDON, J. C. (1835) *The Gardener's Magazine.* [History of *M. grandiflora* 'Exmouth'.] 11, 6 : 70. 72–3, 174

— (1838) *Aboretum et Fruticetum Britannicum. Magnolia.* 1 : 259–84. 15, 58, 59, 61, 71, 72, 73, 84, 133, 173, 178, 180, 181

MCDANIEL, J. C. (1965) Securing Seed Production in *Magnolia acuminata* and *Magnolia cordata.* Reprinted in *Newsletter of the American Magnolia Society.* [Proceedings of the International Plant Propagators Society, Eastern Region, Thireenth Annual Meeting, 1963.] 2, 1 : 4–6. 126, 145

— (1966) A new-old Magnolia Hybrid. *Illinois Research.* [Details of the re-creation of *M. × thompsoniana.*] Fall 1966 : 8–9. 182

— (1966) Variations in the Sweet Bay Magnolia [*M. virginiana*]. *Morris Arboretum Bulletin.* 17 : 7–12. 45, 75

— (1966) 'Cairo' – An Illinois Cultivar of *Magnolia grandiflora. Ibid.* 17 : 61–2. 75

— (1967) Self-unfruitfulness in some Magnolias. *Ibid.* 18, 3 : 64–9. 87

— (1967) *Newsletter of the American Magnolia Society.* [Notes on pollination of flowers of *M. virginiana* by honey-bees and other *Hymenoptera.*] 4, 1 : 8. 46

— (1968) Magnolias from Middle America. *Ibid.* 5, 1 : 2–3. 189

— (1970) 'Spring Snow' and 'Ballerina'. Two New Cultivars of the Loebner Magnolia. *Ibid.* 7, 1 : 1–3. 162

— (1970) President's Paragraphs. *Ibid.* [Notes on the advancement of flower-bud development on M. sprengeri 'Diva' by grafting on to *M. × soulangiana*] 7, 1 : 8. 110

— (1970) Seventeen Magnolias U.S.A. *Ibid.* [Refers to American towns named Magnolia.] 7, 1 : 7. 5

— (1970) Did *Magnolia grandiflora* Borrow some Genes? A Detective Story. *Ibid.* 7, 2 : 4–7. 77

— (1971) Chip Budding: a Reliable Method for Propagating Trees. *Ibid.* [University of Illinois Advisory Leaflet, revised October 1971.] 9, 1 : 10–12. 205

— (1973) Illinois Clones of *Magnolia × brooklynensis. Ibid.* 9, 1 : 13–14. 149

— (1973) Sharpening our Sights on *Magnolia acuminata. Ibid.* 9, 2 : 9–14. 128

— (1973) Variations within *Magnolia liliflora* [*M. quinquepeta*] *Ibid.* 9, 2 : 20–3. 135

McDaniel, J. C.—contd.

— (1974) '*Magnolia cylindrica*', a Chinese Puzzle. *Ibid.* 10, 1 : 3–7. 121

— (1974) 1974 Observations on *Magnolia acuminata*. *Ibid.* 10, 2 : 21–2. 146

— (1975) A Beauty from New Zealand. Notes on Magnolias 'Iolanthe' and 'Mark Jury'. *Ibid.* 11, 1 : 16. 159, 163

— (1975) New Cultivars in *Magnolia macrophylla*. *Ibid.* 11, 2 : 3–4. 61

— (1976) Evergreen Magnolias. *Ibid.* [Reprinted from *The Texas Horticulturist*. 2, 3.] 12, 1 : 18–22. 45, 46, 77

— (1977) *Ibid.* [Notes on *M. virginiana* var. *australis*.]. 13, 1 : 25. 46

MAGNOL, P. (1676, 1686, 1688) *Botanicum Monspeliense*. [Magnol's reputation as a botanist was highly esteemed by his contemporaries. In 1703 Charles Plumier coined the generic name *Magnolia* to commemorate him. Then in 1756 and 1759 Linnaeus based his *Flora Monspeliensis* on Magnol's *Botanicum Monspeliense* and acclaimed the very high standard which Magnol had achieved long before the introduction of the Linnaean system of latinized binomial names for flora and fauna.] 1

MAKINO, T. (1929) *Journal of Japanese Botany*. [Natural distribution of *M. stellata*.] 6, 4 : 8. 113, 172

MANETTI, G. (1825) *Catalogus Plantarum Horti Regii Modoetiensis*. [List of Magnolias growing at Monza.] 178

— (1842) *Catalogus Plantarum Caesari Regii Horti prope Modiciam*. [A supplementary list.] 178–9

MAXIMOWICZ, C. J. (1872) Diagnoses plantarum novarum Japoniae et Mandschuriae. *Bulletin de l'Académie Impériale des Sciences de St.-Pétersbourg*. Decas II, 17 : 417–56. 113, 124

MEYER, F. G. (1971) Two New Hybrid Magnolia Cultivars. *Newsletter of the American Magnolia Society*. [Details of 'Freeman' and 'Maryland' with photographs of mother trees and close-ups of flowers.] 8, 1 : 7–9, Figs 1–4. 153, 154

MICHAUX, A. F. (1803) *Flora Boreali-Americana*. 1. *M. macrophylla*: 327. 60
 M. acuminata: 328. 126, 128
 M. fraseri: 381. 58

— (1819) *The North American Sylva*. *M. tripetala*. 3 : 90. 55

MICHEL. (1828) Traité des Arbres et des Arbustes qui se cultivent en France en plein terre *Magnolia soulangiana*. *Du Hamel*. Ed. 2, 224 : t. 66b. 175

MILLAIS, J. G. (1927) *Magnolias*. Describes both temperate and tropical Asian and American species and hybrids. Written at a time when many Asian species had not flowered in cultivation and now largely outdated as to nomenclature but still useful for historical information. Magnolias of Yunnan (chap. 3) by George Forrest. Key to the Species (chap. 4) by J. E. Dandy, whose name is mis-spelt Dendy throughout the book.
 xv, 25, 47, 50, 64, 76, 84, 87, 89, 94, 101, 118, 125, 134, 135, 169, 176, 177, 179, 181, 187

MILLER, P. (1731) *The Gardener's Dictionary*. [*M. virginiana* as *Tulipifera arbor Virginia* and *M. grandiflora* as the 'Laurel-leav'd Tulip Tree'.] Ed. I : 82. 44, 72

— (1759) *Ibid*. [Description and drawing of *M. grandiflora*

as *Magnolia foliis lanceolatis persistentibus, caule erecto arboreo*. Ed. VII : Fig. 172. 72

— (1760) *Figures of Plants*. [Similar description and drawing.] 2 : 115, Pl. 172. 72

MILLER, R. E. (1975) The Deciduous Magnolias of West Florida. *Rhodora*. 77 : 64–75. 59

MIQUEL, F. A. G. (1866) *Annales Musei Botanici Lugduno-Batavi*. *Magnoliaceae*. 2 : 257–8. 125

MULLIGAN, B. (1959) *Magnolia kobus* 'Wada's Memory'. *Journal of the Arnold Arboretum*. 22 : 20. 160

MUNDEY, G. (1952) A Method of Propagating Magnolias [by budding]. *Journal of the Royal Horticultural Society*. 77 : 449–50. 206

NAKAI, T. (1933) *Magnolia* section *Oyama*. *Flora Sylvatica Koreana*. 20 : 117–20. 31, 62, 64

NICE, C. G. (1973) Magnolias at Nymans by Natural Fertilization. *Rhododendrons 1973 with Magnolias and Camellias 76*. 150, 188

NICHOLSON, G. (1883) Magnolias. *The Garden*. 24 : 508–13. [The Magnolia figured as *M. parviflora* on p. 508, t. 417 is the earliest Western illustration of *M.* × *wieseneri*.] 188

— (1895) The Magnolias. *The Gardeners' Chronicle*. [Suggested parentage of *M.* × *thompsoniana*.] 3, 17 : 515–16. 181

OHWI, J. (1965) *Flora of Japan*. *Magnolia*. 467–8. 113, 123, 134

PALMER, L. (1967) A cold Chalk Garden Throughout the Year. *Journal of the Royal Horticultural Society*. 92, 1 : 12–13. 87, 192

PAMPANINI, R. (1910) *Nuovo Giornale Botanico Italiano*. Nuovo serie, *M. biondii*. 17 : 275, and 18 : t. 3. 118

— (1915) *Ibid*. *M. sprengeri*. 22 : 295–6. 107

— (1915) La *Magnolia sprengeri* Pamp. et la *Magnolia aulacosperma* Rehder et Wilson. *Bulletino della R. Societa Toscana di Orticultura*. 40 : 99–102. 76, 118

— (1915) Le Magnolie. *Ibid*. 40 : 127–34, 151–4, 170–3, 181–4, 199–202, 213–18, 229–34, 59

— (1916) *Ibid*. 41 : 6–8, 23–6, 40–5, 58–62, 77–8, 101–7, 122–5, 135–41, 151–7, 167–73, 183–9. 67, 76, 177

PARMENTIER, P. (1896) Histoire des Magnoliacées. *Bulletin Scientifique de la France et de la Belgique*. 27 : 159–337. 65

PARSONS, S. B. (1875) *The Garden*. [*Magnolia stellata* as *M. halleana*.] 8 : 67. 113

— (1878) *Ibid*. [Colour plate of *M. halleana (stellata)*.] 13 : 572, t. 132. 113

— (1883) *Ibid*. [Colour plate of *M.* × *wieseneri* as *M. parviflora*.] 24 : 508, t. 417. 118, 188

PEARCE, S. A. (1952) Magnolias at Kew. *The Gardeners' Chronicle*. 3, 132 : 154. 126, 160

— (1959) *Journal of the Royal Horticultural Society*. *M.* × *kewensis* and M. 'Charles Coates.'] 84 : 426. 150, 160

P'EI, C. (1933) Vascular Plants of Nanking II. *Contributions from the Biological Laboratory of the Scientific Society of China*. Botany Series 8. *Magnolia zenii*. 9 : 291–3, Fig. 20. 112

PFAFFMAN, G. A. (1975) A trip to see the rare Mexican magnolia tree species *Magnolia dealbata*. *Newsletter of the American Magnolia Society*, 11, 2 : 8–15. 12, 13

PLUMIER, C. (1703) *Magnolia. Plantarum Americarum Genera.* [Earliest publication of the generic name *Magnolia*.] 38, t. 7.
1

PUCCI, A. (1907) *Bulletino della R. Societa Toscana di Orticultura.* [*M.* × *wieseneri*.] 6 : 162.
187

PURSCH, F. (1814) *Flora Americae Septentrionalis. M. pyramidata.* 2 : 382.
59

— (1814) *Flora Boreali-Americana. M. tripetala.* 2 : 381.
55

REDOUTÉ, P. J. (1827) *Choix des plus belles fleurs.*
174

REHDER, A. (1939) *Journal of the Arnold Arboretum.* 20. *M. wilsonii* f. *nicholsoniana*: 91.
67

    M. × *proctoriana*: 412.
126, 165

— (1940) *Manual of Cultivated Trees and Shrubs Hardy in North America.* Ed. 2. *Magnolia*: 246–52. *M. fraseri*: 246.
58

    M. acuminata var. *subcordata*: 247.
129

    M. wilsonii f. *taliensis*: 249
67

    M. liliflora var. *gracilis*: 251.
134

REHDER, A. & WILSON, E. H. (1913) Wilson Expedition to China. Sargent, *Plantae Wilsonianae.* 1, *Magnoliaceae*: 391–418. 49, 50, 51, 66, 67, 70, 99, 101, 104, 108, 111, 118

— — (1927) Lignaeus Plants of Anhwei. *Journal of the Arnold Arboretum. M. cylindrica.* 8 : 109.
119, 120

REICHENBACH, H. G. L. (1841) *Der Deutsche Botaniker. Magnolia.* 1 : 192.
25, 33, 81

ROBINSON, W. (1875) *The Garden.* [*M. stellata* as *M. halleana*.] 8 : 69.
113

— (1878) *Ibid.* [Colour plate of the above Magnolia.] 13.
113

ROYAL HORTICULTURAL SOCIETY, THE. (1950) A Survey of the Genus *Magnolia* together *Manglietia* and *Michelia* by J. E. Dandy, M.A., F.L.S. *Camellias and Magnolias Conference Report.* 64–77.
xv, 16, 25, 29, 81, 83, 92, 97, 100, 165, 182

— (1956) *Dictionary of Gardening. Magnolia.* 3 : 1230–4. 134

SALISBURY, R. A. (1806) *Paradisus Londinensis.* [*M. heptapeta* as *M. conspicua*.] 1 : t. 38.
81, 82, 83

— (1807) *Ibid.* [*M. quinquepeta* as *M. gracilis*.] 2 : t. 87.
132, 134, 135

SANTAMOUR, F. S., JR. (1965) Biochemical Studies in *Magnolia*, I. Floral Anthocyanins. *Morris Arboretum Bulletin.* 16 : 43–8.
164, 182

— (1965) Biochemical Studies in *Magnolia*, II. Leucoanthocyanins in Leaves. *Ibid.* 16 : 63–4.
182

— (1966) Biochemical Studies in *Magnolia*, III. Fruit Anthocyanins. *Ibid.* 17 : 13.
182

— (1966) Hybrid Sterility in *Magnolia* × *thompsoniana. Ibid.* 17 : 29–30.
182

— (1966) Biochemical Studies in *Magnolia*, IV. Flavonols and Flavones. *Ibid.* 17 : 65–8.
182

— (1969) Cytology of Magnolia Hybrids, I. *Ibid.* 20 : 63–5.
155, 159, 166

— (1970) Cytology of Magnolia Hybrids, II. *Ibid.* 21 : 58–61.
166, 211

— (1970) Cytology of Magnolia Hybrids, III. *Ibid.* 21 : 80–1.
166

— (1970) Implications of Cytology and Biochemistry for Magnolia Hybridization. *Newsletter of the American Magnolia Society.* 7, 2 : 8–10.
211

— (1975) Cyanide in *Magnolia*. Some Further Observations. *Ibid.* 11, 2 : 5–7.
110

— (1976) Recent Hybridization with *Magnolia acuminata* at the National Arboretum. *Ibid.* 12, 1 : 3–9.
147

SANTAMOUR, F. S., JR. & TREESE, J. S. (1971) Cyanide Production in *Magnolia. Morris Arboretum Bulletin.* 22 : 58–9.
110

SARGENT, C. S. (1891) *The North American Silva. Magnolia.* 1 : 1–16.
128, 129

— (1894) The Magnolia Family. *Forest Flora of Japan*: 8–16.
125

— (1908) *Trees and Shrubs. M. kobus.* 2 : 57–8.
122

SAVAGE, P. J., JR. (1965) Magnolias in Michigan, Part I. *Newsletter of the American Magnolia Society.* 2, 1 : 2–3.
112, 124

— (1966) Magnolias in Michigan, Part II. *Ibid.* 3, 1 : 3–4. 44

— (1967) Magnolias in Michigan, Part II (cont.). *Ibid.* 4, 1 : 2–3.
56

— (1967) Magnolias in Michigan, Part III. *Ibid.* 4, 2 : 2–4.
44

— (1969) *Ibid.* [Notes on *M. fraseri*.] 6, 1 : 6.
58

— (1973) *Ibid.* [Notes on *M.* 'Orchid'.] 9, 2 : 23.
164

— (1973) An Amateur's Method of Growing Magnolias from Seed. *Ibid.* 9, 4 : 7–15.
147

— (1974) The Beautiful Ivory Nude. *Ibid.* [Discussion of *M. heptapeta* as *M. denudata*.] 10, 2 : 3–9.
111

— (1976) Sights and Scents among the Hardy Umbrella Trees. *Ibid.* 12, 1 : 14–17.
152

— (1976) An Orchid Corsage. *Ibid.* [Further notes on *M.* 'Orchid'.] 12, 1 : 23.
164

SCHLECHTENDAHL, D. F. L. VON. (1864) *Botanische Zeitung. M. schiedeana.* 22 : 144
78

SEALY, J. R. (1962) *Gardeners' Chronicle,* [*M. sieboldii* × *M. tripetala*.] 3, 152 : 77.
150

SIEBOLD, P. F. VON. & ZUCCARINI, J. G. (1846) *Abhandlungen der Mathematisch-physikalischen Classe der Königlich Bayerischen Akademie der Wissenschaften.* 4, 2 : 185–8.
34, 49, 63, 112, 113, 124

SIMS, J. (1807) *Curtis's Botanical Magazine. M. coco* as *M. pumila.* 28 : t. 977.
15

— (1809) *Ibid. M. fraseri.* 30 : t. 1206.
57

— (1809) *Ibid. M. pyramidata.* 30 : t. 1208.
59

— (1814) *Ibid. M. heptapeta* as *M. yulan.* 39 : t. 1621.
15, 81, 84

— (1818) *Ibid. M. grandiflora* var. *lanceolata* ['Exmouth']. 45 : t. 1952.
71, 73

— (1820) *Ibid. M.* × *thompsoniana* as *M. glauca* var. *major.* 48 : t. 2164.
180, 181

— (1820) *Ibid. M. macrophylla.* 48 : t. 2189.
60

— (1823) *Ibid. M. acuminata.* 50 : t. 2427.
126, 127

SKAN, S. A. (1906) *Ibid. M. hypoleuca.* 132 : t. 8077.
49

SMALL, K. J. (1933) A Magnolia as a New Border Plant. *Journal of the New York Botanical Garden.* [*M. macrophylla* subsp. *ashei*.] 34 : 151–2.
30, 61

SMITH, W. W. (1915) *Notes from the Royal Botanic Garden, Edinburgh. M. taliensis.* 8 : 341.
67

— (1920) *Ibid.* 12. *M. mollicomata*: 211.
93

    M. nitida: 212.
79

    M. rostrata: 213.
53

SMITH, W. W. & FORREST, G. (1920) *Ibid. M. tsarongensis.*
12 : 215.   *65*

SOULANGE-BODIN, E. *(1819) *The Gardener's Magazine.*
[Exposition on Gardening in France.]: 222–3.   *172*

— (1831) Beau Phénomène de Fructification, *Magnolia
macrophylla – Magnolia yulan. Annales de l'Institut Royal
Horticole de Fromont.* 3 : 150–1.   *61, 133, 170, 173, 174*

— (1843) Nouvelles Variétés de *Magnolia soulangiana. Ibid.*
6 : 46–8.   *170, 173*

SPACH, E. (1839) *Histoire Naturelle des Végétaux. Phanérogames. Les Magnoliacées* 7 : 427–90.
                         29, 30, 32, 33, 35, 49, 71, 81, 126

SPONGBERG, S. A. (1976) Magnoliaceae Hardy in Temperate North America. *Journal of the Arnold Arboretum.*
[Advocates major changes in the established nomenclature
of several well-known Asian species and hybrids, some
being reduced to synonymy. This publication will have
far-reaching implications in future Magnolia literature,
listings and labelling.] 57, 3 : 250–312.
                    *xv, 38, 46, 60, 61, 64, 66, 67, 76, 81, 99,
                    100, 101, 111, 121, 124, 125, 126, 130, 131,
                    143, 158, 159, 160, 161, 166, 182, 186, 189*

SPRAGUE, T. A. (1909) *Curtis's Botanical Magazine. M.
delavayi.* 135 : t. 8282.   *47*

— (1913) *Ibid. M. salicifolia.* 139 : t. 8483.   *124*

STANDLEY, P. C. (1926) Trees and Shrubs of Mexico.
Contributions from the National Arboretum. M. schiedeana.
5 : 275.   *78*

STAPF, O. (1923) *Curtis's Botanical Magazine. M. wilsonii.*
149 : sub t. 9004.   *66, 67*

— (1927) *Ibid. M. sprengeri diva.* 153 : t. 9116.   *108, 111*

STEARN, W. T. (1974) *Festschrift für Claus Nissen.* [Prof.
Stearn revues Magnol's *Botanicum Monspeliense* and
Linnaeus's *Flora Monspeliensis.*] 612–50.   *1*

STERN, F. G. (1938) *The New Flora and Silva.* [*M. sinensis ×
M. wilsonii.*] 10 : 105–7.   *158*

— (1967) Trees at Highdown. *Journal of the Royal Horticultural Society.* 92 : 104–8.   *48*

SWEET, R. (1827) *The British Flower Garden. Magnolia
soulangiana.* 3 : 260.   *174*

SWITZER, S. (1718) *Icnographia Rustica.* [Account of Bishop
Compton's gardening activities at Fulham Palace.] 1 : 70–1.
                                                           14

THANG, S.-W. (1083) *Cheng Lei Pen Tschoa*
(1108) *Ta-Kuan Pen Tshao*
[Reclassified Pharmaceutical Natural Histories with
mediaeval Chinese texts and drawings depicting medicinal
Magnolias.]
   Hsin i [*M. heptapeta*]. 12 : 346
   Mu lan [*M. quinquepeta*]. 12 : 349
   Hou phu [*M. officinalis*]. 13 : 368.   *9, 52*

THIEN, L. D. (1974) Floral Biology of Magnolia. *American
Journal of Botany.* 61 : 1037–45.   *146*

THUNBERG, C. P. (1784) *Flora Japonica. Magnolia.* 236–7.
                                                          131

— (1794) Botanical Observations on the Flora of Japan.
Transactions of the Linnean Society, London. 2 : 326–42.
                                                       49, 131

TING, Y.-C. (1977) Collecting *Magnolia biondii* in China.
Newsletter of the American Magnolia Society. 13, 2 : 19–20.
                                                          119

TOPF, A. (1852) *Magnolia Lenneana. Gartenflora.* 1 : 244, 86.
                                                          177

TRESEDER, N. G. (1968) Early introductions of *Magnolia
grandiflora* from North America. *Journal of the Royal
Horticultural Society.* [Discusses early records of trees
imported into France and England.] 93, 8 : 347–50.   *72–3*

— (1969) *Magnolia* × *watsonii. Ibid.* [Includes reference to *M.
wieseneri* Carrière.] 94, 4 : 185–7.   *188*

— (1972) Magnolias and their cultivation. *Ibid.* [Lecture given
on 14 March 1972.] 97, 8 : 336–46, Figs 159–63.   *56*

— (1975) *Magnolia cylindrica. Rhododendrons 1975 with
Magnolias and Camellias.* [Discusses history and introduction
and expresses doubt as to identity.] 70–2.   *121*

UNITED STATES DEPARTMENT OF AGRICULTURE. (1967)
Magnolia 'Freeman' (Hyland). P.I. 27763. Plant Inventory
No. 169.   *153, 154*

VASAK, V. (1973) *Magnolia hypoleuca* in Nature and in
Cultivation. *Newsletter of the American Magnolia Society.*
[Includes reference to a spontaneous hybrid of *M. hypoleuca* × *M. tripetala* growing in a local park near Prague.]
9, 1 : 3–6.   *51, 158–9*

VENTENAT, E. P. (1803) *Jardin de la Malmaison. Magnolia
quinquepeta* as *M. discolor.* [Colour plate by Redouté.]
1 : t. 24.   *132, 173*

VOS, C. DE. (1876) *Nederlandsche Flora & Pomona: Pomologische vereeniging.* [*M.* × *thompsoniana.*] 131 : t. 43. *180*

WADA, K. (1974) Some Magnolias in Japan. *Newsletter of
the American Magnolia Society.* [Extracts from two letters to
Prof. McDaniel in 1974.] 10, 1 : 14–16.   *149, 175*

WALTER, T. (1788) *Flora Caroliniana. Magnolia fraseri.* 159.
                                                           57

WEATHERBY, A. C. (1926) A New Magnolia from West
Florida. *Rhodora.* [*M. ashei*, now known as *M. macrophylla*
subsp. *ashei.*] 28 : 35.   *61*

WHITAKER, T. W. (1933) Chromosome Number and Relationship in the Magnoliales. *Journal of the Arnold Arboretum.* 14, 4 : 376–85.   *211*

WILDER, L. (1932) *The Fragrant Path.* [Fragrance of flowers
of *M. virginiana.*]   *44*

WILKINSON, J. (1944) The Cytology of *Salix* in Relation
to its Taxonomy. *Annals of Botany.* 8 : 269–84.   *211*

WILLIAMS, C. (1951) *Magnolia campbellii* White Form.
Journal of the Royal Horticultural Society. 76 : 218.   *90*

WILLIAMS, F. J. (1965) Notes on the Caerhays Gardens.
Journal of the Cornwall Garden Society. 8 : 13.   *92, 107*

— (1966) The Garden at Caerhays. *Journal of the Royal
Horticultural Society.* 91, 7 : 279–86. *93, 107, 166, 167, 198*

WILSON, E. H. (1906) The Chinese Magnolias. *The Gardeners' Chronicle.* 3, 39 : 234.   *83*

---

* The name is hyphenated in the text of this book to conform
with quotations from contemporary French horticultural
literature. However, Soulange-Bodin used no hyphen in his
publications, many of which are simply initialled 'S.B.'.

—(1911) *Photographs of Vegetation in Western China. Magnolias.* 305–8.

—(1923) *Magnolia kobus* var. *borealis. The Gardeners' Chronicle.* 3, 73 : 301.   *123*

—(1927) Magnolias of Yunnan in J. G. Millais's *Magnolias*: chap. 3.   *101, 102*

WYMAN, D. (1960) Magnolias Hardy in the Arnold Arboretum. *Arnoldia.* 20, 3–4 : 17–28. [*M.* × *proctoriana.* Pl. 7 : 27.]   *114, 163, 165*

★ Indicates tropical Magnolias mentioned but not described in this book.
Italic figures indicate where Magnolias in colour plates are mentioned in the text.

cv. = *cultivar*　　　　subsp. = *subspecies*　　　　f. = forma,　　　　var. = *varietas* (variety)

MAGNOLIA SPECIES

MAGNOLIA HYBRIDS AND CROSSES

Except where quoted from other works, the parents are listed in alphabetical sequence.
Hybrids known only by a cultivar name are listed separately under 'Named Cultivars'.

NAMED CULTIVARS OF *MAGNOLIA*

mentioned in this book

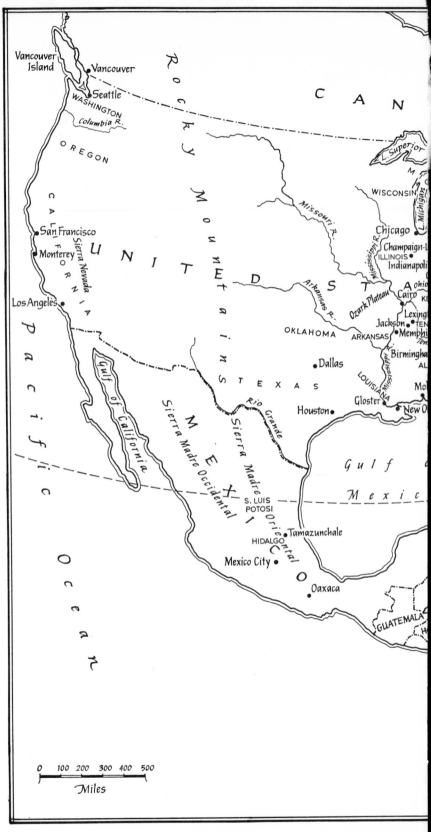

Map showing natural distribution of the western Magnolias